Paradise Lost

‹ ›

PARADISE LOST

‹›

California's Experience, America's Future

UPDATED WITH A NEW PREFACE

Peter Schrag

UNIVERSITY OF CALIFORNIA PRESS
Berkeley · Los Angeles · London

University of California Press
Berkeley and Los Angeles, California

University of California Press, Ltd.
London, England

First Paperback Printing 1999

Library of Congress Cataloging-in-Publication Data
Schrag, Peter.
    Paradise Lost: California's experience, America's future, Updated with a New Preface / Peter Schrag.
        p.   cm.
    Originally published: New York : The New Press, 1998.
    Includes bibliographical references and index.
    ISBN 0-520-24387-0 (alk. paper)
    1. California—Politics and government—1951–   2. Populism—California.   I. Title.
    [JK8716.S37   2004]
    320.9794'09'045—dc22   2004003821
                                                                    CIP

Published by arrangement with The New Press, New York

DO RE MI
Words and Music by Woody Guthrie
TRO © Copyright 1961 (Renewed) 1963 (Renewed)
Ludlow Music, Inc., New York, NY. Used by permission.

Printed in the United States of America

13   12   11   10   09   08   07   06   05   04
        10   9   8   7   6   5   4   3   2   1

Printed on Ecobook 60 with 90% recycled content, containing a minimum of 60% postconsumer waste, processed chlorine free. The balance contains 10% Forest Stewardship Council-certified, no old growth tree cutting, virgin fiber PCF. The sheet is acid-free and meets the minimum requirements of ANSI/NISO Z39.48-1992 (R 1997) (*Permanence of Paper*). ∞

For
Trish

Contents

<>

PREFACE TO THE 2004 PAPERBACK EDITION

<>

California is a garden of Eden, a paradise to live in or see,
But believe it or not, you won't find it so hot
If you ain't got that do re mi . . .

Woody Guthrie, 1937

California is an ever-mutable place, and for much of the nation, a confusing one as well. How else could one characterize the historic recall of a centrist Democratic governor in what was supposed to be a safely Democratic state, less than one year after he'd been reelected, and his replacement by a Republican with an Austrian accent—a bodybuilder and actor acknowledging "bad behavior" toward women—who had never sought public office before?

But the more things change in the Golden State, the more they seem to stay the same. The recall itself, though unprecedented, was also an extension—and very possibly an escalation—of the plebiscitary politics that have dominated California in the generation after 1978 and that constitute the centerpiece of this book. In the view of some experts, among them Bruce Cain, director of Berkeley's Institute of Governmental Studies, the 2003 recall could well mark the start of a time when office holders become even more risk averse, and impatient and distrustful voters are even more prone to direct action at the ballot box.

Many of the changes have been obvious. In the dozen or so years between 1991 and 2004, the state has gone from recession to boom to yet another recession and, very possibly, a new period of economic growth, though hardly one to match that of the late 1990s. But the landslide election of Gray Davis as governor in 1998, following Bill Clinton's decisive California victories in 1992 and 1996, seemed to signal a major shift in the state's political balance. Not only was Davis the first Democrat in twenty years—and only the second since 1962—to win the state's highest office, but he did it with a twenty-point margin that included a strong labor vote and overwhelming support from Latinos. Both suggested the emergence of new political forces in California that might persist long after the 1998 election was forgotten.

The labor vote had been energized by the reaction against Proposition 226—an initiative proposed by outgoing governor Pete Wilson that would have severely curtailed the political fundraising of public employee unions—and by the decision of Wilson's Industrial Welfare Commission to eliminate the eight-hour standard for overtime pay. Likewise the Latino vote had been spurred by backlash against Wilson's embrace and exploitation of Proposition 187 during his 1994 re-election campaign. The initiative, intended to deny schooling and other public services to illegal immigrants and their children, was subsequently overturned by a federal court.

The reaction to Proposition 187—and to Wilson campaign commercials in 1994 that seemed to attack not merely illegal immigrants, but all immigrants—together with the fear generated by the prospect that immigrants would be denied services, prompted hundreds of thousands of California Hispanics to become naturalized U.S. citizens and, along with many who were already citizens, to register immediately as voters. The ranks of Latino voters—the vast majority of them Democrats—swelled from 9 percent of the electorate in 1990 to about 14 percent in 1998. Given that Latinos in 1998 constituted roughly 31 percent of California's population and that 70 percent of all voters were still white Anglos, the Latino share wasn't great, but it was still significant. And whereas about 40 percent of Latinos voted for Wilson when he first ran in 1990, Dan Lungren, the Republican who sought to succeed him in 1998 (the first election after the Proposition 187 fight), got barely 17 percent. In the Latino community, "Wilson," without further identification, became the villain of the 1998 campaign. "Adios Pete Wilson" was the message of the bumper stickers and the post-election celebrations organized by Hispanic activists in Los Angeles.

More important perhaps, beginning in the late 1990s, the Latino caucus became a significant force within the Democratic majority in the legislature, and thus in the legislature itself. (With nine members in the forty-member Senate and fifteen in the eighty-member Assembly, Latinos had better representation in the legislature than they had in the electorate at large.) In the era after the passage of Proposition 209 in 1996, which prohibited race preferences in public employment and education, the caucus helped to drive fundamental changes in the admission policies of the University of California. Those changes included a shift to "comprehensive review"—meaning de-emphasis of grades and tests on which blacks and Latinos generally scored lower than whites and Asians in favor of a broader and more subjective assessment of the full range of each applicant's qualifications. The caucus was also instrumental in pushing through the legislature the bill giving illegal aliens the right to obtain California driver's licenses that would contribute so much to Davis's problems both in 2002 and in the recall of 2003.

In 2002, Davis narrowly won reelection over businessman Bill Simon, a weak Republican opponent. But since Democrats swept the election, winning every constitutional office from lieutenant governor to insurance commissioner (all of them by close votes), since they had safe majorities in California's congressional delegation and in both houses of the legislature, and since both Bill Clinton and Al Gore had carried California in the previous presidential elections, California, which until 1988 had been thought of as generally Republican, was firmly categorized as generally liberal, increasingly dominated by minorities, and thus forever safe for Democrats.

Even before 2002, the state was being seen more as a political exception than as a model. George W. Bush would be wasting his time campaigning in California, wrote Fred Barnes in the conservative *Weekly Standard* in 2000 in a piece called "California doesn't matter: The political future once happened there. No more." He could win the presidency without winning California (as indeed he did). The Golden State was no longer the nation's political bellwether because it was demographically and politically so different; it was no longer the nation's envy because its quality of life had deteriorated and its schools and other public services were so lousy.

Three years later, in a similar vein, "Lexington," the U.S. columnist for the *Economist* magazine, labeled California the "left-out coast," a state "that used to be a trendsetter [and is now] stuck in a time warp." And then there was (in Lexington's view) the implosion of a state GOP that would rather be far right than win and had thus yielded control to a Democratic Party "controlled by its most extreme elements." California was more skeptical of the Iraq war than the nation as a whole, Lexington said. It was relatively indifferent to terrorism because the September 11 attacks took place three thousand miles away; it was not much concerned with geo-strategy.

Some of that, of course, was true. The state GOP had marginalized itself by taking positions, particularly on social issues, that were too conservative for California and by failing to reach out effectively to Latinos and women. Meanwhile the Democrats were, in many instances, too concerned about the interest groups at the heart of their coalition—public employee unions, trial lawyers, ethnic minorities, Indian casinos—to focus on broader problems. What seemed certain however, at least in conventional political wisdom, was that California had become a state apart, one where, as the 2000 census recognized, there no longer was any ethnic majority, and one that was too liberal to be representative of anything. Democrats would be in charge forever.

But beginning two years after his election, Davis, who came to office with high approval ratings and a positive agenda of education reform, was hit by two major shocks, neither entirely of his own making, that would prove to be his undoing. The first was the energy crisis of 2000–2001 with its rolling blackouts. Long before it overwhelmed Davis, the governor's pollster, Paul Maslin, predicted that the energy crisis could become the political perfect storm. It grew not from any act of Davis but from a misbegotten power deregulation plan passed in the Wilson years that opened the state to what subsequently turned out to be widespread price manipulation by Enron and a half-dozen other major energy marketers. The other crisis, the budget crunch that followed the bursting of the economic bubble of the late 1990s and the corresponding dive in California's capital gains tax receipts, left the state with what Davis himself eventually estimated was a two-year gap of about $38 billion.

California was hardly the only state with a huge budget deficit in the first years of the new millennium, nor was its three-year slide in 2000–2003 from budgetary surplus to deficit proportionately any larger than that of the federal government in the same years. But in both instances, Davis, whose victories in five statewide elections had always depended more on negative campaigning than on any fierce loyalty from friends, was widely believed to have dithered when he should have candidly confronted the problem.

In the case of the energy crisis, which at times drove the wholesale price of power to astronomical levels, Davis, fearful of the political consequences of decisive measures and ignoring the advice of most energy experts, was unwilling to allow his Public Utilities Commission to let retail rates rise enough to generate greater consumer awareness of the real cost of electricity. If that move had been combined with "real time" metering of peak-load rates informing consumers of the cost of the energy they were consuming at that moment, it would almost certainly have reduced consumption during the early evening hours when spot prices were the highest, dampened the rate spikes, and prevented many of the blackouts. Worse perhaps, he waited until the Pacific Gas and Electric Co., the state's largest utility, had filed for bankruptcy before agreeing to allow the state's energy companies to negotiate long-term contracts, which by then had become much costlier than they would have been had he acted earlier. Quicker action on Davis's part would have sharply reduced the state's dependence on the volatile and very manipulable spot market.

Similarly his failure—and that of the legislature as well—to recognize and confront the state's looming budget crisis made him an obvious target for political opponents and for voters beset by economic anxieties and frustrated by the state's continual budget confusion and gridlock. That, too, was hardly all Davis's fault. The state's extraordinary constitutional provision requiring a two-thirds vote in each house of the legislature to pass a budget or any other fiscal measure—California is one of only three states to require such a high margin—gave the legislature's minority Republicans, outvoted on most other legislation, an effective veto over the budget. And since the Republican minority refused to back any solution that included new taxes (as Republican Wilson had done in 1991 in response to a similar crisis) they forced Davis to mend the gap with an ugly patchwork of expedients—borrowing, deferrals, and severe cuts.

Among those expedients was restoration of the fee imposed on the license of every motor vehicle, a fee that had been cut in good times a few years before—one of a series of tax cuts approved during the boom. That increase in the "car tax," which roughly tripled the cost to each vehicle owner, combined subsequently with Davis's approval of the highly controversial bill granting illegal aliens the right to a California driver's license, was the symbolic straw that broke Davis's back. Davis had vetoed the driver's license bill twice before, an act which, in the view of authorities on the Hispanic vote, sharply depressed the Latino turnout, from the 14 percent of 1998 to a bare 10 percent in 2002. (Nonetheless, had it not been for black and Latino voters, Davis would not have been reelected.) His politically questionable decision to sign the bill in 2003, an obvious (and desperate) move to shore up his base, probably cost him more votes—60 percent of all voters opposed the bill—than it gained him.

Was the recall of 2003, to use writer Carey McWilliams's words, yet another great California exception, even compared to California's normal politics? Most political experts agreed that Schwarzenegger couldn't have a won a regular GOP primary: his positions on abortion, gay rights, gun control, and other social issues made him far too liberal for the GOP regulars. The structure of the recall, which involved no primary and where, if the governor were recalled, only a plurality, not a majority, was required to win the election for a successor therefore gave Schwarzenegger not only an unusual opportunity but, with his celebrity status and his very deep pockets, a considerable advantage in a race that eventually included 135 contenders.

From the moment the opinion polls showed that the deeply disliked Davis was likely to lose and that Schwarzenegger would probably replace him—it was to be a convincing victory—all the talk about California being irrelevant was replaced with speculation about what the recall would mean for the nation as a whole. Would Schwarzenegger, the social moderate and fiscal conservative, move the whole California GOP toward the center? Would he put his state in play for future GOP candidates, both in presidential elections and in races for the U.S. Senate? Or would the man who was now the second most visible political figure in the nation and, overnight, among the most important, be as much at odds with his own party as he would be with Democrats? The mere possibility that California might be again be competitive in both state and national elections, thus forcing Democrats to spend millions to hold the state, could make it easier for Bush and other Republicans to win elsewhere.

What was certain was that Schwarzenegger's election and his personal political heft once again seemed to change Sacramento's political dynamics. Even before the new governor took office, legislative Democrats talked about repealing the controversial bill allowing illegal aliens to obtain California driver's licenses that they'd approved just a few months before. Attorney General Bill Lockyer, a Democrat and a likely candidate for governor in 2006, announced that while he had opposed the recall, he'd voted for Schwarzenegger over his fellow Democrat, Lieutenant Governor Cruz Bustamante, the first Latino to be elected to statewide office since the nineteenth century, to succeed Davis should he be recalled. (Bustamante, breaking ranks with his party, whose leaders believed that voters should have no choice but Davis or a Republican, had jumped into the successor race, proved himself a terrible candidate, and was trounced by Schwarzenegger.) Meanwhile, in Washington, Schwarzenegger and California's congressional politicians staged a high-visibility post-election event that was closer to a bipartisan public love-in than anything anyone could have imagined only a few months before.

The combination of term limits and political districts engineered to be virtually guaranteed for one party or the other had made California primaries, which drew mostly the party faithful, the real election contests. Those primaries produced Democratic legislators who were more liberal and Republican legislators who were more conservative than the average voter, generating a climate of ugly and often personalized partisanship both in Sacramento and in Washington that made any compromise or accommodation difficult. Now here was Schwarzenegger promising to support Senator Dianne Feinstein's bill banning assault weapons and to push for some sort of federal buy-back of off-shore oil leases. Here were politicians of all stripes and genders pressing to have their pictures taken with a man who, only a month before, had been accused of entertaining narcissistic power fantasies and groping a dozen or more women during his Hollywood career. Still there was hardly any certainty that the good feeling would outlast the moment.

The recall also raised more fundamental questions—many of them about the state itself. California voters, following the leadership of Hiram Johnson and the victorious California Progressives, had written the initiative, the referendum, and the recall into the state constitution in 1911. But while there had been dozens of attempts to recall governors and other statewide officials in the following ninety-two years, and while there had been countless recalls of local officials—school board members particularly—as well as of a few legislators, no recall of a statewide official had ever qualified for the ballot in California. Indeed, in the nation as a whole, only one governor had ever been recalled, and that was Governor Lynn J. Frazier in North Dakota in 1921.

So why did it happen now, and why did it happen to this governor under these circumstances? Through the seventy-six days between July 23, when the recall qualified for the ballot, and the October 7 election, California was deluged with journalists, commentators, and political scholars—American, Mexican, Brazilian,

Canadian, German, French, Swedish, Danish, Dutch, Japanese, Swiss—asking what it all meant. Was this another populist uprising that, like the tax revolt triggered by Proposition 13, would sweep the country? And since hundreds of thousands of new voters registered for the political circus that was captivating the world, wasn't this a wonderful recharge for California's tired, incestuous politics? Was it not, indeed, a healthy transfusion for a political system that had so alienated citizens that each year fewer showed up to vote at all? Or, looking at the long, bizarre list of would-be governors—actors, smut publishers, bail bondsmen, porn queens, newspaper columnists, all of whom qualified by paying a $3,500 filing fee and submitting sixty-five signatures—was this just another piece of California craziness? Did it portend a national wave of recalls or, at least, would it make American politicians at every level more cautious, more likely to look over their shoulders, lest they too incur the wrath of the voters? And, more fundamentally, what was its significance for democracy? America, after all, was the paragon of modern democracies and California was (once again) America's exemplary state.

Part of the answer to "why now?" lay in Davis's own vulnerability—his lack of a loyal base, his obsessive "pay to play" fundraising, his seeming arrogance, as in his declaration early in his first term that it was the legislature's duty to "implement my vision," and his disdain for people and groups that should have been his friends. That vulnerability was compounded by Davis's unprecedented—and ultimately successful campaign—to undermine former Los Angeles mayor Richard Riordan, the strongest potential challenger to his reelection hopes in 2002.

In what many people regarded as an egregious act of political incivility, Davis spent some $10 million to discredit Riordan in the 2002 Republican gubernatorial primary. That campaign ultimately helped give the primary victory to Bill Simon, a man who would run a terrible race in the general election and who, in any case, was far too conservative to have any real chance of winning in California. That drove down the turnout and angered thousands of voters who believed that Davis's stratagems, not the conservative GOP primary voters who picked Simon, had deprived them of a real choice. In response to charges that the recall was another GOP attempt to steal an election (as in the Bush v. Gore fight in Florida in 2000), undermine a legitimately elected Democrat (as in the Clinton impeachment), or illegitimately change the rules (as House Majority Leader Tom DeLay was then doing in his drive for a second reapportionment of the Texas legislature), a great many Davis opponents responded that it was Davis who, in effect, had stolen the California election.

But partly, at least, it was just another example of California's turn to direct democracy. Ted Costa, the anti-tax activist who started his career with Paul Gann during the campaign for California's property-tax cutting Proposition 13, which had passed twenty-five years before, began planning for the recall barely one month after Davis's 2002 reelection. Costa, who directed an organization called People's Advocate, had run a long list of anti-establishment campaigns, from an abortive attempt to privatize Sacramento's publicly owned electric system, to an initiative imposing congressional term limits, to efforts to cut the legislature's pay. He'd also run for county supervisor, for State Assembly and for the state Board of Equalization and lost each time.

Like many of those forays, the recall campaign seemed to be going nowhere. What saved it was the decision of millionaire Darrell Issa, a San Diego–area congressman who wanted to become governor himself, to write the large checks—all told nearly $2 million—for the direct mail campaigns and the paid petition circulators who collected the nine hundred thousand valid signatures required to get the recall on the ballot. (After the election, recall proponents claimed that they'd collected some two million).

That brought into play the same people, techniques, dynamics, and principles that had been staples of California's initiative process for a generation and that this book discusses in some detail. The first of those principles was that with enough money, almost anything can qualify for the ballot; without the money, almost nothing can. As in initiative campaigns, money alone doesn't guarantee success in the voting booth after a measure qualifies. But the 2003 recall triggered a deeper anger, one that went far beyond Gray Davis's alleged malefactions. Some commentators pointed out that California seemed to have one of these political earthquakes roughly every dozen years: the election of Ronald Reagan in 1966; the passage of Proposition 13 in 1978; the enactment of strict legislative term limits in 1990; the Davis recall of 2003. But that's far too simple. The recall makes far more sense seen in the context of California's on-going hyper-democracy—the increasing disdain for representative government and its replacement with initiatives that has characterized the state's politics ever since the 1970s.

This book was first published in 1998. Since then, Californians have continued the intensive pace of direct democracy that they set in the prior generation. In 1996, voters passed Proposition 215, legalizing the medical use of marijuana. In 1998, they approved congressional term limits (a law later thrown out as a violation of the U.S. constitution); sharply curtailed bilingual education in the state's public schools; approved a tobacco surtax to expand early childhood development programs (despite a $30 million negative campaign by tobacco companies); imposed stiffer penalties for juvenile crimes and expanded the crimes for which juveniles could be tried as adults; and, after a record-breaking campaign in which Indian gaming interests spent $70 million and Nevada gambling casinos spent $30 million against them, approved Proposition 5, a vast expansion of slot machines and other gambling at Indian casinos.

In 2000, voters passed a "definition of marriage" act that limited marriage to partners of different sexes, a measure requiring treatment instead of incarceration for a long list of drug offenses, and an initiative lowering the vote threshold for passing local school bonds from 67 percent to 55 percent. And, in 2002, they enacted a measure (funded by Schwarzenegger) to take about $500 million annually from the general fund for after-school programs. Along the way, they also approved a ban on the slaughter of horsemeat for human consumption and on the use of body-gripping traps to catch fur-bearing animals, despite pleas from public officials that it would impair animal control efforts. They did, however, respond to a $40 million campaign by the electric utility industry and rejected an initiative that would have shifted the cost of writing off failed nuclear power plants from consumers to shareholders. All told, California voters passed nine initiatives in the 1960s, twenty-two in the 1970s, forty-five in the 1980s, and sixty-two in the 1990s, not counting hundreds of local measures, many of them seeking to slow or stop development in one place or another. Call that ballot-box planning and zoning. In an October 2000 poll by the Public Policy Institute of California asking voters which they trusted more in making major decisions, the governor and legislature or the initiative process, the initiative process won 56 to 24 percent, with 20 percent unsure.

The widespread view by recall supporters that voter anger against Davis was yet another revolt against "the system" thus was touched by more than a little irony. Given California's recent social and political history, direct democracy itself had become as much the system as the elected officials in Sacramento. It was certainly true that traditional governmental institutions, with their checks and balances and their deliberative processes operated—indeed were designed to operate—at an eighteenth-century pace, even as the rest of the world became increasingly habituated to click-of-the-mouse responsiveness and instant feedback. But while those older public institutions were as prone to venality and self-service as most other large organizations, the plebiscitary remedies themselves—legislative term limits, ballot-box budgeting for everything from parks to schools to children's services, voter-mandated prison terms that drove up the cost of corrections to record levels, super-majority tax formulas that made it easy to cut revenues but nearly impossible to raise them—contributed considerably to the legislative paralysis.

Perhaps more troubling still, there was no sign, despite the early rounds of mutual deference between the new governor and the old pols, that this, finally, was a turning point toward the restoration of traditional government. On the contrary, as Schwarzenegger took office, the next wave of ballot measures was already gathering steam, among them a measure seeking to repeal the driver's license bill; another to overturn a law granting domestic partners some of the same legal rights as legally married spouses; a third to prohibit any California government from ever imposing another car tax; a fourth to take reapportionment of political districts away from the legislature and give it to a panel of judges; a fifth to eliminate party primaries in favor of an open primary in which all candidates would run and where, if no candidate won a majority, the two leading contenders would face each other in a runoff, even if both were from the same party; a sixth, already qualified for the ballot, that would lower the constitutional threshold for passing a budget or raising taxes from 67 percent to 55 percent; plus a string of others, from a measure to regulate the treatment of pregnant pigs to yet another effort to cut services for illegal immigrants. Plus ça change.

The most striking—and furthest reaching—characteristic of the truncated Davis era, and particularly of the boom years that the state enjoyed in the late 1990s, is that so little was done to restructure or reform the state's dysfunctional fiscal and political system. Davis, among the most risk-averse governors in California's history, had little interest in basic reforms. A little more money went into schools and more (from a series of bonds) was appropriated for school construction, but California's per-pupil spending remained well below the national average and far below New York, New Jersey, and other major industrial states. Its school libraries remained the most poorly staffed; its secondary schools, especially those serving poor children, badly lacked qualified teachers, and some classes had no permanent teachers at all. The schools were still bereft of counselors to give students real guidance, their music and arts programs were as underfunded as they'd ever been, and their classes remained among the nation's largest, despite the class-size reduction program that Wilson instituted in the primary grades (a program that was hastily designed and, after five years of operation, showed little in demonstrable results that could confidently be credited to it). In 2001, after a group of civil rights organizations sued the state for its failure to make certain that children in high poverty schools had regular teachers, sufficient textbooks and other materials, functioning toilets, and vermin-free schools, Davis hired a high-powered Los Angeles law firm to prove that such problems were not the state's responsibility and that the student-plaintiffs could learn quite adequately in dirty buildings and didn't need textbooks to take home for homework.

Meanwhile, as the recession deepened in 2001–2003, college and university fees—which had been raised during the recession of the early 1990s, then cut in the boom years—were suddenly raised again to even higher levels than before. Access was cut to classes and programs at all levels, as it had been in the prior downturn, and transfers from the community colleges to the University of California, always a key part of the state's once-grand master plan, were curtailed. Despite recommendations from a blue ribbon panel that the state should even out its boom-bust cycle in higher education, nothing was done.

In the same vein, a string of commissions on finance, state government reform, and other key issues recommending fundamental changes—some of them based on this book—produced nothing of substance, despite the opportunity that the spike in state revenues might have made possible in the early years of the first Davis administration. Even as the state's high-tech economy was widely regarded as the world's leader and as the private wealth of California's richest residents reached unprecedented levels, California's government, its tax system, its rundown physical infrastructure—roads, bridges, water and sewer systems, school buildings—and its public programs languished in another era. Although services, from lawyers and accountants to computer consultants and dog groomers, became an increasingly large part of the state's economy, and as an increasing share of its goods were sold over the Internet, the state's sales taxes covered only goods—and then only those sold over the counter. A book bought from the local bookseller was taxed; one bought online was not, a difference that not only cost local governments money but was also unfair to the local merchant.

And of course, the tax revolt remained alive and well. There have been proposals since this book was first published for a split roll that would tax commercial property at a different rate, or assess it on a different basis, from residential property. There has also been a lot of talk about—and some abortive bills seeking to enact—tax swaps that would give local agencies a greater share of the property tax and return more sales tax revenues to the state. That measure would, at least in theory, reduce the tendency toward "fiscalization of land use"—the intense pursuit by local agencies of big sales tax sources like auto malls and shopping centers instead of balanced development that includes middle income housing in proximity to businesses that bring good jobs. As this edition went to press, an initiative sponsored by the California Teachers Association and actor Rob Reiner was being circulated that would institute a split roll and use the additional revenue for teacher salaries, smaller classes, and some system of universal preschools. But even that proposal is a bittersweet item, linking preschools to across-the-board teacher salary increases without putting in place any system of incentives or guaranteeing good teachers to the schools that most need them. It is also another proposal for ballot-box budgeting that would increase tax revenue but give elected government no discretion in how to spend it. For voters who don't trust government, that may be the only way to raise and appropriate money. But when needs and revenues are unpredictable and priorities change, it's hardly wise policy, no matter how worthy the purposes to which the money goes.

In her 2003 book, *Where I Was From,* Joan Didion, Sacramento's native daughter, deconstructs the myth of California's exceptionalism, the nostalgic belief of every generation, beginning with the children of the first people to cross the plains in the 1850s, that they were independent, self-made individuals and were thus entitled to some special treatment and consideration—and that those in every generation after them were the spoilers of California's providential perfection. In fact, she argues, California, like the rest of the West, always depended on government—on federal subsidies for the railroads, on land grants and cheap water for agriculture, on huge flood control projects to make cities like Sacramento relatively safe from the annual spring deluge, and on defense contracts to spur the wartime and Cold War booms of Southern California. California has no special exemption from tragedy and self-delusion.

What Didion doesn't mention is the essential American dilemma that lies beneath that myth. If we began in perfection, how could there be progress? As she suggests, Californians, who believe they originally came to or were born in that place of original impeccability, are forever trying to restore its perfection, often with the quick, one-shot fixes of the initiative, the referendum, and the recall. Both Schwarzenegger and Tom McClintock, his principal Republican opponent in the recall campaign, spoke about what a wonderful place California had been when they first came there, McClintock (from the East Coast) in 1965, Schwarzenegger (from Austria) in 1968. But as fiscal conservatives, neither was able to acknowledge that their golden age was a time in which California was a high tax state. The year 1965 came at the end of Pat Brown's great surge of public investment, when the voter restiveness that led to Ronald Reagan's election was already stirring. The year 1968, Schwarzenegger's dream moment, came right after Governor Ronald Reagan supported and signed the largest tax increase that had been passed in any state up to that time.

What has unquestionably changed since then is that non-Hispanic whites have ceased to be the majority in California's population—there is now no ethnic majority. Within twenty years, whites will be outnumbered by Latinos among what are projected to be some fifty million Californians. (Roughly 75 percent of California's growth in the forty years since it became the nation's most populous state has been Hispanic or Asian.)

All manner of issues confront the state in wake of the recall, not least among them the question of whether Californians, after a generation of deteriorating schools, roads, and government, are really willing to pay for the high quality of services they said they wanted—or indeed, whether they really still want them. But the issues that continue to fester under most of those questions are immigration and ethnicity. Almost every time that I write about overcrowded schools or stressed public services, e-mails arrive telling me that if it weren't for all those Mexicans, California wouldn't have such problems and that they'll be dammed if they'll pay higher taxes for the education of "those" children. "As for the illegal aliens," said one writer, "the civil war is-a-comin'." The issue has troubled California for a century and a half—Chinese exclusion, Japanese land laws, the internment of Japanese

Americans in World War II, Proposition 187, and the uproar over the driver's license bill come to mind—and it's likely to continue to trouble the state in the years to come.

Given the magnitude of the demographic changes, it's hardly surprising that there is stress and anxiety. California is leading the nation in something that's never been done anywhere in human history: take millions of people from an enormous diversity of cultures, languages, and ethnicities; educate their children to a high level of proficiency for a post-industrial, high-tech economy; and forge them all into a good society with a common political system and common social values. And in many respects, it seems to be working.

The economic and social ambitions of first-generation Hispanics, Vietnamese, Indians, Poles, Russians, and Cambodians, among many others, in California seem not all that different from those of their East Coast predecessors a century earlier— they start businesses, buy homes, send their children to school— with one significant exception. The new "communities" to which the first immigrant generations belong are likely to have fewer connections to any immediate geographic base than to what has been described as a "global entrepreneurial community," which is to say that Indian engineers and technicians in Silicon Valley may spend more on supporting schools in their native villages than on the school down the street. The new Chinese professionals in Los Angeles or Los Altos may be much more closely linked to their backers and/or relatives in Hong Kong than to the Latinos on the other side of freeway. In turn those Latinos, though successful, may feel more loyalty to a village in Chihuahua than to their black fellow-citizens in the next neighborhood. Remittance payments from Mexicans working in the United States to relatives across the border—and sometimes to churches and schools as well—are now estimated to exceed $14 billion a year, making them, after oil, the second largest source of Mexican revenue. In partial recognition of that fact, the Mexican government now allows the new Mexican American citizens to retain their Mexican citizenship, thereby letting them enjoy economic benefits, including land ownership, on both sides of the border.

Since the children and grandchildren of that new wave of immigrants now outnumber the first generation, and since the assimilated—people buying homes, starting businesses, and joining civic groups—are becoming the norm rather than the exception, that too may change. But that change is no more certain than the speed at which California's non-Hispanic voters accommodate to the new world around them. For the moment, California, like much of the West, seems to be the precursor of an entirely new set of social and political arrangements and attitudes, a place inhabited by what Robert Kaplan calls "resident expatriates." These global citizens, regardless of race or ethnicity, have only a tentative loyalty to the place where they live or to anything—other than perhaps their own ethnic group, or native village, or gated development, or elite school—that would resemble a nation or community. That vision of California—not the economy or the climate, but the commonweal—looks like a very different place from the one Americans used to dream about. Californians all, regardless of ethnicity or place of birth, are immigrants in this emerging new society. How well it works will be crucial not only for the state but for America and, more than likely, for the world as well.

Oakland, California
February 2004

SOURCES AND
ACKNOWLEDGMENTS

<>

This book rests heavily on the resources and generous help, extending over the better part of twenty years, of a long list of official state agencies, universities, and private institutions and organizations. Although many have suffered significant funding cuts as a result of California's straitened public finances, they continue to provide a rich array of information on a vast range of matters.

Among the most important of them are the California Department of Finance, which generates and analyzes information on everything from population trends to tax receipts, and which annually publishes the highly useful *California Statistical Abstract*; the Office of the Secretary of State for election results, campaign expenditure records, voter registration data, and the texts of official ballot measures; and the nonpartisan Legislative Analyst's Office, which each year issues a detailed *Analysis of the Budget Bill*, and reports on many other major public policy issues. Additionally, individual agencies—the Department of Education, the Department of Social Services, the Department of Corrections, the Department of Health Services, the Department of Transportation, the University of California, the California State University, the California State Library, the California Postsecondary Education Commission, among others—collect detailed data on everything from

Medicaid services to the staffing of local libraries and the graduation rates of California schools.

Those sources are reinforced by the research and databases of a number of major university-related institutions and private think tanks. Among them: the Institute of Governmental Studies at Berkeley; the California Policy Seminar, also at Berkeley; the private Public Policy Institute of California in San Francisco; the Center for the Continuing Study of the California Economy in Palo Alto; the California Institute for Rural Studies in Davis; the California Taxpayers Association, the California Budget Project, and the California Tax Reform Association, all in Sacramento; and the Center for Responsive Government in Los Angeles.

I've also drawn extensively on data provided by the Center for Budget and Policy Priorities in Washington; the National Conference of State Legislatures and the Education Commission of the States in Denver, and the National Council on Crime and Delinquency in San Francisco; the American Council on Education and the College Board; as well as countless organizations and interest groups representing every sector of public life. In addition, no journalist dealing with policy and politics in California can function very long without drawing on the poll data of the Field Institute, which polls constantly on all sorts of public issues and whose records now go back many years. In addition—and almost routinely—I have relied freely on data from federal sources which, as they come on-line, are increasingly easy to use, among them the U.S. Census Bureau, the National Center for Education Statistics of the Department of Education, the U.S. Immigration and Naturalization Service, the Department of Transportation, and the Bureau of Labor Statistics.

In most instances, the immediate source is cited in the text or in the endnotes, accompanied, where possible, with its Web address, but since much of the material in this book is also drawn from personal observation, from formal interviews, and from countless informal conversations—and, of course, from the writing, reporting, and background of colleagues—much more is not listed or is not given the kind of emphasis that the help deserved.

Among individuals to whom I owe special recognition, not

merely for particular help on the book but for the long-term help that they provide to journalists like me, week after week, year after year, are Elizabeth Hill, the California Legislative Analyst; Thomas Hayes, former California Director of Finance, and others in that agency; Michelle Lee, Melissa Warren, and Shirley Washington at the Office of the Secretary of State; and to many other civil servants who rarely get the recognition they deserve. I'm also much indebted to Professor Steven Sheffrin of the University of California at Davis; Professor Elisabeth Gerber of the University of California at San Diego; Maureen DiMarco, former Secretary of Education and Childrens Services for Governor Pete Wilson; Lenny Goldberg of the California Tax Reform Association; Joel Fox of the Howard Jarvis Taxpayers Association; Michael Shires of the Public Policy Institute of California; Jean Ross of the California Budget Project; Davis Campbell and Kevin Gordon of the California School Boards Association; Mary Bergan, president of the California Federation of Teachers; Frank Mecca, executive director of the California County Welfare Directors Association; Ruth Holton, former executive director of California Common Cause; Fred Silva, former staff director of the California Constitution Revision Commission; Harry Snyder, California Director of Consumers Union; Pat Callan of the California Higher Education Policy Center; Susie Lange, Doug Stone and Jan Agee of the California Department of Education; and Paul Goldfinger, Ray Reinhard, and Bob Blattner of School Services, Inc.; as well as to Edward Blakely, Lydia Chavez, Terry Colvin, Mark DeCamilla, Ward Connerly, Vic Fazio, William Fulton, James Gomez, Bob Greenstein, Gary Hart, Pat Hayashi, Bill Honig, Phil Isenberg, Sherry Bebitch Jeffe, Clark Kerr, Kelly Kimball, Michael Kirst, Steve Levy, Dan Lowenstein, Gerald Meral, Tony Miller, John Mockler, Frank Newman, H.D. Palmer, A. Alan Post, Charles Price, Joe Remcho, Bill Rukeyser, Dan Schnur, Al Sokolow, Bob Stern, Jim Shultz, Richard Simpson, John Vickerman, Don Villarejo, Tracy Westen, William Whiteneck and Jim Wilson.

I also owe special thanks to former Dean Eugene Smolensky of the Graduate School of Public Policy at Berkeley, who invited me to teach a course on the California initiative process at the Public Policy School in the spring of 1997, and thus allowed me to discuss many of my ideas with a group of able and very challenging graduate students; to David Lyon, director of the Public Policy Institute of California, whose invitation to join PPIC's Advisory Council has given me early access to some of the best policy research now being conducted in any state; to Professor Susan Rasky, formerly of the *New York Times*, now of the Graduate School of Journalism at Berkeley, whom any journalist would be proud to call a friend and mentor; and to Professor Bruce Cain of the Institute of Governmental Studies at the University of California at Berkeley, and to Tom Goldstein, formerly dean of the Berkeley School of Journalism, now dean of the Columbia Journalism School, for many considerations, not least of them their willingness at an extremely busy time to review early drafts of this book.

But the largest portion of gratitude goes to my own former colleagues and associates—questioners, enlighteners, challengers, helpers, friends—at the *Sacramento Bee*, the *Fresno Bee*, the *Modesto Bee*, and McClatchy Newspapers: Pete Basofin, Jim Boren, Becky Boyd, Jim Brown, Claire Cooper, Susanna Cooper, David Cummerow, Rosie DeLacy, Edie Decker, Gregory Favre, John Hughes, Albert Hunter, William Kahrl, Tom Kirwan, Maury Landsberg, Lisa Lapin, James McClatchy, Frank McCulloch, Bob Markson, Debbie Meredith, Russ Minick, Bill Moore, Robert Mott, Mark Paul, Erwin Potts, Gary Pruitt, Jewel Reilly, Dennis Renault, Leo Rennert, James Richardson, Rick Rodriguez, Ginger Rutland, Marty Smith, Roger Tatarian, Howard Weaver, Rhea Wilson, Jim Wrightson, and, most particularly to John Jacobs, a great political journalist, who read the penultimate draft, made many useful suggestions, helped me avert more than one horrendous factual error, and kept countless sentences in this book from being as long as this one. Without knowing it, they have all been wonderful teachers in any number of ways.

The greatest of my teachers, however, was the late C.K. McClatchy, son, grandson, and great-grandson of the Golden West, who represented the finest traditions of his state and his profession and who, as editor of the *Bee* during my first decade there, was the kind of mentor and exemplar only a few of us are ever privileged to have.

PART ONE
Introduction

‹›

I

In the generation immediately following World War II, and to some
extent even before, California was widely regarded as both model
and magnet for the nation—in its economic opportunities, its social outlook, and its high-quality public services and institutions.
With a nearly free and universally accessible system of public
higher education, a well-supported public school system, an ambitious agenda of public works projects—in irrigation and flood control; in highway construction and park development—and a wide
array of social services and human rights guarantees that had no
parallel in any other state, California seemed to have an optimism
about its population, possibilities, and future whose largest flaw was
the very excess of expectations on which it rested.

Now, forty years on, having come through the sharp recession
of the early 1990s, the state, with a robust but substantially different
economic base, is again at the world's economic and technological
frontiers: in electronics and software, in biotechnology and a vast
array of other scientifically based industries, in foreign trade, and
in the convergence of the old Hollywood and the new computer-
based graphics and design ventures that have grown up around it.
It is even enjoying a revival of the aerospace industries that were
devastated by the recession and defense cutbacks of the late 1980s
and early 1990s.

But California, even with a large burst of new postrecession revenue, is no longer the progressive model in its public institutions and services, or in its social ethic, that it once was—had indeed ceased to hold that position long before the last recession began. California's schools, which, thirty years ago, had been among the most generously funded in the nation, are now in the bottom quarter among the states in virtually every major indicator—in their physical condition, in public funding, in test scores—closer in most of them to Mississippi than to New York or Connecticut or New Jersey. The state, which has almost doubled in population since the early 1960s, has built some twenty new prisons in the past two decades. But it has not opened one new campus of the University of California for nearly three decades. Its once-celebrated freeway system is now rated as among the most dilapidated road networks in the country. Many of its public libraries operate on reduced hours, and some have closed altogether. The state and county parks charge hefty admission fees. The state's social benefits, once among the nation's most generous, have been cut, and cut again, and then cut again. And what had once been a tuition-free college and university system, while still among the world's great public educational institutions, struggles for funds and charges as much as every other state university system, and in some cases more.

In 1994, Californians, who after World War II had reveled in their own growth and appeared to welcome every comer, voted overwhelmingly to exclude all illegal-alien children from their public schools. Two years later, they voted to prohibit every form of race- or gender-based affirmative action in public employment, contracting, and education. In 1997, California's Industrial Welfare Commission, a body appointed by the governor, abolished a rule dating back to the Progressive Era that required most nonfarm employers to pay overtime to any worker who worked more than an eight-hour day. In the meantime, the gap between the state's upper-income groups and its poorest workers is growing even more rapidly than the national average, not so much because the affluent are making so much more (though they are making more) but because the incomes of the bottom ten percent of the working population have fallen so much further. Thus, as the state celebrates its sesquicentennial—the 150th anniversary of the gold rush of 1848–49; admission to the Union in 1850—California's social policies and governmental structures can be seen more readily as an urgent cautionary tale, and as a high-stakes test for a nation that will increasingly be faced with similar challenges—indeed already is—than as a shining standard.

The most obvious question arising here is as complex in the answering as it is short in the asking: What happened? Why now, why in California, why in this form? What happened in the decades between the ebullient 'fifties and 'sixties and the anxious 'eighties and 'nineties? What occurred particularly in the interplay between the monumental demographic changes of a California where whites will soon be a minority among other minorities and the state's political evolution? What's the relationship between those changes, the enactment of the radical tax limits in Proposition 13 in 1978, the orgy of other voter initiatives that followed in its wake and that have gripped California for the better part of a generation, and the erosion of public services that they brought with them? Can a system that was created, and that flourished, for one kind of population maintain (or regain) its optimism and vitality for another? Put another way, are California's once-splendid public services and its promise of social equity sputtering and coughing because they became overloaded with social burdens? Or is the problem caused by some combination of hostility and indifference on the part of a body of voters that isn't sure it wants to carry this kind of load for *those kinds* of people? Californians seem to have regained some of their optimism, but many of the effects of the changes of the past generation will last long into the future. Could it all have been negotiated to better ends with better leadership?

Some twenty years have passed since the passage of California's Proposition 13, which set in motion not merely the holy crusade against taxes in which much of the country now seems irretrievably stuck, but a condition of permanent neopopulism in California, and to some extent elsewhere, for which there is no real precedent, even in the Progressive Era of the early years of the twentieth century. During the two decades since the passage of 13, California has been in nearly constant revolt against representative government. During that period, voters have passed one initiative after another—tax limitation initiatives; initiatives capping state and local spending; measures imposing specified minimum spending formulas for schools; term limits for legislative and statewide offices; three-strikes sentencing laws; land conservation measures; the measures abolishing affirmative action in public education, contracting, and employment, and seeking to deny public schooling and other services to illegal immigrants, and dozens of others—each of them mandating or prohibiting major programs and policies, or imposing supermajority requirements. Collectively, those initiatives sharply circumscribed the authority and discretion of the legislature, county boards of supervisors, school boards, city councils, and the courts. In addition, countless reform measures have emanated from the legislature that were themselves spurred by the plebiscitary populism that has marked California politics in the past generation.[1] Because of the constraints those initiatives impose on governmental discretion both at the state and local levels, California, in the words of one policy analyst, can be prosperous "and still be in a budget squeeze."[2] At a time when responsibility for welfare and other major federal programs is being shifted down to the states and local governments, those constraints have left many of California's counties, where the ultimate burden of serving needy people resides, in particularly tough cirumstances.

The passage of Proposition 13 serves as a convenient way of dividing the post–World War II era in California between that postwar period of optimism, with its huge investment in public infrastructure and its strong commitment to the development of quality education systems and other public services, and a generation of declining confidence and shrinking public services. Just as significantly, the state's latter-day populism, and the squeeze on taxes and public services it brought, occurred precisely during the period when the state was undergoing those demographic changes: from a society that thought of itself (and in many ways was) overwhelmingly white and middle class to one in which whites will soon be just another minority and where Hispanics, Asians, and blacks already constitute a sizeable majority in school enrollment and in the use of many other public services.

It is hard to prove that those demographic changes produced the political reaction and social neglect. There are other sources of stress in crime, the emergence of crack and other virulent street drugs, and the pressure that increased health costs have put on public budgets. And there are other states—Texas, Florida, New York—that have also been heavily affected by new waves of non-European immigrants. But no state has lived with such extraordinary expectations of social perfection or been subject to such large gaps between what its people once thought they ought, almost as a matter of right, to have, and the burdens they are willing to bear to get it. Those who now disproportionately depend on public services and who suffer the consequences when they're reduced are those new California immigrants and their children. Meanwhile, those who dominate the voter rolls are still white and middle class.

Because of the semipermanent revolt against government that Proposition 13 helped set in motion, and the growing use of the initiative that accompanied it, what had been designed (in 1911) as a Progressive Era instrument whereby "the people" could from time to time check the excesses of a state government that was then dominated by the Southern Pacific Railroad and a handful of other powerful interest groups has increasingly become the prevailing instrumentality of government itself. In the past two decades, the initiative has more often been used by well-organized political and economic entities, on the left and the right, and by incumbent politicians, from the governor down, than by anything that can be called "the people." It is still "the people" that vote on the initiatives that appear on the ballot. But it is those interest groups, backed by media consultants, direct mail specialists, pollsters, and others, that usually finance the costly signature drives, running into the millions, to get measures on the ballot, and the advertising campaigns that put them over—or that block the measures of opponents.

II

Paradoxically, the further the initiative process goes, the more difficult and problematic effective citizenship becomes. California has not just seen a sharp decline in the quality of public services—education, public parks, highways, water projects—that were once regarded as models for the nation. It has also seen the evolution of an increasingly unmanageable and incomprehensible structure of state and local government that exacerbates the same public disaffection and alienation that have brought it on, thus creating a vicious cycle of reform and frustration.

Each measure, because it further reduces governmental discretion, and because it moves control further from the public—from local to state government, from the legislature to the constitution, from simple majorities to supermajorities—makes it even harder to write budgets, respond to changing needs, and set reasonable priorities. And since many of those measures have irrationally—though sometimes necessarily—divided authority between state and local governments and among scores of different agencies, the opportunity for buck passing is nearly unlimited. To cite the most glaring example, because Proposition 13 specifically (and ironically) transferred a great deal of effective spending authority from local governments to the state, the state legislature, itself increasingly constrained by constitutional limits and mandates, allocates funds for local schools. But local school boards have, at least in theory, and, again, within the constraints of their own limits, the authority for spending it.

Thus, when funds run low or programs have to be cut, it is nearly impossible to determine whether accountability rests with the state's elected politicians for not providing enough or with the local board for spending it wastefully. Something similar is true for county governments. And since spending is so hopelessly tangled in formulas that have been written into the constitution—directly by measures like Proposition 98, which established mandatory minimum state funding requirements for the schools; indirectly by a three-strikes initiative that threatens to devour a large part of the state's discretionary funds in escalating prison costs—the system often runs largely on autopilot, beyond the control of any elected official. The whole fiscal system, in the view of Elizabeth Hill, California's nonpartisan Legislative Analyst, has become "dysfunctional." It "does not work together to achieve the public's goals."

Those problems have been compounded by the passage of the nation's most stringent legislative term limits, Proposition 140 in 1990, under which no member of the assembly may serve more than three two-year terms in a lifetime and no state senator more than two four-year terms, and which sharply cut the legislative budget and the professional staff that had once made California a national model as well. California does very little of consequence without excess.

Even before term limits passed, the state legislature had begun to lose a good deal of its luster. Beginning in the early 1980s, it had been afflicted by a series of scandals and embarrassments, including convictions for bribery and extortion that sent a number of its members to jail. More broadly, its effectiveness and stature visibly deteriorated, partly because of the increased complexity and diversity of the state; partly because of the fiscal constraints of Proposition 13 and other constitutional restrictions on legislative discretion and accountability, and the increased partisanship they brought with them; partly because of the increasing cost of campaigns and the political "arms races" they fostered; and partly because of the wider incivility in all public life. But rather than bringing on the "Citizen Legislature" promised by some of its advocates, term limits has generated even more partisanship and incivility among members, a growing inability to compromise, a legislative leadership with greatly reduced powers, and a sharp decline in legislators' comprehension of, and interest in, the complexities of the issues that they are supposed to deal with. When major fiscal committees handling billions of dollars or trying to deal with the intricacies of insurance regulation, school finance, welfare policy, or water law are chaired by people who have been there for no more than six months; when the speaker of the assembly will necessarily be someone with four years' experience or less, and when the professional staff is as thin as it has become, the quality of the work inevitably declines.

In 1997, after all assembly members first elected in 1990 or before were already "termed out," a federal trial judge overturned part of the law, ruling that its lifetime ban is unnecessary to achieve its prime objective, which is to enhance rotation in office and reduce the power of incumbency. The decision, upheld by a three-judge panel, which ruled (incredibly) that the voters really didn't know what they were endorsing, was ultimately overturned by the Ninth Circuit Court of Appeals. Term limits in California, together with sharp cuts in professional staff, are here to stay. The net effect is increased power for interest group lobbyists and agency bureaucrats, who are under no term-limit restraints and who will increasingly become the major source of legislative information. What is likely to increase even more in the face of legislative deprofessionalization—as in some respects it already has—is the power of chance, of error, of gridlock, and of nonfeasance.

But that's only the beginning of this story, which is as much about process as about outcome, as much about unexpected consequences as about those that were intended. Because Proposition 13 froze property values at 1975 levels and only allows them to be reassessed when title changes hands, the owners of identical parcels—say, two neighboring homes of precisely equal value—can pay vastly different amounts in property taxes, and often do. The same is true for business property, something that puts an increasingly large burden on new business and business development, rewards speculative land-holding, and discourages new investment. And because the state has allowed local jurisdictions to keep the sales tax but has shifted a large chunk of property tax revenues (already curtailed by Proposition 13) to pay for its constutionally mandated school support, many jurisdictions prefer sales-tax paying businesses—shopping malls particularly—to new manufacturing plants and other industry, even though the latter usually generate better jobs. The one pays for itself in new tax revenues, the other does not. Thus, in many communities, the developer of a shopping center has often gotten warmer treatment from zoning boards, planning commissions, and city councils than has the new assembly plant. In California, it's called the fiscalization of land use, and its skewing effect on patterns of development appears to be considerable. Although California's economy has grown vigorously in recent years, a lot of people in the business community believe it might grow more vigorously and rationally if the nexus between economic development and improved local public services were more apparent.

Despite these and other distortions, however, Proposition 13 and its progeny remain sacrosanct, icons of a public policy that no politician dare attack. For a whole generation of middle-aged and elderly home owners, the escalating property taxes of the mid-1970s were a searing experience similar to the impact of the Depression on an older generation, and Proposition 13 akin to the New Deal, a measure credited with preserving the homes and economic security of millions of people. In the 1996 election, the voters, rather than easing property tax restrictions, made them even tighter, requiring votes of property owners (in one case) or of the general electorate (in others) for *any* assessment increasing property-based fees or other exactions. In California, no taxation without representation has been replaced by no taxation without a vote—in many cases without a two-thirds vote—of the people.

This book focuses on this neopopulism, its roots in the state's changing political economy and demographics—white, affluent, elderly taxpapers who vote, as against the younger, preponderantly black and Latino people who use the services but vote in much lower numbers—and its consequences in public services, many of them services used primarily by children. The most obvious of those consequences is the relative slide, already mentioned above, in California school spending from sixth or eighth in the nation per pupil to fortieth; the crowded classrooms, the unmaintained buildings with leaking roofs, falling ceiling tiles, and unusable toilets; the layoffs of school counselors, librarians, and nurses; and the reductions in course offerings in everything from art to zoology. Writer Jonathan Kozol found rotting school facilities in the inner cities; California has them in the suburbs as well.

But the consequences of the state's political shifts also include the ironic decision of the financially strapped University of California to offer across-the-board early retirement to thousands of professors whose salaries it could no longer afford, among them some of the same stars that it had so proudly recruited a generation before. They include the reduced hours and resources of the public libraries; the deteriorating highways; and the increasing reliance on fees to run public parks, pools, and other amenities that had once been virtually free (and the broader anticommunitarian fee ethic that comes with them). And they are reflected in the various efforts of a growing number of people, through gated communities and the creation of new secessionist "cities," to withdraw from the larger commonweal altogether. Some of these things have also occurred, and are still occuring, in other states, but in none has the difference between before and after been anywhere near as great as it has been in the Golden State.

Inevitably, the story also touches on the roles of the principal players in this complex drama, from the California Progressives who led the drive to write the initiative into the state constitution, to Governor Edmund G. "Pat" Brown, the master builder and exemplar of California's public dynamism of the 1950s and 1960s. The cast also includes Howard Jarvis and Paul Gann, the antitax organizers, often called "antitax crusaders" in the media, who invented Proposition 13 and whose professional campaign managers created new political technologies in the effort to get it passed. And it includes people like Gerald Meral of the Planning and Conservation League, who adapted them for environmental, medical, and other causes generally described as liberal.

Together the men and women who refined the uses of the initiative and made it the centerpiece of latter-day California politics have brought into existence a whole new set of political practices and organizations. On the one hand, there is a large network of consulting and initiative marketing firms that not merely work for groups seeking to pass ballot measures (or to block them) but sometimes test market issues for their feasibility to generate funds through direct mailings, and then shop for a group to back them. On the other hand, California has witnessed the creation of semi-private legislative practices whereby an environmental organization will package hundreds of locally backed projects into a statewide bond measure—acquisition of park land, for example, or designation of wildlife refuges—in return for financial and other support from local sponsor-groups in getting the measure on the ballot and getting it passed.

All of this, of course, has had—and continues to have—

broader national influence and implications. Just as Howard Jarvis and Paul Gann began the national tax revolt of the late 1970s and helped point the way for the presidential policies of Ronald Reagan, so California's hyperpopulism, its off-again, on-again forays into immigrant exclusion and its growing penchant for autopilot solutions, have resonated at the federal level—in the push for a balanced budget amendment and for a constitutional amendment requiring congressional supermajorities to increase public revenues; in term limits; in the drive for more restrictive immigration policies and against race- and gender-based affirmative action; in flat tax proposals; in mandatory judge-proof criminal sentencing laws, and in the wider neopopulist climate that underlies them. These things did not all originate in California, but they have generally found their most powerful launching platforms there.

From its start in America in the 1890s, that populism has had both its dark and its affirmative, optimistic sides. Both have been opportunities for some of the nation's most influential politicians: from William Jennings Bryan, Robert M. LaFollette, and Hiram Johnson to Huey Long, George Wallace, and Pat Buchanan—as well as those, like Governor Pete Wilson of California, who, though they are not of it and are temperamentally unsuited for it, have nonetheless exploited it. Proposition 187, which passed in 1994, was hardly the first instance when California tried to have the cake of its cheap immigrant labor and shut those workers and their families out at the same time. Californians excluded Asians from a whole range of economic and educational rights—in issuing business licenses, in the right to attend school with whites, and in a variety of other areas—and the Progressives were hardly immune to such temptations. Less than three years after California's Progressive revolt emerged triumphant in the election of 1910, Hiram Johnson, who had pushed scores of reforms, including tougher utility and railroad regulation, direct democracy through the initiative and referendum, and women's suffrage, gave in to the pressure of the Asiatic Exclusion League and signed the Alien Land Law that denied Japanese aliens the right to own land in California.[3] That dark side has always been inseparably interwoven with the more hopeful elements.

[handwritten margin note: Another example of discrim. in CA.]

But California's latter-day populism nonetheless tends to be a different kind of political impulse, not because it is primarily a populism of the right whose prime objective is the enervation of government itself, but because it is not particularly interested in civic engagement or in increasing the effectiveness of the citizen in government at all. It is not primarily a movement to cleanse and regain control of the affairs of state through governmental institutions more responsive to the popular will. It is often more like a parody of the Newtonian system of checks and balances written by the framers into the U.S. Constitution, a mechanical device that's supposed to run more or less by itself and spares the individual the bother and complexities of any sort of political engagement.

Woven through that California-style populism is the seemingly irresistible myth of excessive taxation. When he came into the governor's office in 1991, Pete Wilson was forced by recession and a looming $14 billion state deficit—and by the need to deal with a Democatic legislature—to balance spending cuts with a set of temporary state tax increases. But he took a terrible pummeling for those tax increases, particularly from members of his own party. He has pushed, with considerable success, for major tax cuts ever since. Those cuts have disproportionately favored corporations and higher-income taxpayers. Along the way, he continues to insist— and most voters continue to believe—that Californians are over-taxed compared to people in neighboring states, despite the fact that as a percentage of personal income, Californians' taxes are now at just about the national average, and that they pay a smaller share of their personal income in state and local taxes than all but one of their Western neighbors. (Something similar is true, of course, for the myth that this country is overtaxed as a nation.) It is hard to imagine that those arguments would be made with as much vehemence if the beneficiaries of the public services that those taxes support were believed to be the same people, or the same sort of people, as those who go to the polls and vote, or if more voters had someone living at home who is under eighteen.

But the new populism also reflects (and reinforces) the declining stature of, and respect for, virtually all major public institutions and establishments, from the judicial system and the media, to the universities, to the ideal of commonweal itself. We appear to be on the verge of a time when unedited information and unmediated media—the talk show, the computer news group and bulletin board—will radically change (and perhaps undermine) traditional politics and social relations. For the first time in history, the unfounded rumor, the fragment of suspicion, the wildly false "fact," is something not just shared over the back fence but spread in megabytes and milliseconds, without editing, review, or check, to an audience of millions—peasants with pitchforks on the Internet.

It's impossible to determine exactly how all those forces contribute to the new populism; they are evolving too fast and reacting on one another in too many ways. But there's not much doubt that all have contributed to the anticommunitarian, market-oriented ethic of our politics. The recent history of the California initiative system has demonstrated the essential irony of that process: that as the public trusts the system less and less, it becomes ever more susceptible to untested quick-fix remedies that, instead of resolving the problems of the moment, limit public choice and make long-term solutions even more difficult. But it has hardly deterred it.

III

This book attempts to look at those forces, and at how they have shaped California in the past forty years, and particularly at the period since the beginning of the tax revolt in the mid-1970s. It is divided into five major sections. The first two deal with the before-and-after *what* of this story; the next two with the historical *how* of the past forty years; the last with the future-oriented question of *what now*:

- A section briefly describing California's heyday of post–World War II optimism, itself probably founded on excessive expectations, that peaked in the era of Pat Brown—roughly 1958–66—and an examination of the demographic, economic, and political stresses that so quickly began to undermine it.
- A snapshot of California today, focusing on the state's Mississippified public services and infrastructure and

the fundamentally changed government structure and social relations that California's tax revolt and its political progeny have produced.

- A section on the causes of the radical tax revolt that's associated with Proposition 13, and its consequences in California's ability to manage its affairs. Although 13 has become its enduring symbol, the attempt to mandate fiscal policies has run through scores of other ballot measures, some of them (in reaction to the tax limits) mandating certain kinds of spending, most further restricting either revenues or spending.

- An elaboration of the history, dynamics, and broader implications of California's orgy of plebiscites, as well as a discussion of the major measures of the past two decades, and their consequences both in substantive policy and in the increasingly constrained exercise of policy choices imposed on representative government in California.

- A brief coda examining the possibilities for a new political integration and a revitalized social ethic in California, describing the contrary forces pushing even further toward a market-based governmental ethic, and appraising the national implications and the stakes that ride on the outcome of the conflict between them.

Those subjects, which deal both with the politics and policy consequences of the changes in California, are inextricably interrelated. Certain threads and social motifs—the impact of California's new immigrants, for example, and the complex effects of California's contorted tax and fiscal systems—run through all of them and will therefore recur in different ways in different parts of the book. For nearly a generation, there has been increasing focus among scholars, politicians, and journalists on the growing gaps in California—ethnic, social, economic—between those who exercise political power and the larger population, and particularly those who are the most immediate users of its public services. What has gotten little discussion is the dynamic of the plebiscitary process itself. While it's ad hoc in nature—each measure is decided by voters on its own apparent merits without much reference to the wider context—it has a larger cumulative effect through which statewide majorities restrict the powers of local political majorities, which are often nonwhite. Almost by definition, it is also a device of impulse that tends to be only marginally respectful of minority rights or interests, and that lends itself to demagogic wedge campaigns designed to boost voter turnout for other political purposes.

Place the new political demographics alongside the increasing use of the initiative in setting social policy, and you therefore have an extraordinarily complex set of questions that bear both on the majority's ability to govern and on the rights of the state's (and the nation's) growing social and political minorities. They are loaded with implications for the future of an increasingly diverse American society.

Making the story even more complicated are the unintended consequences of the plebiscitary process, and particularly the growing confusion of government functions that makes it increasingly difficult for anyone outside of government (and often even for those inside) to know who's accountable for what. The voters who overwhelmingly passed Proposition 13 were certainly trying to reduce their residential property taxes. Almost assuredly they were not at the same time trying to shift the political balance of power further from local government toward the state. Yet that was what they did. Neither were they explicitly trying to reduce services to the new immigrants who, even then, constituted a substantial share of the state's school enrollment. The only poll on the issue (taken more than a year after the fact) indicated that Proposition 13 carried among all ethnic groups except blacks; the polls showed it carrying narrowly among Hispanics.

Yet it's hard to imagine Proposition 13 passing if school financing and its benefits had still been perceived in the same terms as they had been in the 1950s, when their enrollment was overwhelmingly white. According to one respected tax economist, the very attempt to equalize funding between have and have-not school districts, ordered by the state supreme court in the early and mid-

1970s, fatally weakened support for high local school taxes and thus helped make Proposition 13 possible. If that theory is correct, it's another striking illustration of the power of the unintended consequences of well-intentioned reform. It's also a clear sign that people have always been willing to pay more if the money is spent close to home.

What seems equally clear is that while the initiative has frequently been used as an instrument both against government and against minorities of various descriptions, it's nearly impossible to try consistently to define the new populism in purely ideological terms—as just (for example) a right-wing phenomenon, even though on individual issues it often is. In November 1996, the same voters who passed yet another stringent tax limitation measure also balloted overwhelmingly to raise the state's minimum wage and legalize the medical use of marijuana. And they came within a hair of restoring higher marginal tax brackets for upper-income tax payers. The ad hoc nature of the initiative process tends to elude anything resembling a consistent pursuit of policy. At the same time, the process is certainly one that, over time, reflects the class and economic impulses of those who use it, and that has reinforced the already sizeable economic and social gaps between California's voters and its larger (nonvoting) population.

This is primarily a journalist's book, not a work of social science. It comes from intense observation and analysis, spanning more than a generation, of developments in what may well be the democratic world's most fascinating political community. The observations have included conversations with most—if not indeed all—of the major public figures in that community: politicians and community leaders at all levels, among them three governors, a former governor, and countless would-be governors; scholars, social activists, and hundreds of representatives of every major interest group: from the bar, from business, from environmental and health organizations, from public employee and other labor groups, from a broad range of minority and ethnic groups, from the universities, the community colleges, and the public schools, and from county welfare offices and public libraries, not to mention the taxpayer organizations, the professional policy analysts, the lobbyists, and the political consultants. And since most of those conversations, backed by thousands of reports and studies and countless follow-up interviews, were conducted from what may well be the best single vantage point in the state—the editorial board of one of the state's major newspapers, as well the major state capital newspaper—they surely qualify, at the very least, as that first rough cut of history that journalism modestly claims for itself.

Given the complexity of the issues in California and the rapid way that event follows event, history's first cut may turn out to be very rough indeed. Yet the changes that have occurred—in government, in public services, in public outlook—are stark and dramatic. And the questions they raise for the nation as a whole are equally stark. Joan Didion was echoing historian Frederick Jackson Turner's classic invocation of the frontier as the crucial influence in American democracy when she declared a generation ago that things had better work in California because it is there that we run out of continent. But that has to be accompanied by another, equally portentous—and much more urban—wish: Things had better work here, where the new American society is first coming into full view, because if it fails here, it may never work anywhere else either.[4] California is America's most important test for that emerging society, and so far the outcome of that test remains very much in doubt.

PART TWO
Altered State

‹›

Golden Moment

‹›

I

In the fall of 1962, the national media discovered California once again. The networks came, *Newsweek* came, *Look* came, *Life* came, and before the decade was out, so did *Saturday Review, Time, Ladies Home Journal*, the *New York Times Magazine, Better Homes and Gardens, Holiday*, and *National Geographic*, many of them devoting entire issues to the California phenomenon. The formal occasion was the moment, sometime that fall or winter, when California, which then had a population of just a little over 17 million people and was drawing between 1,000 and 1,500 new residents a day, would forever surpass New York as the nation's most populous and dynamic state. Governor Edmund G. "Pat" Brown called it "the greatest mass migration in the history of the world."[1]

But the real story, for the editors, for California, for the country, was bigger—the re-rendering of the old myth of El Dorado into yet another form: California not as promise but as the embodiment of the American future—the dream made flesh. "No.1 State: Booming, Beautiful California," said *Newsweek's* cover line. "Tomorrow's hopes and tomorrow's headaches are here today in our soon-to-be largest state," said *Look*. "California Here We Come—and This Is Why," said *Life*. "California: A State of Excitement," said the headline in *Time*. It may turn out to have been the last great burst of regional mythmaking in America. Not since 1893, when Frederick Jackson Turner declared the frontier closed, had there been such a celebration of new territory and possibilities.[2]

Probably the most effusive of the new discoverers was George B. Leonard, then a senior editor at *Look,* who would susbsequently become a leading denizen of the Esalen Institute and one of the more vocal apostles of California's encounter culture. "California," he wrote, "is a window into the future. The powerful, almost incomprehensible new forces that are reshaping the lives of men everywhere are at their strongest here; the traditional patterns of institutions, community and class (which hold back change) are at their weakest."[3] Here, he said:

> is the most fertile soil for new ideas in the U.S. The migrating millions who vote with their wheels for California are responding not only to the lure of sunny skies, but to the lure of opportunity. Already, this state shows the way with a revolutionary master plan of higher education for practically everybody; with an increasingly egalitarian society; with unprecedented opportunities for personal pleasure and fulfillment. Most important of all, California presents the promise and challenge contained at the very heart of the original American dream: here probably more than at any other place or time, the shackles of the past are broken. In helping to create the society of the future, a man is limited only by the strength of his ambition, the dimension of his concern and the depths of his courage to face the dangers of his own creation.

This was not the California of the old frontier and Virgin Land, not the California of the Gold Rush, or of some Eastern fantasy, or even of Hollywood, though there was surely a lot of that. In some respects, California, even then, did not regard itself as a single entity at all—not in the way there is a Kansas or an Iowa—except, of course, for those looking at it from outside. Even then most people thought of themselves as San Franciscans or Angelenos, or residents of the North Coast or the Gold Country, or The Valley

(San Fernando, San Joaquin, Sacramento, take your pick), regions that were often in sharp conflict, particularly over issues such as water, and whose residents were sometimes deeply contemptuous of one another. But the label had to do because there was no other: What it now described was California as it appeared to have become, the dream in place, as it was being lived by increasing millions of Americans.

There was no end of material to support the tone of gee-whiz: the citrus groves that were giving way, at a rate of hundreds of acres a day, to the new housing tracts of Orange County; the beaches, the parks, the backyard swimming pools; the Nobel laureates at Berkeley and Stanford and Cal Tech; the deep thinkers assembled around the table at Robert Hutchins's Center for the Study of Democratic Institutions in Santa Barbara; the great network of junior colleges "where you're not just a name on an IBM card"; the huge water system that Governor Pat Brown was developing in the Central Valley; the great California freeways he was building from one end of the state to the other; and the freeway fights that even then were breaking out among developers, engineers, and environmentalists.

There was the fragrant variety of lifestyles (what *Look* would call "the Way Out Way of Life"); the health fads (a California housewife undergoing a strenuous regimen at her health club and observing that her legs were firmer this year or, in *Newsweek's* verbal snapshot, "wealthy dowagers in bikinis basking in the sun like fat lizards musing over nothing deeper than caloric count"); the exotic homes in every style imaginable—Spanish, Egyptian, French chateau, complete with gold-plated bathroom fixtures, forty-foot sofas, and "automatic rain"; making the scene on the Sunset strip, the nudes on San Gregorio beach, the surfers, the "Zen cultists finding serenity near San Francisco," and the even more exotic politics, cults, and fads that had already become clichés in the Southern California landscape. And, of course, the ultimate symbol: "the California teen-ager, [emblem] of the child-centered and oddly childlike culture," as *Newsweek* described him, "one hand on the wheel and the other around a girl or a beer can, as if the freeway, and all it leads to, were designed solely for him."[4]

Everyone made lists, or even lists of lists. "Among things that California has more of," said the *National Geographic* in May 1966, "are national parks, national forests, military bases. It also has more teachers, students, automobiles, superhighways and motorcycles—not to mention more major league baseball teams (three) and more members of the National Geographic Society (630,000) than any other state." (It had, in fact, been the shocking departure to "the Coast" of two of New York's three baseball teams in the late 1950s—the Dodgers for Los Angeles, the Giants for San Francisco—that had, as much as anything, prefigured the inevitable shift of continental gravity.) California—Berkeley, Cal Tech, Stanford—was the engine of the nation's new intellectual and technological energy, "the farthest frontier [in Leonard's words] of the great Scientific Revolution that is reshaping the world." It was said to be the source of a "new human equation" in the way people related to one another, to their families, their communities, and their society: California, as Wallace Stegner put it at the time, "unformed, innovative, ahistorical, hedonistic, acquisitive and energetic," whose "version of the Good Life, its sports, pleasures and comforts, are increasingly copied by the envious elsewhere."[5] Like the rest of America, only more so.

But most of all, to judge from the prevailing imagery, it was the home of millions of well-educated young families (all white, needless to say) with good jobs at Aerojet and Lockheed; at Hughes and North American and Douglas; at Ford and General Motors (which then still had large California plants); at JPL, the Jet Propulsion Laboratory in Pasadena; at TRW and at the scores of electronics firms that had begun to cluster in what is now Silicon Valley below San Francisco, many of them still-modest operations—Hewlett-Packard, Fairchild—that most people had then barely heard of.

Nearly all of those new Californians had been washed by the Hollywood fantasies of the Depression, which were, of course, largely about itself. And those fantasies were themselves nourished on earlier myths, going back four centuries and more to the dreams of El Dorado—was it not the hot sun that made gold?—and the fabulous Seven Cities of Cibola. The opening chapter of the WPA guide to California, first published as *California: A Guide to the Golden State* in 1939, was titled "El Dorado Up to Date."[6] But hundreds of thousands of them had first seen California (one is tempted to say "the real California," but that might be asking for trouble) during the war, either in uniform at the state's huge military bases—Mare Island, Long Beach, San Diego, Mather, McClellan, Edwards, Pendleton—or as workers in the state's defense plants (the largest single year of California in-migration up to that time was 1943, when a net of 664,000 people moved into the state). Now they were back, moving into those tract houses, a few hundred down, plus $60 a month for thirty years, and demanding the best in schools and community colleges, in freeways and parks and playgrounds, for themselves and their children. What they wanted, according to the prevailing image—no, what they had—was the Good Life.

> You can't talk about the California woman [said the *Ladies Home Journal* in 1967] without a sense of discovery, of excitement, because she is gradually changing the American concept of femininity. She has greater total freedom, more mobility, yet greater personal security as a wife and mother. She has slipped the old orders and mores; the "back home" social structure has evaporated. She has become scandal-proof. She is with it intellectually . . . This Western woman lives in todays and thinks in tomorrows, no matter what her age. There are jobs and positions and fortunes to be made, and she is taking advantage of them.[7]

To be sure, a lot of people, in and outside California, were already voicing deep concerns—about crowding, pollution, resource depletion, about "the impact of unbridled growth," in a state that was adding upwards of 500,000 people a year, about the impact on land and people of the mechanized agriculture in California's Central Valley, and about the ultimate consequences of the science that was going on in those labs. "When I wrote *Brave New World*," Aldous Huxley, by then a longtime California resident, told Leonard, "I had no idea how soon so much of it would come true,

I had no idea—I don't think anyone did—how swiftly science would develop, how fast the population would increase, how effectively people would be organized in larger and larger groups. Already, we are working out most of the techniques for controlling the mind as I saw them in my book. What's more, our power for controlling—or devastating—the outside world already has proceeded beyond what I could have foreseen."[8]

Huxley was hardly the first, much less alone, in his concern about the state's destructive potential. For more than a half-century, American literature had been occupied by the demonic underside of all that sunshine and promise—in the works of Frank Norris, of John Steinbeck, of Nathanael West, of Raymond Chandler; its history replete with a century of exploitation, exclusion, bigotry, and strife: in the fields and farm labor camps, at Manzanar and the other Japanese internment camps, on the docks, and in the streets of the big cities. There was the bombing of the *Los Angeles Times* in 1910; the brutal longshoremen's strike in 1916; the uprising of the Wheatland hop pickers; the frame-up, after the fatal bombing at a San Francisco Preparedness Day Parade in 1916, of the Socialist activist Tom Mooney, who spent some twenty years in jail before he was pardoned in 1938. Those who cared to had seen Dorothea Lange's haunting documentary photographs and read *Factories in the Field,* Carey McWilliams's descriptions of the latifundist industrial agriculture that dominated California's rich valleys.[9] And of course, a lot of middle-class groups, like California Tomorrow, a private planning organization, were already warning about the excesses of all that growth—"the sloppy, sleazy, slovenly, slipshod semi-cities" that a lot of California was becoming or had already turned into—and wondering how polluted "can a bright land become?"[10]

But few of those things, though cited, were integrated into the image: California in the 1960s seemed to have been discovered fresh, without history, without the original sin of conquest, exploitation, and development, as if it been made overnight. One was immediately struck, said *Time*'s new correspondent in San Francisco in 1969, "by how much of the California legend was true—the climate, the geography, the hordes of new Californians shucking off old ways and values and experimenting with the new." And if there were problems, as Leonard said, "the best place in the world" to face them was California, "where the future is happening every day [and where] ordinary people must cope with the novel and difficult dilemma posed by plenty, bigness and change . . ."

Just as important for the image, the place, whatever its problems, appeared to have freed itself of the American past. "California's sprawling population does not live in a coal scuttle culture. It is short on oppressed minorities, and it breathes the heady confidence of the postwar boom," wrote T George Harris in the same issue of *Look*. And so "California's political message is clear: The needy minorities of the past are becoming the prosperous majorities of the future. The have-nots now vanish into a society of near-equal haves." The assassination in Dallas of John F. Kennedy was still a year off, the campus demonstrations first sparked by the Free Speech Movement at Berkeley would not begin for another two years; the Watts riots were three years off, and no one had ever heard of Charlie Manson. Hard as it may be to believe now, according to the 1960 Census, the most common native language of California's foreign-born residents (the largest number of whom were then British or Canadian) was English.[11]

There was reason for the excitement. Although many of the state's great public works monuments—the Bay Bridge, the Caldecott Tunnel, and the Golden Gate Bridge, for example—had been completed before the war, thereby opening the Bay Area to the boom of development that began in the late 1940s, and while California had benefited enormously from the WPA and other federal programs, which constructed hundreds of attractive schools and other public buildings in the 1930s, no state had ever invested in public services and development as California did in the 1950s and 1960s.[12]

There was the enormous burst of highway construction, calling for some $10.5 billion in new freeways and expressways, one-third funded by the huge federal highway program begun in the Eisenhower years, the rest coming out of Calfornia's own vehicle fuel taxes and auto-registration fees, that was supposed to add 12,500 miles of new freeways over a twenty-year period—not to mention countless miles of other roads. That system would, in Governor Pat Brown's words, "connect every county seat and every city of 5000 or more people, serve every major industrial, agricultural and recreational region, and return an estimated two dollars in benefits to highway users for every dollar invested." It was, according to the Brown administration (quoting federal highway officials), "the finest job of planning a highway network in history." Even if traffic volume were to double, as it was expected to do, "it will still flow smoothly and safely."[13]

There was the unprecedented $1.75 billion bond issue to start the huge California Water Project that Brown, who was never ashamed to call himself a liberal, negotiated through the treacherous shoals and narrows of the state's fiercely competitive water agencies—not to mention the competing regional interests in the legislature—and then to approval from the state's voters. At the time it was approved, the CWP, a system of sixteen dams, eighteen pumping stations, nine power generating plants, and hundreds of miles of aqueducts, canals, and levees that would complement the huge federal Central Valley Project, was by far the largest public works project ever undertaken by a state—ultimately, it was expected to cost more than $3 billion. And even at that, Brown regarded it only as the beginning of an even more grandiose forty-year California Water Plan that would, by his own estimate, run to as much as $11 billion.[14] Of necessity, it had something for almost every region and interest group, providing flood control for Northern California ("harnessing the turbulent Feather River") and moving water south from the Feather and Sacramento Rivers to San Joaquin Valley growers—"California Irrigated Agriculture," the roadside signs would say, "Feeds the World"—and pumping it over the Tehachapi Mountains to urban users in Southern California. There was plenty of water, Brown said. The trouble was that "we do not have enough water when and where we need it [and] we have too much water when and where we do not need it."[15]

There was the string of new campuses for the University of California and the California state colleges; there were the thousands of new classrooms being constructed, at a rate of twenty a day, to house the 200,000 new elementary and high school students that were streaming into the schools each year; there were countless new state parks and other major projects, and there was a cheerful willingness to raise taxes, particularly by establishing new brackets for high incomes, when necessary. Brown later recollected a conversation he had with Fred Dutton, his executive secretary in 1959–60 before Dutton joined the Kennedy administration. Dutton was worried about the cost of the water project.

" 'You're going to drown the kids in water,' " Brown recalled Dutton saying, " 'because you won't have enough money to do both.'

"I said, 'We'll find enough money to do both. We'll build the water project and we'll build new universities and new state colleges and new community colleges and elementary schools, too. We've got plenty of money and we have to do it.' "[16] It was something that no California governor—and probably no other American governor—would ever say again in the same way. He believed, his daughter Kathleen Brown said many years later, "in the absolute destiny of California to grow."[17]

The postwar public works boom had begun under Brown's progressive Republican predecessors, Earl Warren and Goodwin Knight, well before Brown was elected governor in 1958, and in considerable measure even before that, and it would continue for some years afterward. "The Californian of today," said the WPA Guide in 1939, "feels a personal pride in the State's gargantuan public works: highways, bridges, dams and aqueducts. And most of all, of course, he exalts in the region's 'happy future.' " Still, it was the Brown era (1959–67)[18] that marked its high point and still symbolizes it. UC's Davis campus, which had been the university farm since 1908, was turned into a regular university branch in 1959. During the same period, the university launched its San Diego campus, an outgrowth of the Scripps Institution of Oceanography; built two entirely new campuses, one at Irvine, the other at Santa Cruz, each with an innovative academic and residential plan that differed sharply from the established institutions at Berkeley and Los Angeles, or indeed from all other large public universities; vastly expanded its campus at Santa Barbara; opened three new medical schools; and launched countless other professional schools and programs. In the meantime there was an even bigger boom in construction of junior colleges and of campuses of the state colleges, the mid-level segment of the state's three-tiered higher education system, which had begun as a collection of teachers colleges, and which is still training more than half of the state's teachers. A total of nine new state colleges were opened between 1957 and 1966.

It was a stunning run. When Brown was elected, the University of California had two major branches, plus a couple of satellites and two medical schools (one in Los Angeles, the other in San Francisco). When he left, there were eight campuses, five medical schools, and scores of other operations, a "multiversity," in President Clark Kerr's newly minted word, that, in its graduate faculties and programs, quickly became the equal of any research university on earth, an enterprise so vast, ambitious, and all-encompassing that it awed even those who created it.[19]

> The University of California last year had operating expenditures from all sources of nearly half a billion dollars [Kerr said in his Godkin lectures at Harvard in 1963], with almost another 100 million for construction; a total employment of over 40,000 people, more than IBM and in a far greater variety of endeavors; operations in over a hundred locations, counting campuses, experiment stations, argricultural and urban extension centers, and projects abroad involving more than fifty countries; nearly 10,000 courses in its catalogues; some form of contact with nearly every industry, nearly every level of government, nearly every person in its region. Vast amounts of expensive equipment were serviced and maintained. Over 4000 babies were born in its hospitals. It is the world's largest purveyor of white mice. It will soon have the world's largest primate colony. It will soon have 100,000 students—30,000 of them at the graduate level; yet much less than one third of its expenditures are related to teaching. It already has 200,000 students in its

extension courses—including one out of every three lawyers and one out of every six doctors in the state.[20]

Kerr would later acknowledge that sometimes his new creature troubled even him. There were already the "walking wounded" within the multiversity, students who "began to visualize themselves as the 'lumpen proletariat'—or, in more modern terminology, as prisoners of the campus ghetto; and a few students wanted even then to make the campus into a 'fortress' from which society might be attacked."[21] And for its part, "the public was worried about how far, and how fast research discoveries may change the lives of everyone. The university was accelerating its racing car named Science, hardly noticing that the public was getting ready to reduce the supply of gas."

But at the time Kerr was so busy building it, recruiting the academic stars that became the world's envy, and constructing the huge research apparatus they required, that there was hardly time to notice. In 1959, one incredulous Eastern college president, Charles W. Cole of Amherst, returned from a Western trip to tell his faculty that in California, Kerr was *stockpiling* professors that he didn't yet need—which, Kerr later acknowledged, was precisely what he was doing. By 1963, as Kerr pointed out, California already had 36 percent of the nation's Nobel laureates in science and 20 percent of the members of the National Academy of Sciences, and its universities had become "bait to be dangled in front of industry, with drawing power greater than low taxes or cheap labor." In 1964, Kerr recalled, twenty-eight of Berkeley's academic departments were rated among the top six in the nation, the first time that a UC campus topped Harvard in the American Council on Education ratings as "the best balanced distinguished university" on earth.[22]

And if the numbers were impressive, so was the Master Plan for Higher Education, approved in 1960, largely at Kerr's instigation, that governed and regulated California's higher education system, a scheme that became a model for the world. In essence, the Master Plan was two things: a formal division of turf among the three sometimes jealous segments of the state's higher education system, and a commitment from the state that it would provide higher education, at virtually no charge, to every Californian who could benefit from it, something that historian Kevin Starr would later call, with no hint of irony, an attempt at creating an educational utopia.

The University of California would be the state's paramount research institution and the only public university in the state authorized to give doctoral degrees and run doctoral programs; it would admit only the top one-eighth of the state's high school graduates to its undergraduate programs, but would also accept juniors who were successful graduates of the community colleges. The state college system—since renamed the California State University, a name and an ambition that Kerr had vehemently opposed—would be primarily a teaching institution and would accept the top third of the state's high school graduates. And the junior colleges, offering both technical and vocational programs and lower-division academic courses for students expecting to transfer to four-year institutions, would be open at no cost to all, regardless of their records, provided only that they could somehow benefit from the process—what the admiring Organization for Economic Development and Cooperation was to call "a distinctive attempt to reconcile populism with elitism." Kerr, in retrospect, said he and others had managed "to seize upon history and shape it rather than being overrun by it."

Given all its growth, particularly in the elementary and secondary schools—and given the fact that this was laid-back, sunny California—it wasn't surprising that there were momentous problems as well. With the surge of new people, particularly in Southern California, local districts couldn't build the schools or hire the teachers fast enough. As a consequence, the state even then had some of the nation's most crowded classrooms, as well as 160,000 students—out of some 3 million—who were attending schools on double sessions. And like other states, California was caught in the backwash of Sputnik, launched by the Russians in the fall of 1957, which generated a decade of criticism about America's supposed space-age shortcomings.

The first items on that list were the academic inadequacies of the public schools: their allegedly excessive focus on "basket-weaving" courses and Progressive Era "life-adjustment programs," their corresponding lack of disciplinary rigor, particularly in math and science, their failure to put enough stress on such "fundamentals" as writing "with ease and logic," and their inadequately trained teachers. If those deficiencies weren't corrected, the Russians would continue to beat this country's brains out in math, science, and engineering, with heaven only knew what dreadful consequences in the Cold War. In Southern California, where the Birchers had become increasingly active, in some cases managing to recall school board members they regarded as too liberal, the criticism, focused on the neglect of "basics" in reading and math, and the alleged one-worldism and lack of patriotism in the civics and history courses, was particularly virulent.[23]

Some of the criticism was almost certainly correct: There were schools where the academic program was flabby, especially compared to the academically more rigorous suburban schools of the Northeast and Midwest, and many people who had seen both were struck by it. While there were few reliable measures in the 1950s and 1960s to compare performance among students of different states, in 1955 the American Council on Education, an organization primarily of research university presidents, tested a sample of high school students in English, math, science, and other fields, and rated California thirty-fifth in the nation.[24]

Yet even if those measures were reliable, the flabbiness in California probably had more to do with the surrounding culture than with the excesses of Deweyan Progressivism—a vision of education not necessarily for superior academic performance, but for the Good Life. Parents demanded a lot of their schools, more than parents did in other parts of the country, the school people told visitors, but what they wanted was also different. Although there were schools and teachers that imposed rigorous demands on students, and parents who wanted them—at Lowell High in San Francisco, at Berkeley High, at Grant High and Taft High in the San Fernando Valley, at Fullerton High in Orange County, and in countless middle and elementary schools, schools that sometimes took advantage of California's informality to find innovative ways to engage their students—most were less concerned with high intellectual intensity than with providing launching platforms for the rich and varied existence that California seemed to promise—and with finding ways to deal with the anxieties and stresses that it often imposed. Sunshine was an integral, if unrecognized, part of the curriculum: In California, Robert Hutchins was supposed to have said, "the high school is the place where the band practices."

Through it all, however, the importance of the enterprise was rarely challenged, nor was the need to keep investing in it or to provide the rich array of counselors, music and art and dance classes, driver-ed and driver training, sports, and the endless list of other programs—during the school day and after—that were offered by the better California schools. Nor did anyone quarrel with the assertion that the state had to build nearly 7,000 classrooms a year to handle the growth in enrollment, plus a few thousand more to ease the overcrowding and replace obsolete facilities. And while many of the new schools of the 1950s and 1960s were unimposing structures thrown up as fast as the tract housing around them—most of them "campus style" arrangements with an amplitude of open areas, breezeways, lots of glass, and lots of green play space—a large proportion of the bonds submitted to local voters were approved. At the same time, the state began to take major steps to correct perceived academic deficiencies—a law, for example (which turned out to be much shinier in promise than in implementation), that asked all California schools to require students to take a foreign language beginning in the sixth grade; and the Fisher Act of 1961, which toughened the state's teacher credentialing system, raised the academic preparation required all of the state's new teachers, and stopped California's new teacher trainees from majoring in what Pat Brown described as "so-called method or how-to-teach courses."

And despite the complaints, California's instructional staff was the highest paid, on average, in the country, excepting only Alaska: $6,600 per year in 1960 dollars, compared to a national average of $5,200, a figure that's particularly notable since many of them were new and young and thus at the lower end of the salary scale.[25] The state's teachers (again despite the complaints) were also among the nation's best trained—for that era—when measured in the percentage (91) who had four or more years of college. And at a time when living costs in most parts of California were still relatively modest, the state was consistently among the top ten in the nation in what it spent per pupil to educate its children: It was tenth in the country in 1959–60—$424 per child as opposed to $375 per child for the nation as a whole ($1,932 per year in 1990 dollars)—and fifth in 1964–65, spending roughly 20 percent over the national average.[26] In the early 1960s, half of California's high school graduates were going to college, compared to an average of about one-third in the rest of the nation. That in itself seemed to be evidence that things were working splendidly: Opportunity made up for a lot of qualititative deficiencies.

The clincher—and, with hindsight, the high point—of the postwar go-go era came that same year, with the election of 1962, when Pat Brown, running for a second four-year term as governor, easily beat Richard Nixon, then attempting a political comeback after his defeat in the 1960 presidential race. It was clear, even at the time, that Nixon really didn't want to be governor, something he denied and then reconfirmed with a dreadful Freudian slip during an election-eve broadcast, which he began with "When I become Pres . . ." When he caught himself, he began again: "When I become governor of the United States."[27] That simply reinforced the visceral dislike of Nixon that many Californians seemed to feel even more acutely than most other Americans about a man who had gotten his start in national politics with gutter campaigns against two respected California Democrats. But the vote also seemed to reconfirm the course Brown and California were taking.

The 1962 election is chiefly remembered now as the one in which Nixon berated the press on the morning after for its alleged unfairness with the declaration that "you won't have Nixon to kick around anymore because, gentlemen, this is my last press conference."[28] (Brown, like a lot of other people, was sure Nixon was finished. "I thought," he said later, "that he was as dead as Kelsey's nuts.") It had been a dirty campaign, with charges echoing about slush funds, about Brown allowing Communists to speak on state college campuses (in fact Brown had "weasled," in his words, by bucking the issue to the regents) and ultimately with a Nixon charge, during the tense moments of the Cuban missile crisis that October, that Brown had utterly failed to plan for the construction of nuclear fallout shelters, thus leaving the state "completely naked" in the event of a Soviet attack.

But what may have been most significant about the race is that, rather than attacking Brown's programs, Nixon pledged, for the most part, to do more of the same. Nixon, to be sure, lambasted Brown for raising taxes, and he called for anti-Communist courses in the state's schools and (prophetically) for a sort of three-strike law that would subject all drug pushers with three convictions to the death penalty. But, significantly, he also called for higher pay for school teachers, more water projects, more freeway construction, more cops.

And so the great celebration continued to echo—in some respects echoed deceptively—for another decade: about the beauty of the landscape, about the state's burgeoning high-tech industries, about the new trends and life styles emerging from this new El Dorado, about this new man (echoing earlier echoes), _Homo Californicus_—and, of course, the new California woman and those healthy, blond, unworried, sun-bleached California children who sometimes looked like a new genetic type altogether.

What was almost never asked was the crucial question, a question that had resounded through much of the history of the frontier: Was this the beginning of something or the end? What was there beyond all that freedom and all those possibilities? More freedom and possibilities? Where, ultimately, could something go that supposedly began in perfection? There had always been two wests—the West of the East, of dream and fantasy and escape; and the West in place, of which California was only the most recent (and, most probably, the last) example. "California," Joan Didion would write, "is a place in which a boom mentality and a sense of Chekhovian loss meet in uneasy suspension; in which the mind is troubled by some buried but ineradicable suspicion that things had better work here, because here, beneath this immense bleached sky, is where we run out of continent."[29]

That raised the stakes to a dangerous level: It brought excessive expectations and, very probably, a fatally depleted ability to tolerate failure. "Big Daddy" Jesse Unruh, the 260-pound speaker and boss of the California state assembly during much of the Brown era— who, in another indication of the great California bemusement, was chosen as a Chubb fellow at Yale at almost the same time that Kerr delivered the Godkin lecturers at Harvard—put it another way. It was because of the sunshine that California grew so many fruits and nuts. What if things didn't work here?

II

The boom mentality began to show fine cracks even before the cheering stopped, as if, beneath it all, it had always been, like much of California itself, built on a fault—a stage set perhaps, or a performance for the envious easterners who came through to visit.

The first sign of trouble, hardly noticed at the time, appeared on the very day of Pat Brown's victory over Nixon, when Californians elected a hard-line conservative named Max Rafferty to be their next state superintendent of public instruction. Rafferty, who had been superintendent of a small Southern California school district, had seized on the post-Sputnik criticism of California schools as fatally infected with progressive, child-centered learning, and had caught the first scent of backlash against left-wing demonstrations (for Fidel Castro, for example, and against the old House Un-American Activities Committee) and against the beatniks and counterculture, which was just then beginning to emerge, particularly in Berkeley and San Francisco.

Three days of demonstrations against hearings held by the House committee in San Francisco, and the televised pictures of helmeted cops dragging demonstrators by their long hair down the steps of San Francisco's city hall in May of 1960, had an enormous impact in fusing those themes and in activating both the right and the left. The forty-five minute HUAC-sponsored propaganda film *Operation Abolition*, which followed the next year, and which got wide circulation among church and patriotic organizations, reinforced that right-wing impact.[30] Rafferty ran on a platform of phonics, fundamentals, and patriotism, replacing Dick and Jane with *McGuffey's Readers*; "indoctrinating" (his word) California's children against Communism—and cleaning up their behavior and cutting their hair. And while the job to which he was elected had almost no real power, it nonetheless was a platform, and the election a sign that something out there was not quite right.

Brown had generated trouble for himself even during his first term, particularly with his well-publicized indecision in 1960 about the execution of the convicted murderer and rapist Caryl Chessman. Prompted by his son Jerry, then a student at Berkeley, he gave Chessman a sixty-day reprieve, then allowed the execution to go forward, thereby alienating all sides and bringing upon himself the label "Tower of Jello." In the succeeding weeks, he said, "wherever I went I was booed."[31] But that was relatively insignificant against what occurred during the second term with the passage in 1964, by an overwhelming vote of nearly 2–1, of Proposition 14, an initiative, later blocked by state and federal courts, that sought to overturn the state's 1960 Rumford Fair Housing Act prohibiting discrimination by race in rental housing, one of the measures of which Brown had been particularly proud. And then, in short order, came the student demonstrations and sit-ins that began in December of 1964 on the Berkeley campus, and, what may have been the biggest blow of them all, the Watts riots of August 1965.

For California, Watts was a stunning moment. During five days of rampage (to quote the official McCone Commisssion report), "perhaps as many as 10,000 Negroes took to the streets in marauding bands. They looted stores, set fires, beat up white passers-by whom they hauled from stopped cars, many of which were turned upside down and burned, exchanged shots with law enforcement officers, and stoned and shot firemen." At the end, 34 people were dead, more than 1,000 were injured, and nearly 4,000 had been arrested. Hundreds of shops were looted and torched over an area that covered some 46.5 square miles.[32]

There had been riots in other cities the previous summer—in New York, Chicago, Philadelphia, Jersey City, Rochester—but none had been remotely as violent as Watts. More important, California was supposed to have an exemption from the stresses that brought urban riots. Watts had been a relatively bucolic place of detached houses where, well into the 1940s, people had large gardens and raised animals, and where no one worried much about urban tensions. As the McCone Report put it,

> There was a tendency to believe, and with some reason, that the problems which caused the trouble elsewhere were not as acute in this community. A statistical portrait drawn in 1964 by the Urban League which rated American cities in terms of ten basic aspects of Negro life— such as housing, employment, income—ranked Los Angeles first among the sixty-eight cities that were examined. ("There is no question about it, this is the best city in the world," a young Negro told us with respect to housing for Negroes.)[33]

Under Brown and Unruh, California had been in the forefront in enacting a string of civil rights and poverty bills—not just fair housing, but a law outlawing discrimination in employment, still known as the Unruh Act, backed by a Fair Employment Practices Commission to enforce it, and a landmark welfare bill that centralized and professionalized welfare practices and considerably increased the benefits they delivered. Watts occurred a year after passage of the federal Civil Rights Act of 1964 and just five days after Lyndon Johnson signed the Voting Rights Act of 1965. Why did this riot happen—and why, of all places, in California?

In its efforts to explain, the McCone Commission came up with a now-familiar list of reasons—inadequate schooling and training, a shortage of available jobs, the lack of public transportation to those that might be available—although its report did not speak specifically of the widespread and often systematic exclusion of blacks from construction work, aerospace, and other semiskilled jobs, or about the abusive behavior, since become notorious, of the Los Angeles cops—then still lionized by "Dragnet" and the other TV cop shows the LAPD itself helped produce—toward minorities.[34] This outburst, too, began with the arrest of a black motorist who was driving under the influence.

But between the lines there was one explanation in the report that was new and significant: the frustrated expectations of the hundreds of thousands of southern blacks looking, like all other Californians, for a better life, who had poured into Los Angeles since the start of the war. During that period, the population of Los Angeles County tripled, but its black population, most of it concentrated in the South Central parts of the city, had increased nearly tenfold, from 75,000 to 650,000. And as the Commission pointed out in what almost seemed like an afterthought, its major recommendation—for better education and training and job opportunities, and for more effective and community-sensitive policing—applied also to Mexican-Americans, "a community which is almost equal in size to the Negro community and whose circumstances are similarly disadvantaged and demand equally urgent treatment . . ."[35]

Whatever the cause—the lack of opportunity; the frequently callous treatment of minorities by the LAPD, which even then had become increasingly militarized in tactics and attitude; the black anger (cited by the Commission) over the passage of Proposition 14—Watts was a reminder for those millions of new Californians searching for perfection, blacks as well as whites, that they were not exempt from history or from the conflicts and tragedy that afflicted the rest of the nation. On the contrary, Watts was a powerful signal that, for all its sunshine and beauty, this new and fragile place provided no guarantee against the dark and the demonic in American life. Just a generation earlier, Nathanael West, in *Day of the Locust*, had imagined how it would be at the end—a sweeping canvas called "The Burning of Los Angeles"[36] that anticipated a great deal, both in work like Chandler's and in countless films, of what would come to be called Los Angeles *noir*.

> Across the top, parallel with the frame, he had drawn the burning city, a great bonfire of architectural styles, ranging from Egyptian to Cape Cod colonial. Through the center, winding from left to right, was a long hill street,

and down it, spilling into the middle foreground, came the mob carrying baseball bats and torches. For the faces of its members, he was using the innumerable sketches he had made of the people who came to California to die; the cultists of all sorts, economic as well as religious, the wave, airplane funeral and preview watchers—all those poor devils who can only be stirred by the promise of miracles and then only to violence . . . No longer bored, they sang and danced joyously in the red light of the flames . . .

Like a lot of others, Didion would recall the image during the riots, for "what struck the imagination most indelibly were the fires. For days one could drive the Harbor Freeway and see the city on fire, just as we had always known it would be in the end."[37]

By 1967, Pat Brown was gone, buried in a Ronald Reagan landslide in the election of 1966, and so was Clark Kerr. Brown had imagined that Reagan, the old movie actor, would be easy to beat: He was delighted when Reagan rather than the moderate George Christopher won the GOP primary. But Watts and the increasingly militant student uprisings that began at Berkeley in December of 1964—originally against a university edict prohibiting on-campus organizing and fund raising for off-campus political activities, then against the cops and the university administrators who tried to clear them out—gave Reagan issues that Brown could not overcome, despite the fact that Brown himself had authorized the use of the cops. Berkeley was, after all, the preeminent symbol of California's enlightened programs and outlook, for which the state's taxpayers had been asked to shell out so generously, and here were those scruffy ingrates trying to shut it down.

"You don't realize," Brown said later, "that the people who don't go to the university—they regard [it] as a sort of elitist organization, and even though I was tough, I was looked upon as soft. They tied it up with my opposition to capital punishment, and then you couple that with the Watts riots and I had been good to blacks. I had gone above and beyond the call of duty with fair housing and all those things. I had shown great sympathy to minorities. So you couple the abolition of capital punishment, the Free Speech Movement, and the Watts riots, and you add all three together, and I think they were absolutely disastrous."[38]

California's commitment to active government and high levels of service did not suddenly vanish with Reagan's election in 1966, despite Reagan's repeated campaign promise to "clean up the mess at Berkeley," his antigovernment campaign rhetoric, and his subsequent reputation as a tax-cutting president; despite the growing fractures in the state's (and the nation's) optimism—and despite a recession in the state's economy in the late 1960s and early 1970s that was more severe than the trough in the national economy during the same period. (That California recession in many respects resembled the recession of 1990 − 93.)[39]

The new governor, warning about insurrection, cracked down on student demonstrators, ultimately sending helicopters and riot cops to tear-gas the Berkeley protestors in what would henceforth always be known as People's Park. He also encouraged the University of California regents, already restive over the campus demonstrations, to get rid of Kerr. To this day, it's not clear to what extent Kerr had been asking for a vote of confidence, and thus invited the firing, and to what extent, as Kerr still believes, it was gubernatorial pressure that caused it. What is certain is that eighteen days after Reagan took office, Kerr was sacked.

But if the regents succumbed to Reagan on Kerr, they resisted his demands for sharp fee increases, forcing Reagan to be relatively generous with the university—considerably more generous than his Democratic successor, Jerry Brown, would be. And while he carried on a feud with the academic establishment, he was, as one of the state's budget analysts who worked with him later put it, "an evangelist, not a doer." During his eight years in office, state spending for higher education increased by some 136 percent, considerably more than the overall state budget. To finance the deficit that Pat Brown left and pay for the projects he set in motion, Reagan also acceded, under only slight pressure from the Democrats who controlled the legislature, to a substantial income tax increase, and to property tax relief that put greater reliance on a sharply graduated state income tax, thereby making the state's tax structure considerably more progressive even than it had been under Pat Brown. And while he succeeded in reducing eligibility for welfare, and thus in slowing the growth of the California welfare rolls, the Democrats in turn extracted from him the most progressive welfare support schedule ever adopted in this country—with an annual cost of living adjustment written into law that would remain virtually immutable until the California recession of the early 1990s.[40]

Nor was that all. Under Reagan's Director of Parks and Recreation, William Penn Mott, California launched a sweeping program of parkland acquisition, one so ambitious that the state never succeeded in finding the funds to develop and manage large chunks of it. Work on the highway program and the California Water Project continued. And it was in Reagan's first year as governor that the legislature, under a constitutional amendment pushed by Jesse Unruh and approved by the voters in 1966, began to operate as a year-round, full-time body. For five-plus years, Speaker Unruh had been enlarging the legislature's professional staff—it grew from five people to sixty between 1959 and 1966—many of them former academics, business people, or journalists whose job was analysis of budget and policy, not political hack work, and who were treated as experts on the state's increasingly complex issues, and often were. Now their numbers and expertise would increase even more.

The two things together, the full-time legislature and the professional staff, ended the days when that body—which had been a sink of corruption in the 1930s and 1940s under Artie Samish, "King of the [booze and gambling] Lobby," who proclaimed himself "governor of the Legislature"—was fatally beholden to, and dependent on, lobbyists for information.[41] It probably never became an institution either as pure or professional as its subsequent portrayal as national model made it—it was, after all, a political body—but compared to most other state legislatures it deserved its reputation. There were always hacks, but in the succeeding two decades—roughly from the mid-1960s to the mid-1980s—many of its members and, even more significantly, its professional staff were people of extraordinary dedication and talent. That was particularly the case (and still is) for the professionals in the nonpartisan Legislative Analyst's Office and, to a lesser extent, in the office of the State Auditor as well.

By 1970, however, the beginning of Reagan's second term, the boom-era enthusiasm that marked the first two postwar decades was gone, replaced, most immediately, by fears over the increasingly apparent disproduct of all that growth and development. Henceforth, government would turn ever more attention to coastal protection, air pollution control, growth and ground water management, and protection of endangered species.

Even in 1962, Pat Brown's ebullient promise that on the day when California became first in population he would arrange "the biggest party the state has ever seen," ultimately called "California First Days" and scheduled, quite arbitrarily, for the last three days of the year and the first day of the new year, had been a bust. There had been bands and fireworks and speeches here and there, and Indian dancers and performances by a group calling itself the Kit Carson Mountain Men, but in Los Angeles, it was the Rose Bowl game and the Rose Parade that, as usual, got the attention, and in San Francisco, where not much of anything happened, the impeccably Establishment *Chronicle* huffed, as many San Franciscans probably did as well, that this was not an event to celebrate but to reflect upon.

"What is there to celebrate?" the *Chron* asked, and then, quoting Chief Justice (and former governor) Earl Warren, called for somber reflection: "symposia and public meetings to consider and find solutions to the problems arising from population bloat." (The *Chron* also complained that the gubernatorially proclaimed holiday would involve double-time pay "for certain indispensable servants in the public employ.)" Boards of supervisors, city councils, and mayors should be required to attend these symposia, the *Chron* concluded, "for it is they who have the power to do something about the blight and the miseries that planless growth has brought to this golden state."[42]

But against everything else, worry about growth and environmental degradation became only one shadow on the larger screen of disenchantment. By the end of the 1960s, there had been no end of blows to the nation's optimism, many of them with a particular California bite: Tet and the general debacle of Vietnam; the assassinations in 1968 of Martin Luther King and Robert Kennedy, the latter in Los Angeles a few hours after Kennedy's big victory in the California presidential primary; the election later that year of Richard Nixon, who was very much alive after his defeat in 1962; the demonic Manson murders of the actress Sharon Tate and three others in Los Angeles in 1969; the evolution, real or perceived, of the flower children of the Haight and Venice and Berkeley into Weathermen and acid-heads; the ongoing and increasingly ugly campus confrontations over the Vietnam War and over university policies of all sorts, including a particularly violent one at San Francisco State in the spring of 1969.

And, as if to cap the decade, in the last month of 1969, there was the bloody fiasco at Altamont, an auto raceway forty miles southeast of Berkeley, where 400,000 people had gathered for what was supposed to be a repeat of the happy vibes of Woodstock—the Rolling Stones were there, and the Jefferson Airplane, and Crosby, Stills, Nash and Young. It ended in a drug-frenzied melee—what a lot of people called the end of innocence of the counterculture—with four people dead, one of them beaten to death by the drunk and drug-crazed Hell's Angels who were supposed to be the event's security force.

Journalist Carey McWilliams, who had worked as chief of the state's Division of Immigration and Housing under Governor Culbert Olson in the late 1930s, called California the great exception, a place "that has not grown or evolved so much as it has been hurtled forward, rocket-fashion, by a series of chain-reaction explosions. . . . Europeans have long marveled at the driving force, the 'restless energy,' of America, but it is only in California that this energy is coeval with statehood. . . . In California the lights went on all at once, in a blaze, and they have never been dimmed."[43]

But California had never really been a great exception to very much of anything, although it sometimes did a lot of things better (or at least did them first) and often to greater excess. It was perhaps, as Wallace Stegner said, just like the rest of the country, only more so. And by decade's end, an increasing number of Californians at last became aware that there were few exemptions. The next governor, Pat's son Jerry, came (in 1974, the year of the Watergate climax, the year Nixon resigned), not as the voice of growth for progress, but as the clean government antipolitician heralding the era of limits and lowered expectations. One of his (several) gurus was E.F. Schumacher, and his mantra was "small is beautiful." Many years later, one of California's smartest politicians, Bill Lockyer, then president pro tem of the state senate, wistfully looked back on the administration of Brown *père*. "Pat Brown," he said, "was the last governor who wanted to do great things."

III

In the early 1990s, California became the focus of yet one more flash of media attention—this time to report the dark symmetry of the golden age, what *Time*, in a 1991 cover story, predictably called California's "Endangered Dream."[44] The precipitating event was the recession that, beginning in 1990, hit the Golden State (which some people had once regarded as recession proof) much harder, and longer, than it hit the rest of the country.

With the closing of major California manufacturing plants in the 1980s, the GM Southgate Assembly plant in 1982, the Ford Pico-Rivera plant in 1984, the Goodyear and Firestone tire plants, the sharp downsizing of what had been a large U.S. Steel plant in the East Bay, and the final collapse in 1986 of the great Kaiser Steel Mill in Fontana, which once employed 5,000 people, California's deindustrialization had been ongoing, almost unnoticed, for some years. And with it, of course, went hundreds of thousands of the relatively well-paid semiskilled jobs on which the region's new immigrants—whites as well as blacks and Hispanics—had been counting. (In Fontana, the ghostly site of the huge old mill—part of it—is now occupied by "Ecology Auto Wrecking" and by acres and acres of other wrecking yards and, next to them, even more appropriately, the California Auto Speedway, which opened in the summer of 1997.) But it was the large cutbacks in the defense and aerospace industries that began in the late 1980s, and the waves of base closings that hit the state beginning in 1990, that drove California unemployment figures to over 9 percent (and briefly over 10 percent) in 1992, where they stubbornly remained for the better part of two years.

In California, however, there was (as usual) much else besides to note on the social index—not just unemployment and tumbling real estate values in a fatally overbuilt market, but a disorientation of the westward-pointing national compass. Again there was a rediscovery: This time it was the exodus of middle-class families—fleeing recession, crime, smog, crowding—to neighboring states. Now, instead of counting the migrants rushing toward El Dorado, the media, taking their cue from Governor Pete Wilson and the leaders of the Chamber of Commerce and the California Manufacturers Association, who blamed California's problems of the early 1990s on high taxes, a costly and corrupt workers compensation system, and excessive environmental regulation, counted the number of U-Hauls and Ryder trucks that were being rented in California, taken out of state, and brought back empty.[45] The Claremont Institute, a conservative think tank, pointed out that even when the rental companies offered huge discounts to people who might rent them for the return trip from Oregon or Washington or Arizona, they found few takers.

Between 1991 and 1994, when the state's economic recovery began, California had a net domestic out-migration of over 600,000 people; population continued to grow because of natural increase and foreign immigration, legal and illegal, but more Americans were leaving than coming.[46] (California, Wilson also announced, had become a welfare "magnet," an assertion for which he could never adduce any evidence.)

> California's fabled magnetism [said *Time*] is reversing itself, repelling as well as attracting many of the get-up-and-go Americans who have flocked to the Golden State in search of the California Dream . . . The escapees are being driven away by an accelerating deterioration in

the quality of life: clogged freeways, eye-stinging smog, despoiled landscapes, polluted beaches, water shortages, unaffordable housing, overcrowded schools and beleaguered industries, many of which are fleeing, with their jobs, to other states. The very qualities that have lured millions to California for 50 years are threatening to disappear.[17]

This wasn't the first time that in-migration into California had declined during a period of recession, but it was probably the most dramatic. And the series of natural disasters that accompanied it was almost certainly unprecedented, and certainly got unprecedented, and often breathless, attention. In the period between 1991 and 1993, the *New York Times* published story after story—there were close to a dozen in 1991 alone—about California's decline and doom: "Nature Humbles a State of Mind: 5-year Drought Is Only the Latest Trouble in Paradise"; "Building on Sand: Pain Repays Reckless California"; "They Came to California for the Good Life: Now They're Looking Elsewhere."

Many were not just about the fires, floods, drought, mudslides, layoffs, or economic migration that were their ostensible subjects; they were, in the best California *noir* tradition, stories resonating with doom and apocalypse. In one, headlined "In California, Nature Refuses to Be Mastered," about the effects of the devastating fire that consumed some 3,000 homes in North Oakland and Berkeley in the fall of 1991, Robert Reinhold, the *Times*'s man in Los Angeles, managed to get the words "grim," "symbolic," and "deadly" into the first three lines and the words "arid," "artificial," "harsh," "fragile," "dangerous," "unnatural," and "unstable" into the first three paragraphs. Instead of pictures of happy young families by the pool, or backpackers at Yosemite, these stories had photos from the archives, of San Francisco after the 1906 earthquake, the Santa Monica Pier after it was destroyed by a Pacific storm in 1983 (eight years before the *Times* story appeared), an earthquake-twisted freeway structure, and a calamity map labeled "Living on the Edge."[48]

The stories were done, if not with satisfaction, then certainly with a sense of the fearful symmetry of California's hubris. Much of this land, said one of Reinhold's pieces, had not been suitable for human habitation in the first place; to make it livable required "a massive rearrangement of the environment [dams, acqueducts, free-ways, bridges, houses hanging from canyon walls and encroaching into natural fire zones] that snubbed nature": They asked for it.

Again there were lists, this time of disasters, natural and eco-nomic, and sometimes of the two rolled together: Los Angeles's famous "see-through" buildings, elegant high-rise office towers built (many of them with Japanese money) in the boom years, scores of them that were virtually empty; employer survey data (which later turned out to be partly false and partly exaggerated) showing that one in seven businesses was thinking of moving out of state; reports (also misleading) that while "many skilled workers are leaving Cali-fornia, immigrants from Asia and Latin America are entering the state";[49] plus *Time*'s list of "eye-stinging smog, despoiled landscapes, polluted beaches, water shortages, [and] unaffordable housing." (Maybe, someone suggested sardonically, the writer was thinking of New Jersey.)

There was a governor naming blue-ribbon commissions—one headed by former Secretary of State George Shultz, the other by former baseball commissioner Peter Ueberroth—to prove (in an effort to drive down taxes and reform the costly and unfair Cali-fornia workers compensation system) that his own state's business climate was terrible, and implying that anyone would be crazy to move a business there, or to think about starting a new one. In those same years, state budgets were approved only after prolonged political battles and weeks of gridlock, budgets that ran ever-deeper into the red. And there was Wilson's state finance director issuing reports to show that California had a structural problem, irrespec-tive of business cycles, in which the users of taxpayer-supported services—schoolchildren, welfare clients, prison inmates, people on Medicaid (called MediCal in California)—were inexorably in-creasing on a curve that was rising much more steeply than the state's capacity to support them.

There is "a deep disenchantment," Neil Morgan, in 1991 still the editor of the *San Diego Tribune*, told *Time*, "that I've decided goes a lot beyond the traffic, smog, crime and too many neighbors . . . a dejection born of overblown dreams . . . We all came out here because it was going to be the Golden State, where all of our dreams were going to click and fall into place and all of a sudden—presto!—the vision of a magic society that we have all raved about since the Gold Rush, it's threatening not to happen. We see the same things happening here that happen—do I dare say it?—everywhere else."[50]

IV

Even if one recognizes that the foundation of the state's 1960s boom mentality was neither as solid as had once been predicted nor as fragile as the tales of apocalypse depicted, it's still striking how radically the state changed in little more than a generation, not because it suddenly became poor but because of vast demographic changes and the equally large transformation of outlook, public will, and public policy priorities that came with them.

The most obvious element of that change is the simple fact of a relentless population boom. It took California roughly 110 years to grow to the 17.5 million people that made it the nation's most populous state in 1962 or early 1963. It took just another 35 years of natural increase and immigration to nearly double that total: "In the last twenty years," said Kevin Scott, the former executive director of the state Commission on Finance, "we've added all of New York State."

But these new Californians did not come with U-Hauls and Ryder trucks, and most—nearly 85 percent—were no longer young families from Iowa or Wisconsin or Pennsylvania, or their blond, blue-eyed California-born offspring. They were Mexicans, Guatemalans, Salvadorans, Hondurans, Filipinos, Chinese from Taiwan and Hong Kong, Vietnamese, Hmong, Cambodians, Koreans, Indians, Pakistanis, Poles, Samoans, Tongans, Palestinians, Iranians, and Russians, most of them people from long-restricted ethnic and national groups for whom the gates had been opened by the repeal of the national origins quotas in 1965, and by a series of subsequent measures, culminating in the 1986 Immigration Reform and Control Act, which allowed more than 2.5 million illegal aliens, roughly half of them in California, to get amnesty and become legal residents.[51] There was, in addition, an echo wave of illegal immigration in the wake of amnesty in the late 1980s, which seems to have been composed in significant part of relatives of newly amnestied aliens coming to join their newly legalized brothers, fathers, and husbands.[52]

Since neither the U.S. Census nor the state counted Hispanics as a separate category in 1960, one can only guess at the numbers for the early 1960s. But a fairly clear picture emerges from the fact that in 1960 only 1.3 million of California's 15.7 million residents were foreign born, that only 1.3 million—roughly 8 percent—were listed as "nonwhite," and that the majority of even the foreign born were native English speakers from Britain and Canada. As recently as 1970, the earliest year for which the demographers at the California Department of Finance collected (or projected) such data, 78 percent of California's 20 million people were white; 7 percent were black, 12 percent were Hispanic, and 3 percent were "other." By 1996, only 52 percent of the state's 32 million people were white, 7 percent were black, 30 percent Hispanic, and 11 percent "other," most of them Asians, and the department projects that by 2002, whites will be a minority. Put another way, while the white population of California grew by about 2.1 million people between 1970 and 1996, the Hispanic population grew by 7.7 million (from 2.4 million in 1970 to 10.1 million a generation later), and the "other"—meaning primarily Asians and Pacific Islanders—by 3 million (from 600,000 to 3.6 million).[53]

Collectively, they are changing the landscape—have already changed it, on the one hand loading enormous new problems on the schools (where they now make up more than 60 percent of the enrollment) and a wide range of other social services; and, as they always have, filling many of the state's most exploited jobs as farm workers, dishwashers, maids, cooks, janitors, and day laborers, on the other, bringing new vitality and talent and creating thousands of new businesses, many of them in or at the fringes of the computer industry and other high-tech sectors—many begun with capital brought from the Far East—others in retail merchandising, in small manufacturing, and in a huge array of services. At the same time, they are revitalizing older neighborhoods and bringing a mind-boggling range of foods, restaurants, clubs, bookstores, music, and churches to what had, in many cases, been white-bread communities.

How the assets of economic contributions—wages earned, taxes paid, communities strenghtened—and the liabilities of social dependency, the cost in medical care, schooling, and other public services, balance out is a matter of endless dispute; there are studies proving almost any argument.[54] One Los Angeles County study, published in 1992, indicated that while immigrants, legal and illegal, paid more in taxes than the county's costs of providing education, health, and other public services, most of those taxes went to the federal government, creating a gap between local tax receipts and the cost of services. Another report, projected from a San Diego County study, concluded that statewide local and state agencies were spending $3 billion more on illegal immigrants than they received in taxes from those groups.[55]

It was largely on the basis of the latter that Governor Wilson began to issue repeated complaints that illegal aliens were draining the state of billions annually for education, health care, and prison costs, complaints that a recent study by a twelve-member panel of the National Research Council seems to bear out. The NRC report concludes, among other things, that California taxpayers pay considerably more for services to new immigrants than the immigrants pay in taxes. It also observes that while "under most scenarios the long-run fiscal impact is strongly positive at the federal level," it is "substantially negative at the state and local levels," and particularly in states, like California, that receive most of the new immigrants. Nonetheless, even the NRC report is necessarily indefinite about the long-term trade-offs between immigrant earnings (and taxes paid) and the costs of the services they and their children receive, all of which depend, as the panel points out, on a whole range of unpredictable economic, social, and demographic factors. "Under one plausible set of assumptions," the NRC report says, "the net present value of an immigrant with less than a high school education is -$13,000; in contrast the net present value [of an immigrant] with more than a high school education is +$198,000."[56]

What's certain is that the impact of different groups—depending on social and cultural background, on immigration status, on income—falls unevenly in different places and at different times. The NRC report also gives strong support to the conclusion that while immigrants—and particularly illegal aliens—may pay their share in federal taxes, they can still be a net burden on the local agencies that provide social services; they may do society's dirty work and still take jobs from unskilled citizens. Meanwhile, the same politicians who, in times of economic growth, call for easier entry for Mexican workers, often complain loudest in tough times about how illegals are straining public services and taking jobs from American workers. There is mounting evidence that the second generation of Latinos is, in effect, following previous immigrants, gaining economic ground and forming an increasingly stable middle class.[57] But it's also certain that in California so far, the social costs, particularly in public services, are more immediate, and far more visible—and have gotten far more attention—than the benefits.

Like previous waves of immigrants, the new groups often cluster, following relatives or acquaintances, in certain communities, even if they first landed somewhere else. The state is dotted with ethnic enclaves, as older Eastern cities once were and often still are—the Hmong in Fresno, the Russians in Sacramento and West Sacramento, Vietnamese in Little Saigon in Westminster. There are Japantown and Little Korea in Los Angeles, and Latino barrios in virtually every city in the state. The Orange County seat of Santa Ana, which had 31,000 people on the eve of World War II, is now a city of 300,000, of whom more than 70 percent are Hispanic and more than half are foreign born. It's hard to imagine that the people who pulled up the orange trees after the war ever dreamed that within two generations their century-old community's shopping streets would be wall-to-wall with *abogados* advertising *divorcios; viajes a México; seguros de auto; fótos y cópias; clínicas médicas: para la mujer de hoy;* and places where "PARA MAMA, *envio dinero hoy y la recibe mañana*"—or that one of its main streets would one day boast a Salvadoran consulate.

Inevitably also, there are multicultural mixes, in music and language and menu, that belong to no group and create categories of their own: Thai BBQ; Viet My Food To Go; Clothes Buena Bonita Y Cheep, or (the generic illustration favored by Shelby Coffey, the editor of the *Los Angeles Times*) kosher burritos. At Newcomer High School in San Francisco, the students, who come with a dozen languages and cultures, none of them English, often learn the foreign idioms and epithets of their classmates before they learn the speech of their new country. Conversely, the Korean bookstore—Smart Books and Toys—at the Oxford Center shopping mall in Los Angeles is crammed with a whole education for American wannabes: primary and intermediate English readers and workbooks, SAT prep manuals, vocabulary books, wall charts with the English names of fish and animals and parts of the human body, star-spangled booklets outlining American "rights and responsibilities," a glossy-covered magazine with a color photo of a Korean toddler wearing a Yale T-shirt on the cover.

There are 1,800 Trans in the Orange County phone book, and 4,300 Nguyens (nine pages of them), not counting Ngs and Nghiens; among Orange County home buyers, there are more people named Nguyen than Smith. In Los Angeles there are shopping plazas on which the illuminated sign at the entrance is in four or five different languages, none of them English. There are towns in the San Joaquin Valley and the Salinas Valley—Gonzalez ("Heart of the Salad Bowl") or Greenfield, or San Miguel—where "bilingual" on the sun-baked main drag means that someone speaks something other than Spanish.

There is Pacific Boulevard in South Central, which had been largely abandoned by white businesses in the years after the Watts riots and is now reoccupied by Latino shops and service outlets. There are those same Los Angeles Dodgers, who integrated baseball in 1947 and abandoned Brooklyn in 1957, whose starting pitchers in the mid-1990s included a couple of Mexicans, a couple of Dominicans, a Korean, and a Japanese, and whose games are now regularly broadcast and telecast to Los Angeles area fans in English and Spanish, and occasionally in Korean and Japanese as well. And not far away, at the Rose Bowl in Pasadena, there is the

Los Angeles Galaxy soccer team, which has been drawing over 38,000 people a game, far more than any other team in the new professional Major Soccer League. At their opening in 1996, they drew more fans, some 70,000, than the Dodgers drew to their home opener. Judging from the cars in the parking lot—the big Chevy low-riders, the souped-up Pontiacs—you'd know that this is not a crowd of suburban baseball fans. But these players, too, are now getting commercial endorsements.[58]

To what extent, and in what way, that population change is the direct cause of the social disengagement and erosion of California's public services in the past two decades, and to what extent it's merely the result of the political demographics that the new immigrants have produced, is going to be debated for years. But who can doubt that there is a connection? The rise of the new minorities and the decline in services occurred in proportion over precisely the same period (which, of course, is when the services are most needed) and at roughly the same rate. The mail of editors is too full of angry letters, the rhetoric of politicians too full of references about the costs "they" impose on the taxpayers, to leave much doubt; the political record too full of legislation and voter initiatives, many of them passed with overwhelming public support, that in one way or another seek to reduce services to those new residents, or eliminate them altogether.

The polls indicate that California voters make a distinction between legal and illegal aliens, as Governor Pete Wilson said he was doing when he based a large part of his 1994 reelection campaign on Proposition 187, the successful initiative—subsequently blocked by a federal court—that would have barred illegal aliens from public schools and all but emergency health services. But the policy record and the rhetoric of California politicians, and of a great many other people, often belies that. "Everything is mucho good," went the little piece of doggerel that California Assemblyman Pete Knight circulated among a few of his colleagues a few years ago. "Soon we own the neighborhood/ We have a hobby—it's called breeding/ Welfare pay for baby feeding."[59] Knight was later forced to apologize, but the message was clear enough.

"They just keep coming," said Wilson's 1994 campaign commercials over pictures of hordes of Mexicans running across the state's southern border, and there was no doubt who "they" were. Although a million aliens were naturalized in this country in 1996, a third of them in California—which the Immigration and Naturalization Service says is a record—and although they made themselves felt in a number of legislative and congressional elections, the vast majority have never voted.[60] The electorate remains what it has always been: disproportionately white and middle class, even as the consumers of public services—school enrollment particularly—have become predominantly Hispanic and Asian. That imbalance is probably the most salient element in California's political history of the past twenty years.

Good-bye El Dorado

<>

I

When California politicians talk about the state of the state these days, history is divided between the recession years (1991–94) and the postrecession boom in California's economy, which began sometime in 1994 (although it wasn't really reflected in state revenues until the beginning of 1995). But the roots of the California of the last years of the twentieth century, with its shrunken public services and its convoluted governmental structure, did not grow primarily out of recession, much less from the series of natural disasters—drought, floods, earthquakes, fires—that California suffered along the way and that, for all the attention they got, always seemed more symbolic than causal.

The out-migration and disenchantment of the early 1990s were real enough. But what almost no one noticed was that the decline in social morale had begun long before the recession, before the big defense cuts, before the base closings. It began before the Loma Prieta earthquake of October 1989, which stopped the first cross-Bay World Series, jolted San Francisco and Oakland, and a good part of the Peninsula, and knocked a span of the Bay Bridge onto the lower level. It began before the devastating Northridge quake of 1994, before the seven-year drought of the late 1980s and early 1990s, and before the rash of floods and forest-and-brush fires and the other Biblical plagues that lashed the state during Pete Wilson's first term as governor (1991–95). It began before the deadly riots that followed the 1992 acquittal, by a white Simi Valley jury, of the Los Angeles cops who beat up Rodney King. And if the disenchantment had set in while the state's economy was still healthy, and when few people were quoted on the subject of leaving the state, its effects would be profoundly felt after the California economy started to roar back and the recession was officially declared at an end.

The spectacular bankruptcy of Orange County, one of the most affluent places in the country, got plenty of national attention, particularly on the financial pages. But few people remarked on the rigid fiscal constraints imposed by Proposition 13 and its successors that helped bring on the pattern of high-risk investment that led to Orange County's disaster, or on the fact that several other California counties, including Los Angeles, saved in 1995 only by a last-minute federal bailout arranged by Bill Clinton, were (and remain) on the verge of insolvency. Nor was much notice given to the adamant refusal of Orange County voters to approve even a modest tax increase to bail themselves out, much less to the debacle that it left in its wake. Because of it 3,000 county jobs were eliminated; major public assets sold or mortgaged, including the county administration building; special flood control, redevelopment, and transportation funds bled to repay creditors—among them school districts and various other municipalities that had joined in Orange County's wild ride—and virtually every county service sharply reduced. The county's resolution of the bankruptcy, which it called a "Robin Hood" plan, will leave those services strapped for years to come.[1]

In 1994, after the Northridge earthquake devastated parts of the Los Angeles area, Paula Boland, a conservative Republican assemblywoman whose own home in Granada Hills was damaged, and who was then sleeping in her car, showed something of the same spirit when she declared that she would oppose even a small temporary sales tax increase to help repair quake-damaged roads, schools, university buildings, and other infrastructure. "Californians," she declared, "are already paying too much in taxes." It was the feds who should pay. "The President owes us. They've taken our military bases and all those jobs. They're going to have to start giving something back to California."[2] There was an earthquake, but there was an almost equally ferocious determination—come hell, quake, or high water—not to allow anything to nuzzle up tax rates.

As subsequent parts of this book will outline more fully, a lot of the damage in California was indeed self-inflicted, but the causes of the decline—most of them—were a lot more prosaic than the rhetoric of hubris, exploded dreams, and nature defied suggested, yet also more basic than any count of U-Hauls, unemployment rates, foreclosures, and bankruptcies indicated. They date back to a series of deliberate public policy choices, to the radical tax and spending limitations imposed by Proposition 13, and to a long string of other policy mandates, imposed through voter initiatives, that began some two decades ago and have continued through good times and bad.[3] Together, in the words of the California Budget Project, they "insure that budgets are increasingly balanced with spending reductions, not revenue increases, regardless of demand for public services."[4]

By 1989–90, just before the California recession began, state and local revenues, as a percentage of personal income—meaning California's *willingness* to pay for public services—had slipped from ninth among the states in the mid-sixties, and fourth in 1971–72, the beginning of Reagan's second term in office, to twenty-fourth; by 1992–93, they dropped further, to twenty-seventh. At the same time, California's level of taxation, according to the Advisory Commission on Intergovernmental Relations, slipped from approximately $137 per $1,000 of personal income (in 1970–71) to roughly $114.[5] And while the tax burden per $1,000 of personal income also fell slightly in many other states during the same period—in part as a result of the national California-fueled tax revolt—none declined as much. The average decline for the nation as a whole was 5 percent.[6] In California, in the decade after the passage of Proposition 13 in 1978, the corresponding decline was closer to 20 percent. As might be expected, California's public services soon followed.

The most glaring example of that erosion, as might also be expected, came in the sector that had always consumed the largest share of state and local spending, the public schools. In the 1960s, California had ranked among the among the top ten states in the nation in annual per-pupil spending—California was still tenth in 1969–70, spending about 10 percent more than the national average. By 1988, before the recession, California had slipped to thirty-second among the states, just above West Virginia and just below North Carolina, and the lowest among the country's ten largest states. In 1988–89, California was spending about $4,500 per child per year (in 1990–91 dollars)—roughly $600 below the national average, far less than any of the other major industrial states. By the early 1990s, its spending declined further, down $300 per child in real dollars between 1990 and 1995, and down even more relative to the other states.[7] By 1995–96, the latest year for which comparative figures are available, it was forty-first among the states, spending roughly $1,100 per child (roughly 20 percent) below the national average, and roughly half of what New York or New Jersey spend.

The state's conservatives argue that, those figures notwithstanding, the state's inflation-adjusted per-pupil spending is higher than it was in 1970. But given the huge chunk that, under federal law, must now be devoted to special education for handicapped students, the higher demands that the economy makes for trained people and its lack of places for dropouts and school failures, and the enormous demographic and social changes in school enrollments and the increased burdens they bring, particularly in California, flat dollar comparisons with the past are simply not relevant. What is relevant is that California spends far less of its personal income on schools than it did a generation ago.

That decline, which began even before the passage of Proposition 13, and before a series of other tax-cutting measures that followed in its wake, but was precipitously hastened by them, had such profound effects that even after the recession ended and the state put large chunks of new money into the schools—an increase of about $650 per child between 1994–95 and 1997–98 (roughly

7 percent in inflation adjusted dollars), most of it in the primary grades—California was still spending roughly $1,000 less per child than the national median. And it was less than California itself had spent, in real dollars, a decade earlier.[8] While Proposition 13 cut all property taxes, it virtually destroyed the ability of schools and other local agencies to increase their operating revenues through higher taxes, even where local voters favored such increases.

The effects are, with one major exception, obvious almost everywhere. The state's teachers' salaries, supported with the clout of the California Teachers Association, by some measures the state's most powerful political organization, and its local affiliates, have more than kept pace with inflation and have remained among the top ten in the nation. As a consquence, everything else in the schools has given way even more than it might otherwise: arts and music offerings, counseling services, school nurses, books, laboratory equipment and computers, and a whole host of academic programs. Building maintenance was deferred, and then deferred again, until, in many districts, only the most obvious emergencies got attention at all.

In 1986, during a decade of economic growth, a federal survey found that California was thirty-eighth in the country in what it spent per pupil on library books, forty-fifth in computer software, and forty-ninth in audiovisual materials. There are still reference works on California school shelves that have Eisenhower as president, science encyclopedias published in 1955 that speak hopefully about how one day man might go to the moon, colonial-era geography books that know nothing about Zaire or Zimbabwe, and etiquette books advising girls not to try to beat boys at their games. (In 1997, someone estimated that the average publication date of books in California school libraries was 1973.) In 1991, California had 1,200 full-time school librarians for its 8,000 schools, fewer than Alabama (which has 1,300 schools) and roughly one-third as many as Texas.[9] No one knows how many classrooms in California do not have a full set of textbooks and how many children, therefore, can't bring even their texts home to do their work. One estimate by the National Education Association and the Association of American (textbook) Publishers found that 54 percent of California teachers don't have enough books to send home with their students. The national figure, itself shameful, is 39 percent. In Los Angeles, high school students spend countless classroom hours copying material from texts they have to share with other students.

For California, one-fourth of whose school enrollment is now composed of students whose native language is something other than English (a similar number come from welfare families and single-parent families), where *one-third* of the state's half-million first-graders begin school speaking only limited English, and sometimes no English at all, and where, with the exception of newly reduced classes in the first three grades (which are discussed more fully below), it is still not unusual to find elementary school classes of thirty-five in which five or six different native languages are represented—Spanish, Tagalog, Hmong, Russian, Korean, Vietnamese—the paucity of resources puts nearly intolerable burdens on schools and teachers.

In the Los Angeles public school system, the second largest in the country, nearly half the students, and almost 60 percent of elementary students, are listed as limited-English-speaking. They speak some eighty different languages at home, and they represent every race, color, and shade on earth. Nor is Los Angeles unique.[10] There are hundreds of similar places: The new California, particularly the California of the public schools, is a state of all shades, accents, cultures. From one classroom in Hayward, in the East Bay south of Oakland: Ashly Augerlavoie, Ronald Benjamin, Carlos Andrade, Noleen Nath, Ruth Seumanu, Brenda Ton, Trang Tan, Leanne Gates, Francisco Garcia, Javier Tapa, Richard Mackowjak, Joseph Craig, John Vu, Roosevelt Hardaway, Kisshan Kumar, Kunaal Nand, Mark Robinson, Veronica Solorio, Danelle Ybarra, Ruth Willis, Fritzj Modi, Melissa Martinez, Ronnie Smith, Royce Moreno, Richard Singh, Shamil Mohammed, Aileen Mendoza, Jonathan Cabuco, Neha Vaid, and Shamia Hawkins.

That can mean all sorts of things, but one thing it certainly means, as Los Angeles School Superintendent Sidney Thompson (who retired in 1997) liked to say, is that "you better not try to fit the kid to the assumptions of the 1950s."[11] How does a teacher, with the best will in the world, deal with the spectrum of languages and cultures found in a growing proportion of California's classrooms? How does she pursue a standard lesson plan or enforce standards in a classroom where the twelve-year-olds have to take two buses to take their little sisters to some other school before they can go to school themselves? How does she handle the anxieties of children who seem to spend as much time dealing with their dysfunctional mothers as the mothers spend taking care of them? How does one do it in a classroom of thirty-two kids without an aide and without enough textbooks to go around? Among the graduates of the Los Angeles district, 20 percent go on to postsecondary education. For the rest, Thompson says, graduation means "a party, a trip to Disneyland, and a piece of paper."

In 1994, the most recent year for which state comparisons are available, California, repeating its dismal 1992 scores, outperformed only Louisiana in fourth-grade reading among the thirty-five states that participated in the National Assessment of Educational Progress (NAEP), with 18 percent of those fourth-graders rated as proficient or advanced in reading, and 56 percent reading below what NAEP defines as the "basic" level. In 1996, California was at the very bottom, tied with Tennessee, among the forty states that participated in the NAEP survey of eighth-grade math proficiency; and near the bottom, above only Alabama and South Carolina, among the forty-three states that participated in NAEP's fourth-grade assessment of math proficiency. In NAEP's rankings, 54 percent of California fourth-graders were reported to be failing in basic skills; nationwide, 36 percent of children fell into that category. In 1996, California eighth-graders were thirty-ninth among the forty-four states participating in the NAEP science survey (the only grade in which state-by-state comparisons were made). Equally troubling, even when comparisons were made within ethnic groups, California students scored poorly.[12]

The dismal reading scores were widely pinned—in part, probably correctly—to an excessive emphasis, beginning in 1986 or 1987, on "whole language" instruction in the state's primary grades, and (echoes of Rafferty) to a corresponding neglect of phonics and other basics. That, in turn, has recently produced a sharp change of direction in the state's reading program toward phonics and the other "basics" of reading instruction.[13]

Similarly, the low math scores were attributed to too much reliance on constructivist math instruction—the "new-new math" that empasizes comprehension of math principles above rote memory of multiplication tables and other "math facts." But since the NAEP survey included a significant proportion of constructivist math items, and considering everything else that was going on, or not going on, in California at the same time, and particularly the shortage of almost every conceivable resource and the high concentrations of limited-English-speaking students in schools with high turnover rates, misguided approaches to reading and math instruction cannot possibly have been the whole explanation. Certainly they could not be the whole explanation for the low math scores.

Compounding the crowding is the deteriorated physical environment in which both teachers and students must work. Jonathan Kozol, in his book *Savage Inequalities*, describes the horrendous conditions—the leaky roofs, nonfunctioning toilets, broken windows, peeling paint—of the inner-city schools in the Northeast and Midwest. The worst schools in California, where puddles form on the floor and where parents pull kids out of school on rainy days "for fear they will be hit by ceiling tiles or shocked by exposed wiring," can easily match that.[14]

In California, as one California education consultant said, "We've got Kozol schools everywhere," not just in the inner cities. During one heavy rainstorm a few years ago, fifty-two of the seventy-five schools in the suburban (Sacramento) San Juan School District reported serious leaks, and that's minor compared to some elementary schools in the Sierra foothills that have been so overcrowded that students eat lunch in tents—which also leak during rainstorms—or to districts where graduation ceremonies and other special events have to be held in neighboring districts because there are no auditoriums or multipurpose rooms.

There are schools where ceilings are flaking, bare wiring hangs down, and floors buckle; where rotting planks make walkways dangerous; where library books mildew from water damage; and where principals report high levels of bladder infections because the toilets are broken or so filthy that students can't use them. There are middle schools of 1,200 students that are entirely housed—"gyms," office, lunchroom, everything—in portable "temporary" classrooms, some of which have been around so long and are so poorly maintained that floors and foundations are rotting themselves. There are places like Oakland's Castlemont High School, where weeds grow in the cracks of the locker room showers. There is Lynwood High School in Los Angeles County, where they could have shown you the place where the teacher fell through the rotten floor, and there is no counting the places where whole buildings smell of rot and mold.

When Delaine Eastin, now the state's superintendent of public instruction, ran for the office in 1994, she pointed out that California had fewer computers per child in its schools than any other state. What she did not know then is that even if someone had found the money to buy those computers, thousands of California schools couldn't have used them because their electrical wiring wasn't adequate. In 1989, at the end of a long boom in the state's economy, DuWayne Brooks, the state's director of school facilities planning, estimated that as a result of a decade of tight budgets and perennially deferred maintenance, 55 percent of California's school buildings were in poor condition—"$50 billion in assets, and you're just letting them rot"—a judgement confirmed by a pair of surveys prepared for Congress in 1996 in which the General Accounting Office found that 71 percent of California schools needed major plumbing or electrical work or roof repairs, and which listed California school facilities as being in the worst physical shape of any state, overall, excepting only the notoriously derelict schools of the District of Columbia.[15]

In March 1996, California voters, having rejected a previous school facilities proposal, passed a $2.025 billion school repair and construction bond, as they have in most election years during the past decade. And in the spring of 1997, with the improving economy and what appear to be increasingly sophisticated and unconventional tactics, the percentage of local districts that mustered the difficult-to-achieve two-thirds vote necessary under California law to pass bonds to build and repair schools went up considerably. (In local elections in June, twenty-six of thirty-eight school bond measures passed, all thirty-eight got over 50 percent, but the rest failed to get the required two-thirds majority.) Paramount among those spring flowers was Los Angeles itself. There, in a low-profile election for a huge $2.3 billion bond, much of it to repair, expand, and upgrade six hundred of the worst schools in the county, the bond campaign managers carefully targeted voters whose children were forced to attend the city's unconscionably neglected schools, Hispanics particularly, without arousing opponents who might have turned out in a more visible campaign. Only 26 percent of the registered voters cast ballots, but that helped significantly in getting a 71 percent approval vote, comfortably above the two-thirds needed, a supermajority of a minority.[16] It was the first school bond the district, with its exploding enrollment, had passed since 1971.

For all the success they've brought, however, and despite the momentarily strong public support for schools—in California as elsewhere around the country—those bonds are barely a start on a long road. It's not easy to undo the effects of two decades of deterioration and neglect, even with the best intentions, and virtually impossible without sustained, long-term effort. And since the best estimate of the current need for school facilities in California runs to $17 billion—not counting the additional demands of the state's current class-size reduction program—and for the next ten years may reach as much as $40 billion, and since maintenance of a sustained and costly effort is always difficult, it's hardly time to start cheering.[17] In affluent Orange County, no local school bonds have even been proposed since the passage of Proposition 13.

Underlying the difficulties in building and refurbishing local schools—and distorting all California school governance almost beyond recognition—is the larger mess created by the fiscal restrictions and spending mandates that California voters have imposed on California government. Those restrictions and mandates, more fully delineated in the next section, both curtail revenues and dictate how a large portion of them must be spent. Those mandates necessarily centralized appropriations in the legislature (and often tied them to constitutional formulas beyond even its reach) even as they left spending decisions to local boards. In doing so, they created a structure that couldn't have been more perfectly designed to undermine accountability among the state and local officials who were supposedly charged with the management and control of the state's public agencies.

If a school district runs out of money, or a county verges on bankruptcy, who is responsible: the elected local board that overspends its budget, or the state legislature that fails to appropriate the funds or, as often happens, appropriates them so late that no reasonable local budgeting and planning is possible? Something similar is true in capital expenditures. Since both funding and design approval for school construction and renovation—what there has been of it—is now partially a local responsibility and partly the province of not one but a half-dozen different state agencies, it has been virtually impossible for any local citizen—or, indeed, even many professionals—to understand what has to be done to get a new school built, or whom to blame for the delays or for the fact that sometimes it never seems to get built at all.

"The birth of a new school facility," in the words of the state's official Little Hoover Commission, "comes about only after an elephantine gestation that involves the participation of the local school district, the [state] Department of Education, the [state] Office of Local Assistance, the State Allocation Board and the Office of the State Architect," and involves hundreds of fiscal and architectural regulations on everything from roof overhang to the maximum size of each classroom, a process that is not only slow and conducive to buck-passing but, in most instances, precludes anything but the most mundane school design. "One official estimated that if every step is performed correctly," the commission said, "from the time a decision is made to build a school it will take about six years to open the schoolhouse doors to students."[18]

Compounding all that is a fractured school policy structure that couldn't have been more perfectly designed to defeat accountability. An independently elected state superintendent of schools, with little direct authority over local districts, is subject to—and often in conflict with—the policy decisions of a state board of education appointed by the governor. In conjunction with the legislature, the governor has budgetary authority but, because of the elected state superintendent, is not generally seen to be accountable for the schools. Thus, in April 1997, when the White House announced that State School Superintendent Eastin had endorsed the president's national testing proposals in reading and mathematics, State Board President Yvonne Larsen quickly sent the administration a letter (drafted in Governor Pete Wilson's office) stating that Eastin had "exceeded her authority." Larsen humbly apologized for the confusion and declared that California intended to go its own way on standards and testing. The collective political message of those state officials, elected and appointed, is that the local boards should be given autonomy to set their own course and held accountable for the results, even as the state imposes major curricular and fiscal mandates—fiscal restrictions, new reading and math programs, class-size reduction, and endless others—that make a mockery of their rhetoric.

Meanwhile, at the local level, court decisions requiring the state to equalize funding between tax-rich and tax-poor districts, combined with Proposition 13 and its progeny, have fostered a different sort of distortion. For once school boards lost the authority to raise local taxes, the interest and engagement of local business communities, once among the most important sources of candidates, expertise, and funding for school board races—and of civic engagement generally—also seemed to wane. A government without the power to raise taxes no longer commands the attention of business groups that it did when it had real power to impair the bottom line. No representation without taxation.

California is not alone in some of these problems. Communities in other states have suffered similar declines in public engagement. As more women take full-time jobs, broad-based parents' organizations have withered everywhere. But those changes appear to have been not nearly as severe as those in California. Nowhere else does the fiscal structure provide as little incentive for citizen engagement at the local level; nowhere was the disengagement of the business community, despite all the rhetoric about the need for better schools, been more apparent. Nowhere has there been as much opportunity for buck-passing between the locals and the state.

The result has been a major shift in the character of those who run for school boards, and in the source of their support. The declining engagement of business and other community organizations, and the corresponding paucity of leading citizens—lawyers, merchants, accountants, and other professionals—willing to run for office has left a vacuum that's been filled by special interest groups: the Christian Right, which has managed to gain at least temporary control of a handful of districts in Southern California, but more often the public employee unions—UTLA (the United Teachers of Los Angeles) and the California Teachers Association and its various local affiliates, which have become the dominant political force in California education. In places like Orange County, the organized Christian conservatives, backed by deep-pockets contributors like billionaire (Home Savings and Loan) banking heir Howard F. Ahmanson, Jr., and local affiliates of the CTA, are often the sole combatants in school board elections. They can generate campaign funds, running into the tens of thousands of dollars, even in small suburban districts, that make the old-fashioned volunteer-based, door-bell-ringing school board campaign a thing of the past.[19] Often no one else is even in the field.

But statewide, the unions are the dominant force. They constitute the largest single source of revenue for Democrats—the CTA contributed a total of $1.37 million to legislative candidates alone in the 1993–94 election cycle, and its local affiliates contribute a few million more—far and away the largest share—to local school board races, and often find the candidates, either from the ranks of teachers in neighboring districts, or from the general community, to run. In 1987, the CTA estimated that of the 110 candidates it backed that year—often with the only major funding in the race—75 percent were elected. The previous year, of the three people elected to the seven-member Los Angeles school board, two were backed by the union, and union-backed board members have dominated the board ever since; the same has also been true in

Sacramento, Santa Ana, Modesto, Fresno, and other California cities.

That does not always mean that the unions call all the shots—"we've been electing more and enjoying it less," CTA President Ralph Flynn said a few years ago; for the most part, he said, he preferred "the one-stop shopping at the Legislature." But in the larger districts, the local union is always a major player, particularly when it comes to seniority rules and other working conditions. It is also true, in varying degrees, in other public sectors. California is first in the nation in its per-capita spending for fire protection, third in spending for police protection, and fifth in corrections, not because of the demands imposed by its spectacular forest and brush fires, or because its prisons are models of penology, or because it has made its streets so safe, but because the political clout—and thus the pay and extraordinary benefits of its fire fighters, cops, and corrections officers—is so formidable.[20]

Perhaps the most vivid example of the power of the teachers' unions in California came in Los Angeles shortly after a divisive strike in 1989 that was ultimately settled with a rich contract. It granted a three-year wage increase of roughly 27 percent that the district couldn't afford and that drove it to the edge of bankruptcy three years later. In an election with a dismally low turnout, an unknown twenty-seven-year-old named Mark Slavkin, whose only notable strength was his union support, was elected to the seven-member board. Julie Korenstein, an incumbent who supported the contract, was re-elected with the strong support of the union. The board member who had most vehemently resisted the union's demands was defeated. There was nothing subtle about all this. "The message," said Wayne Johnson, who was then the UTLA president, "is you better listen to us or you are in political trouble."[21]

In 1996, as if trying to cap both the craziness of California's top-down school mandates and their own assertiveness, the leaders of the UTLA qualified a statewide "Educational Efficiency Initiative," called "95–5" for short, that would require local districts to spend no more than 5 percent of their total budget on administration, the rest in the classroom, from where, of course, much of the money would go on the bargaining table.

The measure was so ill-defined that it was not clear what was to be included within each category: What portion of the cost of capital projects should be counted as part of the 95 percent allocated to classrooms? "The measure," said an analysis prepared by the state Department of Finance and the Legislative Analyst's Office, "contains conflicting statements on whether administrative costs for maintenance, cafeteria operation, capital projects, and other enterprise funds are to be included in the portion restricted to 5 percent." And what would happen if a district were suddenly hit with a large unexpected legal expense—say a damage award to a student for sexual harrassment, either by a teacher or another student—would it then have to fire the superintendent to stay within its limit?[22] And what would the tight formula do to the willingness of any district to begin the costly process of firing a teacher? But with its deceptively simple idea, and the blessings it received from politicians of both parties, among them Los Angeles Mayor Richard Riordan, a Republican, who contributed $50,000 to the signature campaign, and Senator Dianne Feinstein, a Democrat,[23] it very nearly passed. That it came so close—the final vote was 45–55—made it another example of a quick-fix top-down plebiscitary perfectionism[24] that seemed like good sense at the time but would have further hamstrung accountability and governance."

The declining community engagement, and the growing control of the schools and community college districts by their own employees (and to a lesser extent, the employee dominance in some city and county governments as well), produce not merely what one Fresno journalist called board "arrogance in dealing with parents" and other citizen groups—arrogance that often includes unvarnished abuse of those who want to be heard at board meetings. They also produce the shift, already described, of resources from program to salaries.

The contractual clout of the union—which in some respects is all the greater when a financially strapped district has little to give in negotiations other than control over work rules—also circumscribes the districts with so many rules on job assignments and seniority—about how, where, and in what order of seniority teachers can be assigned to what school—that it's not unusual for parents to find that even by the third or fourth week of school, there is still no regular teacher assigned in their children's classroom. Firing incompetent or malicious teachers is virtually impossible; all demands for merit pay or other performance-related incentives are stoutly resisted, and, in some urban districts, it has not been unusual to find personal attacks in teacher union literature on the leaders of the little parents' groups, often with no more than three or four active members, that still have the temerity to challenge the constraints that the teacher contract imposes on school reform.

In a high-cost state that puts such enormous burdens on its schools and teachers, the high level of compensation for teachers (perhaps even their clout in politics and bargaining) is hardly out of line; many teachers spend sizeable chunks of their own money, sometimes running into the hundreds of dollars each year, to buy classroom supplies that their districts can no longer afford. But given the fiscal constraints under which the system operates, the cost of those salaries in program and other services is immense: The power and compensation of teachers have been the granite in the Proposition 13 current; everything else is sandstone.

In light of their resource and space shortages, and the demographic and social problems they confront, it's striking how well some parts of the system are still performing. There are, despite all pressures to the contrary, still extraordinary individual schools, and not just those in exclusive enclaves like Beverly Hills and well-tended suburban gardens like La Jolla. Lowell High in San Francisco, for example, is perhaps the most academically intensive school in the state. And individual districts also excel, even some that, like the Lenox Elementary District in Los Angeles, operate under the toughest conditions.

Lenox, located directly under the flight path in and out of Los Angeles International Airport, is hunkered down against its environment. Its newest school has no windows; it was built almost entirely underground—what rises above ground looks a little like a Maginot Line concrete pillbox—and the windows of its older schools have been boarded shut against vandalism, the occasional gunshot that rings out in the neighborhood, and the deafening roar of the jets passing overhead. Yet its teachers, most of them bilingual and all assembled by an extraordinary superintendent named Ken Moffett, since retired, generate a combination of energy, intelligence, and caring that's rare even in the most advantaged places. A majority of its children begin school speaking little or no English. Some 94 percent are from non-English-speaking homes, most of them Hispanics, and 82 percent are eligible for free or reduced-price lunches. Some live in cars. Most are ready to "transition," as the expression goes, into mainstream classes within three years. Despite these odds, most finish elementary school reading at grade level or better. The district is now sprinkled with teachers who themselves began there in the first grade.

More broadly, and almost as unnoticed in the larger picture, between 1983 and the end of the 1980s, the state, driven by an energetic and uncompromising state superintendent named Bill Honig, and by the general "nation-at-risk" reform ethos, adopted model high school graduation standards. These standards pushed local districts to require at least four years of English, three years of math, and two years of science before granting diplomas, a model that many districts, though hardly all, have followed.[25]

California led the nation in upgrading its curricula in history and science and in adopting more rigorous textbooks, often in the face of vehement opposition from all sorts of ideological groups. These groups ranged from fundamentalists demanding equal time for creation science and sniffing texts for signs of secular humanism and sympathy for witches to Afrocentrists calling for material showing that European civilization began in Africa; from liberals counting uses of the word "nigger" in *Huckleberry Finn* to gays and lesbians demanding that Tchaikovsky and Michelangelo be explicitly recognized as homosexuals in the curriculum.[26]

Spurred by tougher formal admission requirements to the state colleges, California also shifted more of its resources from dead-end programs and other Mickey Mouse courses toward core academic areas (which could well be an unintended blessing of the budget cuts). As a consequence, the percentage of students taking and passing Advanced Placement examinations increased sharply. The number taking solid academic courses—four years of high school English, at least three years of math, two years of science—went up, and SAT scores, while no higher than the national average, crept up, despite the increasing percentage of minority students who now take them. (Not suprisingly, given the large enrollment of students who are not native English speakers, the state's SAT scores are higher than the national average in math, due particularly to the high achievement of Asian students, and lower on the verbal portion.) And although a sizeable proportion of University of California freshmen—many of them non-native English speakers—are required to take remedial English, the entering students at the University of California are, in the view of UC President Richard Atkinson, "the best prepared in history."[27]

But in most schools, the success, when it comes, is there despite the lack of resources, both in poor and in middle-class schools, and often it's not there at all. California's high school dropout rate remains considerably higher than the national average. The graduation requirements in English, math, science, and foreign languages in most high schools remain softer, despite the reforms of the 1980s, than those of comparable states. Many of the course offerings that were cut after the passage of Proposition 13, among them school-funded driver training, once regarded as a California birthright, have never been restored. In some high schools, said a University of California official, it is impossible to do outreach, because those schools do not offer the academic preparation that the university requires. (In a state that prides itself as being the keystone of the Pacific Rim, fewer than one-fourth of California high schools offer Chinese or Japanese in their small menu of foreign languages.) In many high schools, the seventh period of instruction, which vanished in 1978 (and sometimes the sixth), has never been restored. And because of its endless fights over educational doctrine and ideology, California, which under Honig was a national leader in setting standards in the early 1980s, had no statewide testing program of any kind for nearly a decade.

In 1994, the state introduced a new performance-based test

called CLAS (California Learning Assessment System), which included a great many nontraditional, open-ended items—often called "prompts" these days. But the test, produced with much fanfare under the aegis of old-line Progressives in the State Education Department, was so unreliable and so poorly explained to the public, that it became an easy target for the state's right wing, whose members were quick to discover suspicious-sounding passages in literature questions. The test also became a source of concern for middle-of-the-road parents. Instead of directly testing reading comprehension, it asked students to fill in balloons with phrases describing what they thought about the passages on the test. In the same spirit, it included a fifth-grade science exercise on recycling that culminated, not in the articulation of some scientific principle about conservation of energy or matter, but with an assignment to write a letter to the governor urging him to support recycling legislation. CLAS died a quick death. A standardized test was finally put in place in 1998.

The most telling indication of California's school problems, however, may be the difficulty the state faces even as its economy thrives and its revenues grow. Because of the requirements written into the California constitution by Proposition 98, a constitutional initiative approved by voters in 1988 that sets a minimum that California must spend on its schools, the state has no choice but to put a large part of its increased postrecession state revenues into the schools and community colleges (which had probably taken even bigger hits in funding than the schools). Under the complex Proposition 98 formula, which allows the state to defer some school spending in bad times but requires restoration of funding when revenues improve, that restoration came to better than 60 percent of the state's new general fund money—the difference between what had been going into the general fund in 1994–95 and what was available in 1996–97. And when the state in 1997–98 unexpectedly found itself receiving an additional $2 billion in tax revenues, the bizarre Proposition 98 formula, all other urgent needs notwithstanding, dealt virtually every cent of it to schools.[28]

The choice California could make, and is making, was to devote a great proportion of that money to class-size reduction in the primary grades, which has become perhaps the most popular education initiative undertaken in California in the past generation. Under the formula proposed by Governor Pete Wilson and ultimately adopted by the legislature, only districts which reduce class sizes in the first four grades (kindergarten through grade three) to twenty students or less can get that money (at a rate of $800 per child). Wilson's move initially was designed, not for its popularity, but as a way to keep a large chunk of money off the bargaining table and away from the unions that the governor has often been at odds with.

For Wilson, it had looked like a particularly elegant way to get even with the CTA, which ran sharp anti-Wilson commercials during the 1994 gubernatorial campaign focusing on the state's overcrowded classrooms. Those commercials helped generate the climate of support for something that gave Wilson the best press he had enjoyed in his entire gubernatorial career. The CTA, like most public employee unions, strongly prefers unrestricted state funding that puts most of the money on the local bargaining table. CTA's Democratic allies in the legislature initially attempted (probably with good reason) to question the broad sweep of the class-size plan as requiring too many adjustments too quickly. But the ads had created an atmosphere that made it impossible for anyone to resist Wilson's decision.[29] (At the same time, in yet another piece of irony, Wilson's stick-it-to-the-CTA proposals also represented a great gift to the organization, since they brought thousands of new teachers into the system, most of whom immediately became dues-paying CTA members who brought the union an additional $4 million a year.)

By the summer of 1997, the end of the first year of the class-size program, virtually all first-grade classes had been reduced to twenty students, along with a considerable number of second grades and some kindergarten classes as well. The biggest exceptions, as might be expected, were schools in inner-city neighborhoods, which have no space, even for additional portables in the playgrounds; the biggest winners were a few affluent districts that, notwithstanding state equalization formulas, had managed to operate with primary classes of twenty-five kids or less, and thus got the additional money with relatively little effort.

The reduced class sizes in grades K–3, where they were implemented, got almost universal raves from primary-school parents and teachers, many of whom declared that for the first time in their careers they were able to work with individual children. They also elicited marginal indications that some people who had escaped from the crowded and dilapidated schools and put their children into private schools were bringing them back.

But the cost has been high. Since nearly all those new classes are housed either in portables or crammed into whatever corner the schools can find—in libraries, computer rooms, auditoriums, faculty lounges, teacher preparation rooms—and since the new state money has not been sufficient to cover the additional costs of the new classes in many districts, school resources, already tight, have been squeezed even harder for all other classes and programs. Some districts, like Pomona, rented space in shopping malls. Many are taking back the space they had been providing to organizations like the YMCA and other operators of neighborhood day care centers. Others sought waivers from state earthquake standards to rent space in empty office buildings and industrial facilities. Still others simply stuck little partitions into larger classrooms and let teachers handle the chatter from the other side as best they can. In Florida, there has been great political agitation over the fact that nearly 10 percent of students are now housed in portables. In California that number is closer to 20 percent—perhaps one million students—and there is every indication that it will grow ever larger. As a consequence, many California schools now look more like migrant camps—row after row of drab wooden boxes of uncertain safety, most of them painted brown—than like temples of knowledge. There is, the saying goes, nothing as permanent as a portable.

There are, in addition, unresolved questions about the qualifications of the new teachers who have been—and are still being—hastily recruited, more than a fourth of them without credentials, for the thousands of new classes that the class-size reduction program has generated. By June 1998, many of them had qualified for tenure under state law. The result is that almost everything else has become even more crowded and other programs even more constrained, particularly in the inner cities. And since California's average class size was so large to begin with, even the new reforms have not brought the statewide average to much under twenty-seven, still among the largest in the nation.[30]

By June of 1998, 70 percent of all K–3 students were expected to be in classes of twenty or less, but with "districts running out of low-cost options for new facilities," as the Legislative Analyst put it, the possibilities of quickly extending that percentage in the following year were slim.[31] And the new input of money still left California's resources for everything from roof repairs to course offerings to staffing for counselors and the nurse's office among the worst in the nation and, in all but those primary classes, sometimes even worse off.[32] In the summer of 1996, the Los Angeles Unified School District, with its 660,000 students, announced its intention to hire a total of sixteen new music teachers in the next five years, in addition to the seventy-three it then had, a decision that would permit music to be offered at least once a week at every one of the district's four hundred elementary schools. But the district acknowledged that this long-range plan would still mean that kids at the district's larger schools would seldom get a music lesson. The price of twenty years of neglect and decline, as California has discovered, is monstrous.

In the summer of 1996, Robin Greene, the parent of two elementary schoolchildren who had recently moved from the comfortable Southern California suburb of Thousand Oaks to the equally comfortable town of Pittsford, New York, a suburb of Rochester, sent a report about the changed school circumstances of her children back to *The Los Angeles Times*:[33]

> The average class size at Park Oaks [in California] was 32 students, while Thornell Road in New York averages 24 (and parents are outraged by the overcrowding). Park Oaks [with 525 students in grades K–6] has 17 regular teachers while Thornell Road [450 students in K–5]

has 19. Thornell Road also has three full-time teaching aides. . . . There's a full-time physical education teacher and some parents are lobbying for another woman P.E. teacher to instruct the older girls. At Park Oaks, two of our PTA moms, not credentialed teachers, served as part-time P.E specialists.

Thornell Road has a full-time music teacher who specializes in vocals. Another part-time music teacher visits the school to teach instrumental music. Park Oaks had a part-time uncredentialed music teacher who spent five hours a week at the school. To help compensate, our principal at Park Oaks, Leean Nemeroff, spent a half-hour every Friday afternoon singing with the third graders.

Thornell Road has a full-time registered nurse who also teaches safety and health to the students. Park Oaks had a part-time nurse/clerk and a wonderful secretary who ministered to cuts and bruises.

The list goes on. The Thornell Road staff includes a full-time school psychologist, guidance counselor, speech and language therapist, reading teacher, librarian-computer teacher and art teacher . . . Park Oaks had none of these. Instead it had a full-time special education teacher and three other part-time reading and language specialists . . . and the librarian was a dear woman who worked full-time for a part-time salary to keep the books on the shelves.

In the face of such shortages, parents and other school groups in many California communities, sometimes backed by sympathetic local businesses, struggle to raise private funds to replace a little of the tax money lost over the years. Scores of school districts now charge parents $150 a year or more for transportation to and from school; under state law only students who are on some sort of public assistance have the right to ride free. In many other districts, coaches, uniforms, equipment, and the travel of athletic teams is largely underwritten through parent contributions, often under a no-pay, no-play policy, something that was unheard of in California before Proposition 13. Some booster and parent groups, as at Sacramento's suburban El Camino High School, run twice-weekly bingo nights. In other places, foundations have been established to raise funds for music and art programs, and to buy computers and other classroom technology and create small CD-ROM libraries; there is even a California Consortium of Educational Foundations in San Francisco, which estimates there are some 275 of them, most of them created since the passage of Proposition 13.

A few foundations in affluent communities, like the shorefront Los Angeles County district of Palos Verdes, which generates some $700,000 a year, raise substantial sums of money at elegant dinner dances to fund after-school enrichment programs and provide what are, in effect, direct subsidies to teachers. But for the most part, the private efforts come closer to begging and scrounging than anything that could be called philanthropy. In some sex-ed classes, menstruation is discussed with the aid of pamphlets, complete with order blanks for free samples from tampon manufacturers. In still other places, schools, which used to restrict paid advertising displays to football scoreboards, now shamelessly sell advertising space on cafeteria walls for Cheetos and M&Ms and put logos on sports practice uniforms for local auto dealers and fast food outlets. (They would sell space for commercial patches on regular uniforms as well if state law did not prohibit it.) But those efforts, which probably generate no more than an average of $100 per student per year, roughly 2 percent of overall costs, don't make much of a dent in the overall picture. What they may do is keep at least some people in the community informed about the shape the schools are in.[34]

The real difference between California and many other states, as Greene pointed out, is a few thousand dollars a year ($3,200 vs. $6,660 in her illustration) in property taxes on homes of roughly similar value. That, she said, is a small difference if it buys education "in a school that boasts scores nicely above the national average. It would cost me a lot more to send two children to private school . . . Has it occured to anyone that California's housing slump may be partly attributable to its public schools?" New York, she might have pointed out, spends nearly twice per child what California spends.[35]

But for twenty years, the majority of voting Californians, their professions of support for schools notwithstanding, have not shared that view. In an extensive comparative survey of state education programs and resources published by the authoritative industry journal *Education Week* in January 1997, California got devastating ratings, particularly for its poor funding and the inadequate conditions of its schools. It got a grade of D- in school climate, D- in school resources, both the lowest in the nation, and an overall comment that the state's school system, "once [a] world-class system, is now third-rate."[36]

II

In the early 1980s, as the fiscal constraints imposed by the sharp revenue cuts resulting from California's tax-cutting began to pinch, George Deukmejian, the Republican who succeeded Jerry Brown as governor in 1982, began to pursue what was, in essence a two-track policy. He gave the University of California and, to some extent, the middle-tier California State University relatively generous funding, even as the per-student share of spending for the huge but politically weak community college system languished and funding for public schools, relative to other states (and to needs), continued its steady decline.[37]

In part, the decision reflected the embarrassment that Deukmejian suffered in his first term when it was announced that Sematech, a major new scientific research center, was to be set up in Austin, at the University of Texas, not at Berkeley or Pasadena's Cal Tech or in the Silicon Valley (where Californians expected such establishments, by a sort of divine right, to go). In part it was consistent with the social attitudes and the political priorities that Deukmejian brought with him to office. It was also, of course, a relatively cheap course, since any significant increase in per-pupil spending for the large K–12 system is so much more costly. Even after University of California President David Gardner pleaded with Deukmejian for higher fees, Deukmejian, who really believed in low-tuition education, even for the upper-middle-class students who dominated UC's enrollment, resisted. But Deukmejian showed no similar tenderness for the working-class students in the schools and community colleges, which, of course, is where two-thirds of California's college students go.

By 1990, however—before the recession—the state's self-imposed tax restrictions and the rising costs of competing health care and corrections budgets were already reducing inflation-adjusted state revenues for its collegiate institutions.[38] Recession and the change of administration from Deukmejian to Pete Wilson, who was much less sentimental about things like free tuition, turned that reduction into a steep slide. Historically, California had never charged students for "tuition," the cost of instruction, only (in theory) for peripheral things like laboratory expenses, parking, and building and library maintenance, all lumped together as "fees." Even now there is no charge called "tuition" in California. But between 1991 and 1995, the state's general fund spending for higher education declined by more than 20 percent in real dollars (down 16 percent for the University of California between 1991 and 1994), and California's essentially tuition-free higher education system became history.

Over that four-year period, the University of California's basic charges more than doubled, from just under $2,000 a year to over $4,000 a year (plus room, board, and other expenses), with proportional increases in the tuition (still called "fees" in California) charged by the California State University and the community colleges. That still left California's charges no higher than the average for comparable four-year public institutions in other states, and it left the annual $390 fee at the state's community colleges at about one-third the national average for junior college fees. It also enabled UC to increase its funding for financial aid. By the mid-1990s, it claimed it was able to enroll a somewhat larger percentage of low-income students than it had five years earlier, though certainly not in numbers that were proportional to the population, much less in the kind of proportions that would offset and justify the higher costs imposed on lower-middle-income students and their families.[39] Overall, financial aid remained low.

What was certainly clear is that one of the basic props of the "utopian" Master Plan, the guarantee of near-universal access at little or no cost, was gone. After the recovery in 1996–97, when Democrats threatened to seize the popular fee issue, Wilson, understanding the political dangers, "froze" fees three years running.[40] But, even after funding increased again in the mid-1990s and after a 5 percent fee cut was approved for 1998–99, no one spoke seriously about rolling them back to pre-recession levels, much less those of the 1960s. The years from 1990–91 through 1993–94, said a report from the independent California Higher Education Policy Center, "witnessed a virtual collapse of the state's recognition of the Master Plan's elements."[41]

The core of that collapse rested on one simple change. Instead of access being the state's driving principle in higher education, as it had been since the 1960s, support for California's colleges (to use the words of Warren H. Fox, who heads the California Postsecondary Education Commission), became "budget-driven, not enrollment-driven."[42] The result was that, for the first time in California history, both the number and percentage of Californians in higher education went down. In 1990 there were about 1.7 million students (1.2 million in the community colleges, 160,000 at UC, 350,000 at CSU) in California's public institutions. By 1993–94, there were 200,000 fewer—the equivalent of about 60,000 full-time students—than there had been three years before.[43]

That decline can't be blamed entirely on the budget cuts or the corresponding increases in tuition: It resulted at least in equal part from a monumental lack of planning and coordination. (California, said researcher Michael Shires in a report issued by RAND, "appears to be in a state of denial regarding the ongoing viability of the Master Plan.")[44] In fact, it had never occurred to the state's policymakers, either in the legislature or in the universities, that other than perhaps having to accommodate to the effects of short-lived economic dips, there would ever be any long-term need to retrench.

Even as the pressure tightened, tenured UC professors, on average, were teaching no more than three courses every two semesters, meaning they spent roughly four and a half hours in class a week, half of the average teaching load during the good old days of the Clark Kerr era.[45] (In higher education, someone said, when the ship hits an iceberg, the captain and crew get in the lifeboats first.) For a time in the early 1990s, both the University of California and the California State University simply reduced the number of scheduled classes and sections, often without plan or priority. Both seemed almost intentionally to be making it hard for undergraduates, some of whom would sit all night in waiting lines to enroll, and in some cases nearly impossible for students to find seats once they were enrolled. The tougher choices—eliminating outdated, ineffective, or otherwise marginal graduate or research programs, or indeed phasing out entire departments—were not made. "In universities," wrote Donald Kennedy, the former president of Stanford, "sunset is an hour that almost never comes."[46]

Perhaps even more telling, when the financial crunch became unavoidable, UC, which had a well-funded pension system, simply offered senior professors of a certain age and longevity an across-the-board golden handshake, without making any of the distinctions, used by other institutions that had to retrench during the same period, between those it really valued and those it could have done without. The 2,000 who accepted the offer, faculty and administrators, therefore included some of UC's great stars, among them some of the same people—policy analyst Martin Trow, cybernetician Lotfi Zadeh, sociologist Neil Smelser, Nobel Prize-winning economist Gerard Debreu, Nobel Prize-winning physicist Donald Glaser—that Kerr had lured so proudly to California during the University's golden years a generation earlier. Berkeley's Physics Department lost 40 percent of its faculty; the History Department 30 percent; its Music Department four of the five members in its distinguished division of music and musicology.[47]

Some of those stars would stay on, doing research under government grants or teaching part-time as emeriti, although some also took lucrative jobs elsewhere, thus virtually doubling their incomes. And through it all, UC's graduate programs continued to be ranked in the top ten—and often at the very top—among American research universities in the decennial surveys of the National Research Council and similar rankings by other national academic research organizations. Some of those surveys, however, were done before the early retirements took place and not announced until after. And, as always, none made a clear distinction between the current quality of a program and the lingering glow of glories past.

Either way, however, for those who recalled the optimism of the era of Kerr and Pat Brown, and who understood how essential higher education, and UC particularly, are to the state's high-tech, high-value-added, economy, both the real loss and the symbolism were clear enough. In the context of those faculty cutbacks, Governor Pete Wilson's ability, in the summer of 1995, to coerce swiftly the regents into ending the university's affirmative action programs, despite the strong opposition of both UC's faculty and administration, was a particularly severe blow, both to its ability to maintain a vaguely representative student body and to its academic independence from political interference. Shortly after the regents' decision, Richard Atkinson, who had been chancellor of UC's San Diego campus and had just become the system's president, tried, with the quiet urging of some UC chancellors, to delay its implementation. But he moved unilaterally, without consulting the regents—simply announced that UC would take another year to do what his board had ordered. Predictably, that raised the wrath of the governor, who quickly forced the president of the nation's most highly regarded public university to issue a humiliating public apology declaring that he had "erred" and that he understood that it was the regents (i.e., Wilson in this case) who were the policymakers. That left the university even more bruised.[48]

California wasn't alone in having to scale back; other states went through similar recession-driven cuts at about the same time. Higher education, it has been pointed out, is among the first things to be cut in state budgets during hard times, and among the first to be restored when revenues increase after the hard times end. But California's general fund spending on higher education declined twice as much as that of the nation as whole.[49] And while education funding began to rise again in 1995, the amount the state appropriated in 1996–97 for the University of California, after the recovery was in full swing, was exactly the same as it had been a decade earlier, notwithstanding a 30 percent increase in the cost of living. This was the budget of a governor who had himself attended Berkeley's Boalt Hall Law School at virtually no cost, said Jess

Bravin, the student regent in 1996–97, and had thus benefited from a university "that gave—rather than *sold*—him one of the finest educations in the world."[50] Journalist James Richardson, a 1975 graduate of UCLA, put the loss even more forcefully:

> For decades, Californians had enjoyed the promise of a *free* education from kindergarten through college. And it was a truly extraordinary promise. In the early 1940s, both of my parents went to UC Berkeley, then the nation's finest public university. They paid for only books and board. Nothing like a UC education, in Berkeley, Los Angeles and across the entire system as it expanded up and down the state, was offered anywhere else in the United States.
>
> California's modern blueprint for its colleges and universities, the Master Plan, enacted in 1960 and still in force, pledges as a matter of public policy a tuition-free education to all who are qualified. But over the past three decades, California's commitment to its future has steadily eroded as "student fees" first crept, then shot upward.[51]

The recovery brought enrollment back to prerecession levels at the University of California (though not at the California State University and the community colleges), but the changes that had been wrought in the meantime were permanent. UC's student–faculty ratio, which had been 14–1 twenty years earlier, stood at 19–1, and was expected to remain there indefinitely—not bad for most public universities, but a quantum decline at places like Berkeley and UCLA, institutions which had been in a league by themselves. Conversely, at both UC and the California State University, which is supposed to be primarily a system of teaching institutions, the proportion of courses taught by transient (and generally underpaid) part-time lecturers has increased considerably, though no one is quite sure by how much. At California State University at Hayward, for example, which had employed 407 tenured or tenure-track teachers and 142 lecturers just before the recession, there were 373 tenure-track people and 330 lecturers in 1995 who taught roughly one-third of all classes, and considerably more in some increasingly "faceless" departments that, in the warning of one faculty member, are on the verge of becoming "a shell without substance."[52]

The increase in untenured teachers—"highway fliers" who may be teaching at two or three different institutions simultaneously—is hardly unique to California, and may not be all bad: It could well reduce faculty deadwood and bring in people who are more current as teachers (and perhaps as scholars), but it does little for institutional continuity and loyalty and provides even less assurance than before about quality of instruction. And here, too, as in many other things, California fell further. Here, too, it ceased to be the great exception—in considerable part because, in the decisions they made on budgets and taxes beginning in the early 1990s, California voters and political leaders implictly chose to be merely ordinary, and sometimes much less. UC's leaders, meanwhile, determinedly began to turn the institution into a semiprivate entity funded increasingly through federal grants, corporate underwriting, and other private resources, plus tuition (and the federal loans that made it more or less affordable), thereby shifting costs from the current generation to the next.[53]

And they made those decisions, whether by coincidence or otherwise, just as the state's high school graduation classes ceased to be dominated by whites and became increasingly Latino and Asian. In 1993, for the first time in the history of any major American state, more than half of the state's high school graduates were nonwhite, and within a decade more or less, the entire state workforce will be predominantly nonwhite as well. Thereafter whites will never be a majority again, either in the schools or the labor force. "In the 1960s," said Patrick Callan, who headed the California Higher Education Policy Center until the spring of 1997, "we moved heaven and hell to accommodate the baby boomers. We're not doing that now."[54]

Of even greater concern than the reduction of higher education spending, the reduction of college access, and the increased burdens—now amounting to several billion in loans—placed on the next generation are the long-term trend lines in the state's spending priorities. California, again like many other states, saw a sharp increase in gang- and drug-related crimes beginning in the mid-1980s and has been in a fifteen-year crime frenzy fanned both by police organizations, and particularly by the Los Angeles Police Department, which issued dire warnings about the growth of gangs—LA alone was said to have 50,000 gang members—and by a combination of sensational crimes fully exploited by the state's hyperventilating ("if it bleeds, it leads") television news programs.

In 1986, voters, balloting in one of the periodic reconfirmation elections to which all appellate judges are subject under the state constitution, removed Chief Justice Rose Bird and Associate Justices Joseph Grodin and Cruz Reynoso from the seven-member state supreme court. All three had been appointed by Governor Jerry Brown; all were regarded as too soft on crime, and particularly too slow in imposing the death penalty—a fourth, Otto Kaus, anticipating the bloodletting, had already quit. They were replaced by a group of tough-on-crime judges named by Deukmejian, a conservative governor who, notwithstanding his attachment to low University of California tuition, had few priorities other than a balanced budget, prison building, and tough-on-crime legislation: Among his major accomplishments as a legislator had been the bill restoring the state's death penalty law, which, like other state capital punishment laws, had been ruled "wanton and freakish" and struck down as unconstitutional by the U.S. Supreme Court in 1972.[55]

Deukmejian, though famously dull, was a thoroughly honorable and decent man, but he did little to make up for the Reagan-era cuts in federal funding for summer jobs and the other Great Society youth and employment programs—the Comprehensive Employment and Training Act, the Job Corps, the Neighborhood Youth Corps—that had been regarded as factors in crime prevention and that were then rapidly disappearing from California's cities.

On both counts—eliminating preventative programs and toughening the crime laws—Deukmejian's policies signaled a southward shift in the state's Brown-era outlook on criminal justice issues, from a place whose laws, judges, parole boards, and sentencing practices had been moderately progressive in outlook—more like Minnesota than Texas or Florida on such issues as the death penalty, youth crime, and the possibilities of rehabilitation of criminals—and helped make them into some of the toughest in the country. He stoutly resisted proposals to name a sentencing commission to rationalize the state's crazy quilt of criminal sentences and consistently named former prosecutors to be judges in the state's trial courts. Even Reagan, as governor, had approved some mild prison reforms, including a limited program of conjugal visits.[56]

Consistent with that shift, and with the state's tough-on-crime voter initiatives, the legislature began to pass bill after bill increasing sentences—more than 400 have passed just since 1990. In 1994, California passed the nation's toughest three-strikes sentencing law, which was both enacted by the legislature and then, just to make certain the legislature didn't change its mind, redundantly passed again as an initiative by the electorate.[57]

In combination with an increasing drug-driven crime rate, those stiff mandatory sentences drove up California's prison population nearly sixfold over the course of a generation, most of it in the eighties and nineties, from just under 25,000 in 1969 to nearly 160,000 in 1998. And as the effects of three-strikes, which doubles most sentences after the second serious felony, and increases them to twenty-five-years-to-life after the third, begin to be fully felt, prison population was certain to climb even further. In 1970, California spent 4 percent of its general fund on corrections and 14 percent on higher education. By 1998, those numbers had converged, with 8.5 percent going to corrections and 12.9 percent going to higher education, with no clear sign that the long-term trend would soon change. And since higher education and corrections (now joined by the postreform welfare program, the wildest of the budgetary wild cards) are two of the large items in the budget not mandated or protected by some formula, either in the state constitution or in federal law, there were increasingly urgent warnings in the mid-1990s that corrections and higher education were on a collision course.

The most gloomy of those forecasts came from two RAND reports, one, by criminologist Peter W. Greenwood, issued in 1994, the other, by Michael Shires, issued in 1996, which warned that under the spur of three-strikes, by the year 2004–05, the 8–9 percent that was spent on prisons in the mid-1990s would balloon to 20 percent, meaning that health, welfare, corrections, and K–14 education (the schools and junior colleges) would consume between 93 and 99 percent of the budget.[58] That would leave between 1 percent and 7 percent in the general fund for higher education and everything else the state does, from the highway patrol and pesticide regulation, to fighting forest fires and running the Department of Fish and Game, to the courts, the attorney general's office, and the public defender. If something didn't give in that nearly impossible squeeze, Shires said, the additional 500,000 students, above the 1.7 million enrolled in 1994–95, who were expected to be eligible for California's higher education system just after the turn of the century—what Kerr called Tidal Wave II—would have no place to go.[59] "Access deficits," said Shires, "are here to stay."[60]

Those projections soon turned out to be excessively gloomy. While California's prison population and costs continued to grow, the inmate population, even with the effects of the three-strikes laws, has not been rising nearly as fast as first predicted. As elsewhere, California's crime rate began to come down sharply in the mid-1990s, in part due, most probably, to the temporary decline in the population of young, crime-prone males, in part due to an easing in the drug-turf wars, in part because of an improving economy, and in part, almost certainly, because more criminals are in prison. At the same time, California judges, in sentencing criminals for offenses they don't regard as sufficiently onerous to merit the harsh consequences of a second strike (a doubling of the normal sentence), have found ways around some of the mandates of the law.[61]

Yet even in the face of those changes, no one expects the long-term trend in the prison population—currently rising at a rate of 11,000 (about 8 percent) per year—to be anything but up, both in absolute terms and as a percentage of the population—and, of course, in cost. And those numbers will probably rise more sharply as the percentage of the population in the crime-prone years—which tends also to be the college-going years—starts up again at the beginning of the next decade.[62] Even if crime rates stay down, the state's stiffer second-strike sentences will drive the prison population up. "It's the second strikes," a prison official said, "that are killing us." And as the third-strike, twenty-five-years-to-life terms begin to be felt early in the next century, they, too, will drive up the prison population and the costs that go with it.

The RAND predictions may be too gloomy on the higher education side as well. In a high-tech age, there are expedients other than forever replicating traditional research universities, each with a full complement of graduate programs, each offering conventional lectures and seminars in the same way that they've been offered since the early days of Paris, Bologna, and Oxford, each giving diplomas every spring to students who have recorded the seat time—credits, hours, semesters—prescribed by the faculty.

Yet a lot more space will be needed, even with the full development of whatever high-tech distance-learning resources the state can muster. And California has begun no new University of California campus since Pat Brown left office in 1966. It has opened just two campuses of the twenty-one-campus California State University, one of them the fortuitous result of a federal gift of land and buildings to mitigate the effects of the closing of the large army base at Fort Ord, near Monterey, shortly after Bill Clinton was elected. Corrections, and the construction of corrections facilities, meanwhile, have become far and away the state's largest growth sector.

Since 1984, California has opened twenty new prisons, in addition to the twelve it built in the previous 130 years, creating a vast correctional archipelago stretching from one end of the state to the other. (It is hard to drive California's freeways nowadays without coming to signs showing an exit to some correctional facility.)[63] In addition, according to the projections of the Legislative Analyst, by the year 2005, the state must build *fourteen more* prisons, at a cost of some $3.5 billion, to handle present overcrowding, now running at roughly 180 percent of capacity, and the anticipated increase in inmates, whose numbers are projected to rise to 200,000 early in the next decade and to 250,000 by the year 2005.[64] California, according to James Gomez, who headed the state Department of Corrections until early 1997, "has the most crowded prison system in the nation," its prisons (in 1996) filled to 188 percent of their design capacity.[65] Each third strike, he said, "is a $500,000 invest-ment, but California politicians want to punish without paying."[66]

But in fact, the state was paying a huge amount. In the fifteen years after 1980, California's corrections budget increased 847 per-cent; its spending for higher education rose 116 percent. In 1988, for the first time in California history, those 160,000 inmates in California's prisons, who cost the state an annual $22,000 each to maintain, was projected to top the enrollment—graduate and undergraduate—of the University of California.[67] There are 27,200 black students in California's four-year colleges and univer-sities; there are 45,000 blacks in California's prisons.[68]

III

Almost no public service has been exempt from California's ero-sion. But it's the counties and the services they provide—public clinics, mental health, welfare and general assistance to the down-and-out, children's protective services, jails, acute home nursing care, probation, abused women's shelters, drug counseling—that have taken the hardest hit for the better part of twenty years. The blow comes in part because the state's crazy-quilt fiscal structure gives the counties no independent way to raise new revenue; in part because the legislature and governor have raided local coffers to meet their own constitutional obligations—including the transfer of some $3.6 billion in annual property tax revenues from local agencies (over 70 percent of it from the counties) to the state in the early 1990s—and in part because many of those services, though often mandated by state law, have little popular support. It is the counties that are the ultimate dirty workers in the job of keeping the scruffy, the mentally ill, the addicted, the drunk, the chronically ill, most of whom are not organized and don't vote, out of the way and the neighborhoods—and the sight—of respectable citizens, and few people really care how it's done. As a consequence a number of those counties (as already noted) teeter on the edge of bankruptcy.

Up and down the state, social workers triage complaints of child abuse, and then triage again, so while the state's official caseload is held down, the number of child abuse reports not investigated continues to grow. So does the number of children—many more than those in cases sensational enough to make the occasional headlines—who die from beatings at the hands of parents and "family caretakers" (often the boyfriends of parents) whose records and histories are known to the system. State bureaucrats issue figures showing that staffing for county children's services relative to caseload has hardly changed since the early 1990s. This is hardly suprising, since counties are so strapped for money that, according to Frank Mecca, head of the California Welfare Directors Association, they "are turning back federal and state funds because they can't find the local money they need to match them." And so, as one county welfare director put it, hard-pressed welfare agencies open files on only the most dangerous cases, a self-defense strategy in which "supply drives demand."[69]

In Los Angeles, the county jail has been so crowded, in large part by people awaiting trial, that the average inmate serves only 25 percent of his or her sentence—even as a new $373 million, 4,000-bed "state of the art" jail stood empty for more than a year because the county couldn't afford to run it. In many places, the cops no longer investigate fraud and other routine white-collar crimes, and everywhere probation officers are so overloaded that they can provide almost no supervision or counseling for the majority of their clients. The number of probation officers has remained about the same in the past twenty years, but the number of probationers has increased from an estimated 30,000 to 400,000, and each worker's "intensive caseload" has gone up from fewer than 25 to an average of close to 100. "You're lucky," said Susie Cohen, the executive director of the California Parole, Probation and Correctional Association, "if you get a postcard from a client once a month."

According to Cohen, 46 percent of the state's probationers commit new crimes.[70]

While funding for the services that the public demands— sheriff's patrols, for example—is partially protected both by law and political pressure, and while support for mental health has been "stabilized" through state allocation of a certain portion of sales and other taxes to mental health services, albeit at a lower level than inflation and the growth in the state's population, many more have been cut again and again.[71] Clinics and county-funded libraries have been shut, job training and housing assistance for the disabled cut, general assistance reduced to the down-and-out, and unpaid mandatory "furloughs" instituted for all nonemergency personnel. (In a few rural counties in Northern California, governments have been so strapped in recent years that even public safety gave way: A few simply stopped putting any deputies on night patrol.)

Meanwhile, California's landscape has been marked by public libraries that can no longer afford to buy books and are operating on reduced hours, often with volunteer help or with librarians who donate part of their time, or shuttered altogether. Even as San Francisco, where, some years ago, voters set aside a specified portion of local taxes for libraries, was building a new high-tech main library (and then indiscriminately dumping more than 100,000 volumes it decided it didn't have room for into a landfill),[72] the Los Angeles County library system closed ten of its ninety-two branch libraries and sharply reduced its materials budget.

In Merced, a county-seat city of 60,000 in a rural Central Valley county of 200,000, the main library, which was on the verge of shutting down altogether after the nearly broke county cut its budget, is open thirty hours a week, ten of them supported by voluntary donations, but it is, as its director, Charleen Renteria, said, "just a reading room" that can afford no interlibrary services and virtually no new books or periodicals.

In Shasta County, it's twenty-seven hours, and in many smaller cities, it's less than twenty. In the capital city of Sacramento (pop. 400,000), the new central library, which was partially funded through exactions from developers, is open just thirty-seven hours a week—and never in the evenings or on weekends—because the city has no funds to staff it. In some rural areas, libraries are barely open at all, and in most, the purchases of new books and materials have been cut to zero.[73] At Lake Tahoe, said the head of the local Friends of the Library, "our computerized guide to the periodicals was repossessed because we couldn't pay the lease. It was either that or cut the hours we're open to students, and that's already down to six or seven hours a week."[74]

Statewide in the twenty years since the mid-1970s, per capita public library spending declined by nearly 20 percent, staffing by an equal amount, and service hours by over 40 percent. In 1992–93, the last year for which data are available, the state was dead last in the nation in its per capita library services, forty-seventh in the nation in the number of librarians per capita, and forty-sixth in the number of paid staff per capita, ahead only of Texas, West Virginia, Tennessee, Delaware, and Arkansas.[75] Although a number of jurisdictions voted increased local sales taxes for libraries in the mid-1990s, it's unlikely that the picture has changed very much since.

Little has been left untouched. In the mid-nineties, Sacramento County, which has a population of roughly 1.2 million people, and which is not untypical for urban counties, cut its discretionary spending by half and, for the period from 1996 to 1998, was facing the prospect of having to cut that half—about $90 million—by another $35 million. That would mean further reductions in staffing for the already overcrowded courts, where civil litigants often have to wait years before they can come to trial, and in probation, mental health, animal control, parks, and the various administrative services—zoning and planning reviews, building permits, tax assessments, for which there were also already inordinately long waits—that the county provides. (It would also mean more hardship and more homeless people sleeping in doorways and hanging out in the downtown shopping areas, where the merchants were already complaining about competition from the suburban malls.) Because federal and state law mandate certain services in jails, the county has fourteen recreation workers in its jails, but only four in its county parks.

*   *   *

Yet few of these problems compares with what the counties, and the people they serve, were facing in the consequences of state and federal welfare reform. Ironically, it was California's relatively generous welfare benefits that, until the end of the 1980s, were the most resistant to deep cuts. Written into law by Assembly Speaker Bob Moretti and the wily group of Democrats who controlled the Legislature during Reagan's second term as governor (1971–74), they included annual statutory cost-of-living increases in Aid to Families With Dependent Children (AFDC) as well as other benefits that could only be waived or repealed by a two-thirds vote, thereby giving the legislature's most liberal members something approaching a veto.[76] As a result, the COLA for AFDC, an autopilot program of the left, remained all but immutable for nearly a generation, even after virtually all other services began to erode, and despite nearly a decade of efforts by two Republican governors to trim or repeal it altogether.

In the five-year period beginning in 1989–90, however, mounting pressure, both fiscal and political, drove the legislature to reduce the monthly AFDC award for a family of three from $694 a month to $607 and then still lower, when federal waivers were no longer required. In the high-cost urban counties, the benefit was capped at $565 a month, a cut of 24 percent in inflation-adjusted dollars over a five-year period; in the rural counties, it went to $538.[77] While that still left California AFDC benefits higher than those of most other states, in the face of California's high cost of living and the fact that California, unlike most other states, provides almost no housing subsidies, it was a massive cut.[78] In the 1980s, California had also created an innovative workfare program called GAIN (Greater Avenues to Independence) to induce welfare recipients to go directly into jobs, even very low-wage jobs, rather than routing them through extensive periods of orientation, education, and other work-skills preparation. GAIN produced positive results in the two counties where it was seriously tried. Like other serious workfare programs, however, GAIN, which provided child care and other support, was expensive and never fully funded.

With the passage of federal welfare reform legislation in August

1996, most of that is now moot. California's economic boom, its declining welfare rolls, and the additional funds they generated left state officials in unexpectedly good circumstances for cushioning the huge impact that welfare reform was expected to have on California. The new revenues permit the state to put more money into job training and subsidized child care for ex-welfare recipients and other marginal workers than Pete Wilson had originally proposed. And they forced the governor to compromise with the state's Democrats on his demand for punitively tight time limitations on how long able-bodied aid recipients would be allowed to receive aid from the state before they were driven off the rolls of what is now called CalWorks.

But the new revenues and the compromises they produced hardly eliminated the blow. The compromise time limits, permitting no able-bodied person to receive more than eighteen months of aid in any three-year period—twenty-four months in cases where a county allows it—are still more stringent than the federal law requires. That's likely to create a particularly severe problem in California, where in the middle of 1997, when the new welfare plan was adopted, one million people were still out of work, most of them more skilled and experienced than those coming off welfare. And while the state's growing economy was expected to create some 350,000 new jobs a year, at least in the good years, those jobs were barely enough to accommodate new entrants to the state's workforce, let alone the several hundred thousand adults who headed welfare families and had no jobs in 1997.[79] In mid-1997, legislative officials calculated that, in addition to the 800,000 adults on welfare, the state had 1.1 million people on unemployment insurance, 500,000 who were underemployed, and 250,000 who had given up looking for work. (One survey, conducted in mid-1996 by the Field Poll for the California Wellness Foundation, had produced even grimmer figures: a total of 2.8 million "discouraged workers"—students, homeworkers, retirees—who said they would like to work but couldn't find jobs.)[80] Nor was there much likelihood that even the relatively generous sums the state planned to put into subsidized child care would be sufficient to enable all those parents to go to whatever jobs they can find. They are barely enough for the first year—before the deadlines fully kick in.

It's estimated that even if half the state's AFDC recipients were to find work before the expiration of the deadlines that the state and the new federal law impose the burden on county general assistance, the last resort for the destitute, could grow immeasurably. Even after Congress restored SSI (Supplemental Security Income) funding to legal immigrants who were elderly and disabled, it was expected that any remaining cutoff of aid—for SSI (to elderly aliens who are not disabled), food stamps, and other benefits—would hit California, with its large numbers of legal immigrants, particularly hard.[81] The reductions in federal food stamps alone were expected to cost Californians—most of them working families—about $3 billion over the next five years. (It was also likely to cost California growers, producers of the commodities that those food stamps buy, a good deal more.) To make things worse, Wilson, instead of using the relatively generous transitional funds that California's congressional delegation had been able to put into the federal law to cushion the blow, proposed to take $562 million of that amount over a two-year period and use it for other state purposes.

The crucial question, which will not be answered until the time limits on eligibility fully kick in, and in many respects not until the next recession—and part of which will almost certainly have to be addressed in Congress and in the courts—is how much of the cost the state will eventually assume, how much will be put on California's already overburdened counties, and how much will simply be left to the market, to families, to chance, and to the ravages of individual destitution. An analysis done in May 1997 for the Public Policy Institute of California by Eugene Smolensky, a welfare expert and outgoing Dean at the Graduate School of Public Policy at Berkeley, made it clear that particularly in states like California, with their large numbers of immigrants and low-wage workers, the conflicting goals in the "iron triangle" of welfare reform—moving people into jobs, protecting children, and saving taxpayers money—would never permit a very satisfactory solution.

To do the first two would almost certainly cost more money, at least initially, and perhaps indefinitely, not less.[82]

In places like Iowa or South Dakota, with relatively light welfare caseloads, high employment, and relatively few legal aliens, only a handful of whom receive public benefits, those are relatively minor concerns. In California, which in mid-1997 still had an unemployment rate hovering around 6 percent, and roughly twice as high among blacks, Hispanics, and people with less than a high school education, they are enormous issues.[83] In Los Angeles, where, even after Congress restored funds to many elderly disabled aliens, tens of thousands of legal aliens were no longer eligible for SSI and the state supplemental payment (SSP) that comes with it. The jobs that are available are often inaccessible to the poor who live in South Central or East Los Angeles.[84] There are similar problems in parts of the Central Valley, of the Salinas Valley, and other agricultural regions, which have their own concentrations of aliens. Seasonal unemployment rates routinely run over 15 percent there, and there are simply no additional jobs for unskilled workers.

It is the counties that, through General Assistance, the last resort of the desperate and destitute, will have to pick up whatever wreckage the rest of the system will not manage. But it is also the counties, which have no ready way to raise revenues and whose resources are already badly overstretched, that are in the worst possible position to do it. "We've already cut our discretionary spending by half. If we have to take this on," said Muriel Johnson, a Republican who is a member of the board of supervisors in Sacramento County, "we will have to shut [the county] down. The governors talk about devolution, but they want to retain control, when it's local government that is required to take care of the poor and provide the services. It's the counties that get hit with the burdens."[85] Ron Roberts, chairman of the San Diego County Board of Supervisors, echoing pleas from the many other counties to the governor, said it even more plainly: If the counties don't get help from the state, especially with medical care and General Assistance, they'll be bankrupt.[86] In the spring of 1997, the most important help Wilson offered the counties, a proposal eventually blocked by the Democrats, was elimination of the requirement that they provide General Assistance at all—in effect an invitation to the callous to dump the hardest cases on those still willing to provide some care. Ultimately, the counties got a $450 million bail-out, but that was barely 15 percent of what the state had snatched away five years before.

Given California's economic recovery and rapidly declining welfare rolls, the prophecies of disaster may well be premature. Until the deadlines begin to arrive in the years 1998–99, the most severe problem may be massive confusion—welfare caseworkers will themselves require job training to turn them into job counselors—and anxiety.[87] Yet however California's welfare policies ultimately evolve—and regardless of what further changes, if any, are made in the federal welfare law—California's social services to the poor, the sick, and the disabled, which had once been among the nation's most generous, will, with the possible exception of Medicaid, be no more than average and, when things finally shake out, perhaps considerably less than that. Much of that, of course, was determined by a Congress and president who turned the well-intentioned but costly aim of moving people off welfare into a budget-cutting device that dangerously undermined both the reform's prime objective and the future prospects of those it was supposed to help. But the state, with its near-bankrupt counties, their inability to generate new revenues, and its broader tax constraints was in a particularly bad position to deal with the consequences. No matter what the state now does, said Dion Aroner, the liberal Assemblywoman from Berkeley who cochaired the joint legislative committee working on the welfare reforms, "we will do significant damage to lots of families and seniors and kids who will be hurt by what the federal government did . . . We can't fix that."[88] And when the next recession comes, said one of those cobbling together the California program, "it all falls apart."

The historical pattern has been roughly similar in Medi-Cal, the state's Medicaid program, which didn't exist until the mid-1960s, and which until recently retained—and in some measure still retains—more of the social tenderness of that era than any other social program. California started to negotiate with hospitals to drive down the costs for its Medi-Cal patients under Jerry Brown in the early 1980s, and has since begun to move more and more of them into full health maintenance organizations—the target was to have 3.2 million of the state's 5 million-plus eligibles in HMOs by 1998. It has thereby managed to reduce its per-patient costs to one of the lowest in the nation, an average of $2,100 per person compared to a U.S. average of $3,300. Only New Mexico and Mississippi spend less. (New York by contrast, spends nearly $7,300 per recipient.)[89]

Even so, with one or two exceptions,[90] there has been no major evidence of a decline in care or access for the state's poorest citizens: On the contrary, because Medi-Cal now pays as well for many services as the bare-bones HMOs and other cost-cutting private insurers (or, conversely, because HMOs have become so tight in what they pay for medical services), primary care appears to be more accessible for Medi-Cal patients than it was a few years ago, and reliance on high-cost emergency rooms, often the last resort of the poor a few years ago, is down. Private providers who, a decade ago, disdained to take Medi-Cal patients now compete vigorously for Medi-Cal contracts. California also provides a relatively generous package of services not mandated by the federal government—dental care, podiatry, outpatient psychological services, acupuncture, speech and audiology services, chiropractic care, and nonemergency transportation. The Wilson administration has tried repeatedly to cut them, arguing correctly that the state provides a wider range than any of the nation's other large states. But the Democrats in the legislature, backed by strong medical and senior-citizen lobbies, have blocked him.

Similarly, in efforts to encourage welfare recipients to get off the rolls, even for some low-paying jobs that provide no private medical insurance, the state also maintains relatively liberal eligibility rules—among the most liberal in the country. Not surprisingly, California is also among the top ten states in the percentage of the population covered by Medicaid and the highest among the major states. In California, families of three with incomes of up to $11,208, 86 percent of poverty, are eligible. That is hardly generous for those struggling to pull themselves up but is more liberal than the eligibility rules in any other major state.[91]

All those things having been said, however, California faces a major health care crisis. Because so many working Californians lost job-related health care coverage in the late 1980s and early 1990s—an estimated 1.28 million people fell off the rolls between 1989 and 1993, itself a reflection of the new economy—just over half of California workers are now covered by private medical insurance, making the "working uninsured" into California's "newest and fastest growing vulnerable population group."[92] Even with the state's relatively liberal eligibility rules for Medicaid, and with the expanded federally funded child health insurance program the state instituted in 1997, the percentage of California's nonelderly population that has no coverage of any sort—nearly 24 percent in 1994—is among the nation's highest. The 48 percent of California two-year-olds who are fully immunized is lower than the percentage in all but six states—the District of Columbia, Arkansas, Utah, Nevada, Georgia, and Texas—and the percentage of its new mothers who have no prenatal care in the first trimester is among the nation's highest.[93] Until 1997, twenty percent of the state's children had no medical coverage of any kind and while the state's newly enacted child health insurance program will reduce the number substantially, it will hardly eliminate the problem. That particular statistic made Governor Wilson's self-defeating rush to cut off prenatal care to illegal aliens, nearly all of whose children will be born in this country and thus be American citizens, even less defensible. All begin life at much greater risk, both to themselves and to the taxpayers who will have to subsidize the additional cost of their health care in the future.

There is a seamlessness in California's medical-care distress that may be unique—or at least prefigurative. The state leads the nation in the percentage of private patients enrolled in HMOs, which had once seemed like a bright solution and which, in relentlessly pressing to hold costs down, have increasingly become a major part of the problem. More broadly, California's health care system is leading the nation on the road to a nonsystem, a patchwork of partial programs and services—public clinics, nursing homes, migrant health centers, for-profit Medi-Cal mills, AIDS clinics, county health facilities, public hospitals, private hospitals, university teaching hospitals, burn and trauma centers, AIDS mental health facilities, senior centers, Indian health clinics. Each is supported by a different array of funding sources, each picks up some fraction of the patients, shoving others out the door, and each is desperately trying to find some payer to pick up the bills.

Those providers, particularly those serving the uninsured, are increasingly squeezed, on the one hand, by rising health costs and the growing numbers of people over sixty-five, and, on the other, lashed by intense HMO-driven marketplace competitition that leaves less and less leeway for shifting costs of uncompensated care to private payers. (Those pressures are also leaving the medical schools and teaching hospitals, whose high overhead for research and teaching was always partly supported by shifting part of the cost to private patients, nearly frantic. Because of them, and because of the sharp cutbacks in the funding for indigent care that bankrupt Orange County had once provided, the University of California's teaching hospital in Irvine, another Kerr-era addition, was put on the block.) Under such a combination of assaults, "California's health safety net," in the words of a major report by the foundation-supported Institute for the Future, "is unraveling [and] will not be repaired through local or private action or through limited reforms of current programs. If state action is not taken, the ultimate disintegration of the safety net will send tremors throughout the state's landscape." That safety net, as the institute put it, "is not a marketplace," nor can the publicly funded health care system "be reformed without affecting the private health care system and vice versa; the two systems are virtually one story." And, not to put too fine a point on it, they are both in deep trouble, with consequences that will reverberate through the state's economy.[94]

Maybe the strangest outgrowth of California's shrinking public sector budget and the resulting stress on public services has been the proliferating "rent-a-judge" system—something between arbitration and the ordinary judiciary—increasingly used by well-heeled corporate clients who can afford not to wait in line for their day in California's crowded courts. Here again, California is not unique, but because of the pressure of the three-strikes law and other criminal cases involving long mandatory sentences, which cause more and more defendants to go to trial rather than plea bargaining for a lesser charge, nowhere has it become as widespread. For well-heeled clients who don't want to wait—often for the better part of two years—or to suffer expensive delays and postponements as judges are assigned to higher-priority criminal cases, it's a system that offers not only arbitration but full-blown trials with their own juries and, in some cases, their own appeals, few of them open to public scrutiny.

Many of California's appellate court justices, and hundreds of other California judges, now retire at the earliest opportunity to "catch up economically," as one of them put it, by joining that private system, which pays them as much as $600 an hour (although the going rate for most is closer to a more modest $375–450 an hour) to judge those disputes.

There are now some 400 of them, working either for organizations like Judicial Arbitration and Mediation Services, the American Arbitration Association, or a handful of private firms, or for themselves. That would not be so different from more ordinary forms of arbitration, or from ordinary deals between corporations, were it not for the fact that in its pervasiveness it creates a strong sense that there are two systems of justice, one for the rich and one for everybody else. When a private litigant appeals a privately litigated decision to higher courts, he is at the front of the line, far ahead of the ordinary people who started through the public civil justice system at the same time and may still be waiting for their first day in court.[95]

There is also the unconfirmed but nonetheless persistent suspicion that even when they are still on the public bench, some of those judges are now tilting decisions to make themselves marketable to prospective private clients. Some, said Sacramento County Muncipal Court Judge Barry Loncke, are "negotiating with private interests to exploit their offices for future gain." Loncke said he'd even seen a judge who was still on the bench passing out business cards during recess to lawyers for one of the parties trying a case before him. Such charges have been indignantly denied by others, who argue that, in any case, the private judging eases the pressure on the regular court system. But that hardly mitigates the heightened sense, strong under the best of circumstances, that even in the halls of justice there are two classes. Certainly it's done nothing to make judges bashful about advertising, often with full pages in the legal newspapers, once they are on the market. "If you want justice in the southland of Los Angeles," former Associate (Supreme Court) Justice Armand Arabian told the *Wall Street Journal*, "you wire 213-ARABIAN and you got me." In the ads, he is the "Arabian Knight."[96]

IV

By now, the California economic recovery of the late 1990s has become almost as much a cliché as the recession and its attendant calamities were at the beginning of the decade. But it has been a curious comeback. The job market that has emerged, and the society the new California economy is producing, bear only a rough resemblance, either in population or in public policy and vision, to the economy and society of the 1960s, or even to the California of the 1980s. Silicon Valley, parts of Orange County, and the state's other high-tech regions—the centers of telecommunications and other information technology and biotechnology—are booming. So are tourism and the Southern California entertainment industry, the apparel and fashion design industries, and the Pacific Rim Trade, each of which has generated tens of thousands of new jobs since the recession in what is not only a recovery but a major restructuring from traditional manufacturing to knowledge-based enterprises and industries, sometimes in the same facilities. In a resurgent Burbank, for example, which had long been home to the NBC studios and other film and television facilities, but where Lockheed Aircraft was once the largest employer, former aircraft parts and assembly plants have been converted and taken over as studios by Disney, Warner Brothers, and other entertainment complexes.

And with the recovery, not surprisingly, California has also reversed the out-migration to other states of the early 1990s. According to the boosterish Center for the New West, California is adding two jobs in entertainment for every job lost in aerospace. As a consequence, average household income in the San Francisco Bay Area ($63,000) was the highest of any metropolitan area in the nation in 1995. (The same is true for the cost of housing: In San Francisco, the median price of a house in 1996 was $257,000; in suburban Marin County, it was $323,000.) "The emerging face of California—ethnically diverse, technologically advanced, entrepreneurial, globally minded, and highly innovative—holds out an enormous promise for most of the state residents," said a breathless report from the New West Center which, in its syntax, sounded not all that different from George Leonard's at the beginning of the sixties:[97]

> Nowhere is California's lock on "knowledge value" more obvious than in the field of science-based industry. Despite the many predictions that California would lose momentum in those critical fields, the state has actually consolidated its dominant role as the premier center for innovation and research. The state's market share in high-technology employment has actually grown by one-third since the mid 1970s.

Yet the economy and society that are emerging not only seem less ebullient than the prerecession California, with per capita income, which once hovered at about 10 percent above the U.S. average, expected to level off with a "premium" of no more than 4 percent; they also begin to have worrisome resemblances to the third world economies that California, as a booming trade center, is increasingly engaged with.[98]

Many of the new jobs—in service occupations, in Los Angeles's small new manufacturing plants, even in Silicon Valley electronics assembly work—pay less than the manufacturing jobs in aerospace and other heavy industry that disappeared in the 1980s. There are thousands of new jobs, for example, in Southern Calfornia's little garment factories—shops employing large numbers of illegal aliens, most of which are not in full compliance with the labor laws and are always dependent on low wages for survival. And those that comply are always pressed by the competing sweatshops at their fringes.[99]

California boosters like to talk about its high-tech industries, but apparel manufacturing—often in those minimum or subminimum sweatshop jobs—employs 160,000 workers, almost twice as many people as computer manufacturing, and its growth as an employer since 1990 has been much more vigorous. Agriculture and canning, which have always been low-wage seasonal industries heavily dependent on immigrant labor, still employ more people— well over 400,000 all told—than all high-tech manufacturing put together.[100] And practically unnoticed by the California high-tech boomers, the use of low-wage farm labor appears to have increased as growers upgrade from field crops like wheat to more intensely cultivated fruit and vegetable crops, which require more workers, most of whom continue to be illegal aliens and of whom, in the words of Don Villarejo, who heads the California Institute for Rural Studies, "there is an unlimited supply," and probably a surplus.

In a significant recent study funded by federal agencies and private foundations, the Institute found that in scores of Central Valley farm communities, there are tens of thousands of invisible people, and perhaps more, living in "back houses"—toolsheds, garages, old barns without postal addresses—who, in towns like the Fresno County community of Parlier, make up more than 20 percent of the population, but have been counted by no one—not the Census, not the Bureau of Labor Statistics, nobody.[101] Income of California farm workers is about $6,500 a year, and their wages, instead of rising, are going down.[102] Recent surveys commissioned by the Department of Agriculture show that pay (much of it in piecework) of U.S. farm workers has fallen from just under $7 an hour in 1980 to slightly over $6 now; in California, it's fallen from just under $7 to just over $5.[103]

Even in software and high-tech development, not all is extravagant prosperity, much less old-fashioned security. According to California Controller Kathleen Connell, at least 15 percent of the new high-techies are self-employed or working in part-time jobs (which, among other things, "makes them angrier and less likely to support funding for public services"). In the Silicon Valley around San Jose, an estimated 27 to 40 percent of the workers hold part-time, temporary, or other "contingent" jobs.[104] Those are the workers—some of them—who once had health care and other benefits but have them no longer.

All those findings are consistent with the broader observation that the state's job growth has taken place at the high and low ends of the wage scale, not in the middle, a phenomenon even more pronounced in California than in the nation generally. As a consequence, the spread between the most affluent 20 percent of the population and the poorest has been growing even faster in California than it has elsewhere in the country. According to a comprehensive study issued by the Public Policy Institute of California, a cautious and rigorously independent think tank on state policy issues, since the mid-1980s, that gap, already among the largest in the nation, has been getting larger, and at a more rapid rate than elsewhere. That growing California gap stems not so much from relatively large gains in income at the top (although there were gains among those in the top brackets), but because those at the bottom have been losing ground faster than low-wage earners in other parts of the country. In the nation as whole, the income of those in the bottom 10 percent of families declined 13 percent (in inflation-adjusted dollars) between 1976 and 1994; in California, family income for the bottom 10 percent declined 36 percent, much of it since 1987, the year the Immigration Reform and Control Act began to provide amnesty for large number of illegal aliens and when they, in turn, began to send for their relatives, thus generating a second wave of illegal immigrants, which further softened the job market for low-skill workers.[105]

The pattern holds for household incomes as well as for the incomes of single wage earners, whether male or female, and there is every reason to expect it to continue into the future. In projections compiled early in 1997, the fastest growing California job categories for the period 1993–2005, with their 1995 median hourly pay, are waiter/waitress ($4.25), general manager ($23.00), retail salesperson ($5.50), cashier ($5.00), general office clerk

($6.00), instructional aide ($8.00), secretary ($9.00), receptionist ($8.00), food prep worker ($5.00), and registered nurse ($16.72). By the year 2005, the state will have new jobs, according to those projections, for 43,000 more systems analysts and 109,000 waiters and waitresses. By all accounts, moreover, as former welfare recipients compete with the working poor for low-ends jobs, welfare reform will almost certainly further depress low-end wages.[106] California, which once saw itself as a state of middle-class, middle-income, homeowners where the suburban single family home was the preeminent artifact of civic cohesion and the good life in America, is now among the bottom two or three states in the nation in home ownership—55 percent of families own their own homes, compared to a national average of 64 percent.[107]

Those widening income gaps, rather than being mitigated by California's postrecession tax policy, have been exacerbated by it. To deal with the recession, Wilson and the legislature not only cut services but increased sales and use taxes, raised the top income-tax rate, suspended the renter's tax credit, and took a number of other revenue-enhancing measures. (They also raided the public employee pension fund for about $1 billion, which the courts have since ruled was illegal).[108] When the recession ended, the taxes that hit primarily the poor were kept in place. The renter's tax credit (which had been increased after the passage of Proposition 13 to provide a little marginal relief to those—mostly people of modest incomes—who did not own residences) was suspended again. (In 1998, after an extended fight over the disposition of the state's growing revenues, the renter's tax credit was partially restored for some middle income renters, but was not made refundable for the poor, who paid little or no income tax.) The sales tax increases were made permanent.

In the meantime, the increases on upper income-tax brackets were allowed to lapse, and corporate and business taxes were cut by $2.3 billion a year.[109] Because of its progressive income tax structure, California has historically had what the liberal Citizens for Tax Justice calls "one of the least regressive tax systems" in the nation. And the Wilson tax shifts, in the words of CTJ Tax Policy Director Michael P. Etlinger, "aren't going to put California in the ranks of the terrible ten."[110] Still the changes represent a substantial shift of the tax burden downward on the income scale.[111]

The people at the upper end of those income scales—the corporate executives, the accountants, the designers, the entertainment industry producers, the real estate operators, the writers of software for every industry and enterprise imaginable, the bankers, lawyers, traders, and the various other Pacific Rimmers, like the organizations for which they work, each of them modemed, cell-phoned, electronically banked—are themselves, of course, much more closely connected to their peers in New York or Tokyo, or Hong Kong or London, than they are to the people on the street below. They are members of a "community," real or virtual, that has no fixed geographical base and fewer real communitarian loyalties with each passing day, people whose dreams seem, perhaps for the first time in our history, to be connected to no geographical region or place—certainly few that celebrate social diversity.

Meanwhile, those who still retain a sliver of the old dream are pursuing it in ever larger numbers into gated communities, another social development in which California, with its shrivelled public services and shrunken sense of commonweal, has become the hands-down national leader. Edward J. Blakely—another early retired Berkeley faculty member, who had been chairman of its Department of City and Regional Planning and is now the dean of the School of Planning at the University of Southern California—estimates that nearly a million Californians now live in developments behind gates ranging from "elaborate two-story guardhouses manned 24 hours a day to roll-back iron gates to simple electronic arms."[112] Even outside those gates, there aren't many affluent areas in places like Los Angeles or Palm Springs where neighborhood associations haven't hired private patrols: In the upscale West Side neighborhoods of Malibu and Pacific Palisades, and in the high-income East Bay enclave of Piedmont, the most common lawn sign is that of Westec Security, with its large yellow letters warning "ARMED RESPONSE." In San Marino, probably the wealthiest city, per capita, in California, the parks are closed on weekends in an effort to exclude the rabble from Pasadena and other neighboring communities.[113]

To be sure, it's not just Californians who are looking for gates, fences, and armed patrols; nor is it just the rich: A growing number of middle-class apartment and condo projects in places like the San Fernando Valley have erected road barriers and other security devices to keep strangers out; in Sacramento, owners of low-rent apartment units in a marginal area called Franklin Villa, a complex of 900 condos and rental townhouses, many of them occupied by families at or just above the poverty level, have pleaded with the city council to impose a special tax on the complex, which is already gated, so they can hire security guards and install other security measures against the gang and drug problems that plague the area.

But the model is much more likely to be a suburb like Canyon Lake than an inner-city enclave like Franklin Villa. One of the largest gated California communities, the walled city of Canyon Lake, about 75 miles southeast of Los Angeles, is an incorporated town of some 14,000 people—some wealthy, some solidly middle class, some of them people who commute three or four hours a day in order to live there. Canyon Lake maintains its own eighteen-hole golf course, 380-acre lake, equestrian center, tennis courts, and virtually every other amenity of the California good life. Blakely, no fan of gated isolation, calls it "a typical suburb that happens to have a gate around it."[114] Still, it means that no uninvited people appear on the streets—neither Jehovah's Witnesses passing out tracts nor environmentalists circulating petitions, much less homeless people pushing carts between shelter and soup kitchen. No one comes through the gate who is not invited by a resident. The outer world stays out. That kind of fortress mentality, as planner George Sternlieb said, is "not simply racist." It's the fear of many "in the New America [of] falling off the housing train"—or the hope of recapturing the dream before it slips away.[115] But sometimes it's hard to separate the two.

Whatever the motives—fear, hope, fantasy—it's the rich and the middle class in California who are leading the march to the wall, with social implications of enormous importance. Blakely, using data provided by the state's Building Industry Association, estimates that nine out of ten new middle- and upper-income housing developments in California are "forting up" as gated communities. "The Los Angeles area is the new archetype of metropolitan spacial segregation [which has led] groups within the hypersegregated environment to wall and secure their space against the poor," he writes. "Those who try to escape poverty by moving away are using walls to prevent it from reaching their newfound oasis."

In the effort to guarantee such an escape, many of these communities "also privatize civic responsibilities such as police protection and community services." Thus they "create a private world that shares little with its neighbors or the larger political system."[116] That, as planning consultant William Fulton says, has been reinforced by California's post-Proposition 13 "welcome stranger" tax structure, which blocks new taxes on existing property and shifts much of the burden for urban services, and particularly for new infrastructure, to new development. One of the primary devices for doing that is a system under which developers and large landowners can create "Mello-Roos districts" to issue bonds for water, sewers, schools, drainage, and other infrastructure, which are then repaid out of increased taxes on the property located in those districts. But while the costs are borne by new property, some of the benefits may go to the larger community. That, as Fulton points out, leads "to a breakdown of community identity and the atomization of citizenship. Once your city requires you to pay what is, in effect, an entry fee for schools, roads or the view, you're not likely to think of your community and its facilities in the same generous spirited way that people used to. A public park becomes one bought and paid for by you and your neighbors."[117]

> Nowhere [said Fulton] is this atomization occurring more quickly than in the fast-growing Inland Empire (east of Los Angeles). There, financially strapped school districts are obtaining new construction funds through growth taxes imposed on homeowners in "Mello-Roos" taxing districts. These homeowners are often led to be-

lieve that the Mello-Roos taxes, which can cause a home-owner's property tax bill to double, will allow the local school district to build schools in their neighborhood. Instead, the money is thrown into a big pot devoted to expanding classroom capacity districtwide. The result is that the Mello-Roos kids are frequently bused long distances to attend schools with kids whose parents live in older tracts and don't pay Mello-Roos taxes. Enraged parents complain that their kids should not have to mingle with those who come from lower taxpaying classes.

Obviously, these parents do not really expect "public" education. What they expect—and it's not surprising, given the way the Mello-Roos taxes are marketed by developers—is private education in their neighborhood, administered by a public school district. They paid their money. So, where's their school? This is not the kind of attitude that fosters community identification, especially in a just-constructed tract.

Inevitably, it also reinforces preexisting restiveness about the idea of public schools. In 1993, the school establishment, backed by $14 million from the California Teachers Association and the National Education Association, with which it's affiliated, easily beat a private school voucher initiative in California that would have provided an immediate taxpayer subsidy to parents of the 500,000 California children who are attending religious or other private schools—as well as, of course, to the many other families whose children might have made the break had the voucher passed. But the threat of another voucher, with all its anticommunitarian implications, seems to lurk perpetually in California's political shadows.[118] The accompanying social system, with its immutable class structure and pauperized underclass, declining homeownership and gated communities, is still waiting to fully emerge. What it certainly is not is the place where (to echo T George Harris's words of the early sixties) "the needy minorities of the past are becoming the prosperous majorities of the future [and where] the have-nots now vanish into a society of near-equal haves."[119] In San Diego, where hundreds of new software companies and other small research-based high-tech businesses are regarded as a model comeback economy, 40 percent of public high school students, most of them Latinos, drop out. The model, and the advisor, for San Diego's economic development program, came from Singapore.[120]

V

In the end, the story of California's public sector over the past generation is a chronicle of a place that has been living on, and drawing down, its accumulated social capital. After California's huge investment in public services and public infrastructure during the 1950s and 1960s—estimated to have averaged a staggering 22 percent of all total state spending between 1950 and its peak in 1967—the state began a long slide of neglect during which (in the words of the Washington-based Center on Budget and Policy Priorites), it "has been squandering these advantages."[121] Since 1980, through good times and bad, capital expenditures have averaged less than 5 percent of total state spending: The Center estimates that the value of California's basic infrastructure—roads, bridges, water and sewer systems, schools—declined by 18 percent, relative to population, in the period between 1974 and 1988 (and certainly hasn't grown since).

What may be most startling in that picture are the numbers for roads and freeways, once one of the paramount symbols of the new California. Since the early 1980s, according to figures compiled by the California Taxpayers Association, California's spending for highways, a proud cornerstone of Pat Brown's program and once the ultimate California symbol, has been among the lowest and often the lowest, per capita, in the nation, as many people driving the state's roads and freeways have surely noticed: In 1992, the U.S. Department of Transportation ranked California eighth from the bottom in the nation in the percentage of highway mileage it rated in poor condition.[122] And while the state's motorists pay far less per mile in fuel taxes than they did thirty years ago, as virtually all Americans do, and less than any of their western neighbors,

California's politicians, fearful of voter backlash, have adamantly refused to raise them since voters approved a modest graduated four-year increase, beginning in 1991, from 9 cents a gallon to 18 cents. In 1995, with those increases in place, California collected precisely what it did in 1970 in fuel tax revenues, measured in constant dollars. In the meantime, vehicle miles traveled had increased nearly 90 percent.[123]

Most of California has no severe weather problems, which of course should make road maintenance easier. But it now has a severe earthquake retrofit problem in its road and bridge structures, particularly in the Bay Bridge, which by itself requires close to $1.5 billion worth of work—most probably the construction of an entirely new span for the two-mile stretch at its eastern end. With the state's fund for highway and transit improvements already in arrears by more than $3 billion, that makes the outlook for road maintenance and highway improvements even more uncertain.[124]

There is no satisfactory explanation for the highway phenomenon, which goes back at least to Jerry Brown's era of limits and to the powerful streak of slow-growth environmentalism on which it floated. And yet unlike schools or colleges—let alone welfare—the roads are everybody's public service, and since they are largely supported by dedicated state and federal funds, most of them derived from the gas tax, one might expect them to be exempt from the narrowness that has affected school funding in the past twenty years. Road maintenance and improvements can be funded even if welfare is starved. But somehow the miasmic combination of concern about smog and crowding and the general suspicion of government projects seem to have stifled even this echo of the old communitarian optimism.[125]

No one can accurately measure the accumulated effects of a generation, more or less, of rotting public services, of noninvestment and disinvestment, or the cost of the deferred maintenance, much less the consequences of the economic opportunities missed, or the damage to confidence in the most basic public services. Nor can anyone really calculate the cost in community and in human health, social pathology, and miseducation. But some signs—the dismally low reading and math scores of California students on the National Assessment of Educational Progress, for example, or high school dropout rates, crime rates, and teen birth rates that are all among the ten highest in the country—are hard to miss. Mervin Field, who has been polling Californians for half a century, observed how, even after California's economy turned up again, "the outlook of the average Californian doesn't match the economic indices." How much that's the cause of the state's evolving social policies and how much is consequence is hard to say. Probably it's a little of both.

Whichever way that question is answered, the issues behind it resonate with the now-prevalent myth—the antimyth of the 1960s, when Kerr talked about the value of research universities as "bait" in drawing industry—that states and communities have to offer low taxes and minimal regulation to remain competitive. And that theory of bargain-basement public services makes no sense. In the words of Stephen Levy, who heads the Center for the Continuing Study of the California Economy in Palo Alto, for California to try to turn itself into "a high risk social area in an effort to compete with Asia" is futile and probably worse. When high-wage businesses hesitate about moving to California, concern about the poor condition of the schools and the social infrastructure appears to loom as large as taxes and the cost of housing. "The issue isn't just training of workers," Levy said, "it's that there's no decent place for the employees' kids to go to school."

The same goes for other services. "Recreation and cultural facilities nearby are hugely important," says Levy. "What this economic base wants is a little fancier than South Carolina—Opera? You damn well better have an opera."[126] But on that score, too, the state has a problem: affluent California, the center of the entertainment industry, provides about 40 cents per California resident in public funding for the arts, less than all but seven states, and about one-fourth what New York or New Jersey spend—South Carolina spends twice as much as California does —and nothing whatever for public broadcasting.[127] At the very moment when San Diego was celebrating its economic recovery, the San Diego Symphony, one of the better regional orchestras, filed for bankruptcy and folded. Within six months, Sacramento's once-vital symphony orchestra, scratching for both corporate and municipal support, went under as well.

In 1991, when Governor Pete Wilson issued a set of gloomy, recession-driven projections about the nearly impossible burden that, in his estimate, the state's rapidly growing number of tax consumers—schoolchildren, welfare recipients, prisoners, the aged, blind, and disabled—would soon put on the state's taxpayers, Tom Hayes, Wilson's impeccably conscientious and capable finance director, described it not as a temporary effect of recession but as a sort of inexorable Malthusian destiny. Even though things might go right with the rest of the country, California was being ground between a stagnant tax base and out-of-control demands for public services: California as the great exception *noir*. By the year 2000, he predicted, 14 million California taxpayers would have to support 18 million tax-eaters.[128] (Nor was Wilson alone in those gloomy forecasts. In the summer of 1993, California Senator Barbara Boxer, a liberal Democrat by almost any definition, was asking whether the state could continue to afford to educate the children of illegal aliens.)

The Malthusian numbers, even with California's increasing social divisions (and even at the depths of the recession), were wildly exaggerated, in part because Hayes and Wilson counted many of the tax-eaters twice, and sometimes three times—children on welfare, for example (once as schoolchildren, once as welfare recipients)—and in part because Hayes read the sudden upsurge in caseloads as structural rather than as the short-term effects of recession and the one-time impact of the newly legalized aliens who had become eligible for public benefits in the late 1980s. If one assumed instead the more traditional growth rates in welfare and Medi-Cal of the 1980s, it put the total number of beneficiaries of public social services at about 13 million people, most of whom were students in the state's schools and colleges (some of them, of course, also wage earners and taxpayers, or their children), and some 17 million workers. The declining welfare rolls of the postrecession mid-1990s showed how absurd the earlier prophecies of tax-eater entropy had been.

Yet even if the high welfare numbers had not declined as they have, even at the peak of the recession, California had a far lower ratio of dependents than the state supported in the go-go 1960s and early 1970s. In 1970, California had 4.6 million children in its public schools, supported by 7.5 million workers—one child for every 1.6 workers, almost the same ratio as in 1960. In 1994, it had 5.3 million children in its public schools supported by over 14 million workers—one child for every 2.6 workers. In 1970, enrollment in the state's public colleges and universities totaled just under 1.2 million; in 1994 it was just under 1.8 million—again a lower ratio of tax consumers to wage earners.[129]

Of course, there are other factors—the sharp upsurge, for example, in health costs of the previous two decades (which has since leveled off), the high birth rates among immigrants, the state's growing social inequality—that qualify the numbers, and there are ample grounds for deep concern about the coming squeeze on federal Social Security and Medicare budgets as the baby boomers begin to retire in the first decade of the next century. But the dire warnings in California about the invasion of the tax-eaters don't wash. Even the booming school and university enrollments predicted for the next decade will not bring the proportion of service-dependent California residents to the relative numbers that they had been in the 1960s, when the workforce was much smaller.

In 1968–69, the middle of Reagan's first term, California spent roughly 5.4 percent of its personal income on schools; twenty years later, it was 4.5 percent; the decline in the percentage spent on higher education was even greater. And even at the peak of the recession, in 1992, California's inflation-adjusted per capita income was $21,500, higher than in any year between 1950 and 1983, and nearly double what it was in 1950; in 1992, its top-bracket incomes were higher than they had ever been.[130] Nor was there much chance that the state's tax burden, also lower as a percentage of income, would grow significantly. If anything, after the tax cuts enacted by the legislature in the mid-1990s, and with the growing income levels of the postrecession period, particularly in the upper end of the economic scale, there was a better chance that, with the exception of low-income people, who bore a greater share of it, the overall tax burden would decline.[131]

But two things surely have changed. One is the complexion of those tax-eaters, and thus the perception and politics of the burden—the rising percentage of schoolchildren, now roughly 60 percent of total enrollment, who are not white; the large percentage of Medicaid recipients who are Latino; the Thais and Cambodians and Hmong on welfare; the prisons dominated by inner-city blacks and Latinos; the university campuses where, as at Berkeley and UCLA, the largest single ethnic group is Asian; the increasingly visible black and Latino enrollment of the urban community colleges. With such numbers, it wasn't hard to fathom the reasons for the strong support for Proposition 187, the measure designed to deny schooling to illegal aliens and their children, in the fall of 1994. California went through a fairly severe recession in the early 1970s, with unemployment rates exceeding 9 percent two years running, and welfare rolls rising in proportion, which also squeezed state services. But while Governor Ronald Reagan complained vehemently about the rising cost of what he called "the welfare monster," and while he foreshadowed Wilson's rhetoric in a memo to his staff to place "a heavy emphasis on the taxpayer as opposed to the tax-taker,"[132] there was no shrill campaign about how the state was going to hell because the tax-eaters were about to drive the taxpayers to the poorhouse.

The other change is the growing discontinuity between voters and the consumers of state educational and social services. Twenty years ago, parents with children in school (and in the parks and playgrounds) made up 42 percent of the electorate; now 21 percent of the voters have children in school. And, while 46 percent of parents of children under 18 are white, 78 percent of the voting electorate is white; conversely, 37 percent of the parents are Latino, but even after the ballyhooed surge in Hispanic voter participation in 1996 only 11 percent of the voters are.

As elsewhere, California's voters are older and more affluent than the consumers of state and local public services, only more so: 58 percent of parents (1994) have household incomes under

$40,000, but only 40 percent of the voters do. In the eight years between 1988 and 1996, the percentage of the electorate sixty years old or older increased from 23 to 28 percent, and 75 percent of them were registered. By contrast, of the 17 percent of the electorate in the ages between eighteen and twenty-nine, barely half were registered.

Perhaps even more telling, by the year 2000, of the 6 million children expected to be in California public schools, barely 2 million—35 percent—will be white. Unless voting patterns change radically in the meantime, they will then be even more poorly represented at the polls.[133] A state that had identified itself as a magnet for young families with bright expectations now saw itself as a place inhabited by people who are increasingly Hispanic and Asian (and whose children are even more disproportionately brown and yellow) and dominated by older voters whose children are grown, or who never had any, and who could no longer afford to pay—or were no longer willing to pay—for its public services. "Nothing infuriates me more," went one letter to the *Sacramento Bee*, "than expecting the senior citizens to keep paying for the education of those who will not, or cannot, learn to read, much less anything else . . ." or, in the words of another, complaining about "the methodical pillaging and plundering of the taxpayer, forcing those who have no kids to pay through the nose for someone else's," or, in the words of still another, who was "tired of my tax-payers money going to educate these illegals [when] what we should be doing is shooting them at the border." In Oxnard in 1997, an unsigned flier attributing the area's crowded schools to immigrants was blamed for the narrow defeat of a $65 million school bond proposal.

Neither the letters nor the flier speak for the majority of Californians—and with things like the new willingness to approve school repair and construction bonds, the state may now be show-ing at least a resurgent, albeit belated and insufficient, willingness to support schools. But these things hardly make a summer. Thirty years after its golden moment, probably the most compelling fact of California's new politics is the discontinuity—real and perceived—between the old (white) California dream and the new brown/yellow/black realities.

PART THREE
Mississippification

‹›

The Spirit of 13

‹›

I

Howard Jarvis had been playing on the fringes of California politics long before he and Paul Gann, the former Sacramento realtor, changed history in 1978. In 1962 he had challenged Thomas Kuchel, California's senior U.S. senator, in the Republican primary. Kuchel had been in the Senate since 1952, when Governor Earl Warren appointed him to replace Richard Nixon, who had become Dwight Eisenhower's vice-president, and was in the mainstream among moderate California Republicans of that era—a Republican in the style of Warren himself. But Jarvis regarded him as a liberal Democrat who "voted with the Democrats on every crucial issue, and I thought we ought to have a *Republican* U.S. Senator." Kuchel easily won the primary—Jarvis ran a poor third—and was reelected in a landslide on the same day on which Pat Brown defeated Nixon for governor. In 1970 Jarvis ran for the state Board of (tax) Equalization and ran third again. In 1977, he tried to take on Tom Bradley in a Los Angeles mayoral race and again ran third.[1]

But if some of the claims in his ghosted autobiography, *I'm Mad as Hell*, invite challenge, the persistent Jarvis had done a great deal. (And insofar as anyone has been able to check, in the book, to quote Huck Finn, "he told the truth, mainly.")

He had, at various times in his long career, been the publisher of a string of small newspapers in Utah; the "press man" on Herbert Hoover's reelection campaign train in 1932; the publicist for the Utah State Republican Party; a speculator during the 1930s in Los Angeles real estate ("land in California was gold then," he said, with the enthusiasm of your standard California plunger, "and still is)"; a semipro baseball player, and a small-time professional boxer and Jack Dempsey's occasional sparring partner; the friend of Gary Cooper, Clark Gable, and other Hollywood stars; the manager of a Los Angeles drug supply firm; the founder of a Los Angeles company making rubber pads and various other latex-based products; the part owner during World War II of a company degaussing (demagnetizing) ship's hulls for the navy; the manufacturer of garbage disposal units; the owner of a large business making appliances and airplane subassemblies; and the partner of a man named LeRoy J. Leishman, who Jarvis said had invented the push-button radio. Together, Jarvis wrote, he and Leishman stood to rake in millions in the radio venture but (to make Jarvis's long story short) were cheated out of their patents by the Crosley Radio Company after an extended string of legal actions. Crosley's failure to pay them for their development, Jarvis claimed, was upheld by some New Deal judges carrying out an anticorporate Roosevelt mandate (which Jarvis never fully explains) by ruling that Jarvis and Leishman didn't have a patentable invention.

What's beyond doubt is that, through it all, the blunt, pugnacious Jarvis, a short man with a bull head and thick glasses, never stopped dabbling in politics. He was one of the original backers of Richard Nixon; he was a campaign worker for Eisenhower—he claims he "got to know Eisenhower pretty well" and was invited to a White House dinner where he ended up schmoozing with Winston Churchill late into the night after most of the other guests had left—and he headed an "independent" campaign committee that in 1964 raised $115,000 for the presidential campaign of Barry Goldwater.[2] None of that money ever got to Goldwater—it all went to fees and expenses for Jarvis and his collaborators—and Goldwater eventually sued to shut the Jarvis operation down.

The same thing happened again in 1976, when Jarvis and a collaborator, William Morrison, raised money for S.I. Hayakawa, the semanticist who had become something of a California hero when, as president of San Francisco State University, he stared down student demonstrators on his campus in 1969, and who, in 1976, had been elected to the U.S. Senate. As a senator, Hayakawa soon earned the designation "Sleepy Sam," but he was awake enough to realize that he hadn't gotten a cent from the $60,000 that the Jarvis groups, Friends for Hayakawa, Businessmen for Hayakawa, and Seniors for Hayakawa, had collected from Republican loyalists in Hayakawa's name. Most had gone to a political consulting firm that spent nearly all of it for travel, office expenses, accounting, and legal work. Before the campaign was over, Hayakawa, too, went to court and got the organizations shut down.[3] Jarvis indignantly denied that he took any money for himself. As to a charge by columnist Jack Anderson that he tried something similar with a purported fund-raising campaign for the National Right to Work Commmittee: That was all "manure."[4]

Jarvis's real fixation, however, was taxes, and the property tax in particular: All taxes, he sometimes said, were "felony grand theft," but it was restriction of the property tax that became his highest calling. "I'm going to stay in this tax thing," he told a reporter, "till it either wins or I die."

Jarvis—columnist Richard Reeves once called him "the last angry man"—was hardly the only one working the issue. Philip Watson, the Los Angeles County assessor, determined to show his constituents that he was as much an opponent of high taxes as anyone else, had been organizing tax limitation measures in California since the 1960s. And in his last years as governor, Ronald Reagan himself took up the cause, sponsoring Proposition 1, a constitutional amendment that would gradually have ratcheted state spending down to 7 percent of personal income. But his collaborators and drafters, a John Bircher named Lewis K. Uhler, who later became head of the National Tax Limitation Committee, and the Nobel-winning economist Milton Friedman, an improbable combination, had produced a 5,700-word document that, by his own acknowledgement, even Reagan didn't understand. Although it made it to the ballot, voters rejected it by a margin of about 54–46.

But Jarvis, who had been working the territory since the mid-1960s, was easily the most persistent. In 1972 he had tried to qualify his own property tax limitation measure, then reluctantly joined up with Watson when he couldn't get the requisite number of signatures. Watson, who had already managed to qualify one of his proposals for the ballot, and failed in the general election, was trying again, and now, with Jarvis as a junior partner, he failed once more, this time by a margin of nearly two to one.

The dogged Jarvis was undeterred, however, and immediately set out to try again, this time (again) by himself. By law, valid signatures equal to 8 percent of the total votes cast in the previous gubernatorial election are required—they must be raised within a period of 150 days—to put a constitutional amendment on the California ballot. Jarvis almost made it in 1976, when he got 489,000 signatures, just 10,000 short of the number that he estimated he then needed. When he realized he had fallen short, he hooked up with the soft-spoken Gann, who had been running his own tax limitation organization, called People's Advocate, in suburban Sacramento, and immediately started over. And this time, he would succeed—and succeed more spectacularly than even he probably dreamed.

Jarvis-Gann—Proposition 13 on the June 1978 primary ballot, which was approved overwhelmingly by California voters—did not simply cut property taxes or limit the future taxing powers of all public agencies in California: It set the stage for the Reagan era, and became both fact and symbol of a radical shift in governmental priorities, public attitudes, and social relationships that is as nearly fundamental in American politics as the changes brought by the New Deal. Joel Fox, a native of Boston, who, after Jarvis died in 1986, succeeded him as head of the Howard Jarvis Taxpayers Association, would later take his school-age son to visit the monuments of the American Revolution—Concord, Lexington, Bunker Hill—and make comparisons between that time and this, comparisons that seem charmingly hyperbolic: These were the places, he told the boy, where Americans first fought for liberty and against oppressive taxation. But for twenty years, Proposition 13 has been both the preeminent symbol of protection against imperious government and the third rail of California politics—"touch it and you die"—and, to only a lesser extent, the source of a theology of radical tax reduction and government limitation—in California, in Washington, in Margaret Thatcher's England, and to some extent elsewhere in Europe—not seen in this country since the Revolution.

The beginnings of Jarvis's success went back more than a decade, and while they're complex, they also reveal a great deal about the peculiarities and misdirection of California's perfectionist politics. By now, it's a truism that the immediate source of the Great Tax Revolt that produced Proposition 13 was the spectacular inflation in California real estate values, and particularly in home prices, during the 1970s. That inflation drove up residential property tax bills at astronomical rates, particularly in Southern California, in some cases causing them to double and then double again in a period of four or five years, rising to the point where thousands of people, particularly those on fixed incomes, were genuinely fearful that they would lose their homes. Between 1974 and 1978, the value of an average home in California went from $34,000 to $85,000.

The power of those fears can hardly be exaggerated. For that postwar generation in its new rapidly urbanizing suburbs, the deferred Depression dreams and the wartime reveries about the good life were centered in those Hollywood-Western ranch-style tract houses. Perhaps because so much of California, and Southern California particularly, had been settled so recently, and because there was such a paucity of established institutions—because there was so little else—there is probably no other part of the country where the single family home has represented so much: not only an emblem of economic respectability (as it is elsewhere), but often the only source of attachment, status, and self-esteem in new communities that offered few others. ("O, boy," said the wartime ad, quoting the stereotypical marine in his foxhole in New Guinea, "when I get out of this jungle, I'm going to build me a sweet little cottage in California, and stay there the rest of my natural life. It won't be big, but it'll have every convenience I can cram into it . . . a shower with hot and cold running water in every bedroom . . . a handy little kitchen . . . and a certain girl named Sally who knows how to make a juicy steak . . .")[5]

The landscape of the 1950s and 1960s had been covered with monuments to the search for that version of the golden future: places called Sunset Estates, Magnolia Estates, Sunny Hills Estates, Laurelwood Estates, Hacienda Heights, Anaheim, Garden Grove, thousands upon thousands of acres of citrus groves and wheat fields turned into the American dream of the year 1955—$11,900, $12,600, $14,000 for modern ranch living with three bedrooms, two baths, plus an "extra Jack and Jill room"—all of it available for $995 down (nothing down for veterans), plus $61 a month, or $65 a month or $68 a month.

No base so frail, of course, could have long supported as large a load of expectations as this one was expected to bear, especially as it drew more and more immigrants, foreign and domestic, pursuing the same thing. Its very success carried the seeds of its decay. And so the "slow disintegration" of the "postwar virtuous circle of good jobs, rising incomes, cheap land and quality public services . . . into the present vicious circle of social polarization, expensive land, and a declining public sector" that urban critic Mike Davis speaks about was not altogether surprising.[6] The tax revolt, said sociologist Clarence Lo, "was the California dreamers waking up."[7]

That, however, is hardly the whole of this strange story. Even after the spike of inflation that came with the first energy crisis in 1974, national consumer prices continued to rise steadily through the decade. But California housing inflation, which was much more severe, was driven by a combination of factors that were in many respects unique.

The first was a wave of property assessment scandals perpetrated by a scattering of corrupt assessors in the 1960s that generated a reform law (AB 80, sponsored by a couple of liberal Bay Area legislators and enacted in 1967) that produced consequences almost totally opposite of what had been intended.

The AB 80 reforms were founded on the fatal misapprehension

that because the crooked assesssors, most notably San Francisco's Russell L. Wolden, who was ultimately convicted and sent to jail, were giving breaks to a few well-connected business friends, they were giving breaks to all commercial property, thereby overassessing residential property. But the truth was quite the reverse. The assessors were doing favors for some commercial enterprises that were, in turn, doing favors for them, but the big breaks had been going to homeowners, who, as always, were the voters that the elected assesssors most needed to mollify. Thus, instead of making it easier to hold down increases in residential assessments (as the assessors, crooked or not, had in fact been doing) that would have dampened the effects of the oncoming inflation in values, AB 80 turned the whole assessment process into what someone called "a non-discretionary administrative function"—put it on a computerized autopilot—that required every parcel, commercial or residential, to be reassesssed every three years at 25 percent of market value.[8] The more fully the new law kicked in, the more the tax burden was shifted from commercial to residential property. By the late 1960s, there were bumper stickers in San Francisco: "Bring back the crooked assessor."

There had, in fact, been scattered property tax protests in Glendale, Pomona, West Covina, Alhambra, Manhattan Beach, and other parts of Southern California as early as the 1950s, long before the AB 80 reforms were enacted, even as the polls were showing that voters strongly favored increased spending for schools, mental health, fire protection, and transportation.[9] And while the early protests fizzled, in part because the assessors had the power to mitigate the complaints, the homeowner associations that helped organize those protests grew stronger and angrier. They were also spurred by the incipient slow growth movement arising from complaints about new apartment developments, high rises, new freeways, airport expansion, increasing traffic congestion, air pollution, and city-to-suburb school busing of minority children that began in the 1960s.

In fast-growing areas like the San Gabriel Valley east of Los Angeles, there had long been protests against redevelopment projects, which both brought more crowding and, in the view of the homeowners, sucked property tax money into subsidies for developers and other businesses. In Monterey Park in 1976, residents passed a local initiative (by an 85 percent majority) to restrict the construction of new condominiums; in the San Fernando Valley, homeowner groups managed to get height limitations on new buildings on Ventura Boulevard; and in countless other communities, resistance mounted to virtually anything that threatened to bring more development, more cars, less open space, and new people, especially if they were poorer or browner or blacker.[10]

(In what was probably the most famous instance of no-growth resistance, residents of the funky seaside town of Bolinas just north of San Francisco repeatedly tore down state road signs on nearby Highway 1 showing the road to their town. Ultimately, the state highway department just stopped replacing them.)

In 1960, urban critic Mike Davis pointed out, over two-thirds of new housing units constructed in Orange County below Los Angeles had been single-family units; a decade later, 60 percent of the new units were apartments and condominiums. In the interim, escalating land prices had simply driven the price of the traditional starter home out of reach. And with those escalating prices came "the clouding of the California Dream":[11]

> On the one hand, the open space amenities that supported the life styles and home values of wealthy [Los Angeles area] hillside and beach dwellers were threatened by rampant, large-scale development; on the other, traditional single-family tracts were suddenly inundated by waves of apartment construction. New development was perceived as a categorical threat to the detached culture of low-density residential life. However reluctantly, in the face of entrenched conservative stereotypes and prejudices, elements of the environmental critique advanced by the Sierra Club and California Tomorrow gained currency amongst homeowner activists, who grasped at the notion that the endangered open spaces around their homes—even the "pastoral scatteredness" (aka urban sprawl) of their subdivisions—were conser-

vation values as much as rock piles in Yosemite or wild rivers on remote coasts.

It was those homeowner associations and the perceived nexus between taxation and development, in some places spiced by mounting anger against school busing, that became the backbone of the tax revolt of the mid-1970s. Meanwhile, pressure was also mounting to find ways to control growth and increase environmental protection at the state level. On the same ballot in November 1972, California voters approved initiatives that, for all their apparent differences, reflected similar impulses: one prohibiting the transfer (i.e., busing) of students to any school on the basis of race, creed, or color, and repealing the state law that had made school desegregation state policy; the other creating the California Coastal Zone Conservation Act to control growth and protect open space and public access along the state's shorelines.

The first passed by a margin of 63–37, although, as predicted at the time, it was later ruled unconstitutional and thrown out by the courts, thereby fueling a new set of resentments and protest organizations. The latter passed 55–45 and remains state law.[12] And two years later Californians elected Secretary of State Jerry Brown, son of the master builder, on a platform that, as many people have since pointed out, was loaded with Freudian inferences about the Oedipal problems of the man some people derisively referred to simply as "Junior": slow growth, coastal protection and other rigorous environmental controls, limits on big government programs, and political reform. "People ask me, 'What's your program?'" he once said. "What the hell does that mean? The program is to confront the confusion and hypocrisy of government. That's what's important . . . You don't have to *do* things. Maybe by avoiding doing things you accomplish quite a lot."[13] Jerry was determined not to be like his father. And that's what a growing number of Californians seemed to want of him as well.

One set of complaints fueled the other. In slowing growth, imposing moratoria on new construction, and, most particularly, virtually blocking the development of low- and middle-income housing in many parts of Southern California altogether, the homeowner groups reinforced the run-up in residential real estate prices that, at first, were the source of the self-satisfied chat at the neighborhood Little League games and church socials and that ultimately became the source of fiscal and political disaster: For nearly two decades it was lovely to see what had been a $12,000 tract house go up to $30,000; but when it doubled again, to $60,000, or tripled to $90,000, and the taxes went with it, it was fun no longer. For most people, the run-up in assessed value was nothing more than a paper profit that could not be realized until the home was sold, and perhaps not even then. As the leaders of the tax revolt kept saying, when incomes lagged far behind the run-up in property tax, the higher assessment was certainly not a good measurement of ability to pay. An individual could more or less control his sales tax by controlling his spending, and his income tax only rose when his income rose. But property taxes were beyond the taxpayer's control. Twenty years later, some of their former opponents began reluctantly to acknowledge that on that point, maybe, the tax rebels had been right.

For a time, the disaster was averted, in large part because the shift of the tax burden to residential properties that the reform law inadvertently commanded was partially concealed through a series of mitigating state tax reform measures. Among them were a pair of bills enacted under Reagan that provided (and subsequently expanded) homeowner exemptions and replaced the lost revenue with an increased sales tax and increases in the much more progressive income tax. The Democrats also got Reagan to accede to income tax withholding, something that he vehemently disliked because he believed taxes should be felt and not be lifted more or less unnoticed out of the wage-earner's weekly paycheck, but which also had the incidental effect of tightening tax collection and thus driving up revenues.[14]

By the mid-seventies, however, the inflation in California residential property values far outran the relatively small mitigating measures that the legislature had been able to enact (even as general inflation began to drive middle-class income taxes, which were then still not indexed, into the upper brackets). Total property tax revenues did not increase markedly, largely because of the residual effect of the inadvertent shift in the tax burden from commercial to residential property decreed by AB 80. Commercial real estate, moreover, was not going up nearly as fast as residential property, in part because larger commercial property turned over less frequently than residential property, and in part because it could not be assesssed by computerized formulas. Indeed, as a percentage of personal income, combined property tax bills for residential and business properties were lower in 1978 than at any time since 1970.[15]

But homeowners' tax bills began rising sharply, and in some places they were going through the roof. Between 1975 and 1978, while assessments for commercial and industrial property increased only a relatively modest 26 percent, assessed values more than doubled for owner-occupied homes—and in many cases increased much more than that—thereby increasing the share of total property taxes paid by the owners of single-family homes from 32 to 42 percent.[16] At the same time, there was a perception, partly true, partly exaggerated, that a growing share of taxes was no longer going to schools and cops but to welfare and health, meaning to the poor and to the new foreign immigrants—and that even when it went to schools, it appeared increasingly to be schools for somebody else's children. As early as September 1978, shortly after 13 passed, Jarvis was writing articles complaining about aliens "who just come over here to get on the taxpayers' gravy train," echoing what he and many of his followers had been saying quietly for some time.[17]

For the indefatigable Jarvis—he was then already seventy-five years old—it was an opportunity not to be missed. By 1977, he had become director of a Los Angeles association of apartment house owners, and, despite his previous near-misses—or indeed because of them, and because of the names and followers he had gathered in his unsuccessful runs for office—had become the center of an increasingly active network of Southern California homeowner and taxpayer organizations. In addition, his new partner Gann, the retired Sacramento realtor, who had been trying to work (and had failed with) his own tax protest, brought his list of names and connections, most of them in the increasingly conservative suburbs and the growing cities of the Central Valley.

More important, Jarvis, always the brighter and more aggressive in this team, had learned the lessons of previous failures. His would be a simple scheme that any voter could understand: Property values would be rolled back to their 1975 levels and could be raised by no more than 2 percent a year for inflation until the property was sold and transferred, at which point it could be reassessed at the purchase price. The tax rate would be limited to 1 percent on the value of each parcel, with the legislature determining how that 1 percent would be apportioned among the various local agencies that had previously set their own tax rates. The only exception to that 1 percent would be for the cost of amortizing whatever local bonds were still outstanding. But henceforth, local agencies, including schools, would effectively be prohibited from issuing any new bonds. (The restriction on new bonds would be amended in 1986, when school districts were again given authority to issue construction bonds if they were approved by a two-thirds vote of the electorate—the same rule that had applied before the passage of Proposition 13.) Jarvis believed that schools shouldn't be funded through the property tax at all.[18]

The principle was simple. There was to be no local tax increase without a vote of the people, and no increase in property tax rates under any circumstances. All "general" tax increases (say in the local sales tax) had to be approved by a majority of local voters. Increases in "special taxes" required a two-thirds vote. That provision was originally conceived in an effort to protect economic subgroups within the general population by preventing voters at large from socking it to unpopular interest groups (like the apartment house owners that Jarvis worked for).

As the courts would interpret it, however, "special taxes" came to mean anything earmarked for a special purpose—libraries or police protection or transit. That would also come to be helpful to the cause of tax resistance. Voters were always reluctant to approve "general" taxes that gave politicians money they could play with; the two-thirds threshold made it hard to pass even local taxes earmarked for something that the majority liked. In addition, all tax increases imposed by the legislature would henceforth require a two-thirds vote in each house, with the exception of new ad valorem property taxes, which were totally prohibited.

All together, what that meant, in simple terms, was that the tax on the average home would immediately be reduced by nearly 60 percent at a collective first-year cost to local governments of roughly $7 billion. More important, as Joel Fox would say, for the first time "it was the taxpayer who had certainty instead of the tax collector."[19]

In drawing his proposal and in selling it to the voters, the wily Jarvis conveniently ignored the tax shift that had so heavily favored commercial property at the expense of owner-occupied homes. Nor did he allow himself to be distracted by arguments that big businesses, many of them out-of-state corporations, would save far more than the average homeowner, or by the argument that since there would be less property tax to deduct, a substantial portion of Californians' property-tax savings would be scooped up by the federal government in higher income taxes.

He didn't give a damn about all that crap, he often said. All those arguments were just "manure," "a lot of compost." His interest was in the homeowner—the fertile territory of anger, frustration, and, increasingly, of fear, which the escalating tax bills generated, particularly among people on fixed incomes, some of whom found that the $400 tax bills they had been used to on their two-bedroom tract houses had shot up to $1,200. In some instances, local governments, fearing the wrath of voters, had even reduced tax rates. But often that was difficult, particularly because under the law in effect at that time, each county's share of the cost of Medi-Cal and certain other social benefits was proportional to its assessed property valuation. Thus, as values went up, so did costs, making rate cuts difficult.[20] And because the state has so many overlapping local jurisdictions—cities, counties, school districts, fire districts, park districts, flood control districts, mosquito abatement districts, each with power to set its own rates—the effect of any single jurisdiction's rate reductions on the total tax bill of any individual homeowner was negligible in any case. The tax system had, as writer Robert Kuttner said, "taken on a life of its own."[21]

Jarvis, who had formed an umbrella group called the United Organizations of Taxpayers in the 1960s, worked the Southern California homeowner associations relentlessly, and particularly those in the San Fernando Valley, driving from meeting to meeting, drawing increasingly large crowds, and, as the new assessments kept coming in, becoming a frequent guest on Los Angeles radio talk shows, especially on the program of the conservative George Putnam who, Jarvis said, "was looking for a way to boost his ratings." When the Jarvis people set up tables in the shopping malls, they wasted no time on explanations or details. "We learned," Jarvis said later, "the best approach to use on someone when you want to get their signature on a petition [is just to say]: 'Sign this—it will help lower your taxes.' That usually worked."[22]

Many of the homeowners and voters Jarvis was addressing were the same people who had arrived in the great wave of optimism of the previous couple of decades, but judging from the organization's contributor lists, most of them people putting up $25 or $50 each, the great majority were either retirees or housewives, or real estate operators or investors, who would subsequently describe themselves—and be described in the Jarvis campaign ads and literature—as elderly people unable to pay their property taxes and on the verge of losing their homes to foreclosure. By the time he and Gann turned in their signatures late in the fall of 1977— altogether more than 1.2 million, at least twice what they needed to make the ballot—the image of the prototypical Californian of the go-go years had evolved from the bright young family raising children in new developments to elderly homeowners unable to pay their taxes. One of their leaders was sixty-six, the other seventy-five.

II

As the protests mounted in the summer and fall of 1977, and Jarvis and Gann were collecting their signatures, Governor Jerry Brown and the legislature fiddled. Property values and tax bills were increasing faster and more steeply in Southern California, but no region was exempt, and almost no one questioned that some sort of property tax relief was urgently necessary.

The problem was what sort. California is among just a handful of states requiring a two-thirds majority in each legislative house to enact a budget or pass any other appropriation bill, except those for schools. That provision, which has been part of the constitution since the 1930s, seemed to be no great obstacle in the golden prereform days when legislators—for better or worse—were more collegial, regardless of party, and more inclined to compromise than they are now, and when there seemed to be lots of money to go around. But it became crucial as the state became more diverse and divided in the 1970s and the larger political consensus eroded.[23] Since then, the two-thirds requirement has been the nearest thing to original sin in the California system. More than any other structural flaw, it diffused accountability and brought on much of the budgetary gridlock that California became notorious for in the 1980s and early 1990s, and which on at least one occasion forced the state to issue IOUs to pay its employees and contractors.

And so while the state in 1977–78 was in the fortunate position of sitting on a growing surplus that would eventually exceed $5 billion—itself the result of the ratcheting effect of income-tax bracket creep during an inflationary period—agreeing on reform was next to impossible. The most promising proposals—the creation of a split roll, for example, that would permit the taxation of owner-occupied residences at lower rates than commercial and other property—all required two-thirds votes, both in passing the necessary constitutional amendment through the legislature in order to put it on the ballot (which would, of course, ultimately also require a majority vote of the electorate) and in the state budgetary appropriations that were necessary to fund local property tax relief measures. The two-thirds supermajority requirement gave any determined political minority an effective veto on whatever was proposed.

The upshot was something approaching more than a year of gridlock. While both houses of the legislature were controlled by Democrats in 1976–78 (and indeed, for nearly two decades after that), they did not have the required supermajority in the senate.

Nor were they all the same kind of Democrats, with conservatives favoring direct relief to homeowners, liberals proposing to close corporate tax loopholes and pushing to use at least part of the surplus for larger tax breaks for renters and other progressive redistribution of income (how quaint that now seems), and representatives from the Central Valley and other rural areas complaining that too much relief was going to the cities.

The governor, meanwhile, when he was engaged at all, was pushing for a business inventory tax reduction (not to mention an Office of Appropriate Technology, a state space program, an alternative energy project, and a few other pet ideas for which he needed money). It's conceivable that Brown was also trying to protect some of the surplus to comply with a court-ordered equalization (discussed more fully later in this section) of local school finances. But Brown, who was hoping to run for president in 1980, and eventually did, was also delighted to have the bracket-creep-driven surplus as evidence of his efficient management of California affairs. Much later, Brown confessed that he should have paid more heed to the warnings he got from members of his cabinet about the mounting property tax complaints—a lot of people believed that he could have made the difference in producing an alternative that would have headed off Jarvis-Gann—but that would have required "more time than I had attention span to deal with . . . It was a problem of growing inequality (between business and residential taxpayers) and I didn't have the stomach for it."[24]

They should have known—should have paid attention. As one of the leaders of the tax revolt said later, "if you get a million signatures two or three times" on major reform measures "you have to know that something is wrong." But Brown and the legislature failed to come up with anything in 1977, when there might still have been time to deflate Jarvis and Gann's petition drive. That fall, when a cumbersome compromise bill full of arcane devices—among them a "circuit breaker" that would limit the property tax to some percentage of a homeowner's income—fell two votes short in the senate, the legislature gave up and went home.[25] What was he supposed to do when he went back to his district, asked Walter Steirn, one of the (conservative) Valley Democrats, in explaining his negative vote, "talk to these people about circuit breakers, split level tax concepts, XYZ funds, marginal threshold rates . . . *Marginal threshold rates?"*[26]

In February of 1978, the legislature, with not a vote to spare in either house, cobbled together an eleventh-hour relief measure based on the split roll idea. The measure, designed to give voters an alternative to Proposition 13, appeared beside it on the June ballot as Proposition 8, a constitutional amendment that would authorize the legislature to permit local governments to tax owner-occupied dwellings at a lower rate than other property. It did not authorize any shift of the burden to other property; instead, the loss in local tax revenue would be made up out of what would soon be called the state's "obscene surplus." But the measure did not assure anything. It was coupled to a complicated separate bill drafted by a Marin County patrician named Peter Behr that reflected the political sausage-making necessary to satisfy the various legislative factions. The bill, which included sliding scale exemptions for senior citizens and various small benefits for renters, would have permitted an average residential property tax reduction of only 32–35 percent, compared to Jarvis's 57 percent, a classic case of too little, too late.[27]

Almost the entire establishment—the major industry groups, the chamber of commerce, city and county officials, the big newspapers, the League of Women Voters, Common Cause, the labor unions, the moderate leaders of both parties, even the conservative California Taxpayers Association—backed Proposition 8 and opposed Proposition 13. While the big corporations stood to gain hundreds of millions of dollars in property tax reductions from Jarvis-Gann, the fear was that the legislature would immediately seek to recoup the losses in increased corporation taxes or in a truly radical split roll system that would increase business property taxes beyond the relatively acceptable amounts that business was paying before Proposition 13, or would have to pay under Proposition 8.

All through the spring, as the campaign heated up, public officials and the media were issuing warnings about the consequences to schools and virtually all other public services. In February, some four months before the June 6 vote, state school superintendent Wilson Riles, the liberal who had defeated Rafferty in 1970, announced that Proposition 13 would require the average school district to cut budgets by 38 percent, force the layoff of thousands of teachers, and result in classes with as many as sixty students. "The measure," Riles warned, "would do nothing short of destroying education in California." And since California law required school districts considering layoffs for the following year to notify teachers who might be affected by March 15, district after district was sending formal notices to all its teachers that they might not have a job come fall.

All that, Jarvis said, "is a snow job by some marinated bureaucrats and over-animated popcorn balls." As for Riles, who happened to be black, "he's of low IQ and doesn't understand the amendment. Education has already been destroyed in California by Riles and the school system that doesn't teach kids anything . . . The initiative is to cut property taxes in California and to save a couple of million people from losing their homes. They are a lot more important than twenty thousand schoolteachers."[28]

It turned into an expensive battle. If Jarvis's official spending reports are to be believed, he and Gann spent less than $60,000 to get the signatures and qualify Proposition 13 for the ballot. But in the election battle for the hearts and minds of the voters that followed, each side spent more than $2 million, a large amount by the standards of that day. The various Jarvisite organizations associated with the "Yes on 13" campaign—the United Organizations of Taxpayers, the county homeowners associations, the Apartment Association of Los Angeles County, Gann's People's Advocate— raised and spent some $2,279,000 on direct mail and radio and TV advertising, the opponents nearly as much.

The difference was that most of the "Yes on 13" money was raised in a direct mail campaign by a pair of shrewd Newport Beach campaign consulants named Bill Butcher and Arnold Forde—they called themselves the "Darth Vaders of Direct Mail"—whom Jarvis had hired. It came from thousands of individuals—ranchers, real estate investors, brokers, doctors, farmers—many of them elderly, many retired, in amounts that rarely went over $100.[29] (One of Butcher-Forde's favorite devices, which would be further honed and refined in the 1980s, was to mail their pitches in official-looking envelopes that mimicked the mailings of their archenemy, the tax collector, advising the recipient that there was "IMPORTANT TAX INFORMATION INSIDE" that should be opened immediately. Often that important information included the amount of the recipient's current property tax, a warning that it might soon double, and an appeal to send money at once to stop it.)

In contrast, most of the "No on 13" money came from some of the state's largest banks, utilities, retailers, and other corporations, much of it in five-figure amounts. That made it next to impossible for the antis to sustain any sort of populist counterargument, however true, that the real beneficiaries of Proposition 13 would be big commercial enterprises and the owners of larger condomiunium complexes who belonged to the apartment owners association that Jarvis worked for.

That quandary was compounded by the disorganization and disagreements of the "No on 13" groups. Everybody knew that tax relief was necessary and that the only alternative was Proposition 8, but the corporations were leery of stressing the split-roll idea too much, lest it get out of hand. The only effective argument was that renters would be guaranteed none of the savings from Proposition 13—that landlords, operating in a tight housing market, would simply keep them, a prediction that turned out to be largely correct: Renters got almost nothing after the measure passed. Further complicating the problem of the "No on 13" campaign was the fact that Proposition 8 was the work of the same politicians who were widely regarded as the people who had created the problem in the first place: The only known name among the three people who signed the ballot argument for it was Jerry Brown, a figure who even then was hardly the repository of great public trust. In this fight, it was Jarvis, the pugnacious demagogue, who represented ordinary people. When Jarvis filed his spending and contribution reports with the California Secretary of State's Office in 1978, he described, in printed block letters, his own nonmonetary contributions as "1 million hours—VOLUNTARY—Non Paid Help Extending Over 15 years."

Finally, the antis faced yet one other difficulty that was hardly discussed at the time, and hasn't been noted very much since, but which appears to have been a significant factor in the passage of 13. In two major decisions, both designated *Serrano v. Priest*, one in 1971 and one in 1976 (*Serrano I* and *Serrano II*),[30] the state supreme court, taking on an issue that many other states would later confront, had declared California's property-tax-based school financing system an unconstitutional violation of equal protection principles and ordered the legislature to change it. The court, agreeing with the working-class plaintiff-parents in the case (and with John E. Coons and Stephen Sugarman, the Berkeley law professors who had developed the legal theory on which it rested), found that even when a poor community like Baldwin Park, twenty-five miles east of Los Angeles, jacked its tax rates up to $4.78 per hundred, a near-punitive level, its per-pupil revenue was less than half that of a wealthy community like Beverly Hills, which had a property tax rate less than half that of Baldwin Park. Put another way, in 1976, a tax rate of $1.00 per hundred in Baldwin Park would have generated $170 per child; in Beverly Hills, the same rate would have generated $1,340.[31] "Affluent districts can have their cake and eat it, too," the court said. "They can provide a high quality education for their children while paying lower taxes . . . Poor districts, by contrast, have no cake at all."[32]

The legislature responded to *Serrano* with a bill (AB 65), designed to equalize school revenues over a period of time by "levelling up" funding for poor communities: providing increased aid from the state's bulging treasury for districts that had low tax bases, imposing revenue caps on wealthier districts, and taking some of the property tax of those wealthier districts and redistributing it to poor districts. That, contends Dartmouth economist William A. Fischel, in an intriguing argument, not only committed much of the state surplus so that it could not be used for tax relief—AB 65 was signed by Jerry Brown in September 1977, the same moment that the legislature was gridlocked on property tax relief—but eviscerated voter support for the local property tax.

Many communities "view their school property taxes as a 'benefit tax' rather than an 'onerous' tax," Fischel wrote, even for people who have no schoolchildren but nonetheless see good schools as a major factor in sustaining property values. But after *Serrano II* "declared that the state had to insure near-equality of expenditures per pupil, one of the main reasons that voters had for protecting the painful-to-pay local property taxes evaporated." *Serrano* "converted the property tax from a local benefit tax into a pure deadweight loss."[33] To what extent those considerations actually "caused" Proposition 13, as Fischel claims, and to what extent they figured in the choices voters would make is hard to ascertain—Jarvis often tried to argue, in his characteristically disingenuous fashion, that Proposition 13 would not harm schools because *Serrano* already required state funding—but it certainly undermined one powerful reason to vote against it.

Given the way things seemed to be stacked in favor of Jarvis-Gann, what was suprising was that in the first week of May, a month before the election, Proposition 13 appeared to have only the slimmest of leads in the polls—42 to 39, with 19 percent undecided. At some level, despite the rising tax rates, and despite Jarvis's denials that anything terrible would happen to public services, the voters seemed to understand that they were on the brink of some momentous decision, and were hesitating before it.[34] But then came the news from Los Angeles County where the assessor, Alexander Pope, who had been in office for barely ten weeks, was under growing pressure to make the new assessments—which the county supervisors wanted to keep bottled up until after the election—available to those taxpayers who wanted to come downtown and look at them. Normally those assessments only went out in October, when tax bills were mailed. But three weeks before the election, Pope, breaking with prior practice, gave in, and the numbers were even worse than the pessimists had feared. Under the assessment-reform law passed after the 1960s scandals, roughly one-third of all property was reevaluated every three years, and most of the new assessments this time were in the skyrocketing real estate market on the West Side of Los Angeles.[35] (In 1974, Pope later said, the tax on his own house had been $1,224; in 1978, had Jarvis-Gann not passed, it would have gone to $3,130.)[36]

At that point it was all over: Jarvis, ever the master of blather and hyperbole, had been making what had appeared to be wild predictions that taxes here or there would double. Now, night after night, the evening news on Los Angeles television stations, with their millions of viewers, was filled with pictures of tearful old ladies whose assessments had in fact more than doubled and who told interviewers they saw no alternative but to sell their homes, young mothers declaring that they would have to go back to work to pay the tax man, and public officials scurrying to come up with yet one more fix.

In panic, Jerry Brown and the Los Angeles county supervisors agreed to order Pope to roll back the new assessments (which was illegal under AB 80), but at that point the City of Los Angeles, with its bloated budget and powerful public employee unions, declared that it had been counting on those assessments, and if they were rolled back, it would have to raise its rates, which, of course, meant that there would be tax increases for the hundreds of thousands of Los Angeles city property owners who hadn't been reassessed.

Even the most brilliant political consultants couldn't have dreamed up that sort of campaign publicity, with political leaders scurrying around in confusion and Howard Jarvis rising above them like an avenging prophet. Butcher and Forde had been betting since the beginning of the campaign that Jarvis could be made the centerpiece of the campaign—that he was not just a "goofy old gadfly" but "somebody ordinary taxpayers could identify with"— and the bet paid off.[37] In March, Howard Jarvis, who had always been regarded as something of a hustler and a buffoon—even then, Gann often said Jarvis had diarrhea of the mouth—had been stopped and charged with drunk driving in the San Fernando Valley community of Thousand Oaks. (He would never be convicted.) Now, barely two months later, he was the savior of the small homeowner, the leader of a national movement to be reckoned with, and, in some respects, the most influential political figure in America.

On June 6, in what was an extraordinary turnout for a primary election in a nonpresidential year, 69 percent of registered voters cast ballots, giving Proposition 13 nearly 65 percent of their votes. As might be expected, it carried overwhelmingly among those over fifty, but it seems to have won majorities among almost every segment of the voters other than renters, blacks, who opposed it overwhelmingly, and those younger than twenty-four, many of them almost certainly college students responsive to warnings that with Proposition 13, the days of low fees would quickly come to an end. University of California scholars Davis O. Sears and Jack Citrin, who later conducted a major study on the passage of Proposition 13, concluded that it even carried among parents of schoolchildren, though their data on that question comes from a retrospective survey of some 1,800 adults, not voters, conducted eighteen months after the election—no exit polls raised that crucial question—and conflicts with other poll information about voters in the corresponding age groups. What is indisputable, however, is that the strongest support came from elderly white homeowners who had no children at home, and that the strength of the support increased with income.[38] Along with a measure extending the death penalty to a number of new crimes, which passed the same day, Proposition 13 was the first initiative that Californians had approved in four years. There has not been such a period since, nor is there likely ever to be one again.

III

Overnight, three things happened. The first was that millions of California residents and businesses got whopping property tax cuts. The biggest dollar winners were the state's major corporations and other large commercial property owners. Statewide, the Pacific Telephone Co., got a property tax cut estimated at $130 million, the Pacific Gas and Electric Co. gained over $90 million, and Southern California Edison $53.8 million. Standard Oil got a cut of $13 million in Contra Costa County alone (where it had, and Chevron now has, a huge refinery); Lockheed gained $9.5 million in Los Angeles; IBM got a cut of over $6 million in Santa Clara County.[39] Among the other big winners was the federal government, which recaptured an estimated 22 percent of the savings of

California taxpayers in the form of higher income taxes and, ironically, even the state treasury, which recaptured 14 percent by the same means.[40] All told, homeowners received only 24 percent of the total dollars. But in numbers, the vast majority of the winners (and certainly those who got the attention) were those tax-revolting homeowners, among them some of the same widows who had been crying into the TV microphones just a couple of weeks earlier, and who, in effect, now capitalized their property tax savings into a windfall that drove the values of their properties even higher than they had been before.

And if they were now laughing all the way to the bank, so was the bank. Money that a potential buyer might once have paid for property taxes could now be allocated to interest. The monthly payment would be the same; the only difference was that it went to the bank holding the mortgage rather than the school district or the city tax collector. In a study of the early effects of Proposition 13, Kenneth T. Rosen of the Center for Real Estate and Urban Economics at Berkeley concluded that "each dollar decrease in relative property taxes appeared to increase relative property values by about seven dollars."[41] But now, with assessments frozen at 1975 levels and taxes capped at 1 percent, they could enjoy the appreciation without fear that the tax collector was coming after them. In 1988, David Doerr of the California Taxpayers Association estimated that in its first decade, Proposition 13 saved taxpayers a total of $228 billion, about the equivalent of the annual federal deficit in the last Reagan years, moving the state from seventh in the nation in property tax revenue per $100 of personal income to thirty-fifth.[42] In 1996, Joel Fox of the Howard Jarvis Taxpayers put the estimated taxpayer savings at a slightly more modest $196 billion—plus another $82 billion for the savings from tax indexing, which soon followed. "Our members," he said, "have gotten their money's worth."[43]

(Renters, on the other hand, did not. In places like Santa Monica, where the housing market was already tight, hundreds of landlords sold their properties to take advantage of the run-ups in values, and the new owners, with higher mortgages to pay, instead of lowering rents, as Jarvis had vaguely promised, jacked them up. That quickly brought a local rent control initiative, courtesy of the

Campaign for Economic Democracy, headed by actress Jane Fonda and her then-husband Tom Hayden, as it would in Berkeley, which further skewed and tightened the market, drove many existing properties off the market, and pushed new apartment construction down to near zero.)[44]

The second overnight effect was the conversion of scores of politicians of both parties to the new theology. It wasn't surprising that a dozen or more Republicans had run as "Proposition 13 babies" that November, many of them with funding from the California Tax Reduction Political Action Committee that Jarvis had created after the primary. (One of them, Bill Leonard, a conservative from San Bernardino County who had himself been in real estate management, said that as he called on voters that spring, the only thing he was asked was his position on Jarvis-Gann.) After the November election, those Proposition 13 babies would become a new conservative GOP core in Sacramento who, adopting their opponents' disparaging label, proudly referred to themselves as "the cavemen."

And a lot of others who had opposed Jarvis-Gann soon joined them. Governor Jerry Brown, the prophet of lowered expectations and now dubbed "Jerry Jarvis," not only announced he would do everything he could to make Proposition 13 work, a matter on which he had little choice, but as the chief apostle of the "era of limits," slipped into the new mode with the ease of a man who had always been waiting for it. He had, he said, become "a born-again tax cutter."[45]

In some respects, indeed, he had long been setting the climate for it. For four years Brown had been berating the state's schools and universities for their wastefulness, occasionally threatening to give them not another dime of new money if they didn't shape up. Never, he declared at one regents' meeting, "has education been more irrelevant to more kids." Rarely, he said on other occasions, had public institutions failed the society in so many ways or helped perpetuate so many inequities.[46] And the same, in his view, appeared to be the case for a great many of the other institutions and programs—freeway construction in particular, which he reduced to virtually nothing—that were among his father's proudest achievements. And while he was disdainfully rejecting suggestions that he ought to have a plan, that government ought to be hyperactively doing things, as it had under his father, he was also incapable of providing the tax relief that might have justified the inactivity. (By 1980, when he was trying to unseat Jimmy Carter in the Democratic primaries, he was already supporting a federal balanced budget amendment.) Against such messages, Howard Jarvis could as easily be seen as a liberator than as a barbarian-destroyer. Unruh, the former Big Daddy of the Assembly, who had become California's elected treasurer, later observed that Brown, who had fiddled as the crisis escalated, was the father of Proposition 13 in many more ways than he knew.

The third effect inevitably followed from the other two. What the taxpayers gained, the tax collector lost. Overnight, property tax revenues for local agencies declined by between $6 and $7 billion annually. (They would lose still more later.) That amounted to roughly 27 percent of all revenues for cities, 40 percent of all county revenues, nearly half (on average) of what school districts had been getting, and up to 90 percent for some fire districts.[47] But because counties had virtually no alternative sources of revenues, they were—and would remain—the hardest hit, particularly in the face of reduced federal funding for social services during the 1980s, the escalating costs of medical care, and the rising demand for services.

Because of the $5 billion surplus the state had accumulated, and because its revenues were still running somewhat higher than its needs—and would continue to do so until the early 1980s—the legislature was able to put together hastily a set of bailout bills and cushion the worst of the initial blow. The essence of that first bailout was a transfer of property tax revenues from the schools to cities, counties, and other local jurisdictions, with state funds replacing most of what the schools lost. That shift, in effectively making the state the predominant source of local school funds, had the incidental advantage of speeding compliance with the *Serrano* mandate to equalize school funding.

Nonetheless, the impact of Proposition 13 was quickly felt, despite the bailout. That first year all summer school programs were cancelled, sports and other extracurricular programs reduced, public library hours curtailed, and some branch libraries closed down altogether; maintenance of parks, playgrounds, and other recreation facilties was sharply curtailed, and fees increased (or imposed for the first time) on those who used them. The summer school programs were restored in subsequent years, but the service reductions, the cuts in other school programs, the reduced staffing in everything from park and recreation programs to school counsellors and mental health clinics, the perpetually deferred maintenance, and the fee increases became the pattern of the future. And so, of course were the increasingly complex fiscal and accountability formulas that the state had to fashion (and constantly revise) to allocate what funds were left. California's public schools, which had been among the most generously funded in the nation, began a path of decline from which they have never recovered.

To this day, the Jarvisites regard their triumph as a great victory for small people over big government. They also argue, correctly, that not all of California's problems, fiscal or otherwise, from forest fires to earthquakes to child murders, can be attributed to Proposition 13—even though some critics tried to do so—or that all cuts in service were unfair. Joel Fox later liked to quote a piece by Robert Wright in *The New Republic*, who blamed the miscarriage of justice in the O.J. Simpson trial on Howard Jarvis. The trial, Wright contended, "showed what kind of county and municipal government you can get with an inadequate tax base . . . Sloppy criminologists, a loony coroner and mediocre prosecutors consistently outgunned. All performing roughly as their salaries warrant."[48] Conversely, Proposition 13, as even some liberals acknowledged, forced government to become leaner in its operations, eliminating overhead and moving public employees to more useful services. In any number of police departments, sworn officers who had been doing routine desk work were replaced by lower-paid clerks; the same was true in county jails, where highly compensated deputies were replaced by lower-salaried guards; and almost everywhere, overhead was reduced and procedures modernized. When charges went up for admission to city zoos and county parks, it burdened low-income families; but it was hard to argue that the taxpayers should continue to subsidize the duffers at the municipal golf course.

Still, Proposition 13's negative impact on both services and governance was enormous. Since it delegated the allocation of the local property tax to the legislature and governor—and given the state's preexisting jumble of overlapping local jurisdictions, altogether some 7,000 of them, the only place it could have placed that responsibility—it took power and discretion away from local governments, away from locally elected officials and local communities, who were now sharply constrained in their ability to raise any substantial local funds, and moved them to the capitol in Sacramento. "We need to have a situation where the people can say the Democratic Party is responsible for this disaster, or the Republican Party is responsible for that disaster," Jarvis said. *"We must have a place to put responsibility for our political decisions . . .* [his italics]"⁴⁹ But since the resulting funding formulas and power relationships— particularly those involving the counties and the schools—would become increasingly tangled between the state and the locals, the ability of the citizen to determine who was responsible for what would become increasingly attenuated as well. The same act that seemed at first to empower the voter over his government also enfeebled him as a citizen.

Compounding the effect, though almost unnoticed at the time, was the ratchet effect it created in the state's overall tax system: Jarvis-Gann prohibited the legislature from increasing taxes without a two-thirds vote of each house. But the law still allowed taxes to be *lowered,* and tax loopholes to be introduced, by majorities. It thus constitutionalized unjustified tax breaks for precisely the special interests—in one estimate running to some $6 billion a year—that voters complain so much about. It's "like a roach motel," said one critic of this process. "Once a tax loophole crawls in, it never crawls out."⁵⁰

More fundamentally still, as Sears and Citrin pointed out, Proposition 13, for better and worse, transformed California's dominant political style. "Austerity and self-reliance replaced planning and social reform as symbols of legitimacy. Politicians increasingly came to speak the language of trade-offs and constraints rather than growth and progress. In the pre-Proposition 13 era, policymakers could think first of what programs they wanted to expand and feel confident that revenues would be available. After 1978, the dominant mood forced officials to revise spending priorities to fit fixed revenues. New programs had to be 'marketed', not merely announced, since they took money away from ongoing activities or necessitated raising fees or taxes."[51] (Which, one should add, became nearly impossible.) And it changed the center of social gravity—from the young to the old, from mobility to security.

IV

Within months of the passage of Proposition 13, Jarvis and Gann had a noisy falling-out. Gann was proceeding with a spending limit initiative that Jarvis, recorded by an off-air microphone before the taping of a public television program, said was "shit." He was not going to blast Gann, he told the people around him, and then immediately did. "I don't give a damn. Gann is trying to promote something to make money. For Gann." Asked for a reaction, Gann declared that "Howard has a very difficult problem with the English language. It's hard for him to get above a two-letter word. He says 'I' and 'me' very well . . . Howard and I know how irrational he is."[52] But there was plenty of potential left in the tax revolt and in the larger assault on elective government; separate or together, they were both determined to work it.

Gann in fact would have an easy time getting his measure, Proposition 4, which he called "the Spirit of 13," on a special election ballot in November 1979. It limited the growth of state and local spending to no more than the increase in population plus the increase in cost of living or the increase in personal income, whichever was *lower*, and prohibited what have since become widely known as unfunded mandates—legislative impositions requiring local governments to operate programs or provide services for which no state funds were appropriated. Given the constraints on local agencies, the latter was a good idea in principle, but it turned out to be unenforceable: The legislature would simply pretend that its mandates had no fiscal consequences for counties or cities and do more or less what it pleased. But the other part of Gann was a booby trap. Even in 1979, when inflation was running into the double digits, it was clear to some people that the spending limits, which applied to state government and separately to each local jurisdiction, had great potential for mischief in a region (and in communities) where school enrollment, prison populations, and health costs (as elsewhere in the country) rose unevenly, and often far more quickly than population, and where a growing economy imposed demands on public services (for roads, utilities, and other public infrastructure) that could easily run ahead of inflation. But in the great post-Proposition 13 rush to join up, the Gann limits, cosponsored by Assembly Speaker Leo McCarthy of San Francisco, a fully certified liberal Democrat, had no real opposition and passed overwhelmingly. It was just one of many indications of how far—and how fast—Proposition 13 had moved the political center.

Jarvis, in the meantime, had gone national—and international. Within a week of the election he had become a celebrity, the very incarnation of the mad-as-hell taxpayer who wasn't going to take it anymore, appearing on the cover of *Time*, on the national news talk shows ("Imagine Howard Jarvis from Magna, Utah," he said with mock humility, "being interviewed on 'Meet the Press'"), and being introduced around Washington to politicians eager to shake his hand, first by California's Republican Sam Hayakawa (who had forgotten all about Jarvis's fund-raising hustle two years earlier), and then by Democratic Senator Alan Cranston, "a decent man," in Jarvis's view, who "showed a lack of guts by campaigning all out against 13, and then turning around as soon as he saw the votes come in and start saying nice things about it."[53]

"You certainly had a big victory," Cranston was reported to have told Jarvis. "You certainly got your ass kicked off," Jarvis reportedly replied.[54] By December, Jarvis was in Paris at the invitation of then-mayor Jacques Chirac, and in London, appearing before the Certified Union of Taxpayers, taping a broadcast for the BBC, and meeting with Margaret Thatcher, who was then the Tory leader but had not yet become prime minister.[55]

More ominously, in September his newly formed American Tax Reduction Movement had sent mailgrams to every major party candidate for Congress—870 House candidates, 66 Senate candidates—demanding support for his program to cut federal spending by $100 billion in the next four years and federal taxes by $50 billion (demands that may seem modest by Gingrichian "Contract with America" standards, but seemed hardly modest at the time). Those who supported the plan should "send me a telegram." Those who did not "need do nothing; [but] a failure to respond will automatically list you as an opponent," and all opponents would be targeted by ARM for defeat. At least three hundred candidates took the pledge.

Ultimately, that threat turned to farce. Again Jarvis was soliciting funds from his productive mailing lists for the campaign; again there was no sign that those who took the pledge got very much from Jarvis. Nonetheless—Jarvis's not-uncharacteristic failure to deliver funds notwithstanding—Proposition 13 set off a flurry of Jarvisite tax revolts across the country. None was as radical as California's, which, as ever, was in a class by itself in its uncompromising search for ideal solutions, but the movement was certainly vigorous enough to get the attention of a Republican presidential candidate from California who had himself dabbled in the process. Within a year there were tax limitation measures on the ballot in seventeen states, all but five of which were ultimately approved (by 1980 there would be some sort of tax revolt in forty-three), among them two, in Idaho and Massachusetts, where voters explicitly followed California's lead in approving measures that both cut and limited property taxes. In addition, two others, Colorado and New Jersey, enacted spending limits.

By 1994, virtually all states had imposed some new constitutional restrictions on local or state taxes and/or imposed spending restrictions. Some, like Michigan, which, in 1993–94, faced its own property tax revolt among older voters, had also shifted at least some of their school support from property taxes to the sales tax and other revenues.[56] Jarvis and Gann thereby made tax-cut fever, as the country has long since learned, not only the centerpiece of the Reagan presidency two years later, but a seemingly immutable feature of American politics. "Reagan," Citrin wrote in 1986, shortly after Jarvis died, "quickly polished Jarvis' rhetoric, and his presidency enshrined the gadfly's credo as national policy," an observation that is almost as true now—and maybe as understated—as it was then.[57] In 1996, Oregon voters, who had rejected a property tax limition measure fifteen years earlier, became the most recent to join the parade, approving Measure 47, which, as in California, rolled back property taxes (albeit not as severely) and left it to the legislature to choose among schools and other property tax-dependent services which would take the biggest hit.[58] To Americans who came of age since 1980, it may seem surprising that it was ever otherwise.

But for Jarvis and Gann, and to some extent for the larger assault on the powers and perogatives of government, the real action, now increasingly commercialized and professionalized, remained in California.[59] Unlike the signature campaign for Proposition 13, which had cost almost nothing, Jarvis raised and spent more than $2.1 million to get enough signatures to get Proposition 9, an initiative which would have cut the state income tax in half, on the June 1980 ballot. Much of that money was raised by Butcher-Forde, who now had the invaluable mailing lists generated in the Proposition 13 campaign, and who had not only learned how to use the same piece of direct mail—as ever in the official-looking envelope—to generate both signatures and contributions, but how to test-market issues before there was even a sponsor for them. Thus it was never quite clear whether Proposition 9 really began with Jarvis, by now a valuable piece of marketing property, or with his direct-mail wizards. What was clear was that a great deal of the campaign money—for direct mail, for media campaigns, for consulting services, for polling—went directly into Butcher-Forde's coffers.[60]

In the end, despite its overwhelming lead in the early polls, Proposition 9 was voted down, in part because this time the additional loss—estimated at $4.8 billion in the first year—may indeed have scared voters, in part because many voters were in fact convinced that the biggest gainers would be the rich, and in part because the income tax was generally perceived to be fairer, or at least more predictable, and more related to ability to pay, than the property tax.

Despite that setback, the rollback on taxes went on. (The typical California voter, it has been said, is a white, fifty-year-old housewife in Van Nuys with a household income of $50,000 a year; to this day, polls of such voters indicate that 55 percent believe their taxes are unaffordable.)[61] In June 1982 California voters passed initiatives abolishing all state gift and inheritance taxes, excepting only that portion of the tax that would qualify for an equivalent federal tax credit, and (in another Jarvis-sponsored measure) requiring indexing of state personal income tax brackets for inflation. In 1986, overturning prior court decisions that had chopped a few small loopholes in Proposition 13, they approved a Jarvis-sponsored initiative—passed shortly after his death—restating and tightening Proposition 13's provisions that specifically require approval of any new general tax by two-thirds of the governing body and a majority of voters; special taxes—those designated for a particular purpose—require a two-thirds vote of the electorate. In the meantime, the legislature, catching the spirit of 13, joined the parade, placing before voters a string of constitutional amendments further extending Proposition 13's property tax protections.

All told, there would be sixteen or eighteen of them in the two decades after its passage, some of them originating through the initiative from the Jarvis organization, some from the legislature: one eliminating loopholes in Proposition 13's tax restrictions that creative city or county officials had begun to exploit; another trying to reverse court decisions that limited its application to noncharter cities; others to correct ambiguities and eliminate other problems created by sloppy drafting; still others excluding solar energy systems and new residential fire protections from reassessment; and still others allowing property tax postponement for elderly homeowners, permitting homeowners moving from one residence to another of equal or lower price to pay no more in property tax than they had on the previous home, and exempting replacement residences for the disabled from higher assessments.[62]

The most important, however, allowed the frozen assessment on a family home to be passed from one generation to another. The original initiative permitted tax assessors to reappraise a home at market value when it was transferred from one owner to another. These new amendments provided that when parents transferred a family residence to their children, the original assessment should remain in place ad infinitum—a "dynasty provision" that was eventually extended to cases where property is transferred directly to grandchildren as well—thus formally creating what may be the nation's first legally defined hereditary nobility of property.

The cumulative effect of those measures was not only the massive transfer of control from local government to Sacramento discussed above—hardly what the Proposition 13 rebels wanted—but a massive constriction of the power of all government to manage revenues. Because it effectively ended the real power of local government to control the property tax—and because the state began to shift it around at will, "it is stretching," in the words of one analysis, "to continue to characterize California's property tax as a *local* revenue source."[63]

And in moving fiscal authority to Sacramento, and dividing it uncertainly between scores of state and local agencies whose impact on one another became increasingly unmanageable and incomprehensible, it also produced an explosion of lobbyists and consultants representing cities, school districts, and other local public agencies in Sacramento—hundreds of them. Where once cities and counties had fiscal autonomy and generally relied on their associations to look out for their (generally common) interests, many now hired their own and established full-time lobbying offices in the capital or engaged independent lobbying firms to represent them.

The Los Angeles Public Schools, the City of Los Angeles, Santa Clara County, the City of San Jose, the San Diego Public Schools, San Diego County, the Orange County School Superintendent's Office, and the Kern County Schools all maintain full-time Sacramento lobbying staffs and offices, as do the Metropolitan Water District of Southern California, the Santa Clara County Water District, the East Bay Municipal Utility District, and other major publicly owned utility districts. Hundreds more hire one of the big lobbying firms. And the more efforts were exerted to make the system manageable, the more unmanageable and incomprehensible it became, thus setting off an accelerating cycle of reforms—in the legislature and increasingly by the initiative route—which made the process even more unmanageable.

V

Action and reaction: By the late 1980s, as the clients for state services outpaced the rise in the state's population, Proposition 4, the Gann spending limit, which passed so easily and with so little debate or examination in the high-inflation year of 1979, began to bite. Under Gann, neither state nor local spending could increase faster than population plus inflation. But as inflation, which had been running into the double digits when Gann was passed, abated, and as the state's client populations—particularly school enrollment and prison inmates—began to outrun the rise in the general population, and the Gann spending limits began to pinch, Governor George Deukmejian, the Republican who had succeeded Jerry Brown in 1983, began to squeeze K–12 spending, which represented far and away the largest single part of the state budget, and was thus the largest and most convenient target in any attempt to cut it. That had obvious fiscal consequences for schools, but it also generated great uncertainty for local districts in what they could expect in the way of revenues, making it increasingly difficult to hire teachers and plan budgets in time for each new academic year.

The clincher came in 1987. Although Deukmejian could have dodged, or at least postponed, the spending squeeze by shifting some state funds to local governments, which were not yet brushing up against their spending limits; although many of their facilities—parks, libraries, schools—were rapidly deteriorating for lack of maintenance; and though their services were increasingly stretched, Deukmejian, stubbornly resisting pleas from local officials, refunded $1.2 billion to the taxpayers. In Deukmejian's view, it was what the voters had intended, and thus the only honorable thing to do. The average taxpayer's refund was $71.

In response, Louis "Bill" Honig, California's independently elected school superintendent, backed by Attorney General John Van de Kamp—like Honig a Democrat, and like Honig independently elected—teamed up with the League of Women Voters, the state's association of police chiefs, and a number of other public employee groups to run Proposition 71, an initiative that would have loosened the Gann limits and given state and local governments greater spending flexibility by changing the inflation formula to allow spending to rise either according to the rise in state personal income or the national consumer price index, whichever was *higher*. If there weren't any adjustment, they argued, the state would have to cut deeper and deeper into essential spending for education, public safety, and other services. Deukmejian, as might be expected, opposed Proposition 71.

The measure, which appeared on the primary ballot in June 1988, was defeated by just over 100,000 votes, roughly one percent of the 10 million cast—in 1991, in yet another ballot measure, the spending caps would finally be revised more or less as Proposition 71 had proposed[64]—but the defeat quickly became prologue to something of considerably greater consequence. In response to Deukmejian's decision to refund the tax money, much of which would have gone to school support—and well before Proposition 71 failed—Honig and the well-heeled California Teachers Association had spent $1.3 million to qualify a more direct and aggressive measure, an initiative, which appeared on the ballot as Proposition 98 in November 1988, and which in some respects was almost a mirror-image of Gann.

But instead of limiting spending, Proposition 98's complex provisions guaranteed a minimum of 40 percent of the state's general fund each year to the public schools and community colleges, or annual increases at least equal to the increase in school enrollment and cost of living, whichever would produce higher revenues. In order to prove its reasonableness, they included a clause that permitted, with a two-thirds vote of each house of the legislature, a temporary waiver of the Proposition 98 formula in cases of economic emergency, but that required that the schools be made whole when the emergency ended. (The last provision was revised in 1991 with a clause establishing a complex "Test Three" that would automatically reduce funding in cases of severe recession but would restore the funding base when things improved.)

When Proposition 71 went down in June, therefore, Honig and the teachers union were ready. Arguing that schools were underfunded and badly overcrowded (both of which were true), and that schools should not be subject to the budgetary whims of the legislature, they went all out to get Proposition 98 passed, ultimately succeeding by virtually the same narrow margin by which Proposition 71 failed.

The campaign for—and passage of—Proposition 98 was a milestone in California politics and public finance almost as significant as Proposition 13 itself. As soon as the returns were in, a number of other public officials and agencies, particularly University of California President David Gardner, began to say publicly what they had been saying privately since the campaign for Proposition 98 began.

Honig's move, they charged, was not just an unfraternal act—traditionally the state's health, welfare, and educational establishments, if not always in harmonic collaboration on budget matters, at least tried not to engage in frontal competition—but one that left them out in the financial cold. Gardner and the UC regents feared, quite legitimately, that the school funding mandated by Proposition 98, by locking up 40 percent (and ultimately more) of the state's general fund, would force higher education to compete with prisons and with the state's skyrocketing health appropriations for the increasingly small portion of the state's revenues that were not formula-driven. But at bottom, they had themselves largely to blame. Although Honig had tried hard to get Gardner and the Board of Regents of the University of California to support the measure easing the Gann limits, they refused to buck the governor who had appointed most of them, and who had treated UC better in the mid-1980s than he treated the schools or the community colleges. While Honig and the public sector employees and the

League of Women Voters campaigned to loosen spending limits for all services, Gardner and the regents, having made their separate peace with the governor, sat quietly on the sidelines.[65]

But Proposition 98 would also turn out to be a bundle of ironies. While its provisions guaranteed minimal funding for schools, after nearly a decade on the books it has never managed to move the state's per-pupil school funding back toward the national average, much less return it into the ranks of the major industrial states. California remains in the bottom quarter of all states in per-pupil school funding. And, of course, Proposition 98 confounds all other funding choices. Although there might be pressing other fiscal needs—for health, or higher education, or social services—a formula that never delivers more than 60 cents of any additional tax dollar to those needs undermines any unified effort by social service groups, even the most liberal, to push for new taxes. And because each year's increase in school funding immediately goes into the base for the following year, thereby leaving still less money for future discretion, both Deukmejian and his successor, Pete Wilson, have treated Proposition 98 more as a ceiling than as a floor for school funding.[66] California schools were getting less in inflation-adjusted dollars in 1997–98 than they got a decade earlier, when Proposition 98 was passed.[67]

Proposition 98 had been sold to the education community as a device that would forever "take us out of the politics of Sacramento [and] eliminate the need to beg for funds," but it turned education funding into a zero-sum game in which various interest groups within the school community—special education, the gifted and talented, the unions representing only teachers, and those representing teachers and teacher aides—began fierce battles among themselves over who would get what.[68] The Proposition 98 formulae, moreover, were so complicated that no more than a handful of people, even among the school lobbies, really understood them. (One late-night budgeting session in the governor's office in the early nineties broke into hysterical laughter when Maureen DiMarco, Governor Pete Wilson's Secretary of Education and Children's Services, and Finance Director Tom Hayes, began to hand dollar bills to the people around the table, among them Wilson himself, in a vain effort to explain how the various tests and triggers in the law actually worked.) In May 1997, when California unexpectedly found itself with $2 billion more in revenues than had been expected in January, a combination of numbers—slower-than-anticipated population growth (which raised per capita income), and somewhat larger growth in school enrollment than projected—forced the state to spend *98 percent* of the new money on schools, even though some counties were still on the verge of bankruptcy and a whole host of other services were strapped.

The upshot of these formulae, needless to say, has been a sausage of unintended consequences, except perhaps for those who had little regard or use for public services to begin with. While Proposition 13, in state-izing school support in 1978, began to equalize school funding between affluent and tax-poor communities, as the state's *Serrano* decisions required, and as the courts in Texas, New Jersey, Vermont, Michigan, and many other states have since mandated, the effect, even in combination with the guarantees of Proposition 98, was, in general, quite the opposite of what the school lobbies and the *Serrano* plaintiffs had hoped for. Instead of leveling up, average California school funding, relative to other states and the nation as a whole, has been leveled down. "Shifting funding responsibility from the local level to the state," wrote economists Robert L. Manwaring and Steven M. Sheffrin of the University of California at Davis, "decreased education expenditures."[69]

VI

At the local level, Proposition 13 and the various measures that followed in its wake produced a wholly unprecedented set of distortions. As might be expected, once the property tax was cut and capped, local governments embarked on a determined search to find replacements for the lost funding. The result has been a cluster of fees and assessments on virtually anything that will stand still for an exaction and doesn't require a vote of the electorate: Developer fees—so much per square foot—on most new residential construction to help build new schools, parks, and playgrounds (some of which are never built, or which turn out to be pathetically inadequate even when they are) that are in turn passed on to buyers in the price of their new homes; increased real estate transfer fees; higher business license fees; and new utility taxes, as well as fee increases for virtually every state and municipal service from planning and zoning permits to admission to state parks and city swimming pools.

In addition, the legislature allowed landowners to create "Mello-Roos Districts" (named for the sponsors of the post-Proposition 13 legislation that established the process), whereby they can vote to assess themselves for the repayment of bonds for new infrastructure—sewers, freeway intersections, drainage—in the areas they propose to develop. Those assessments, too, are ultimately written into the taxes for new homes. At the same time, cities and counties began to create large numbers of new assessment districts to improve landscaping or sidewalks or street lighting that (at least in theory) benefit the properties on which the new assessments are imposed but that were increasingly used to fund projects that could only remotely be described as "lighting" or "landscaping" and were often located far from those who are taxed and theoretically benefit. (It was, said one whimsical critic, an attempt to raise revenues with enough stealth "that the hornets wouldn't get mad.") In 1996, in what may the most flagrant example, the Los Angeles Community College District proposed a lighting and landscape assessment district for projects that included a new football scoreboard on one campus and the construction of an equestrian center on another. In theory, these were supposed to be direct benefits to the property of homeowners located thirty miles away. The district's board approved the project; it was only after the ensuing public uproar that it reconsidered and opted to put the measure on the November ballot, where voters soundly rejected it.

Collectively the new fees and assessments couldn't begin to replace the lost property taxes or cover the increased burdens imposed by the disproportionate increases in school enrollment, prison populations, and health care of the 1980s, much less replace the declines in federal funding, particularly in the cities, which lost large chunks in block grants, model cities money, and other funds beginning in the 1980s. Other major states backed in funds to replace some of those programs; California did not. And while conservatives, conjuring up ever-more creative standards of comparison—taxes and fees per worker, for example[70]—sometimes claimed that public spending had returned to pre-1978 levels, the overall California tax burden, as a percentage of income, is now just slightly above average among the states and remains lower than it had been in the 1970s.[71]

Nonetheless, the new expedients contributed mightily to the frustration and distrust among a growing number of taxpayers who argued that all these devices, many of them made possible by a 1992 state supreme court decision holding that Proposition 13 applied only to taxes, not assessments, were shabby end-runs around Proposition 13 and the various other tax limitation measures that were supposed to prevent such levies. In response, the Howard Jarvis Taxpayers Organization, considerably reduced in membership since the golden days of the early 1980s—down from about 300,000 to fewer than 180,000—but still formidable, qualified yet another initiative, Proposition 218, for the November 1996 ballot that closed those loopholes and thus may represent the final round in the tax-cutting cycle that began with Proposition 13.

The measure, which the sponsors called "The Right to Vote on Taxes Initiative," was based on a simple theory: no local tax, fee, or assessment—none—was permissible without a vote: In some instances, it required a vote of the affected property owners—and property owners only; in some it required a vote of the local electorate generally. Further, no charge of any sort for any project that in theory benefitted certain properties (better lights or sidewalks or parks) could be levied without an engineer's analysis showing that the properties on which those charges fell would actually benefit in proportion to the charges. Thus it was no longer possible, for example, for the city of Port Hueneme, near Ventura, to impose an assessment for improving the view of the beachfront on homeowners who did not actually have a view of the beach. After 218 passed, cities woke up to discover that even when they wanted to raise sewer or garbage fees by a few cents, they had to send individual notices to all affected property owners delineating how each would benefit in proportion to the new charges (a requirement that would itself cost hundreds of thousands of additional dollars even in medium-sized cities like Fresno or Santa Barbara). If a majority objected, the fee could not be raised.

Perhaps even more radical, voting on property-based assessments, say for new lights or sidewalks, had to be weighted according to the proportion of the burden that would be borne by each affected property. The more valuable the property, the more votes the owner had: The owner of a parcel who will have to pay $5,000 gets fifty times the number of votes as the one who was to pay only $100, thus giving large corporations, including foreign corporations, a vastly disproportionate voice. Those who own no property get no vote. That voting requirement, moreover, was imposed, not only on all prospective property-related fees and assessments, but retroactively on everything that had been levied without voter approval since the beginning of 1995. Proposition 218 thus not only established another barrier to the ability of elected government to establish priorities but, in true Hamiltonian fashion, gave electoral privileges to the rich and wellborn—and excluded those not so blessed—in a manner that had not been seriously proposed in America since the abolition of the poll tax.

Although the Jarvis organization had only limited funds for a real campaign, and although some of its leaders themselves doubted they would succeed (largely because of the weighted voting that gave large property a disproportionate voice), the measure passed easily: The final margin was 59–41. Unless the courts ultimately sustain the constitutional challenges that have been filed by the City of Los Angeles and a number of other municipalities, which seems unlikely, Proposition 218 could severely restrict most further local assessments or other exactions for infrastructure and for transit improvements and development, and could thereby reduce local revenues by another $2.5 billion a year.[72] That amounts to only 5 percent of what the locals now take in, but at a time when scores of cities and counties are badly strapped already, it is not an inconsiderable amount. Within weeks of the measure's passage, Moody's began downgrading the credit rating of San Diego, Sacramento, and other major California cities, which had already been lowered after the passage of Proposition 13, another notch. For people in the East, where they still let their elected representatives do such things, said one liberal lobbyist, it's an alien notion. But in California people really seem to want to vote on all taxes.

"I don't think California will fall into the ocean because of Proposition 218," Joel Fox said after 218 passed. But 218 added a new level of uncertainty to a whole range of municipal services, from libraries to parks and even public safety, that had relied in part on funds that could be ginned up through property-based assessments.[73] A few months after its passage, the City of Sacramento completed an ambitious excercise in which citizens were asked, through mailings and at well-attended public forums, to make essential choices about the best way to reduce the city's substantial budget deficit. Ultimately they chose a combination of spending cuts and tax increases. But the tax increases they chose all required voter approval, something that could not even be attempted without a costly special election before budget decisions had to be finalized.[74]

Still, Fox was right in one important sense. Proposition 218 did not change the system established by Proposition 13. It just nailed things down more tightly. It does not eliminate its major inequities and distortions. It does not affect the fees that developers pay, as a condition of approval in the planning process, to finance the infrastructure that their projects require. And those fees necessarily fall largely on the buyers of new homes, thereby compounding the "welcome stranger" shift in tax burden from current property owners to buyers of new property that Proposition 13 set in motion. They place the burden for the construction of new schools, for example, not on the entire community, as had traditionally been the case, but on the new residents. Home developers estimate that fees, new infrastructure, and other mandated expenses now run to between $30,000 and $60,000 for each new home "before they begin digging the first hole in the ground."[75]

Even with those "growth taxes," many new developments never get the amenities—community centers, parks, playgrounds—that older neighborhoods take for granted. Sacramento City Manager

William Edgar, for example, acknowledges that South Natomas, the city's first major post-Proposition 13 development, which is located on the north side of the city, pays far more than its share in property taxes and gets far less than its share of community facilities. The same is true in scores of other developments dating to the early and mid-1980s. That may explain why new housing development in California generally has lagged so far behind the economic recovery of the mid-1990s and so desperately far behind the state's housing needs. In 1996, John Wilson, chief economist for the Bank of America, estimated that California was building 85,000 new units a year when it should be building at least twice that many.[76] What the fees do produce is what planning consultant William Fulton called a "cocoon citizenship," in which the new home-owners "identify only with those people who live in their tract . . . everybody outside is them, even if they live in the same city."[77]

To compound the problems, California's increasing reliance on various developer fees to support new school construction only can work in growing suburbs, where there is residential development, not in existing cities, where high birth rates and immigration, not new housing, drive increases in student population. Or as Fulton put it, "houses don't produce students. People do." And while the state itself generates some bond funding to aid school construction, that money, even if matched by local funds as the law provides, has been inadequate. The result is that the old cities are unable to come up with their share of the funds. Students in central-city districts—who account for much of the state's annual increase in enrollment (averaging about 150,000 a year)—will, in Fulton's words, "continue to try to learn in overcrowded schools, portable classrooms and other makeshift arrangements."[78]

VII

As might be expected, the state's fiscal constraints and the social distortions they generate have brought a pervasive, and often explicit, shift from a communitarian ethic to a fee ethic in which, wherever possible (excepting only public safety), the immediate beneficiary alone is supposed to pay for a growing share of the service that government provides. That's been applied not only to the substantial increases in admission charges for state and county parks, or to the development of California's first privately developed toll roads for those who want to avoid the congestion of the freeways (in tax-averse Orange County, of course), something that would have been unthinkable a generation ago in California's *freeway* culture,[79] or to the sharply rising fee structure of the state's college and universities, but, at the margin, to the public schools as well.

In the early 1980s, to cite one illustration, voters approved a constitutional amendment modifying Proposition 13 that again permitted the issuance of school bonds and tax overrides, provided that they get a two-thirds majority of local voters. That law specifically authorizes districts proposing overrides, which are repaid with a parcel tax on each piece of property, not a tax based on assessed value, to exempt elderly owners of residences from the resulting property tax increase. The exception is based on the presumption that the geezers have no school-age children and thus gain no benefit from better schools. Thus, in 1987, the rapidly growing suburban school district of Elk Grove, south of Sacramento, asked voters to approve a $70 million bond proposal that not only put the burden of repayment on new homes ($9.87 a month for each new house, as opposed to $3.87 for each existing one), but gave all property owners who were over sixty-five a 70 percent reduction in rates.[80] That was, in effect, a triply regressive proposal: it favored the old; it taxed expensive homes at the same rate as modest ones; and it taxed new property more steeply than existing property. But in the judgment of the district's bond consultants (which turned out to be correct), the proposal stood a far better chance of passage in that form, and the district desperately needed the facilities.[81]

The main source of California's "welcome stranger" posture, however, is Proposition 13 itself. Because it assesses all pre-1978 owners at 1975 assessments levels and allows property to be reassessed only when it changes hands, owners of virtually identical homes on the same street often find themselves paying vastly different property taxes. In one not untypical example, the *San Francisco Examiner* in 1990 found two neighboring suburban homes of precisely the same general quality and size (2,400 square feet), both built in 1963. One was still inhabited by the original owner; he paid $742 in property tax. The neighbor, who bought his home in 1986, was paying $3,280.

In the late 1980s, one such taxpayer, Stephanie Nordlinger, brought suit. Nordlinger was a Southern California lawyer who had bought a home in the Baldwin Hills section of Los Angeles in 1988 for $170,000 that the prior owners had bought just two years before for $121,500. In due course, she was informed that her property had been reassessed at $170,100, as the law allowed, and received a property tax bill for $1,701. Subsequently she also discovered that neighbors who lived in nearly identical homes that they had owned since 1975 were paying between $300 and $400, a difference in tax burden that the U.S. Supreme Court called "staggering." The court also took notice of the fact that, as her brief argued, some Beverly Hills mansions were paying less in taxes than people living in little houses in far less desirable places. Moreover, the court found that by 1989 the 44 percent of California property owners who had owned their homes since 1975 paid only 25 percent of the total residential property taxes paid by homeowners statewide.[82] (By the early 1990s, the 43 percent of homeowners who were still assessed at 1975 levels were paying just 20 percent the effective rate for new homeowners.)[83] Nonetheless, in a decision handed down in 1992, the Court rejected Nordlinger's argument that she was denied equal protection under the Constitution, reasoning, in Justice Blackmun's words, that:

> [First] The State has a legitimate interest in neighborhood preservation, continuity and stability . . . The State therefore legitimately can decide to structure its tax system to discourage rapid turnover in homes and businesses, for example, in order to discourage displacement of lower income families by the forces of gentrification, or of established mom-and-pop operations by newer chain operations.
>
> [And, second] The State legitimately can conclude that a new owner at the time of acquiring his property

does not have the same reliance interest warranting protection against higher taxes as does an existing owner [who], already saddled with his purchase, does not have the option of deciding not to buy his home if taxes become prohibitively high . . . In short, the State may decide that it is worse to have owned and lost, than never to have owned at all.[84]

Justice John Paul Stevens, in lone dissent, seemed to have the weight of precedent and logic on his side—including a 1989 decision in a West Virginia case by the same justices involving very nearly the same issues.[85]

The selective provision of benefits based on the timing of one's membership in a class [Stevens wrote] is rarely a legitimate state interest. Similarly situated neighbors have an equal right to share in the benefits of local government. It would obviously be unconstitutional to provide one with more or better fire or police protection than the other; it is just as plainly unconstitutional to require one to pay five times as much in property taxes as the other for the same government services.

Stevens sardonically referred to the privileged taxpayers as "the Squires"—squires both among homeowners and businesses—particularly in light of the fact that what he called "the Proposition 13 windfall" can be passed indefinitely from generation to generation, a policy which favors the "housing needs of children with homeowner-parents over children with non-homeowner parents."

The story was, in fact, not as simple. Subsequent studies found that Proposition 13, for all the inequities and distortions it produced, also led, paradoxically, to a more progressive property tax overall than the conventional ad valorem tax, because it was people with high incomes who paid far and away the largest share of the residential property tax. "Both lower-income and elderly homeowners," in the words of economist Arthur O'Sullivan and his colleagues, "benefit from Proposition 13 because they are more concentrated in earlier base years. In California's high priced real estate market, lower-income individuals, on average, are able to own a home today only if they bought it in the distant past."[86] A few years earlier, Jarvis, comparing the new situation with the old, had put it more bluntly: "There are two $50,000 houses next to each other. Someone comes along and buys one of them for $80,000. That raises the taxes on similar property for miles around to $80,000, whether they like it or not. And that is what is really unfair. What we did cured 99 and 99/100% of this thieving system they had before."[87]

But those older and lower income individuals who bought their homes in the distant past, and the children and grandchildren to whom they can leave their homes with the low dynasty provision tax assessments, are, of course, disproportionately white—members of the generation of the fifties and sixties—and those who tend to lose out in this arrangement, and who are sometimes shut out of the housing market altogether are disproportionately young and Hispanic and Asian. And to say that "lower-income individuals . . . are able to own a home today only if they bought it in the distant past" is hardly a celebration of equity in a happy new age.

Yet even if the tax inequities in residential property are defensible as a necessary cost of keeping retirees secure in their homes, they are totally indefensible with regard to business property. If Penney's builds a new store across the road from Gottschalks, it will be assessed at the full cost of the property, not counting the various fees new developments must pay in addition, while its competitor pays on its 1975 assessment or on whatever it paid when it bought or built its facility. (As of 1996, an estimated 50 percent or so of business property paid taxes based on 1975 acquisition costs, pegging the real property tax rates on some business at levels of 0.2 percent.)[88] That, as might be expected, generates still further distortions and impedes competition by giving established businesses a measurable advantage.[89] Equally important, it discourages the most productive use of land. Lenny Goldberg, head of the liberal California Tax Reform Association and consultant to various labor and other liberal groups, who has followed (and engaged in) California's tax wars for many years, points out that rising land values "should help transform inefficient, low-level land uses (e.g., gas stations, used car lots, junkyards) into higher value-producing property. Rising property taxes serve that function by increasing the carrying costs of underutilized land [and] discourage speculative witholding of land from the market . . ."[90]

Proposition 13, instead, gives all the wrong signals, a problem compounded by the slow turnover of commercial property, which is often held and leased long term, "so that it may not change hands for a long period. If a company wants to avoid reassessment, it only need to lease property rather than sell it outright . . . Rising land values and rising incomes earned from the property (thus) are never captured." When Intel builds a plant and equips it, it is not only assessed at market value; it must also pay all the attendant fees, exactions, mitigations, and other charges that are imposed on new development. But the surrounding businesses, which benefit from that activity, and which see the value of their businesses go up as a result, pay nothing. They simply get the windfall. New investment is taxed; the attendant increase in land values is not.

That, too, brought legal action. In 1986, Macy's of California was involved in a leveraged buyout, which triggered a reassessment, bringing a tax bill amounting to several times those of its nearby competitors. Macy's, like those competitors, Sears and Penney's, had had a store at the Sun Valley Mall in Concord, a suburb east of San Francisco, since the 1970s, where leasing was the routine way of doing business. The company, noting that 86 percent of the commercial properties in the Sun Valley Mall had not changed hands and thus were not reassessed, was granted a hearing by the U.S. Supreme Court in a lawsuit charging that Proposition 13 violated both the Commerce Clause and constitutional equal protection guarantees. But as the case began to draw attention, Macy's got so many threats of boycott from the rabid defenders of Proposition 13, some organized by the Howard Jarvis group, some generated by other groups—including thousands of cancelled or returned credit cards—that it dropped the case. Welcome, stranger.

VIII

When the legislature worked out the first post-Proposition 13 division of the local property taxes in the summer of 1978, it gave a substantial chunk of what remained to the counties and cities, then replaced most (though hardly all) of what the schools had lost from its own (momentarily) ample coffers. Even then it seemed unlikely that with tax rates capped at 1 percent, the additional property tax revenues that the average community would gain from new development, and residential development in particular, would be sufficient to fund the additional schools, parks, and other services that families with children would require. Thus, in addition to all the various fees and assessments that local communities imposed, there developed by the mid-1980s what came to be called "fiscalization of land use," planning and zoning choices made not so much from the point of view of what would most enhance the health of the whole community—the attraction of clean light manufacturing operations, for example, that promised well-paying jobs, or the creation of balanced residential development that provided housing for the low- and middle-income families that came with new industry—but what one city manager called "cash box zoning" designed to attract development that would maximize tax revenue.

And since the biggest and cheapest source of local revenue was the sales tax, the planners not only pursued shopping centers, outlet stores, and auto malls; they often did so in preference over employers engaged in light manufacturing, even if they promised better jobs, because their enterprises did not return any sales tax to the local community: You wanted the plant next door, where it provided jobs for your residents, but you wanted the mall inside your jurisdictional limits, where it generated sales tax income for you. In one such instance, planners in Monrovia, a city at the foot of the San Gabriel Mountains about twenty-five miles east of Los Angeles, went all-out to get a Price Club store instead of the high-tech manufacturing plant that Datatape, at that time a subsidiary of Kodak, was considering for the site. Datatape would bring good jobs, but as City Manager Rod Gould said at the time, it would have much in city services as it would have generated in city One indication of how intense the competition has been was his unwillingness, while he was negotiating the deal in 1994, to disclose the name of the firm, because "it might get picked off by one of my neighbors."[91] In another instance, Apple Computer was only allowed to install a new facility in a suburban commercial development after it agreed to put in retail space on the ground floor so that the project would pay for itself in the tax collector's office.

There are, of course, economic development battles all over the country in which communities and states compete to provide tax advantages and other goodies to corporations willing to build new plants—or even to keep existing ones—in the host community. But in California, what Planning Consultant Fulton calls this "sordid and depressing war" is focused largely on sales tax-paying retail businesses. Fulton describes the result in the coastal city of Ventura, where he lives, and where nearby cities were once "intimidated by our Maginot Line of retail establishments, a regional mall, a half-dozen significant shopping centers and hundreds of small, locally owned businesses selling everything from running shoes to darts."[92]

> Recently, however, the neighboring cities have figured out how to slip around our Maginot Line. They have spent the past several years providing tax abatements and other incentives to various businesses, and as a result they have amassed impressive weaponry along the freeway near our border: auto dealerships, outlet malls, movie theaters and, most devastating, that nuclear bomb of retailers, a Wal-Mart.
>
> The result? Our town has lost its once-impressive lead in sales-tax revenues, and our regional mall has been decimated. Now our city manager is busy devising a counterattack. But as in all arms races, the winners are losing as well. The neighboring cities are teetering on the brink of insolvency because of all the subsidies they have proferred to the retailers. So while our mayor gets hammered for not doling out enough goodies to lure

the retailers, the other two mayors get hammered for literally giving away the store.

The prime instruments of the battle for the sales tax have been the state's 350 redevelopment agencies, entities established (at least in theory) to revitalize decayed urban areas. But "what started as a war against blight has mutated," in the words of a Santa Cruz developer and school board member named Doug Kaplan, "into a war between cities for sales tax revenue." School districts can only issue bonds with the approval of two-thirds of the local voters, but redevelopment agencies can issue bonds, which are supposed to be repaid from the tax increments on the rehabilitated property, on the vote of three or four agency directors. As a consequence, California's redevelopment agencies now owe more than $10 billion, several times the bonded debt of all of the state's 1,000 local school districts. And that, of course, sucks a huge chunk out of the local tax base—including the tax base of the schools —"building shopping centers and superstores with money that should have gone to public schools."[93] More than half the state's redevelopment districts have been created since the passage of Proposition 13; by 1990, their assessed valuation represented 6 percent of California's property tax base. "Blight," as some have said, "has been given an overbroad meaning."[94]

There have been other battlegrounds in these beggar-thy-neighbor wars as well, even in the booming years of the 1980s. Probably the most obvious of them has been the wave of new city incorporations—essentially secession from the counties in which those putative cities are located—by residents of places, as in Citrus Heights, a Sacramento suburb, that saw an opportunity to pick off a few lucrative sales tax-paying properties, usually centered around a big shopping mall, and (in the view of their proponents) buy themselves better municipal services, police protection particularly, than the half-starved county had been able to provide, and, where possible, escape from the problems that the cops were there to guard against. In the latter respect, of course, they are not so different from the gated communities to which ever more Californians are moving.

The inevitable outcome of this process is that the county in which the incorporation takes place (and over which the county has little control) is deprived of the sales taxes that the new city grabbed off, and thus left even more impoverished and less able to service its other citizens. In the 1970s, seventeen cities were incorporated in California. In the 1980s there were thirty-four, and in 1991 there were seven more, the largest number for a single year in history, nearly all of them suburban or exurban enclaves with only a vague resemblance to a conventional city: Laguna Hills, Calabasas, Malibu, Lake Forest, Dana Point, Diamond Bar. Some, like Yucaipa and Yucca Valley, were in the fast-growing "Inland Empire" areas east of Los Angeles, but most were in Los Angeles, Orange, or San Diego counties.

Almost none of them, in fact, provide the full range of city services that residents in the East and Midwest are used to—fire protection is handled by the same independent fire district that had provided it before, water supplied by the same utility district as before, parks maintained by the same independent park and recreation district, police services provided under contract by the county sheriff. What the new cities did have was planning and zoning authority—meaning the power to manage traffic and, wherever possible, to control commercial development, check the spread of high-rise office buildings, to which the elected county supervisors, the "downtown" authorities in places like Orange County, with their cozy relationship to developers, were particularly hospitable—and keep poor and low-income housing out.[95]

For every secessionary attempt that succeeded, there were probably three or four that failed—incorporation attempts, attempts to secede from school districts, efforts to split off from one county and create another—either because the voters rejected them or because they were blocked by the courts. In 1982, for example, when an attempt was made to take part of the large Fullerton High School District in suburban Orange County and merge it with the Yorba Linda Elementary School District, the state supreme court, then dominated by the liberal appointees of Pat and Jerry Brown, blocked it, noting that "many in the area may see it as an attempt to isolate the white students of Yorba Linda from contact with a significant number of minority students."[96] But the impulse is always there.

In the early 1990s, a decade too late, the legislature finally enacted a bill that required city incorporations to be revenue neutral and thus reduced the incentive for beggar-thy-neighbor breakaways. But it did not eliminate it, since many of the secessionist groups still saw great advantage in the power to do their own planning and zoning. That can be read either as a healthy attempt to bring that power closer to the neighborhoods that are most affected, or as a subtle form of NIMBYism by middle class and/or predominantly established groups to shut out newer and poorer groups and the social service agencies and low-income housing—what there still was of it—that the powers downtown were seen as trying to impose on them. At one time, the powers downtown had some fiscal flexibility—and a reasonable incentive in the prospect of getting new property tax revenues—to accommodate outlying areas by promising them better services. But since Proposition 13 they have had little of either.

Nor does the new incorporation law, which applies only to new cities within counties, apply to the most far-reaching of those attempts at secession, the campaign of a coalition of business and homeowner groups in the sprawling San Fernando Valley, now populated by over 1.2 million people, about one-third the population of Los Angeles, to secede from the city of Los Angeles itself. This virtually unprecedented effort had been fanned by Paula Boland, the politically ambitious Republican Assemblywoman from Granada Hills who had slept in her car after her home was damaged in the Northridge earthquake, and who was then preparing to run for the state senate. It will probably not succeed, because the economic and political ties between the Valley and the city—water rights not least among them—are intertwined and knotted too tightly. The Valley, moreover, is an amorphous collection of developer-spawned post-office addresses in the northwest corner of Los Angeles—Northridge, Pacoima, Chatsworth, Canoga Park, Van Nuys, Tarzana, North Hollywood, Panorama City, Studio City, Woodland Hills, Encino—that really has no identity other than perhaps its resentment of Downtown and its history of organized resistance to the school busing programs of the 1970s and early 1980s.

Yet the pressure for a new city in the Valley will almost certainly continue, both as a device to negotiate for a larger share of Los Angeles's scarce resources and as a symbol of the decaying power of communities to hold themselves together. Boland did get a bill through the Republican-controlled state assembly that would have made Los Angeles powerless to stop it and that called attention again both to the stresses and the illusions of California's tax-revolt era. (A similar Boland measure authorizing the breakup of the Los Angeles school system was enacted in 1995, although no breakup has yet occurred.) The bill was blocked by the Democrats in the senate—in 1996, Boland herself was defeated in her senate race— but in the spring of 1997, an amended (and much weaker) secession bill sponsored by Bill Lockyer, the Democratic leader of the senate, was again pending in the legislature.[97]

The argument, echoing those in many other secessionist communities, is that the powers downtown are too far away from the Valley and too unresponsive to its needs. The Valley, contrary to its reputation—earned, for example, in its strong early support for Proposition 13, and later in the rapid acquittal by an all-white jury in adjacent Simi Valley of the cops who beat up Rodney King— does in fact have ethnic diversity, if not neighborhood integration (31 percent Latino, 4 percent black, 8 percent Asian), though it still is more affluent, on average, and has a far larger percentage of whites than the city of Los Angeles as a whole.[98] (If it became a city, it would be the nation's sixth largest, and easily its whitest.)[99]

Still, as historian Kevin Starr said, the Valley is not hallucinating in its belief that it has problems. "As the most representatively mid-American portion of the city," Starr wrote in a piece called "Deconstructing Los Angeles,"[100] "it is suffering, with special intensity, that sense of active and present danger, of annihilation even, increasingly seizing the middle classes in the United States." Nor is it so different from hundreds of other American suburbs whose residents slowly find themselves re-engulfed in all the things they tried to escape from.

But the Valley is still radically different from the rest of Los

Angeles—an area dominated by people who moved there in the first place to avoid, or get away from, the problems of Los Angeles, and as a middle class, afflicted with the heightened frustrations that California's excessive Golden State expectations generated. (As the debate was raging, the city's alternative newspaper, *L.A. Weekly,* asked readers to choose a name for the new city. Among the not-so-whimsical choices: Minivan Nuys, Fencino, and Twenty-nine Malls.) In the case of California's property-tax deprived communities, that frustration is further compounded by the inability of local governments to respond to even the most severe local problems. A decade ago, when Los Angeles, pressed by increasing rates of violence, tried to pass a small tax increase to hire more police officers, it failed to get the two-thirds majority that Proposition 13 required.

Meanwhile, the perception of community continues to shrivel, and the competition between neighboring communities to get sales tax-paying businesses increases. Where businesses providing good jobs had once benefited a whole region, regardless of their exact location, the shopping centers and auto malls that are now the apples of the planners' eyes serve almost no one except the particular place in which they are persuaded to locate. Proposition 13, said planning consultant Fulton, decoupled the city treasury from the local economy. "The outlet mall in Oxnard—that's what most California cities now mean by economic development. What they're trying to do is steal sales taxes from the next city. They have no stake in growing the local economy." In 1991–94, the legislature, which had been rolling over an accumulating pot of red ink in the late 1980s and early 1990s and was facing an increasingly severe state deficit, grabbed back between $3 and $4 billion annually in property taxes from the cities and counties in order to meet its Proposition 98 obligations to the schools. After that shift, the pressure to go after sales taxes, and the indifference to development that primarily generated property taxes, became even greater.

The subtext here is not merely the distortion of economic and social priorities but the institutionalization of a slow-growth/no-growth outlook that had been woven into the tax revolt almost from the start. Lenny Goldberg, the liberal tax reformer, notes that the system of developer fees and other exactions for freeway inter-changes, schools, water systems, and sewers has shifted the burden from the general community to new businesses and residences, and from big business to little business, which turns over faster. More-over, it has imposed a large share of the costs for new business at the front end, where it's least affordable, not taxing the business down the line as it becomes more profitable and thus, in a sense, sharing in its growth.

"If local governments thought growth would bring amenities like libraries or museums, they'd act differently," Goldberg says, and many builders and developers agree with him. "But with Proposition 13, people see the costs of growth; they don't see the benefits."[101] That's also fostered the virtually unchecked regulatory climate about which business so vehemently complains and which, in truth, adds significantly to the cost of new development. But since there is little economic downside to environmental and other local regulatory punctiliousness, no one but the developers is in-clined to worry too much. Local goverment in California now re-sponds first to its own treasury, as Fulton said, not to the local econ-omy. Although some cities have, like places all over the country, strained to give tax breaks to manufacturers, most have much less stake in growing the economy than their counterparts elsewhere.

Slow growth/no growth appears to have been part of the Proposition 13 mix from the start. It was certainly one of the things that brought homeowners together in the years before 1978, and, although one rarely hears it from politicians, many of Proposition 13's defenders have been privately saying it for the better part of twenty years. And slow growth has certainly been fostered by the fiscalization of land use that followed the passage of 13, which, as Fulton said, has made housing and other property tax-oriented development a bad deal.[102] Try to argue that the measure needs to be revised because it stifles growth and makes it hard to build the infrastructure that the state needs to accommodate its growing popu-lation, and you hear some cross between "so what" and "great— that's what it ought to be doing." In the two decades since the mid-1970s, real-estate developers may be the only prominent group in California who, as a class, are as disparaged as politicians.[103]

The opponents of Proposition 218, the 1996 initiative which sought to shut the few loopholes local governments had found around the property tax limitations of Proposition 13 and its successors, kept wanting to argue that Proposition 218 would make it still harder for local governments to accommodate growth—to construct the freeway interchanges, fund the transit, develop the parks that new developments required—but found no way to do it without hurting their cause with slow-growth and environmental groups more than they would further it. And, in 1991, when a coalition of developers, school groups, and public employee organizations worked out a deal to ease the Gann spending limits and raise the pathetically inadequate gasoline tax (much of it for light rail and other public transit projects), they had a difficult time persuading the state's environmental organizations not to oppose it. It was approved by voters by the narrowest of margins.

And, as usual, the ethnicity of the new people that growth was supposed to accommodate was subtly woven into the no-growth position. Lo quotes James K. Lee, head of a group called Citizens for Property Tax Relief, in a 1994 interview, on protecting property from the burden of immigrant-newcomers:

> What we've done with current policies in our state is basically unemploy and disenfranchise the educated populace and make sure we get government programs for the uneducated. What we are left with is guys that dress up in their pajamas when they go to school with a backward baseball cap . . . I'd like to see negative growth. I'd like to see a negative outflow. It would help the state, yes . . . I think they also ought to restrict all government services such as umbrella services like that to citizens.[104]

It would be impossible to determine how significantly those ethnic fears and resentments contribute to the slow-growth impulse, and how much is prompted by narrow NIMBYism. Nor, for that matter, is it possible to separate genuine concerns about clean air, open spaces, endangered species, and all the rest from the narrowest property-based fears about new people and immigrants. What's indisputable is that incentives for any sort of balanced community development were sharply undermined. Even as the "welcome, stranger" system shifted the burden of financing the costs of growth from the general community to the new resident or the new business, and thus undermined the growth incentive, the balance of power in local planning also shifted sharply from public authorities to the private entrepreneurs and landowners, who advanced the costs, not only of the roads, water lines, and sewers that had always been associated with their projects, but of the parks and schools as well. California's local governments are now run by officials who have never raised a tax and who don't understand the connection between services and taxes.

Proposition 13 was, of course, a property tax measure, but it has also been a major influence on how California communities are planned and shaped, and on the sense of community—or lack of it—in which they exist. It has both narrowed the sense of place and curtailed the sense of time in which public choices are made, reducing them to a set of ad hoc single-purpose decisions "laid end to end."[105] In 1995, when Orange County, one of the richest places in the country, had sunk into its epochal municipal bankruptcy—in part because of Treasurer Robert L. Citron's acrobatic attempts to replace at least some of the county's property tax-strapped resources with the fruits of high-yield (and high-risk) investments—County Executive William Popejoy, who was brought in to direct the rescue operation, pleaded with voters to approve a half-cent sales tax increase that would have cost the average resident about $50 a year and raised about $140 million, roughly half of the county's discretionary budget, to protect already-shrunken services. But the proposal never had a chance. By a margin of 3–2, the voters refused. "I don't think," sociologist Lo had said at a conference at UCLA in 1994 to examine the long-term effects of Proposition 13, "that we're in a political community any more."[106]

March of the Plebiscites

‹ ›

I

It's easy to get a good chicken-and-egg argument about what came first in California: Was it the breakdown and unresponsiveness of representative government, or was it the hundreds of voter initiatives that have been proposed, and the scores that have been approved by the voters, to deal with them? But there's no doubt that in the spiral of public alienation and disengagement, of constitutional reform, gridlock, unintended consequences, further alienation, and more reform, it was Howard Jarvis and Paul Gann who started the modern plebiscitary cycle and inaugurated California's new political era.

Theirs was the first and the most powerful in a series of lessons in a new civics. It teaches that because of gridlock, special interest influence sometimes bordering on outright corruption, and extreme in-your-face partisanship and ideology—or some unfathomable combination of all three—normal legislative government does not work. Only the initiative really works, according to this new civics, not merely as a check on irresponsible government, but as a driving engine for major policy initiatives on everything from taxes and environmental regulation to control of illegal immigration and the death penalty. "With the Legislature in a state of almost complete paralysis," said Jim Shultz, who for many years headed The Democracy Center, a San Francisco-based political training and consulting operation for liberal organizations, "the initiative has become the center stage for shaping the course of state policy."[1] One can argue about causes, but few these days would dispute the consequences. Proposition 13 not only spawned the network of consultants, direct-mail specialists, and other business comprising what some people now call, with only minor exaggeration, California's "Initiative Industrial Complex," but prompted a seismic shift in the state's political center of gravity as well.

The initiative, referendum, and recall were all written into the California Constitution in 1911. All were part of the first great burst of Progressive reform enacted in the four years—a period that historian Kevin Starr called the Camelot of the California Progressives[2]—that followed the election of Hiram Johnson as governor in 1910 and that brought a Progressive majority into the legislature with him. That first burst was to include a host of other major reforms: women's suffrage (which got a lot more national attention than the initiative at the time), tougher wages and hours laws, strengthened utility and railroad regulation, pensions for teachers, and free books for schoolchildren.

But the chief target, and certainly the blackest villain in this drama, was the Southern Pacific Railroad. It had dominated the California economy with its power to set extortionate rates for every bushel of wheat and every lemon it carried to market. It owned huge tracts of California land and controlled the California legislature, a great many city governments, and many of the state's courts with unabashed arrogance. A series of scandals arising from the political power of the SP and other California corporations, and the cozy relations they maintained with politicians and judges—"your big banker [as Johnson proclaimed], your big merchant, sinning respectably, joining hands with the criminal and the thug"—made the Progressive takeover possible.[3]

Although Johnson was the son of a Sacramento politician who had himself been a faithful voice and vote for the railroads, he was a classic Progressive of his era. As a small-town professional, a lawyer, aghast at the power of the new trusts of the industrial age, he first gained statewide attention when he helped prosecute members of the graft-ridden San Francisco political and business establishment, among them Mayor Eugene Schmitz and the city's political boss, Abe Ruef.[4] The battle, Johnson often said during the 1910 campaign, was between "the great moral masses [and] the corrupt but powerful few." And among those powerful few, it was the SP, the Octopus of Frank Norris's novel (there named the Pacific and Southwestern Railroad), that these three measures of direct democracy were most meant to check.

> The opponents of these reforms [Johnson said in his
> inaugural] believe the people can not be trusted. On the
> other hand, those of us who espouse these measures do
> so because of our deep-rooted belief in popular govern-
> ment, and not only in the right of the people to govern,
> but in their ability to govern; and this leads us, logically,
> to the belief that if the people have the right, the ability,
> and the intelligence to elect, they have as well the right,
> ability, and the intelligence to reject or recall . . .[5]

The toughest fight in the legislature, which had to draft these amendments and put them before the electorate, was over the recall of judges, an idea that even some Progressives weren't too sure about and that the old political establishment attacked as a "spewing of intoxicated radicalism" by "reckless and desperate revolutionary leaders."[6] No mincing of words there. But even the initiative drew strong opposition—most notably, if not surprisingly, from Grove Johnson, Hiram's sixty-seven-year-old father, who had resigned from the legislature when his politically estranged son was elected governor.

"The voice of the people," the elder Johnson said, "is not the voice of God, for the voice of the people sent Jesus to the cross." These were "wicked innovations." The *Los Angeles Times*, at the time as fierce a voice of oligarchic power and reactionary union busting as there was in the West, warned that the "ignorance and caprice and irresponsibility of the multitudes" would replace "the learning and judgment of the Legislature."[7] From other sources came dire warnings that women's suffrage would spell the end of the family, "unsex society," and destroy the gallantry of men; that direct democracy would discourage able men from running for office, that the recall of judges would undermine stable government and make it an instrument of "the radical and turbulent few," and that the whole package of proposals would lead to "the anarchistic rule of the rabble."[8]

Even writers like Herbert Croly, who were inclined to be sympathetic to the Progressive spirit, warned, as early as 1914, that direct democracy was as likely to be susceptible to abuse and manipulation as elected legislatures, and in some cases more so. As Richard Hofstadter summarized Croly's argument later: "Confronted by an array of technical questions, often phrased in legal language, the voters [in the states that had previously adopted the initiative] shrank from the responsibilities the new system attempted to put upon them. Small and highly organized groups with plenty of funds and skillful publicity could make use of these devices . . . [while] those who expected that the public will, once expressed directly, would bring a radical transformation of the old order were surprised to find the voters exercising their prerogative in the most conservative way, rejecting, for instance, the proposals for municipial ownership, the single tax, and pensions for city employees."[9] But perhaps the most thoughtful and telling criticism came from the *New York Times*, which published a scathing editorial a week after the vote called "Anti-Democracy in California":[10]

> While pretending to give greater right to the voters [the initiative] deprives them of the opportunity effectively and intelligently to use their powers. They receive the right to vote much more often and on a larger number of matters than before, but the number and variety of the votes they are called on to cast does away with all chance of really using sense and discretion as to all of them. The new method is proposed as a check on the machines. But the strength of the machines lies in the inattention and indifference of the voters, and the voters are sure in the long run to be more inattentive and indifferent in proportion to the number of questions forced upon them at one time. When the machine man-

agers get familiar with the working of the new method, they will work it for their own ends far more readily than they work the present method.

In the end, all three measures, as well as nearly twenty other constitutional reforms that appeared on a special election ballot on October 10, 1911, were approved overwhelmingly by the voters, the initiative and referendum (which were written into the same amendment) by a vote of 168,774 to 52,093, the recall by an even wider margin of 178,115 to 53,755. As a consequence, wrote C.K. McClatchy, the editor of the *Sacramento Bee* and a lifelong friend and supporter of Hiram Johnson, when he reviewed the Progressive accomplishments about eighteen months later, "Big Business, the Interests, the Southern Pacific, the grasping and greedy public service corporations, the unclean and the vile in politics and in social and commercial life—these no longer dominate in the halls of legislation. The money changers—the legions of Mammon and of Satan—these have been lashed out of the temple of the people."[11] (The women's suffrage amendment was almost voted down; it passed by a margin of some 3,600 votes, out of nearly 250,000 cast, after the outlying votes came in on the third day. The only measure on the ballot that failed, a relic of the bad old days, was one that would have allowed public officials to ride the trains with free passes from the railroad.)

The initiative and referendum were both instruments of direct democracy borrowed from Switzerland via a growing number of American states, most of them in the West and Midwest, that had been adopting them in the previous dozen years. South Dakota, in 1898, had been the first, followed by Utah, Oregon, Montana, Oklahoma, Maine, Missouri, Arkansas, and Colorado. In their California versions, all allowed voters to initiate governmental actions through petition either to recall an official, to repeal an act of the legislature (the referendum), or to initiate new legislation or a constitutional amendment.

All have been amended a number of times since, but their basic configuration remains unchanged. After review by the attorney general's office to make certain that the measure's title and summary are not wildly misleading and that the wording is more or less legally sound, initiative sponsors now have 150 days to gather the necessary signatures to put a measure on the ballot. In the case of a statutory initiative, valid signatures of registered voters equal to 5 percent of the votes cast in the last gubernatorial election are required. In the case of a constitutional amendment, the number increases to 8 percent—currently just under 440,000 for a statutory measure, and a little under 700,000 for a constitutional amendment. As a practical matter, however, a great many more than those minimums have to be collected for a sponsor to be certain that the signatures are valid and that the petitions don't contain a fatal number of duplicates.[12]

Given the magnitude of the changes that the voters instituted, and the vehemence of the politics, pro and con, that attended the debate, the immediate results were, to put it mildly, minimal. Few voter-initiated statewide referenda have ever qualified for the ballot; the most recent success came in 1982, when the voters overturned the legislature's vote to build a peripheral canal that would have diverted a large quantity of Northern California water from the Sacramento-San Joaquin Delta and moved it directly south to farmers in Central California and to urban users in Los Angeles. (A lot, of course, was already being pumped south, but it was being taken from the delta, which made it more vulnerable in drought years to the requirements of fish protection and other competing demands.)[13]

And while there have been countless recalls of local officials, almost no recall petitions against California state officials have made it to the ballot (the last was in 1914). A number of attempts have been made, particularly in the early 1980s, when the state's supreme court justices were under attack as being too liberal because of their failure to vigorously enforce the death penalty. But while a number of appellate justices have been removed when they failed to win majorities at the periodic reconfirmation elections they must face under the state constitution, none has ever been recalled in California.

Until 1978, the same was generally true for the initiative. In 1914, the first year that the Progressive reforms had any practical effect, six initiatives were approved by the voters (only one of which, dealing with abolition of the poll tax, could be regarded as fundamental). But in the sixty-four years between that time and Jarvis-Gann, there has been only one year, the Depression year of 1934, when more than three initiatives were enacted, and a large proportion of those that have passed have dealt with such unmomentous issues as control of boxing and wrestling, regulation of fishing in parts of Northern California, liquor laws, chiropractic practice, and the institution of Daylight Saving Time. (One that nearly passed was the Depression-era "Ham and Eggs" initiative of 1938, which promised to pay every Californian who was over fifty years old the sum of thirty dollars every Thursday, with "the costs," in Carey McWilliams's words, "to be financed by mechanisms of such Byzantine intricacy that no one could understand them.")[14] All told, forty-two initiatives were passed by the voters between 1911 and 1978, an average of slightly more than one during each two-year election cycle.

Proposition 13 radically changed all that, setting a pattern, not only in the use of new media technologies to advance "populist" causes—some real, some manufactured—but, as Shultz said, re-igniting "the romance of the initiative as a source of real political power."[15] Between November 1978 and November 1996, forty initiatives were approved by the voters, an average of four in each two-year election cycle, and nearly as many as in all the years before 1978. At the same time, many more groups are trying to get measures passed and spending huge amounts of money to do so, or to defeat the efforts of others. Between the 1960s, when nine initiatives qualified for the ballot, and the 1980s the total doubled in every decade; in the 1970s twenty-two qualified; in the 1980s that number rose to forty-six. In the 1990s sixty-one initiatives made it to the ballot, not double the number of the 80s, but easily the largest number in any decade in history and, considering the range of topics, and their breadth and importance, probably the most far-reaching. In the November 1990 election, when there were thirteen initiatives on the ballot, the state's ballot pamphlet contained 222 pages of summary, analysis, and arguments, including more than 100 pages of fine print with the text of those measures. The ballot measures in the November 1996 pamphlet took a relatively modest 110 pages, including 30 pages of minute print.

But the numbers only begin to tell the story. While some of the measures on California's post-Proportion 13 ballots can match almost anything that preceded them for triviality, by almost any measure—cost, length, social and economic importance—many are of such consequence that the real policy decisions are now being made in the plebiscitary process and not in the halls of the legislature or the office of the governor, much less at the school board or the city council. These measures include criminal sentencing, taxation, environmental regulation, civil rights, regulation of smoking, auto insurance rate-setting, transportation policy, and alien exclusion. Increasingly, moreover, governors, legislators, and other public officials are using what had been once regarded as the people's remedy against government to advance their political objectives.

The same goes for "the interests"—the insurance industry, the tobacco companies, the trial lawyers, public employee unions, and, in one instance, that very same Southern Pacific Railroad—that are themselves running and/or bankrolling ballot measures to advance their economic agendas. In November 1988, various interest groups qualified five competing measures for the ballot addressing in one way or another the combination of fraud, waste, and rate gouging that had brought a crisis in the auto insurance system. Many people in Los Angeles were paying $1,250 a year for barebones liability insurance, and about one-fourth of the state's drivers had no coverage at all.

Of those initiatives, one (Proposition 104), which was sponsored by the insurance industry, called for no-fault insurance but prohibited tough rate regulation, in the process rewriting virtually the whole state insurance code. Another (Proposition 100), sponsored by trial lawyers and some consumer groups, contained rate regulation and various procompetitive measures but prohibited no-fault insurance and declared that the public did not wish ever to regulate attorneys' fees. A third (106), sponsored by the industry, limited all attorney contingency fees—not just those in auto cases. A fourth (101), sponsored by a single maverick insurance company, called for cutting insurance rates in half but provided that auto insurance carriers would pay nothing toward anyone's medical damages until all of that person's other forms of insurance were exhausted. And the fifth (103), sponsored by California consumer groups and endorsed by consumer advocate Ralph Nader, imposed a draconian rate regulation scheme and created the elected post of state insurance commissioner to oversee a state insurance department that had become a slave to the industry. But it carefully avoided the issue of no-fault, which, by sharply reducing legal expenses, might have been much more effective in driving down rates. Nader, it was said, had himself become too beholden to the trial lawyers.

Collectively those competing industry-sponsored measures ran to some 100 pages of fine legal print, much of it covering similar subjects and referring to a plethora of other code sections whose significance only an insurance lawyer could have understood. California law provides that when initiatives with provisions covering similar subjects are passed at the same election, the provision in the one that gets the most votes prevails. Two of these industry measures, however, contained poison pills specifically overriding the competing consumer measures in toto, were they also to pass. And since there was no way to be certain what provisions in these measures the courts would regard as dealing with similar matters, and given the general complexity of the five measures and the intricate ways they overlapped, it was impossible even for well-informed voters to determine how they would impinge on one another if more than one passed, much less predict which would pass.

What was clear was that each measure promised part of a real solution but prohibited implementation of a complete one: a no-fault system without regulation to make certain that consumers would benefit from the new system; "reform" derived largely by limiting lawyer fees and thus public access to the legal system; regulation without any means of making sure that rates could really be brought down. All this, in the words of the *Sacramento Bee*, which conducted a rigorous analysis of these measures, was "worse than a parody of what the initiative process is supposed to be about."[16]

In the end, all the special interest measures were voted down, despite the fact that the insurers and the trial lawyers had spent some $80 million on their competing efforts, most of it on thirty-second TV commercials. This was more than George Bush spent that year in his entire presidential campaign. (The big insurance companies alone raised some $70 million to carry Proposition 104 and defeat the competing consumer and lawyer-sponsored measures.)[17] And the one initiative of the five that did pass, Proposition 103, the consumer reform proposal, ultimately turned out to be far weaker than advertised. The first elected commissioner, John Garamendi (1990–94), began to clean up the mess in an insurance department that had been run by political appointees of the governor and dominated by the industry it was supposed to oversee. He also negotiated deals through the corporate thickets of the industry to save thousands of policyholders of some large insurers that were on the verge of going bankrupt.

But the great auto insurance payoff never came. Although 103 promised rate rollbacks and rebates, and although some premiums were ultimately rebated, the rate rollbacks never came, even after tort reform had lowered the industry's costs.[18] The insurance companies managed to keep the process tied up in the courts for the better part of four years, until, in 1994, Garamendi, who had sought the Democratic gubernatorial nomination and lost, was succeeded by a Republican legislator named Charles Quackenbush. Quackenbush had run for the insurance commissioner's job largely on some $2.4 million in insurance industry money—70 percent of his campaign funds came from the industry—and was as beholden to the industry as any of the governor-appointed commissioners of the prereform era had been, if not more so.[19] Within two years of assuming office, Quackenbush was severely reprimanded by the state's auditor general for his department's accumulating backlog of complaints, its failure to examine insurers periodically as the law required, and, more generally, its "limited effectiveness in meeting the public's need for protection from unlawful or unfair practices by insurance companies."[20] Worse, the creation of the office further diffused accountability into yet another low-profile elected position that few voters would ever pay much attention to.

*　　*　　*

In some respects, even the "failures" in high-stakes battles between major economic powers bring a measure of success for their backers, since they prevent the enemy from winning and keep play alive for another day. Some measures, indeed, go on the ballot for no other purpose than to confuse voters and/or divert support from competing propositions, and thus preserve the status quo. And if the insurers could be said to have failed in 1988, a great many others have succeeded in other years on other issues. Where the economic stakes are high, even a huge investment is small next to the money that's riding on the outcome. In 1984, when a single company, Scientific Games of Atlanta, a manufacturer of lottery tickets and other gambling paraphernalia, ponied up virtually all of the $2.3 million needed to qualify an initiative and run the campaign for what became the California Lottery, the voters, formally reassured that since one-third of the proceeds would go to schools this was a noble cause and not just a matter of avarice, jumped at the chance. Since then, of course, Scientific Games and other commercial lottery operators have recouped their investment dozens of times over.[21] The schools, on the other hand, have regretted the lottery ever since. Although it provides them with less than 3 percent of their revenues, whenever school officials complain about inadequate funding, they are confronted by questions from people who believe that the lottery was supposed to have solved the problem. The confusion has subsided in recent years, particularly since the lottery stopped using the phrase "and the schools win, too" in its advertisements, but it has not vanished and still remains an excuse of people who vote against school bonds.

Nonetheless, when the nos on an issue have large sums to spend to defeat an initiative, they can usually generate enough uncertainty and confusion to prevail.[22] In 1996, in one of the most extraordinary examples of the power of money in initiative campaigns, a coalition of high-roller law firms that specialize in securities fraud class action lawsuits—some in California, others in New York, Chicago, Washington, and Philadelphia—spent $15 million to qualify and support Proposition 211, an initiative that would have made it easier for individuals, labor union pension funds, and other disappointed investors to sue corporations and their officers on charges of misrepresenting stock in initial public offerings.

But the $15 million wasn't nearly enough. The industries that particularly depend on such offerings—Silicon Valley electronics firms, Wall Street brokerage houses, and other large corporations, many of them also outside California—fought back with a campaign that swamped the proponents. The $37 million they raised was not only sufficient to trump the lawyers' war chest and easily beat Proposition 211. There was enough left over so that state Chamber of Commerce President Kirk West and the other business operatives who were running the "No on 211" campaign were able to take $2 million of that money and put it into the campaign to defeat Proposition 217, a labor-sponsored initiative on the same ballot that would have reinstituted some upper-income tax brackets (10 percent on individuals making over $115,000; 11 percent on individuals making over $230,000) that the legislature had temporarily imposed in one of the state's more extreme fiscal crises and then allowed to lapse. The diversion of funds from one campaign to another may have been illegal—there were loud complaints, even from some of the Silicon Valley firms, among them Intel and Hewlett-Packard, that had contributed large sums to the campaign against Proposition 211, and didn't wish to be tied to the antitax campaign—though formal sanctions were never imposed by state election officials.[23] But it's hard to imagine that when Hiram Johnson and the Progressives wrote the initiative into the California constitution, it was this kind of battle that they had in mind.

II

There are all manner of explanations why California is now such fertile ground for plebiscitary solutions to social and economic problems and such a wellspring for the rhetoric of alienation from government that underlies it. Not the least of them is the state's enormous size and diversity. In the mid-1940s, when he wrote *Inside U.S.A.*, John Gunther observed that "most Californians have great state pride, whether they were born in California or not,"[24] but it's long since become an understatement to say that there is no single

California polity. In some respects the idea of California has long been as much a literary as a political concept. There are at least a half-dozen major media markets, none of which much overlaps with the others. The Bay Area and Southern California have always been in contention, and not just over water, and the citizens of the coast generally regard themselves as no more connected to the inhabitants of the Central Valley or of the Inland Empire, which stretches from the eastern suburbs of Los Angeles through the desert to the Arizona line, than they do to the people of Kansas or Tennessee. For many residents of San Francisco, the Central Valley is merely a hot and inconvenient barrier on the way to Tahoe, Yosemite, or Reno.

In the early 1990s, when a Northern California assemblyman named Stan Statham was pushing yet another proposal to divide the state (this time into three states), citizens of twenty-seven of the thirty-one counties that put the issue on the ballot as an "advisory" vote, most of them in the rural parts of Northern California, backed it overwhelmingly. Of course it went nowhere except on the lists of crazy-California stories; even if the state could ever decide how to distribute its resources on everything from water to higher education, could anyone imagine the U.S. Congress agreeing to the prospect of four, much less six, senators from ex-California? (When Statham ran in the Republican primary for lieutenant governor in 1994, the issue was all but forgotten, although he was sometimes asked which of these would-be states he proposed to lead.) But it does tell something about the state's state of mind.

Compounding that problem is the state's lack of a strong political party structure, which might have served both as a political-messaging device and a mechanism of political compromise and integration. That, too, dates back to Hiram Johnson and the Progressives, who deeply distrusted parties and passed measures making elections for all local offices, from county supervisors to school boards, nonpartisan; instituting cross-filing in the statewide offices that did remain nominally partisan; and otherwise throttling party organizations.[25] When Pete Wilson, then sitting in a relatively safe U.S. Senate seat, was first considering a race for governor in 1990, Stuart K. Spencer, who had worked for Reagan in California and played a key role in the national campaign against Jimmy Carter, and who was regarded as one of California's most astute political strategists, warned him to stay away from it because, in his view, the state was ungovernable.

Even within the state's disparate regions and markets, the chances that people will hear or see very much on television or on radio dealing with any state issue, much less know the name of their state senator or their assembly member, are slim. With just eighty assembly members and forty state senators, the same number it's had since the beginning of the century, California's senate districts, each with a population of some 800,000 residents, are larger than its fifty-two congressional districts, making it unlikely that many voters will have any direct contact with their representatives. No television station outside Sacramento now has a bureau at the state capitol—the last closed its operations in 1988—and few bother to devote any news coverage to state affairs. They get interested only if the story involves a particularly odious political scandal, of which the state has had a number in recent years, or an especially absurd legislative proposal—a bill calling for public paddling of teenage graffiti artists (which failed), or establishing a publicly funded self-esteem commission (which passed)[26]—to which, as is widely known, California has never been immune.

Making governmental accountability even more difficult is the two-thirds supermajority that the constitution requires in each house of the legislature before a state budget or any other appropriation can be enacted, and before any tax can be raised. That supermajority requirement, as noted in the previous section, gives determined political minorities an effective veto; it contributed to the gridlock that prevented the legislature from offering any real alternative to Proposition 13 until it was too late to stop it, and it continues to foster the impression that the legislature is really not responsive to anyone but the well-heeled special interests.

In some instances, as Robert M. Stern, formerly general counsel of the state's Fair Political Practices Commission, points out, the impression is correct. For many years, for example, the legislature, beset by pressure from developers, oil companies, and a range of other property owners, had dragged its feet on demands for some sort of protection against unchecked development on—and decreasing access to—California's magnificent coast. Such protection, as Stern contends, *might* not have been enacted until it was too late without an initiative, Proposition 20, the California Coastal Protection Act, that was spurred in part by the huge oil spill that followed a major accident on a drilling platform off the Santa Barbara coast in 1969. The voters passed Proposition 20 in 1972—on the same day, incidentally, that they approved another ballot measure, Proposition 17, restoring the death penalty in California. But it's important to emphasize the "might," because there is no way to know how soon the issue might have reached a critical mass in electoral politics. In 1970, two years before Congress passed the federal Endangered Species Act, the California legislature, bucking pressure from developers, builders, and other powerful interests, passed, and Governor Ronald Reagan signed, CEQA, the California Environmental Quality Act, which is even now one of the most stringent environmental protection measures in the country.

The argument about legislative unresponsiveness may be more self-evident when it comes to the state's attempts to deal with the medical and social consequences of smoking. Through most of the 1980s, proposals by individual legislators like Assemblyman Lloyd Connelly of Sacramento to raise California's absurdly low tobacco tax to pay for part of the health costs that the state was facing to treat smoking-related diseases—and incidentally to discourage smoking through public education campaigns and, of course, through higher tobacco prices—went nowhere.

Connelly, who had made a specialty of legislation dealing with toxic substances, couldn't even get a second in committee. It was not until he and others combined with the American Cancer Society, the Lung Association, the California Medical Association, and other health groups to qualify an initiative, Proposition 99, for the November 1988 ballot, raising the cigarette tax by 25 cents a pack, that the matter could even be fully aired—and ultimately passed by the voters. To do that, the backers, spending slightly over $1.8 million, most of it from the Cancer Society, the hospitals, and the physicians, had to overcome a $21 million tobacco industry campaign (including nearly $11 million from Philip Morris and $8.5 million from R.J. Reynolds).[27] The tobacco industry campaign featured TV scare ads showing mobsters hijacking truckloads of cigarettes to sell tax-free on the black market.

And, to cite perhaps the most obvious example, it would be highly improbable for a legislature much dependent on large contributions from big donors to enact any real campaign spending reforms; when such measures have passed, the politicians have been the first in court to get them overturned. Yet here again there are caveats. Even though spending-reform measures keep making it on to the ballot, and even though three have passed, not one has yet been fully implemented. Two competing initiatives, Propositions 68 and 73, were approved in June 1988, but after a Byzantine course in and out of state and federal courts, both ultimately were invalidated on different constitutional grounds, the one in part because it conflicted with the other (which got more votes and was then itself overturned in court).

The third, Proposition 208, which was sponsored by Common Cause (and of which Stern, now codirector of the privately funded California Commission on Campaign Financing, was himself the principal author), was approved by voters in November 1996. A federal judge quickly struck it down, and while its ultimate fate in the appellate courts is not yet certain, if it survives, its prime effect may be to give independently wealthy candidates like Ross Perot, and incumbents who had amassed war chests before its passage, huge advantages over all others. It may also put still more force behind the creation of so-called independent expenditure committees, groups purportedly unconnected with any candidate that, under the Supreme Court's First Amendment decisions on political speech, can spend unlimited amounts.

All of which suggests that in some cases at least, the legislature fails to act because acceptable solutions are truly difficult to fashion. In others, the issue, though seemingly of great moment to somebody (and ultimately approved by voters), say the need for a law declaring English to be the state's official language, doesn't deserve any major legislative response. As the framers of the Constitution well knew, there are times when popular passions ought to be resisted. In still others—crime is the most obvious recent example—legislatures have been only too happy to do the people's will, and more, without deterring similar plebiscitary efforts. (That may be particularly true in California, where the electronic media are often the only overarching form of "community," and where over the course of a decade, as crime hysteria grew, legislators enacted hundreds of crime bills, piling sentence upon sentence, regardless of ultimate cost.)

What may be even more germane in California is that the legislators' very fealty to their increasingly diverse constituents and their diverse and disconnected regions, however disproportionately middle-class those voters may still be, combines fatally with the state's supermajority requirements and its initiative-imposed constraints on legislative discretion. You do what your constituents want, but there may not be much that is both constitutionally permissible and that two-thirds of the people can agree on. In the state's disjointed system, it is sometimes structurally easier to get a majority of the voters than it is to get two-thirds of their representatives.

In the good old days, when the state's residents were still overwhelmingly white, as its voters still are, and when the idea and promise that were simply called California had not yet fully given way to regional particularism—when no one had ever heard of such things as media markets—and when there seemed always to be enough money, legislators often seemed able to fashion compromises with a bipartisan collegiality, both during sessions and after hours in the capital's watering spots, that overcame the structural hurdles of the state's constitutional requirements. That was frequently true even on divisive regional and economic issues.

But beginning with the passage of Proposition 13, with its fiscal limits and its crop of new, more partisan, more ideological "cavemen," and, in some respects, perhaps even earlier, the comity began to erode at an accelerating rate. After he left office, the restrained and very conservative George Deukmejian put some of the blame on the state's 1974 political reform initiative, which made it harder to take lobbyists' money for food and drink—and for other things as well—and thus considerably dampened the members' conviviality. (In that sentiment he appeared to echo Jess Unruh, the Big Daddy speaker of the 1960s and an altogether different kind of politician: "If you can't eat their food, drink their booze, screw their women and then vote against them," Unruh was supposed to have said, "you don't belong here.")[28] Even in the Jerry Brown years, when the governor's office and both houses of the legislature were controlled by the same party, the supermajority requirement gave political minorities an effective veto and rewarded hard-line partisanship. In the late 1970s and through the 1980s, budget after budget prohibited state Medicaid funding for abortions because religious conservatives, though themselves in the minority, could block any budget that didn't have such restrictions.[29]

After 1982, when Deukmejian replaced Jerry Brown, partisan tensions, often leading to gridlock, became almost routine, with the legislature controlled by Democrats and, in the case of the assembly, by a group of liberal Democrats under the speakership of the flamboyant Willie Brown of San Francisco. In the face of two fiscally conservative governors, a militantly conservative Republican minority in the assembly that was far to the right of the Republican governor and that had enough votes to block any fiscal measure, and a tax-constrained and increasingly straitened budget, Willie Brown, though speaker, knew that the best he could do was protect as much as possible of the benefits that his constituents, and particularly the poor of the large cities, had been given by a more optimistic and generous state in better days. Brown liked to be a player, and both governors tried to keep him in the center of the play, but often the political forces, in the view of good-government types such as Walter Zelman, then head of California Common Cause, produced "something less than compromise, or perhaps the ultimate in compromise—no action at all. The result has been government by stalemate, failure to deal with critical issues and, ultimately, public frustration."[30]

Yet by the 1980s, the problem had become deeper than mere frustration with the lack of action. Because legislative districts were evenly apportioned by population, not by voters, a much smaller number of black voters in South Central Los Angeles or Latino voters in East Los Angeles elected members to represent those areas than was the case in middle-class white suburbs.[31] As a result, California government not only had a tendency to be divided, and often stalemated, between Republican governors, chosen by the entire electorate (the same electorate, of course, that voted on ballot measures), and Democratic-majority legislatures chosen from low-voting urban and working-class districts that might reflect population, but not the state's voters. It also produced a legislature that was itself sharply split between urban liberals, many of them sounding like holdovers from an earlier era (which, often, they were), who were at least minimally responsive to the growing social and ethnic groups in their communities, and the militant Proposition 13 babies from the conservative white suburbs. Such a legislature was not only distant and anonymous but seemed, with every passing year, to become ever more disconnected from the majority of white, older, Protestant voters who regarded themselves as "the people."

Speaker Brown, of course, was the perfect embodiment of all that: He was from San Francisco, he was black, he was a lawyer who had spent his early years representing pimps and hookers. Brown liked good clothes and fast cars and didn't mind flaunting them. But he was also the smartest politician in the state—and far and away the most interesting—and he managed to hold the speakership and control the assembly for more than fourteen years, twice as long as anyone in history. In the middle of that tenure, the legislature, which was closely identified with him and not long before regarded as a model for the nation, went through an extended set of fund-raising scandals, most particularly an episode called Shrimpscam in which FBI agents, posing as out-of-state business people, managed to snag a half dozen legislators and a number of staff members in accepting bribes—got some of them on videotape literally stuffing money into their pockets—for support on a phony bill to aid in the construction of an equally phony shrimp-processing plant in West Sacramento.[32] (Which, being eighty miles from the ocean and an even longer way from the nearest shrimp beds, had never seen a shrimp that wasn't frozen.)

Although Democrat Brown was almost certainly intended to be

Shrimpscam's major target, all of those caught were from the state senate or from the other party. With the exception of an assembly-woman from Los Angeles who was ultimately acquitted, the only person close to Brown who was caught in any scandal at that time was a Beverly Hills real estate operator named Mark Nathanson, whom Brown had appointed to the state's powerful Coastal Com-mission.[33] Yet the scandals, combined with Brown's flamboyance, his cozy relations with tobacco companies, the trial lawyers, and other interest groups, from which he raised millions of dollars annually, the prowess with which he distributed those funds to other legislative Democrats, his willingness to do little favors even for Republicans, and the undeniable power those things gave him—over every assembly capitol office, parking space, and staff slot—made him into a durable symbol of the legislature's failures and disdain, real and alleged, toward public sensibilities. On more than one occasion, he described himself as the ayatollah of the legislature, and in some ways, he surely was.

In the context of the increasingly illiberal 1980s, the great unap-preciated irony of California's peculiar government structure—and particularly that two-thirds supermajority requirement, which was so beloved by conservatives who thought it helped check liberal spending—is that it permitted urban liberals to block the budget-ary adjustments that the state's fiscal situation probably required. But if liberals like Brown, John Vasconcellos of San Jose, Art Agnos of San Francisco, Tom Hayden of Santa Monica, Nick Petris of Oakland, Tom Bates of Berkeley, Maxine Waters of Los Angeles, and the various legislators who represented the tony West Side of Los Angeles voted for these adjustments, it would have cut not only into the perks of realtors, doctors and lawyers, but sharply into welfare and other benefits for the poor.

The consequence is that traditional services—including schools before the passage of the Proposition 98 school-funding guarantees—were cut more deeply than welfare, thereby reinforc-ing the inchoate sense among conservative voters that the people they thought they had sent to Sacramento (if they but knew their names) were not really representing them, indeed, were really not their kind of people at all. And for that, too, Willie Brown—urban, black, powerful, political from head to well-shod foot—made a perfect symbol, the leitmotif against which a large number of the political campaigns of the 1980s and 1990s have been played.

III

Although there are exceptions such as the passage of Proposition 99, the tobacco tax increase that won despite enormous cigarette industry spending to defeat it, it's probably still true that where there is not a wide, self-evident case for an initiative, such as the tobacco tax, a disproportionate amount of money invested against a ballot measure will beat it. But after Bill Butcher and Arnold Forde took on the work of the Howard Jarvis organization—and ultimately some other hot-button issues of particular concern to the elderly—that hypothesis was supplemented by another principle, stated most simply in an ad from a direct mail firm called Advanced Voter Communication: "We will qualify a Constitutional Amendment, even to 110 percent, in 45 days. And we guarantee specific numbers of valid signatures on a money-back basis."[34]

Put another way, if you spend enough money either on professional signature gatherers or send out enough direct mail appeals to well-chosen lists of voters, you can get almost anything on the ballot. In ordinary years, according to one leader in the business, the cost for conventional signature-gathering on the street runs to maybe 85 cents a signature, but in years when a lot of measures are being circulated, as was the case in 1996, the cost can run to $1.50 or more. "It's become," said Kelly Kimball, who runs Kimball Petition Management, one of the leaders in the field, "a nasty, cutthroat business." But it is also a good business. Even if a measure eventually loses, the campaign consultants, who generally take a percentage of everything, will make a great deal of money. In 1988, for example, when, partway through the time allowed to collect signatures, the auto insurance industry's no-fault measure was declared unconstitutional, it was hastily rewritten and sent out for signatures again at a time when there were only forty-eight days left. By paying a direct mail firm $5 million to collect the 400,000 or so valid signatures it needed, a whopping $12 a signature, the industry got the measure on the ballot in about thirty-three days.[35] The voters, as noted above, rejected it, but that did not prevent the chief campaign consultant on the measure, Clint Reilly of San Francisco, who got a percentage of every ad and every mailer, from raking in a reported $7 million or more in commissions and buying himself an elegant San Francisco house with the proceeds.[36]

Conversely, as Ruth Holton, who served as head of California Common Cause in the early and mid-1990s, pointed out, it's a rare measure, even among the most popular, that can be qualified without at least half the signatures coming from paid signature gatherers—commercial firms available to whoever is prepared to pay the commissions, plus a few dedicated consultants who only serve do-good organizations—that organize the campaign, print the petitions, hire students or others to set up tables in shopping malls and other well-traveled public places, and pay them some fraction of what the firm gets from the sponsor.

Increasingly, the business of signature-gathering resembles farm labor, a system where the petition management firm subcontracts with someone else—a sort of coyote—who employs the workers who actually sit at the tables or go door-to-door gathering signatures. Usually the professionals—Kimball, for example, or American Petition Consultants, another of the dominant firms in the business—will be soliciting for several measures at once. Few of those at the tables will understand, much less explain, the details of the measures they're working for. Many, despite laws to the contrary, may not even live in the jurisdiction where they're temporarily working. The emphasis is on quantity, not civic virtue, what Kimball called the "hoopla process," in which "you say whatever you need to get a signature."[37] If the voter asks too many questions, "you hand them a petition and text sheet. You say come back to me if you want to sign it. After two or three lines, it doesn't become cost effective to argue with a person."[38] The main reason "you sign a petition when you're approached in front of a store," he added, "is first of all you don't want to look stupid." The whole process, he concluded, "sucks."

Holton herself had run a successful initiative campaign at Common Cause in November 1996, qualifying and passing Proposition

208, the campaign finance reform measure, despite a $4 million negative campaign by CalPIRG, the California Public Interest Research Group, a Naderite organization, which was pushing Proposition 212, a competing, and considerably more radical, measure and spending huge amounts of money, much of it from its national affiliate, to get it passed, and to get Proposition 208 defeated. (One index of California's plebiscitary excesses is that sometimes even the good-government groups run competing initiatives against one another; in this case, the Common Cause initiative, Proposition 208, passed handily, while Proposition 212 failed.)

Holton, who had to pay 75 cents apiece for the 300,000 signatures Common Cause could not get through volunteer efforts, regarded the low price—and the relative large number of signatures generated by volunteers—as a triumph. With rare exceptions—the most recent was a measure passed in 1990 making it illegal to hunt California mountain lions and appropriating money to purchase habitat for their protection, for which all of the 675,000 signatures were collected by volunteers from the state's Mountain Lion Foundation and by other environmentalists—the numbers are just too large, and the time alloted too short, to give all-volunteer operations much chance for success.

As might be expected, the commercialization of signature-gathering has generated pressure for reform. But under Supreme Court free speech rulings, nothing has passed muster. In 1974, the California Political Reform Act established a ceiling under which no qualification campaign could spend more than 25 cents times the number of signatures required. That was struck down by the state supreme court after the U.S. Supreme Court declared all mandatory spending ceilings unconstitutional.[39] And when Colorado in 1980 passed a law prohibiting the use of paid signature gatherers as a violation of the populist principle of the initiative, the U.S. Supreme Court struck that down as well.[40]

Although some signature-collectors were being paid as early as the 1930s, the field wasn't professionalized until the late 1960s, when Ed and Joyce Koupal set up shop in Sacramento and Kelly's father Fred Kimball got into the business in Los Angeles. And until the late 1970s, even they had generally been regarded as marginal adjuncts to the volunteer organizations that were presumed to do the lion's share of the work. But after Butcher-Forde came on the scene, the whole initiative process was increasingly automated and commercialized—in some cases to the point where it wasn't clear whether it was the sponsor or the commercial consultants who had conceived and initiated the measure. That was especially the case in the early 1980s when Butcher-Forde, among others, were test marketing issues (called "self-starters") and then pitching them to potential sponsors. Proposition 37, the California lottery initiative, which was funded by the manufacturers of gambling materials and which voters approved in 1984, was first tested by Kimball Petition Management, which was "looking for something we could make money on, and somebody who would fund it."[41]

"People go out and propose these initiatives," said Joe Cerrell, a long-time Los Angeles political consultant, "so they can make money. It's become a straight business." One of the things that helped make it so was Butcher-Forde's discovery that they could gather signatures and raise money with the same mailings, generally with a pitch warning of another impending death blow from the tax collector, and another blast at government fraud, waste, and abuse. These pieces, which often went out in those official-looking envelopes—"Important Voter Information Enclosed. Please Open Immediately," or "Property Tax Statement Enclosed. Do Not Destroy"—were generally mailed under the reduced, heavily subsidized postal rates available to nonprofit organizations.[42]

Butcher-Forde, however, owned two things that no one else had—the Jarvis name, which had enormous credibility, particularly among the elderly middle-class voters who made up the vast majority of the membership of Jarvis's organizations; and the Jarvis list itself, augmented with carefully screened lists of other names, which were worth their weight, and more, in gold. One indication of the value of the right list came from Butcher-Forde's offer (which was refused) to provide direct mail petition circulation services for Proposition 99, the 1988 tobacco tax initiative, in return for the mailing list of physicians, nurses, Cancer and Lung Association members, and other health organization activists who participated in the campaign.[43] But they had the Jarvis list, over which they had gained complete control—Jarvis, Fox said, had given them free use of it for ten years—and by the mid-1980s, according to documents resulting from a lawsuit and a subsequent *Los Angeles Times* investigation, the firm was earning close to $12 million a year out of which they were paying themselves between $3 million and $5 million each. Additional earnings came from rental of the list to other groups.[44]

Most of the money never went further than Butcher-Forde, latterly known as BFC, meaning that even as they were paying themselves those millions, the organizations for which the funds were ostensibly raised—Doris Day's Animal League, James Roosevelt's National Committee to Preserve Social Security, and Jarvis's own organization—got little or nothing from the funds collected in their name. In 1985 Butcher-Forde raised $7.7 million for the Jarvis group: Fund-raising costs took up $3.7 million; Butcher-Forde Consulting (BFC) got another $2.5 million; lawyers' fees took another $735,000, leaving just over $750,000 for the Jarvis cause.[45]

Filings in the suit, which had been brought by a former member of the Jarvis organization who suspected that most of the fundraising was undertaken merely to feed the campaign consultants, indicated, in the words of an FBI investigator who examined the Butcher-Forde records in an unrelated investigation, that "the Jarvis organization, through the acts of BFC, defrauded thousands of people who mailed in contributions under the false pretense that the money was going to pay the expenses of the proposition campaigns."[46] In a similar operation during the mid-1980s, Butcher-Forde, with Jarvis's name, collected $1 million in an abortive campaign to remove the increasingly unpopular Rose Bird from her seat as the state's chief justice, much of it in chunks of $10 and $25. But when the drive was abandoned in 1986, without any tangible sign that any real campaign had ever been conducted, they had virtually nothing left in the till.[47] (Needless to say, the contributors got nothing back.) But for all that, most of the widows and pensioners who belonged to the Jarvis group and responded to the BFC pitches thought no less of him.

In many respects, Butcher-Forde, who in 1988 sold their business and mailing lists for more than $11 million, were one of a kind, and not just in their ethics or their relations with clients. Although other organizations tried direct-mail signature-collection, most found it was more expensive than the conventional shopping mall route and only rarely use it as their sole means of collecting signatures.[48] But in helping turn the initiative into an industry, Butcher-Forde were among the great pioneers. In part because of them, the "initiative industrial complex" has increasingly become, not just a supplement, but a replacement for conventional politics. One revealing study showed that before 1978, initiative campaigns devoted less than 4 percent of their qualification budgets to professional signature gatherers, and many paid nothing; for the measures on the ballot in the 1978 general election campaign, that number shot up to 78 percent; by 1986, it was up to 91 percent.[49] "This is the largest electorate in the world," said Ken Masterton, who runs signature campaigns for Common Cause and various environmental and other public interest groups, "that you can access with one piece of paper."

Once a measure gets to the ballot, the campaign—for and against—is not very different from any other election campaign, with the exception, as one consultant put it, that "ballot measures can't talk back to you." If there is enough money, it goes chiefly into thirty-second TV and radio spots, but a great deal is also likely to be spent on direct mail and slate mailers, cards produced strictly for profit by commercial operators and sent to selected lists of voters that purport to come from "Democrats for a Better Environment" or "Citizens for Reponsive Government" or whatever manufactured name seems promising, a name that rarely has any connection with any legitimate political organization.

Those lists can now be targeted with something approaching the precision of the global positioning satellite—prochoice Republican women in the Fifth Assembly District; Latinos opposed to gun control in the Tenth Senate District. Space on the phony endorsement mailers is then sold, usually to the highest bidder and often with the threat that if A doesn't buy, the opposing candidate or position will be solicited and endorsed. The bought-and-sold endorsements are surrounded with slogans and endorsements, usually without knowledge of the endorsee, that reflect the targeted voter's politics and with which the voter is likely to identify: for Bill Clinton in pieces sent to Democrats; for some "green" initiative in pieces sent to environmentalists; against gun control in pieces sent to conservative Republicans. The profit comes from the slots that are sold. (The law requires any "endorsement" that is sold to be marked with an asterisk, but the asterisks are so small and the footnote in such miniscule type that they easily can be overlooked.)

For some organizations in some circumstances, free media—newspaper editorial endorsements, for example—are still important, especially if the issue is complex and there's no money to do much else. But voters generally get their information from three sources: from mailers, from TV and radio spots, and from the title that appears on the ballot and the official summary—the language, 100 words or less, at the head of the measure in the pamphlet that every voter gets. That language is drafted by the attorney general's office, and because it is so crucial it often becomes the subject of a separate court battle before it reaches the ballot itself: For that reason, said one liberal activist, "we deeply care who the attorney general is. We did much better under John Van De Kamp [a Democrat] than we've done under Dan Lungren [a Republican]." For that reason also, one Sacramento superior court judge, James T. Ford, has become a specialist in fights over ballot titles and summaries. Needless to say, the amount of information the mailers, the ballot title, and the thirty-second ads provide is pitifully small. Bruce Cain, a professor of government at Berkeley and associate director of its Institute of Governmental Studies, points out that "voters are sagacious in their use of cues" to make choices—who endorses a measure, who opposes it. But in many surveys taken as little as two weeks before an election, the "don't knows" will outpoll the percentage of voters expressing a preference 80–20.

As the new campaign techniques were developed and refined, and as the legislature and governor became more bitterly partisan, the question—is it too easy to amend the California constitution?—posed by Cain seemed increasingly to demand an affirmative answer.[50] In fact, as Cain points out, while California's constitution—which covers a huge range of policy subjects, from taxation to gambling, from veterans affairs to environmental protection—has been amended 489 times since its adoption in 1871, only 36 of those amendments came by the initiative route; the rest were put on the ballot by the legislature.

Even so, Cain answers the question with "a qualified yes," particularly in light of the fact that "some of the most critical fiscal decisions have been put into the constitution by the ICA [Initiative Constitutional Amendment] process, and this has limited the ability of elected officials to deal with fiscal crises."[51] But since many statutory initiatives are almost as untouchable by the legislature, and totally untouchable by local governments, and since they often hamstring local government even more severely, they often amount to virtually the same thing—quasi-constitutional amendments as impervious to change as the constitution itself. Most require either a two-thirds vote of the legislature (and sometimes more) for amendment, or, worse, preclude any amendment without another vote of the electorate.

As should already be clear from the sequence of measures that followed the passage of Jarvis-Gann, those conditions have produced a cycle of frustration, reform, and further frustration in which each initiative further constrains the ability of government, state and local, to respond to new conditions and set priorities. Because the initiative does not impose any requirement to consider trade-offs—the impact of a tax cut on services, the budgetary effects on other programs of a spending mandate—the voters can act now and, in the words of one political scientist, "worry about the consequences in services later."[52]

Over the years, that process, because it is so impervious to legislative repair, has both generated new frustrations and whetted new sets of plebiscitary appetites—and opened new doors of opportunity to various interest groups and their campaign operatives. And that, in turn, often leads to yet other ballot measures, thereby beginning the cycle over again: from tax and spending limits to spending mandates, to anger at the unresponsiveness and ineffectiveness of the legislature, to calls for term limits; from constraints on social services to rising crime rates, to tougher sentences and ballooning prisons costs, to yet further constraints on social services. "This is the sad irony of California politics," in the words of University of California political scientist Elisabeth Gerber. "Voters perceive government as unaccountable so they pass initiatives to restrict its actions. This constrains government and prevents it from responding to the state's pressing demands, which further angers voters and provokes them to pass even more stringent constraints." The process has become both medium and substance.

Not surprisingly, the state's increasingly cautious elected officials, watching those developments and sensing that voters are expecting less and less from the conventional governmental process, have often climbed on the plebiscitary bandwagon, on the one hand augmenting what the voters had done or anticipating what they were about to do, on the other showing increasing aversion to taking on tough issues at all. In a growing number of instances, city councils, boards of supervisors, and other local entities have submitted questions to voters in "advisory" ballots—including some highly technical ones such as the closing of a nuclear power plant in Sacramento, for example—that, under the law, they could have decided themselves.

The almost inevitable result of that kind caution is to put still more emphasis on the plebiscitary process. In the meantime, the elected representatives devote a growing share of their energy to serving corporate, labor, and other economic interest groups that, unlike most voters and a large portion of the media, keep at least part of their attention on government. One of the pervasive motifs of that process is that even as the voters demand the right to vote on every tax and assessment, as they create yet more elective offices, and as the ballot in California has grown to nearly unmanageable length—in one recent election in San Francisco, each voter was asked to register choices on more than 100 offices and ballot issues—the percentage of them who actually cast ballots steadily goes down.

IV

Until the mid-1980s, it appeared that the new populism in California, which had been so clearly dominated by the campaign for tax and spending limits and tough-on-crime laws, and so laced with attacks on welfare cheats, waste, and government in general, would remain largely a speciality of the right. A meaningless nuclear freeze measure sponsored by peace activists had passed in 1982, and a number of extremely conservative measures—one that would have banned gays from teaching in the public schools; another, sponsored by the Lyndon LaRouche organization, aimed at a quarantine of AIDS patients—failed.

But in the mid-1980s, California environmental and health organizations began to develop their own techniques to take advantage of the process, thus making groups generally identified as "left" into major players themselves. In 1986, led by David Roe of the Environmental Defense Fund, they qualified and succeeded in passing Proposition 65, an initiative imposing strict regulations on the discharge of toxic materials into the ground and the state's water systems, and requiring warning signs in groceries, restaurants, bars, and virtually every other business where any substance identified by the state as carcinogenic or as hazardous to pregnant women—from wine to cleansers—is sold to the general public. And beginning with the 1988 primary, the state's Planning and Conservation League, spurred by a set of inventive campaign funding tactics devised by the PCL's executive director, Gerald Meral, turned itself into what Jim Shultz of the liberal Democracy Center in San Francisco called "an initiative factory." Under Meral, PCL qualified an ever-more ambitious set of bond measures to finance the acquisition and development of park and recreation areas; build and improve intercity rail services; increase the tobacco tax to fund health care and antismoking education and advertising campaigns; protect mountain lions; and fund a florid array of projects from expansion of various local museums to the cleanup of inner-city playgrounds and vacant lots.

The earliest of them, Proposition 70 (June 1988), was the first park bond proposal that had gotten on the ballot by the initiative route. It called for $765 million in state bonds to acquire new state and local parklands, restore and expand wildlife habitat, and develop urban parkways, and extended even to such details as buying boats to help the state Department of Fish and Game enforce its regulations. In the seventy-plus years before, the state had spent just $1.6 billion on park acquisition; Meral proposed to spend almost half that much in one swoop.

All told, Proposition 70 included some sixty individually defined projects, each with a specified amount, in every corner of the state. That in itself was new: In previous park bond proposals, all proposed by the legislature, the general purposes were outlined, but it was left to the legislature and state agencies to decide how and where to spend the funds. But Meral added something even more controversial: Each of these specific projects was chosen, not only with an eye to maximizing local voter appeal, but in negotiations with local environmental groups, each of which was expected to generate a certain amount in campaign funding or a certain number of signatures to get the measure on the ballot and/or passed, an arrangement that was quickly (and predictably) labeled "park barrel" politics.

Meral denied then—and has denied since—that the projects had been "sold" to local bidders. He said they had been chosen on their merits; he himself had driven around the state in a rented Geo to see the landscape, look at the needs, and meet with local groups.[53] But while there may have been no explicit quid pro quo arrangement, each group was "expected," in the words of a Meral letter, "to contribute either money or signatures in proportion to the benefits we receive." In Los Angeles County, the Santa Monica Mountains Conservancy, which was to get $30 million from the proceeds of the bonds, pledged $50,000 and 50,000 signatures; the Hillside Federation, a coalition of homeowner groups, collected another 50,000; the Los Angeles chapter of the Sierra Club pledged another 50,000. In San Diego County, which was to get $50 million for various projects—"urban canyons" park land acquisition, protection of riparian habitat, coastal protection—a coalition of business people and environmentalists pledged to collect 125,000 signatures.[54]

Proposition 70 generated loud opposition from the state Chamber of Commerce, the Farm Bureau, the Cattlemen's Association, and other agricultural groups, many of which have always looked with suspicion on any do-good attempt to protect rural land from ordinary commerce. The measure, they complained correctly, "abandons the normal process of having park land spending proposals developed by the Legislature and professional park planners." Instead "special interest groups will set the priorities" and establish "a dangerous precedent of allowing special interests . . . to promote their selfish projects."[55] In fact, special interests had always promoted their "selfish projects"; only they had done it in the legislature or in the agencies, sometimes to the considerable benefit of themselves and the public servants they were dealing with. Sometimes they had even done it with their own initiative. Now a different set of interest groups were doing it on their own.

The proposal, which happened to get the endorsement of then-Senator Pete Wilson, who was in those years still in a moderate-environmentalist phase, passed easily, and Meral and the Planning and Conservation League immediately embarked on his next project, a $2 billion rail bond project, which would appear as Proposition 116 in June 1990, to improve interurban and local passenger service in various parts of the state. It would include, among many other things, the acquisition and improvement of railway rights-of-way for mass transit—but incidentally also for freight service through some of the state's most lucrative shipping corridors.

This time, however, Meral's most prominent partner was not the coalition of environmental, wildlife, and park organizations that had been so much involved two years earlier, but the Southern Pacific Railroad, the Octopus of Hiram Johnson's day, which put up more than $500,000 to get the signatures for Proposition 116 and help it pass. And since the SP also stood to acquire the right-of-way for a major freight spur through Los Angeles to the increasingly busy container terminals at the Port of San Pedro, the howls reached unprecedented levels. If the legislature had engaged in these kinds of trade-offs—"buying and selling an initiative"—said state Senator Quentin Kopp, they would have been felonies. Worse, writing bond issues and tax measures this way, as one columnist gently put it, "skews spending priorities by putting them, in effect, up for bid."[56] Kopp did not explain how that differed from measures, such as the lottery, or the no-fault auto insurance initiatives, which were entirely funded by a single interest.

The ever-creative Meral explained, correctly, that the Los Angeles freight spur would reduce the polluting volume of truck traffic that often choked surface streets on the way in and out of the port, that the public strongly supported rail and mass transit, and that if such projects helped the SP, they were also a major plus for both the environment and the state's economy—and would certainly be cheaper if they used existing railroad right-of-way than if whole new routes were developed. Proposition 116 also contained a section locking away a portion of the state's gas tax that had been previously designated for transportation projects but that had often been diverted by the legislature for other purposes. For both good reasons and bad, that provision particularly incensed California's legislators. These decisions had been their prerogatives; they brought campaign contributions and political clout. If anybody was going to wheel and deal on those things, they wanted to be the ones to do it. But Proposition 116 also passed.

By 1994, when Meral and PCL came up with Proposition 180, yet another $2 billion catchall of park, wildlife, and other conservation projects, Kopp had succeeded in enacting legislation designed to curb Meral's kind of logrolling. Kopp's bill kept the sponsors from even mentioning signatures and campaign contributions as they were consulting with local groups about what to include in their measures.

That, however, hardly shortened Meral's list. On the contrary, the initiative that qualified for the ballot included some 400 items: wildlife projects in Merced County; playground development in San Francisco; improvements to the Hollywood Bowl and the African American Museum in Los Angeles; funds for the California Indian Museum and the Museum of Latino History and for the Fresno Conservation Corps; plus some 300 other projects of park development, coastal access, coastal trail construction, and wildlife protection; jobs programs for at-risk-youth in the inner cities (cleaning up graffiti-strewn playgrounds and empty lots); and right-of-way acquisition for future rail excursion lines. There was even a $2 million item for acquisition of land and the construction of a center in Central America along the migratory path of California bird species for the study of biodiversity and tropical biology, a principal purpose of which is the conservation of habitat critical for the preservation of migratory bird species native to California.[57]

Proposition 180 failed, as did every other spending-related measure in that election. This was 1994, the year of the great Republican upsurge and of California's greatest budget crisis since the Depression, when even the most uncontroversial spending items, including a $2 billion state school bond proposal of the kind that almost always passed, went down. But Meral's logrolling and pork barreling would be upheld by two state court decisions striking down Kopp's law as an infringement on the initiative process. The law, said the trial judge in the case, appears to be founded on the belief "that no one must have a base motive to promote legislation," when in fact self-interest "has been at the root of the intiative process from the beginning, not altruism."[58] The law, said the appellate court in upholding the trial judge in a unanimous opinion, violates free speech, and does little to reduce the possibility of corruption. Between the lines, the judges seemed to be saying that in brokering deals between different interest groups, Meral had only been doing in the private sphere what Congress and most legislatures routinely do in the public sphere.

But the judges were also confirming something more significant, and that was a kind of private legislative process that produces not just legislative Christmas trees loaded with goodies for almost everybody, but a different, extralegislative way of creating political coalitions—in Meral's case mostly for middle-class do-good projects. Deep-pockets interest groups had long been able to buy themselves ballot measures; they did not need to broker with others. But in a polyglot state of 30-plus million people with no other overarching sense of political community, Meral's coalitions seemed, for better or worse, to be the closest that anyone had come in many years to creating one. Along the way, the sharp-eyed Meral had even managed to bury into Proposition 117, the mountain lion protection measure that he helped write, a provision appropriating a chunk of the funds raised through Proposition 99, the tobacco tax measure that had passed two years earlier, to help fund mountain lion habitat. "Smokers of California," Assemblyman Phillip Isenberg would say, "were being asked to save mountain lions. The word bold does not begin to describe the imagination and brass necessary to pull this off."[59] By the year 2008, Meral calculates, the four successful initiative campaigns that he and the Planning and Conservation League have been involved in since 1988, will generate more than \$16 billion for health and environmental projects.[60] That's not bad for semiprivate government conducted by a man almost no one in California had ever heard of.

The question, of course, is at what cost in government accountability and responsiveness, and at what cost in more urgent services and programs to real people. Meral, like other activists on both the right and left, argues, correctly, that the voters are deeply distrustful of elected government and would much rather specify and lock down every additional dollar that government gets. He has polls to prove it: the closer to home, and the more specific the allocation, the more likely that the public will support it. In Fresno in 1993, the voters approved something called "Arts to Zoo," which raised the local sales tax by one-tenth of a cent, with the proceeds—about \$5 million a year—going to a specified group of local arts and cultural organizations for a twenty-year period: half for the local symphony orchestra, the art museum, and the zoological society, and smaller parts to libraries, senior citizen groups, and various other organizations.[61] But each turn of what is now widely known as ballot box budgeting eats up an ever greater chunk of the public purse and makes it still harder for government to establish priorities and respond to new needs. Even where a new tax is approved, or an old one increased, or a new set of bonds okayed for a specified purpose, it leaves less fiscal flexibility, and less credit with the bond buyers, for the next need, and particularly for the unexpected.

In California, one need not look far to divine the net result of that process. For the better part of twenty years, there has been a steady shift in the balance of social benefits: Minimum spending guarantees for schools, albeit still low, are written into the constitution, largely on the strength of organized school employee groups; parkland is acquired, animals protected, antismoking campaigns funded, toxic emissions reduced, criminal sentences increased. But as the voter-mandated expenditures—and especially those for schools—scrape against the similarly mandated tax and expenditure limits imposed by Proposition 13 and its successors, particularly when, as in the period between 1991 and 1994, bad economic times take their toll in declining state revenues, there is no give left in the system. And so the Rube Goldberg machine that is now the California fiscal system clanks and creaks, arbitrarily snatching $3.6 billion a year in property tax receipts that had been allocated to the counties and other local governments in the great post-Proposition 13 bailout. It delivers the money to the schools to meet the Proposition 98 guarantees, thereby leaving the counties on the verge of bankruptcy and unable to pay for the social services they provide.

Given the mandates and fiscal constraints imposed on them (and of course the realities of electoral politics), the state's elected leaders probably had little other choice in the middle of a recession as deep as the one California went through in the early 1990s. But what the law (most of it the result of voter initiatives) mandated was, in this case of robbing Peter to pay Paul, also the path of least resistance. It is the counties that do most of the state's dirty work, the things that must be done but that no one much wants to think about, let alone pay for: providing general assistance for the genuinely down-and-out, running the probation systems, operating health clinics for those who have neither private insurance nor Medicaid, finding foster homes for the increasing number of neglected and abused children, operating children's protective services and adult protective services, and cooling out or jailing the public nuisances, the drunks, the wife beaters.

And so, as the recession ended in the mid-nineties and the money flowed again into the state's coffers, the Rube Goldberg fiscal machine did not grind and clank into reverse to return the property tax money that had been lifted from the state's hard-pressed counties. Instead, as noted in the previous section, it delivered the increased proceeds, which were substantial, to the schools (which certainly can use them, and a great deal more) and to the state's public universities (which ditto). It also continued to feed the rapacious growth in prison expenses, whose funding is also written into this increasingly immutable structure through mandatory sentencing laws—all enacted without regard to cost. In 1996, when the legislature acceded to the counties' plea that they be able to keep at least the money derived from whatever growth there might be in the property tax, Governor Pete Wilson vetoed that, too. (And, from his perspective, perhaps, not without reason: In late 1996, the Legislative Analyst issued a warning that despite expanding revenues, there will be new state deficits before the end of the decade if corrective action—changes in Proposition 13 and Proposition 98—is not taken.)[62]

The end result of all this pea-under-the-shell shifting and allocating is that an enormous chunk has been taken from services for the poor and delivered to the middle class. And since the new federal welfare reform law now permits—no, encourages—the states to ratchet down their spending for welfare, now called Temporary Aid to Needy Families, and to cut legal aliens from some programs entirely, which in turn threatens to dump additional people on the last-ditch resources of local agencies, the potential for a ruinous squeeze on the counties is compounded.

One cannot blame people like Gerry Meral, who is the most gentle and socially conscious of human beings, for the shift in priorities, which is hardly unique in California. Nor should one blame the voters of places like Fresno for trying to put a little more money into museums, symphonies, and zoos, or the voters of a number of other communities who for similarly unimpeachable reasons voted to tax themselves a few extra mil in order to support their struggling public libraries.

But one is still left with the conclusion that even at its best, the plebiscitary dynamic—call it the ethics of the initiative—has precious little room for spending that immediately benefits someone other than those who must vote on it. It is not prone to generosity and is rarely respectful of minority rights, much less of minority needs. And while it is true that elected legislators often fail to do what their constituents wish (and often do a great deal worse than they deserve), sometimes they also do a little better for those who are underrepresented in the electoral process, something that the initiative process almost never does. "When the legislative process," wrote former Harvard law professor Derrick Bell:[63]

> is turned back on the citizenry either to enact laws by initiative or to review existing laws through the referendum, few of the concerns that can transform the "conservative" politician into a "moderate" public official are likely to affect the individual voter's decision. No political factors counsel constraint on racial passions emanating from long held and little considered beliefs and fears. Far from being the pure path to democracy . . . direct democracy, carried out in the privacy of the voting booth, has diminished the ability of minority groups to participate in the democratic process. Ironically, because it enables the voters' racial beliefs and fears to be recorded and tabulated in their pure form, the referendum has been a most effective facilitator of that bias, discrimination, and prejudice which has marred American democracy from its earliest day.

That states the case too strongly. The inherent political logic of the plebiscite has little room for any sort of political minority—just as it allows little leeway for legislative nuance or subtlety. By its nature, it tends to wield a blunt hammer that often strikes even those who forged it. But with those qualifications, it hardly invalidates Bell's argument.

V

Bell's point is particularly applicable to California's recent history, where nothing has reflected the tension between majority power and minority rights more clearly than the series of ballot measures and related gubernatorial policies on crime, immigration, and affirmative action that have marked—indeed characterized—California Governor Pete Wilson's career in statewide politics. Nor has the demagogic potential of the initiative been more vividly demonstrated than in the three measures that he made his own and with which his latter-day political efforts have been associated—two for reelection as governor in 1994, one in a dismally unsuccessful campaign for the presidency in 1995–96.[64]

Wilson wasn't the first to venture into this field. For more than a generation, California politicians have exploited—or tried to exploit—the initiative in running for office. Particularly in circumstances where campaign funds are limited, association with a popular measure can create name identification and provide attention and legitimacy that ordinary campaign techniques cannot. In 1974, then-Secretary of State Jerry Brown, as a cosponsor of Proposition 9, the California Political Reform Act requiring reporting and disclosure of campaign expenses and creating the California Fair Political Practices Commission, made it a symbol of his reformist politics and rode it into the governorship. In 1990, Attorney General John Van De Kamp, a Democrat, tried the same thing with three simultaneous initiatives—Proposition 128, an environmental measure cosponsored with state Senator Tom Hayden, called "Big Green"; Proposition 129, a middle-of-the road anticrime measure cosponsored by a group of moderate law enforcement officials that would have provided additional funding for drug abuse treatment and prevention, as well as some additional prison construction; and Proposition 131, a moderate term-limits initiative (to compete with the state's more severe six-years-and-out measure, which passed) that would also have toughened the state's campaign finance laws and expanded conflict of interest provisions. None of the three passed, and Van De Kamp, who had counted on the initiatives in the general election, didn't make it past the primary.

Wilson, however, went far beyond those relatively primitive efforts. In embracing and demagoguing hot-button issues, Wilson used the initiative, not merely to showcase his own candidacy, but as a political wedge to destroy his opponent. In the process, a man who began his career in the state legislature, and in the office of mayor of San Diego, as a moderate liberal Republican, not merely redefined himself but helped shift and reset the state's political climate to boot. If Jarvis and Gann's tax revolt politics moved California sharply from the liberal New Deal style politics of Pat Brown, Wilson took the state further right in its essential social assumptions and ethnic relationships.

The impulse was understandable. By the time Wilson ran for the senate in 1982, moderate liberal Republicans were already an endangered species in California. Wilson, who had strongly supported affirmative action as a legislator and mayor, who was a strong backer of abortion rights, and who had made the near-fatal mistake of supporting Gerald Ford when Ronald Reagan, always a favorite among his fellow California Republicans, took Ford on in the 1976 primary, badly needed to mend his fences with his state's increasingly conservative Republican Party. But while he never gained the trust of the core of his own party, in part because he remained unabashedly prochoice on abortion, the campaign techniques that evolved from the effort were, with the sole exception of the failed presidential race, highly successful, even when he himself changed positions to exploit those techniques. Such flips, as George Gorton, who was Wilson's chief campaign consultant in 1994, pointed out, never damaged a candidate as long as the flip was toward something that the voters agreed with.[65]

The first of the hot-button issues, crime, had been part of Wilson's politics since the beginning. Wilson had latched on to other tough-on-crime measures, most particularly Proposition 115 in June 1990, when he had to beat off a group of conservative opponents in the California gubernatorial primary. Proposition 115, which passed easily, eliminated California's exclusionary law on illegally seized evidence, which had been more protective of privacy rights than federal law; it also allowed the use of hearsay evidence in preliminary hearings and otherwise reduced the rights of criminal defendants. But Wilson's support that year had no potential as a wedge, since his primary opponents were even more conservative than he was, and since his opponent in the general election, Democrat Dianne Feinstein, was herself a hard-liner on crime.

In 1994, after the abduction and sensational murder of a twelve-year-old Petaluma girl named Polly Klaas (late in 1993) had stoked California's crime hysteria, there was ample opportunity. Wilson was hardly the only one to try to capitalize on it: Every

California politician exploited what some people came to call Pollytics. A memorial service for the girl in December 1993 brought out a gaggle of politicians, among them Feinstein, who in the meantime had been elected to the U.S. Senate and who, like Wilson, used the occasion to advertise her own tough anticrime proposals. But it was Wilson who used it most shamelessly and to the most lasting effect.

Wilson, then running for reelection to a second term as governor, had initially appeared to favor a three-strikes bill sponsored by Republican Assemblyman Richard Rainey, who was a former sheriff in suburban Contra Costa County and long-time law-and-order advocate in the legislature. It would have required twenty-five-year-to-life sentences for anyone convicted of a third felony, but counted only violent offenses as strikes. But in the collection of three-strikes proposals that began to sprout like weeds in the spring of 1994, there was an even harsher measure heading for the ballot, an initiative written by a Fresno photographer named Mike Reynolds whose own daughter had been murdered by a felon recently released from prison, and whose story thus resonated in the Klaas murder. The Reynolds initiative counted any felony from murder to bicycle theft as a third strike. When Kathleen Brown, Wilson's Democratic opponent, came out in favor of Three Strikes, Wilson flipped, becoming not merely a supporter of the Reynolds proposal, which ultimately appeared on the ballot as Proposition 184, but the measure's chief advocate. And while Brown ultimately endorsed Proposition 184 as well, Wilson relentlessly attacked her as being soft on crime, especially after she had indicated doubt about a Wilson proposal to put first-time rapists and child molesters in prison for life.

The attacks had particular effect since the political target herself opposed the death penalty. Worse, she was the sister of Jerry Brown, who had named Chief Justice Rose Bird and all those other allegedly soft-on-crime judges to the California bench in the late 1970s, and the daughter of Pat Brown, who had agonized over the execution of Caryl Chessman more than thirty years earlier. Although she described herself as "a different shade of Brown"—implicitly not a flake like her brother Jerry—no voter could fail to make the connection, or see the difference between her and Wilson, who had a long record as a hard-liner on crime. The Legislative Analyst warned that the costs of the extended sentences, which subtantially increased the ordinary prison term for a second felony as well as a third (from 4.5 years for the second residential burglary, for example, to 10.4 years), would increase prison operating costs by $3 billion by the year 2003 and $6 billion by the year 2020, require billions more in new prison construction costs, and quickly eat up a large chunk of the state's discretionary spending.[66] Nonetheless, the voters overwhelmingly approved the Reynolds initiative, despite the fact that the legislature had passed an identical law eight months before.

What was true on crime was even more emphatically true on illegal immigration, an issue that, in that recession year, had almost unlimited potential for exploitation. By the time Wilson ran for re-election in 1994, the issue had been written into yet another ballot proposal, the SOS ("Save Our State") initiative drafted largely by Alan C. Nelson, who had been the head (under Ronald Reagan) of the U.S. Immigration and Naturalization Service and was, at the time, the California lobbyist for FAIR, the Federation for American Immigration Reform. It was sponsored by a number of tough-stand immigration control groups, and its cochairs, besides Nelson, included Harold Ezell, who had been Western Regional Director for INS under Nelson, a crackpot Southern California accountant named Ronald Prince, and an ambitious Republican assemblyman named Richard Mountjoy, who was then preparing a run for the state senate.[67]

SOS, which would would become Proposition 187, declared that the people of California "have suffered and are suffering economic hardship caused by the presence of illegal aliens in this state [and] are suffering injury and damage caused by the criminal conduct of illegal aliens in this state." Its provisions were written to deny illegal alien children access to public schools (a denial which was acknowledged to be unconstitutional, even by many of its backers)[68] and to exclude illegal aliens, adults or children, from virtually all other public services (for most of which, of course, they were already ineligible anyway). But perhaps the thorniest parts of the measure were (first) a provision that required proof of legal residency not only for all children attending public schools but for their parents as well, a device that would, in effect, have denied thousands of American citizens born here to illegals the effective right to a public education; and (second) a requirement under which all California teachers, school administrators, nurses, doctors, and other professionals working for public agencies were to report all people believed to be illegal aliens to the attorney general and to the INS, in effect turning them all into police agents.

Most of the Californians who supported 187 were not the bigots that their opponents made them out to be. There had in fact been a sharp increase in immigration between 1975 and 1995—3 million more immigrants came to the United States during those two decades than had arrived in the preceding forty years. That surge peaked in California in the late 1980s and early 1990s, when estimated immigration to the state, legal and illegal, averaged roughly 400,000 people a year. Those numbers were almost certainly larger than the state could have comfortably accommodated even in the best of circumstances. But they became particularly frustrating in light of the failure of the federal government to honor its promise to tighten controls at the major border crossings, where the border patrol was pathetically understaffed, in enforcing the sanctions against employers who hired undocumented workers that were supposed to be a key provision of the 1986 Immigration Reform and Control Act, in enforcing the general labor laws, and in providing funding for the additional costs of services to the newly amnestied immigrants to which Reagan and Congress had committed themselves when IRCA was passed. In the period between 1989 and 1994 the number of INS agents assigned to enforce the employer sanctions declined by half, and employer sanctions became a joke.[69]

But what troubled the backers of 187 most was the anomaly of providing taxpayer-supported social services in a severe recession to people who, in their view, were by definition lawbreakers—individuals who, instead of being served by public agencies where they deprived legal residents of public resources, should be quickly deported. Still, in its overtones of xenophobia and exclusionism, Proposition 187 echoed a familiar theme that ran back more than a century in California history. The string of California laws and local ordinances denying Japanese aliens the right to own land, effectively excluding Chinese in San Francisco from the right to get licenses to operate laundries, denying alien Japanese the right to fish in coastal waters, and denying all Asian aliens the right to obtain professional licenses is almost endless. Although some were overturned by the Supreme Court as early as the 1880s, others weren't struck down until after World War II.[70]

In the thirty or forty years after 1946, that string seemed to be broken, until, in 1984, California approved Proposition 38, a relatively mild measure instructing the governor to write a letter to the president and other federal officials urging them to end laws that required states with large numbers of foreign-born citizens to provide voting materials in languages other than English. It was followed by the passage of Proposition 63 in 1986, which declared English to be the state's official language and required the legislature to implement that declaration with "appropriate" legislation, something that was, in fact, never done. (No one at the time seemed to recall that California's first constitution, written and ratified in 1849, had been printed, by official order, in both English and Spanish.) But Proposition 187, some of whose early proponents circulated fliers urging Californians to "wake up and smell the refried beans," took those relatively mild outbursts to an altogether different level.

In embracing SOS and becoming its leading spokesman, Wilson, reflecting the state's own long ambivalence on immigration, reversed direction almost 180 degrees. Until the late 1980s, Wilson, then the junior senator of a booming state, had held the standard position of the big California growers who had always been heavy contributors to his campaigns: the looser the restrictions on the entry of low-wage Mexican farm labor, the better. He had fought hard to make certain that exemptions for a minimum of 350,000 farm workers were written into the Immigration Reform and Control Act of 1986. Even after its passage, Wilson pressed the Immigration and Naturalization Service to ease its enforcement of the "burdensome application procedures" of the law to make it easier for Mexican workers to enter the country—crops, he wrote Attorney General Ed Meese in 1987, "were rotting in the fields"—and to stop surprise raids of farms to search for illegal workers. In the end, SAW, the Special Agricultural Worker program that Wilson got written into the law, became an invitation to widespread fraud that led to the legalization of more than 1.1 million aliens, most of them in California.[71]

Wilson's views were hardly unusual; they followed a familiar California course—demanding open borders when the economy was booming, attacking immigrants when things turned sour. But for Wilson, California's rising anti-immigrant agitation provided a two-pronged political opportunity, against both Bill Clinton and Kathleen Brown, who—not suprisingly, given the ethnic constituencies and politics of the Democratic Party—opposed Proposition 187, despite polls showing widespread support for measures to curb services to aliens. The measure had, in fact, been languishing in the signature-gathering process until Wilson, sensing its potential as a wedge against Brown and seizing on it as a way to define his own candidacy, prompted the state Republican Party to put up some $200,000 to help it qualify.

Until the end of 1992, while George Bush had been in the White House, Wilson's complaints about the cost to the state of educating illegal aliens and imprisoning convicts who were illegal immigrants were perfunctory and polite. As soon as Clinton replaced Bush in 1993—and despite the fact that Clinton was more generous in funding immigrant-impact programs than Bush had been—Wilson lost no opportunity to attack the president for the federal government's ineffective measures in controlling the border and for its failure to appropriate the billions that the feds (under Reagan) had promised and allegedly owed the states for health, education, and welfare services to aliens, legal and otherwise. In July 1993, more than a year before the 187 campaign even began, Wilson, perhaps even then positioning himself for a presidential run, bought full-page newspaper ads with an "open letter" to Clinton declaring that "We can no longer allow compassion to override reason." The cost of serving illegal immigrants—which he put at $3 billion a year, mostly for schools—was bankrupting the state, he asserted, demanding that the feds pay what was due. Wilson had a legitimate complaint, but contrary to Wilson's version of things, not all of California's problems came from the federal government's failure on immigration.

Even here there was a further twist. Although Wilson, by then only an echo of the complete moderate, made Proposition 187 his issue in 1994, from the beginning of the campaign he privately assured moderate friends and colleagues (correctly, as it turned out) that if it passed, 187 would get stuck in the courts because it was unconstitutional, and that its more odious provisions (like the statewide requirement requiring teachers, school officials, and health workers to report suspected illegals to the authorities) would therefore never be enforced. Toward the end of the campaign, he even acknowledged it in public. When he was asked during a debate what he would do if he were a school principal forced to throw illegal alien children out of school, he declared that it would never get to that, since it would be stopped in the courts before that could occur. In endorsing it, he said, he was only sending a message.

But the theme of unchecked immigration—conveyed by Proposition 187 and highlighted in Wilson campaign commercials showing those shadowy figures, presumably illegal aliens, running across a road—was also a great wedge to use on Brown and the divided Democrats and, judging from subsequent polls, a major factor in her defeat. "They keep coming," said the narrator in those commercials, a refrain that proved virtually impossible for Brown to answer. It was also a covert, though hardly subtle, assault on all of California's ethnic minorities, despite Wilson's vehement assertion that he was concerned only with illegal aliens and despite his absurd trip, during his abortive presidential campaign the following year, to the Statue of Liberty in New York Harbor, where he sought to underline the point that there was a right way and a wrong way to get into the country. Soon after 187 passed, Wilson, contradicting his own reasoned answer in one TV debate, said its provisions should be implemented immediately, even if it meant throwing schoolchildren onto the streets. Within a year, Wilson was among the most enthusiastic of those who were pushing for a policy, eventually written by Congress into the federal welfare reform bill and signed by Bill Clinton, to get *legal* aliens declared ineligible for food stamps and other federal welfare benefits. Here, too, California's message had been heard.[72] And in the spring of 1997, he used the leeway he got under the federal welfare law to push still harder to deny illegal aliens access to mental health, prenatal care, and other public services.

The topper in this series of politically manipulated ballot measures was CCRI, the California Civil Rights Initiative of 1996, which prohibits all race- and gender-based preferences for, or discrimination against, individuals or groups in California public education, contracting, and employment. CCRI was originally drafted and sponsored by two California academics, Glynn Custred, an anthropologist at Hayward State University, and Tom Wood, the director of the conservative California Association of Scholars. Custred and Wood had become exasperated by race preference programs, particularly in admission to Berkeley and UCLA, the most selective campuses of the University of California system (and easily the most selective public universities in the country), that appeared to go far beyond what the U.S. Supreme Court, in its landmark *Bakke* decision,[73] had contemplated when it permitted the use of race as one "plus factor" in student admissions. Using a rigid point system, UC's selective campuses had in fact been automatically admitting blacks and Latinos with far lower test scores—an average gap of 200–250 points on the combined SAT score (in a range of 1,200 points)[74]—than many of the whites and Asians they rejected, and they gave preference to affluent out-of-state minority applicants over economically disadvantaged Californians who did not come from groups designated as "URMs" (underrepresented minorities). The gaps were even more blatant in admission to some of UC's graduate and professional schools.[75]

When demands began to mount for UC to end race preferences in admission, Jack Peltason, who was the university's president at the time, warned that without such preferences, black enrollment at Berkeley and UCLA might decline by as much as 50 percent and Latino enrollment by some 25 percent. When the university was asked how that was possible if, as UC insisted, nearly all admitted minority freshmen were fully qualified, the response was that if those students couldn't get into their first-choice UC campuses, they would be snatched up by other institutions. That hardly reinforced UC's implicit contention that without preferences, a large number of minority students would be deprived of an opportunity to get a good education, nor did it bolster confidence in UC's defense of its system, which had already been revised under pressure from a federal civil rights investigation on possible reverse discrimination. Custred and Wood also were enraged by continuing efforts by the Democrat-controlled California legislature, twice vetoed by Pete Wilson, to pass legislation to pressure the state's institutions of higher education to pursue, not only ethnically proportional admission rates, but ethnically proportional graduation rates as well.[76]

Custred and Wood, however, had neither the funds nor the political skills to get CCRI on the ballot, and it would have gone nowhere had Pete Wilson and California Republicans not seen it as a wedge with which to drive internal divisions between the blue-collar labor constituencies and the civil rights and minority wings of the Democratic Party. The Wilson campaign organization regarded the CCRI idea as a key element, not only in what it hoped would be a successful Wilson campaign for the 1996 Republican nomination for president, but in the general election campaign of whoever the ultimate standard bearer turned out to be.

Again Wilson flipped. He had begun his political career as a determined proponent of affirmative action: his career as legislator, as mayor of San Diego, and as a U.S. senator had been marked by support for goals and targets in contracting and employment.[77] But Wilson was as good a political trend spotter as anyone in the game and a master at what had by then come to be called "repositioning." And so, by 1995, Governor Wilson had not only embraced CCRI and issued a series of executive orders ending those state affirmative action programs that were subject to his sole discretion, but, with unmatched *chutzpah*, filed suit against his own state to end affirmative action programs that he had once supported. Then, in a stormy meeting in July 1995 that included a bizarre confrontation with civil rights leader Jesse Jackson, Wilson, and Ward Connerly, a long-time friend and political protege whom Wilson had appointed to the University of California regents, rammed resolutions through the board mandating an end to the university's race-based affirmative action programs in admissions and employment.[78]

Like Connerly, a Sacramento businessman (who was himself black), most of those regents were appointees of either Wilson or Deukmejian—many of them political contributors better known for loyalty to the party than for educational statesmanship. Yet it turned out to be a close vote, because even some of them balked. There was, of course, a particular irony in the fact that the University of California, which had fought all the way to the U.S. Supreme Court in defense of its race preferences—and in whose *Bakke* case a very divided court had set the national standard—would become the first major public university to abandon it.

For Wilson, despite all the national attention he got for CCRI, the presidential campaign turned into a short-lived disaster. While he and the state GOP contributed close to $500,000 to get CCRI on the ballot, and while they raised the lion's share of the funds for the general election campaign, the issue turned out to be only marginally useful as a political weapon—in part at least because Clinton had managed to defuse it by ending some of the government's least defensible race-preference programs and more generally with his "mend it but don't end it" position. Wilson continued to push it adamantly: In a teleconference with California Republicans that was accidentally overheard by a journalist, Wilson and House Speaker Newt Gingrich urged strong support for the measure because (in Wilson's words) "it's become a partisan issue . . . that works strongly to our advantage [and] has every bit the potential to make a critical difference [in the campaign]."[79] But none of Wilson's normal group of business backers contributed to it—business was conspicuous by its absence from the effort. Republican presidential candidate Bob Dole, who was already dangerously exposed on the gender issue, endorsed it timidly but hardly spoke about it until the last desperate weeks of the election. In the meantime state party leaders conducted an invidious TV ad campaign linking Clinton's opposition to CCRI with his opposition to Proposition 187, thus rolling immigrant bashing and the campaign against affirmative action into one ugly ball. The clumsiness of that effort became such an embarrassing liability to the cause that it was publicly deplored even by Connerly, who by then had become head of the campaign to pass CRRI, and who vehemently insisted that CCRI was not just an extension of 187.

Despite those difficulties, CCRI, which appeared as Proposition 209 on the November 1996 ballot, passed easily, albeit by a narrower-than-expected margin of 54–46, not the 65–35 percent majorities that the previous year's polls had suggested. It might not have gotten even that many votes had the opponents in the last weeks of the campaign not generated a small backlash to their own efforts with TV ads trying to link support of the measure with the Ku Klux Klan.[80] The polls seemed to indicate that while most voters, including a majority of women voters, opposed race and gender preferences, many felt uncomfortable about ending all affirmative action. Clinton's equivocal statements effectively tapped into that ambivalence. Conversely, it's also possible that many voters began to sense that the issue had in fact been manipulated by the Republicans for blatantly partisan advantage, and that they themselves were the targets of that manipulation.

Yet surely a lot of people heard the message, inside Congress and out. The vote on 209, combined with the residual effects of Proposition 187 and the cuts in food stamps, SSI, and other benefits that were being imposed even on legal aliens by the new federal welfare law, resonated with a series of unmistakable (and familiar) themes for Hispanics and other new California residents. On the one hand, they helped stimulate the unprecedented surge in new citizenship applications that made 1996 a record year in the number of people who were naturalized; on the other, they were a powerful reminder of how much more difficult and convoluted California's class and ethnic picture was becoming. It may also have become a wake-up call for some Republicans, including some in California, who seemed to be starting to realize that, at least for the long run, Wilson's blatant style of race-and-immigration politics was a descending road to electoral oblivion.[81]

Like most of the provisions of Proposition 187, Proposition 209 was quickly blocked by a federal court, in this case a San Francisco judge and former civil rights lawyer named Thelton Henderson, who had been appointed by Jimmy Carter. CCRI's prohibitions against race- and gender-based preferences for, or discrimination against, any individual or group sounded like the very essence of American civil rights principles—were indeed an echo of the equal protection clause of the Fourteenth Amendment. But Henderson, agreeing with lawyers for the American Civil Liberties Union and a range of civil rights organizations, found that in foreclosing local political efforts by minorities and women to secure affirmative action programs, it treated them differently from other groups— veterans, for example—who were not similarly precluded from trying to obtain ordinances or other local laws granting them preferences in employment or education that were permissible (and sometimes encouraged by the courts) under the U.S. Constitution.[82]

But Henderson's decision was swiftly and summarily overturned by a three-judge panel of the Ninth Circuit Court of Appeals that was as conservative as he was liberal. The court declared, with what seemed like flat good sense, that "the Fourteenth Amendment, lest we lose sight of the forest for the trees, does not require what it barely permits . . . No one contends that individuals have a constitutional right to preferential treatment solely on the basis of their race or gender . . . That the Constitution permits the rare race-based preference hardly implies that the state cannot ban them altogether." The judges also went out of their way, with gratuitous excess, to berate Henderson: "A system," they declared, "which permits one judge to block with a stroke of a pen what 4,736,180 state residents voted to enact as law tests the integrity of our constitutional democracy."[83] What if those 4,736,180 residents had voted to intern all of California's Japanese aliens?

Nonetheless, just a year after 209 passed, the U.S. Supreme Court, refusing to review the decision of the three judge panel, effectively upheld it. Unlike Proposition 187, whose most important provisions, the exclusion of illegal alien children from public schools, and the conversion of school officials and social service workers into de facto police agents for the immigration authorities, violate all manner of prior high court decisions,[84] CCRI is clearly consistent with the Supreme Court's recent course in cases involving race-based contracting set-asides, legislative redistricting, and other major civil rights issues. In those cases, the court, under the doctrine of strict scrutiny, is requiring that race-based affirmative action programs must be "narrowly tailored" to implement "a compelling government interest."[85]

Proposition 209 is a blunderbuss prohibiting virtually all good-faith efforts in the public sector to enact measures, other than those ordered by a court to remedy specific instances of discrimination, to undo the effects of past bias, or to make the public workforce more representative and credible, or in any way to target programs in order to increase opportunities for minorities. A few months after 209 passed, Connerly himself allowed that it might have been better if its provisions had allowed for a more gradual approach. He also acknowledged that 209 could make it harder to break up the old boy networks in public contracting and employment. And, as the University of California struggled to maintain some minority representation in its entering classes, he even acknowledged that 209 might need to be amended to permit some race-based targeting of university outreach programs.[86]

But 209 also attacked practices and precedents that are already undergoing judicial reexamination, not least of them the principles of the *Bakke* ruling itself, which a three-judge panel of the U.S. Fifth Circuit Court of Appeals in Houston, going out of its judicial way, had struck down in *Hopwood v. Texas* a few months earlier.[87] Because of the Supreme Court's failure to review *Hopwood*, *Bakke* is now no longer the law in Texas, Louisiana, and Mississippi.

What the Fifth Circuit judges said in *Hopwood*—that because "non-remedial state interests will never justify racial classifications," no race-based admissions program is permissible—is almost precisely what 209 says. Sooner or later that issue will probably have to be addressed by the high court, if for no other reason than to get the country back to a single standard on affirmative action. What the law now encourages in forty-six states, it prohibits in four others. Perhaps more broadly, since CÇRI, whether it's wise policy or not, is almost a dead echo of the Fourteenth Amendment, it is absurd, as the judges on the Ninth Circuit panel said, to argue that a state law that requires equal protection of the laws violates equal protection of the laws.[88] In the end, as Jeffery Rosen put it, the logic of the ACLU attack on 209 seems to assume that any state law or initiative favoring one group over another—insurers over trial lawyers, patients over health maintenance organizations, farmers over railroads—is impermissibly discriminatory, and thus "would invalidate much of the legacy of the Progressive movement, including the initiative process itself."[89] That still left many questions of interpretation, as well as possible conflicts with existing federal law, and thus promised no end of further legal action in lower courts. But the initiative stood.

There seems little question that the new policies of the University of California regents to end race-based affirmative action, approved fifteen months before the passage of 209, were driving down applications from minority students even before they went into effect. But there is no way yet to predict the broader consequences of Proposition 209, or even to know how it will be implemented in the hundreds of different situations to which it may apply. Would the system adapt, as San Jose already has—by demanding that all contractors who have low proportions of minority employees prove that their hiring and promotion policies were, in fact, totally based on legitimate job qualifications and not on race or gender criteria? Or would it prohibit all outreach to underrepresented groups and generate a wave of reverse-discrimination lawsuits from white males demanding proof that the black man or the Hispanic woman hired ahead of them was really chosen on the basis of race- and gender-blind criteria?

For California—the new California—the long run probably allows no other choice than the principles that 209 dictates. In some instances, the race preferences in public employee hiring have already evolved into a system of entitlements leading to sharp interminority battles, particularly between blacks and Latinos.

When the new ethnic groups begin to achieve proportional political power, such preferences could harden into the most virulent forms of discrimination. Equally important, at a time when the Census Bureau itself is beginning to struggle with questions about how to classify individuals, the problem of definition in a society that is as multiethnic as California becomes almost insurmountable. How does one count the children of the increasing numbers of mixed marriages—Latino and Asian, black and white, Filipino and Pacific Islander? What boxes are they to check on the application form? Until the regents ended ethnic preferences, the University of California listed East Indians with whites, treated anyone with a Hispanic surname as an underrepresented minority even if that person was the all-white child of an Argentine banker or a Uruguayan shipping executive, and counted Filipinos, to whom this country presumably owes a special obligation, as a separate ethnic category but gave them no preference. How does one effectively disfavor Japanese and Chinese job applicants, many of whose parents suffered the most brutal forms of discrimination in California? Why should a recent immigrant from Mexico get preference ahead of American-born Asians? And when race- or gender-based preferences are given, say in the awarding of contracts, how wide can they be?

Such questions don't simply drive issues like CCRI; on their answers rests a good part of California's future as a workable society. Unfortunately, to be successful in this new society, the answers and policies based on them will almost certainly have to be complex, nuanced, sometimes even fudged. And those are all the things that neither 209 nor, indeed, any ballot initiative really permits.[90]

VI

Given California's history of progressive innovation in government, Proposition 140, the 1990 initiative enacting tight legislative term limits and imposing other restrictions on those innovations, was perhaps the most telling stroke of all. With it, the circle of government reform that began in the 1960s began to close. California had been among the leaders in enacting tough campaign disclosure laws, limiting the scope of lobbyists, and moving toward a full-time legislature with a highly professional staff. Now with Proposition 140 it became not only the first major state to enact term limits for all elected state officials, from governor to assembly member, it also imposed the most stringent in the nation—three two-year terms in a lifetime for the state's eighty assembly members, two four-year terms for its forty state senators and all other elected state officials. Almost as important, though rarely noticed, Proposition 140 sharply reduced legislative staffing and perks.

California was hardly alone in going down that route—since 1990, some twenty states have imposed legislative term limits, all but one, Utah, through the initiative route—but it certainly led the way.[91] And while term limits can comfortably be classified as a near-perfect example of populist reform—a change in the governmental process that legislatures are unlikely to impose on themselves—it probably wouldn't have happened at all without help from a few conservative deep pockets. Nationally, the most prominent of those deep pockets were two right-wing Kansas oil billionaires named Charles and David Koch, working through a handful of well-funded national organizations; in California, the angel in 1990 was a conservative Los Angeles politician named Pete Schabarum, who was retiring after five years as a legislator and nineteen years as a county supervisor—no term limits for him. Since the law prevented Schabarum from keeping for himself the $1 million-plus he still had in his campaign treasury, he decided he would use it, in combination with major funding from a couple of those national term-limits organizations, to buy his fellow citizens term limits.

While term limits were promulgated in each state as a remedy for the particular ailments of that state, the movement was not just the result of a wild round of coincidental dissatisfaction that happened to sweep every state that had the initiative in its constitution: The legislatures of Maine and California, Ohio and Idaho, Oklahoma and Michigan, didn't all turn into swamps of iniquity at the same time. But since Congress, the prime target of the voters' restiveness, is hard to reach through state voter initiatives, it was the legislatures that got hit, and it's in the states that term limits have stuck. Yet nowhere have term limits been more rigidly drawn than they are in California—no state other than Michigan imposed a three-term limit for assembly members and a two-term limit for state senators *and* a lifetime ban on ever running for that office again. Nowhere else were they so consistent with the populist passions and the plebiscitary impulses that immediately preceded them and so radically different from the state's once-high expectations of a professionalized legislature.

In California they've had an immediate—and in some measure a seismic—effect. Although the state's term limits were sold by Schabarum and his partners as a way to get fresh blood and new faces into government—citizen legislators, including more women and minorities not bound to the old interests and the good ol' boy networks—it was no accident that Willie Brown, the long-term (black) speaker from San Francisco became the poster child of the term-limits drive. And while Brown's assertion that the attacks on him were primarily motivated by race was probably something of an exaggeration, it is nearly impossible to tease apart the racial anxieties and the political restiveness of a large part of the state's disproportionately white, middle-class voters. Certainly no other issue better illustrates how the state's voters used the inititiative to check the power of urban voters in those predominantly minority districts that produced so many of the state's legislative leaders. Brown's glitzy parties, brash fund-raising, and wheeling and dealing with trial lawyers, tobacco companies, teacher's unions, and other interests would have earned any politician some heat. But it was also true, as he told reporters, that "I am in a spot where racial minorities are not supposed to be . . . You could say whatever you wanted about this black man, and it was instantly believable."[92] As Richard Hofstadter pointed out long ago, the impulse toward cleaner government and a more perfect democracy in the Progressive movement was always a little hard to separate from the racist and the xenophobic.

Ultimately, Brown would have the last laugh. He would trade one office for a larger and brighter stage as mayor of San Francisco—and would enlarge *that* simply by being who he was.

But the rest of the state was not as blessed. Because California was among the first to enact term limits, and because its limits are so stringent, it was also the first to experience the results of the change.

By 1996, all of the assembly members who had been in the legislature in 1990, and many of the state senators, were "termed out." With the exception of a few people who had served before term limits took hold, left, and then returned, there has been a total turnover in assembly membership—and the results are hardly what had been promised. Contrary to the rosy predictions of term-limits advocates like columnist George Will, California did not enter a golden age of "civic republicanism."[93] Proposition 140 has not brought the state perceptibly closer to the "government of citizens representing their fellow citizens" that Schabarum promised voters in his ballot argument six years ago. Nor has it done much, quoting the ballot argument again, to "remove the grip that vested interests have over the Legislature [and] put an end to the Sacramento web of special favors and patronage." What it did do was to send a new generation of politicians to Sacramento many of whom were long on partisanship and painfully short on both legislative experience and policy background—and, worse, seemed not much to care.

That's not to say that the proponents were all wrong. Because of term limits, the California Senate, one of whose members, Ralph Dills, has been in public office since 1938, and in politics since 1934, when he was a member of Upton Sinclair's EPIC organization (End Poverty in California), will cease to be what one legislator, with some hyperbole, called "the geriatric ward of California."

That presumably will be true in a lot of other states as well. Because of the high turnover term limits will foster, there is a chance that some legislatures will become somewhat more diverse ethnically and have more women—something that may now be starting to occur at the margins in the increasing representation of Hispanics in the California legislature, where they have always been, and still are, significantly underrepresented. (The number of blacks in the legislature, meanwhile, has declined, and the number of women remains about the same.) And term limits, combined with subsequent campaign spending reform initiatives, will make it much harder for assembly Speakers or senate presidents pro tem, none of whom is likely to serve more than a few years, to accumulate either the power that their predecessors had or the dispensible political campaign funds on which much of that power was based. Often they won't be around long enough even to discipline upstart members, as Brown did, by stripping them of committee chairmanships or suddenly moving their office into some dark capitol corner.[94] Because of term limits, some of the personal arrogance and indifference that characterized some long-term members may be a thing of the past.

But anyone looking for a new breed of citizen-legislators will probably look in vain. By general agreement, the 1995–96 term-limits-crunch session of the California legislature was probably the most mean-spirited and unproductive in memory, a unique combination of instability, bad behavior, political frenzy, and legislative paralysis. In the two years between 1995 and 1997, California had five assembly Speakers, two different Republican assembly leaders, two Republican senate leaders, and eight special legislative elections, not counting runoffs, among them three recalls. Term limits also prompted a frenetic game of musical chairs prompted by the search of the nearly termed-out for jobs of longer and more secure tenure—as lobbyists, consultants, academics, or in other public offices. That, in turn, produced an almost continuous battle over the Speakership, and, with it an unprecedented round of fratricidal vendetti stemming from the attempts of a group of clumsy and inexperienced assembly Republicans to punish those who were insufficiently loyal to the demands of their caucus.

Thus, what began as the high drama of promised democratic reform ended as farce:

In November of 1994, Republican Senator Marian Bergeson, a ten-year veteran of the legislature, knowing she must leave office by 1996, runs for, and wins, a seat on the Orange County Board of Supervisors. This sets up a special election in March that's won (after a runoff in June) by Republican Assemblyman Ross Johnson. He leaves a vacancy in the assembly and thus prompts another special election, which is held in September. In the meantime, Republican Assemblyman Dick Mountjoy, who would have been termed-out in 1996 and was looking for a place with more potential, has won a special election for the senate seat vacated by Senator Frank Hill, who was removed from office in the summer of 1994 after his conviction on a bribery charge. But because of a closely divided assembly (and because a quirk in state law permits it), Mountjoy delays giving up his assembly seat even after his senate victory so that he can cast his vote for a Republican Speaker, in effect occupying two seats simultaneously.

Eventually, in what Republicans call a coup, the Democrats, with the help of one Republican defector, Assemblyman Paul Horcher, oust Senator/Assemblyman Mountjoy from the assembly and return Brown to the Speaker's chair. Mountjoy's assembly seat is thereupon filled in yet another special election. (In the course of that maneuvering, the Republicans, who won a slim majority of assembly seats in 1994, become so intimidated by the uncanny ability of the long-time Democratic speaker, Willie Brown, to use parliamentary devices to delay their hoped-for takeover that one of their members, a former sheriff's deputy named Larry Bowler, cuts the wires of the internal microphones in the caucus chamber out of fear that Democrats might be listening in.)

In anger and revenge, Republicans organize a successful voter recall against the defecting Horcher, who is replaced by Assemblyman Gary Miller. The Republicans also organize a recall against Assemblyman Mike Machado, a Democrat, accused by them of breaking a promise not to vote for the Democratic Speaker. That recall fails miserably, and Machado files an $800,000 claim with the state, under a law allowing public reimbursement of expenses to the survivor of a recall. In the meantime Willie Brown, now running for mayor of San Francisco, steps down as speaker, but since Orange County Republican Assemblywoman Doris Allen is angry at the way she's been treated by the leaders of her caucus, she, like Horcher before her, refuses to vote for the Republican leader, Jim Brulte, for Speaker. (She is also termed-out and thus seems to feel no undue fealty to her caucus.) Instead, she allows herself to be elected Speaker of the nearly evenly divided assembly with the unanimous votes of the Democrats (and her own vote) and over the unanimous opposition of her Republican colleagues.

Allen thus becomes the target of yet another GOP recall (in November 1995) in which she is ousted and replaced by a Republican loyalist named Scott Baugh. Before the recall election takes place, the increasingly embattled Allen resigns the Speakership, but not before she manages to describe her GOP colleagues, in one very public (and much-quoted) statement, as "power-hungry males with short penises." She is replaced as Speaker by another maverick Republican named Brian Setencich, a former professional basketball player and Fresno city council member with barely a year's legislative experience, who, like Allen, is elected over the opposition of all but two members of his own caucus—his and Allen's.

Baugh's election finally provides the Republicans enough votes to replace Setencich and elect their own Speaker, a Southern California Christian conservative named Curt Pringle, but he also brings them another embarrassment: Not long after his election, Baugh, along with a number of Republican staff members, is indicted by the Republican district attorney in Orange County on charges of campaign fraud in connection with their efforts to run a dummy Democrat to split the opposition vote.[95] In the March 1996 primary, meanwhile, less than a year after his elevation as Speaker, Setencich, in what one California columnist called "a terminal case of mad GOP disease,"[96] is himself bumped out of office by a Republican primary challenger whose only backing comes from a well-heeled and powerful group of Southern California Christian fundamentalists associated with Rob Hurtt, the Republican leader in the state senate.

In November 1996, the Democrats, taking advantage of some egregious Republican campaign errors, some committed by their own Speaker—recapture control of the assembly and again choose their own Speaker, Cruz Bustamante, who had first been elected to the legislature in 1993. Democrat Carole Migden, who has been in the legislature less than a year, becomes chair of the Appropriations Committee. At roughly the same time, Marian Bergeson, the former state senator who had started the whole game of musical chairs when she resigned to take a seat on the Orange County Board of Supervisors just two years before, resigns *that* seat in order to take a post in the Wilson cabinet. A few weeks later, Pete Schabarum, who bankrolled Proposition 140 to bring cleaner government to California, and who has since been running an organization in Southern California called Citizens for Better Representation, is indicted by a California grand jury on charges of embezzlement and tax evasion.

It's probably true that none of this—nor the resulting legislative gridlock and high levels of partisan hostility—would have been half as severe, or the stakes as high, had it not been for a redistricting scheme created by judicially appointed special masters after the 1990 census that so evenly divided districts—another great reform ideal—that it was hard for either party to get undisputed control of the lower house (and which, in turn, also helped fuel the legislative money races among those increasingly insecure incumbents). It's also conceivable that were we living in a less ideologically unforgiving time or place, there might have been more of a chance of compromise and professional respect among the members.

But term limits itself sends an affirmative message that experience is not as important as ideological purity and/or faithful representation of the demands of the voters of one's district. Government, said Phil Isenberg, the pragmatic Democratic assemblyman and one of the legislature's most thoughtful people before he was himself termed-out in 1996, is not "like filling sandbags in the flood"—something that a citizen does on a temporary basis, after which it's time to go home and return to normal life.

During much of 1994, Willie Brown, who had been in the assembly for over thirty years and was its speaker for nearly fifteen, tried to train up a new generation of Democratic leaders—potential Speakers, chairs of key committees, and all the rest. But the effort had only marginal success at best, in part because no one who has been there four years or less has time to learn enough about California's complicated issues, and in part because, under term limits, the payoff will be so limited. Who wants to stay up all night learning brain surgery when he can only practice for two years? Henceforth, Brown told reporter Daniel Weintraub, there is going to be no "central force, no central person, who is really responsible or accountable, everyone just doing their own little number . . ."[97]

In the spring of 1997, after the Democrats recaptured the assembly, squabbling and tension among the novice legislators, including potentially dangerous friction between black and Hispanic factions, bogged the lower house down again, sometimes in nasty bickering over such portentuous issues as a motion to adjourn in the memory of a murdered rap singer. (Of the assembly's twenty-seven committees, eleven were chaired by freshmen.) "We are still finding our way," said Assemblywoman Sheila Kuehl, who was one of the state's smartest legislators, and, with three years' experience, among that body's most senior members. "We do not have a unified culture yet because so many people are new . . . We haven't even formed the relationships you form in the first year of college." Four-year veteran Debra Bowen put it even more succinctly. "There are no old timers," she said, "who you can go to when things go sideways."[98]

The effects have been—and always will be—less severe in the senate, with its eight-year limits and with its complement of members who previously served in the assembly. (Just as they will be less severe in states like Oklahoma, Nevada, and Utah, which have twelve-year limits for each house of their legislatures—longer than the average term is now.) And since a number of termed-out senators will henceforth be seeking seats in the assembly, as a few have already done, they may provide some leavening there as well.

More broadly, as Douglas G. Brown, the director of Colorado's Office of Legislative Legal Services, observed about the likely effects of reforms related to that state's term-limits initiative, "the legislative process is remarkably adaptable and resilient." But he did not minimize the dangers: "Experienced members know that disagreement is the default position and agreement takes time and compromise and education to achieve. Experienced members can reason by analogy from previous experiences; new members will not know the lessons of the past."[99] Bill Lockyer, California's senate president pro tem, put it another way: New members arrive "convinced that those people (already in government) have screwed it all up: I'm going to fix it, whatever it is. [But after a while] people tend to meet smart people with different values . . . and they start to say, 'Maybe I'm not absolutely right about this.' "[100] With term limits, that's far less likely to happen.

What term limits have certainly done is to reduce legislative experience and increase instability, which was probably part of their intent, and raise the chance for error and confusion. In a survey sponsored by the National Conference of State Legislatures of the behavior of California assembly members elected since the enactment of Proposition 140, the authors concluded that rather than trying to work out compromises in the fights over the Speakership, "the 54 term limit babies behaved in ways indistinguishable from their colleagues elected prior to term limits." If they differed in any significant way, the authors observed, it was that far fewer of them had served as legislative staffers before they were elected than was the case for their predecessors. Their inexperience "made them ill-equipped for anything but a passive role."[101]

And unless current court challenges ultimately succeed, that's not likely to soon change. Under any rigid term-limits formula, members begin looking for the next slot almost from the moment they arrive (and certainly from the moment they have any legislative experience). The legislature has in effect become like a Greyhound bus station, where some people have just arrived and where others are waiting to leave, and where few have any particular interest in, or loyalty, to the place through which they must pass. In the two-year period between the 1992 and 1994 elections, California had twelve special elections—that's 10 percent of all seats—in which more than $10 million was spent, more per race than the already large amounts, now approaching a total of $80 million every two years, spent in regular legislative elections.[102] By the time all campaign expenses were tabulated, the amount spent in the 1996 election cycle easily broke all previous records. That's not money that comes in $5 donations raised at neighborhood teas and clambakes. In 1996, for the first time, as former California Common Cause director Ruth Holton observed, political candidates were holding fund-raisers in Sacramento—meaning that they were shaking down the special interests—even before they were elected.[103] In 1995, an off year, legislative freshmen raised an average of $165,000 each, considerably more than their veteran colleagues.

In the spring of 1997, more than six years after the passage of the term-limits initiative, Claudia Wilken, a federal judge in Oakland, struck down Proposition 140, ruling that the lifetime ban was unnecessary to accomplish the rotation in office that the measure seeks, thus making it unconstitutionally broad, but stayed enforcement of the decision pending further appeals. Wilken's decision was temporarily upheld in a split decision by a three-judge panel of the U.S. Ninth Circuit Court of Appeals. That further compounded the state's political confusion—could termed-out members now run again after all?—and further encouraged attacks on the meddlesome courts. But in December 1997, just before the filing deadlines for the 1998 elections, both Wilken and the three-judge panel were overturned by a unanimous eleven-judge panel of the Ninth Circuit. The minor constraint on voters' rights that Proposition 140 imposes, the court said, was a small imposition and "is justified by the state's legitimate interests . . . California voters apparently perceived lifetime term limits . . . as a means to promote democracy by opening up the political process and restoring competitive elections. That was their choice to make."[105] When the U.S. Supreme Court declined review, the fight was over.

That could start a whole new term-limits clock on present incumbents, but it is not likely to change the larger picture or bring back the experienced legislators and staff who have already been forced from office—the people of talent and dedication along with the hacks. Nor will it restore the old relations between the institutional legislature and its members.

As Proposition 140's sponsors promised, the flow of money, particularly to members of the assembly, will be less subject to the control of a powerful Speaker, as Willie Brown had been. Even without term limits, it will be a long time, if ever, that any figure in that house will develop the long-term relationships that Brown, for better or worse, managed with trial lawyers, minority groups, public employee unions, land developers, and other major lobbies. For the same reason, it will also be hard for anyone to develop the clout to broker deals among various interest groups—which are now increasingly trying to work their own deals directly with individual members—or to keep caucus members in line, and thus to make parties politically accountable organizations. And that will make it even harder than it has been in California, with its increasingly fractured body politic, to hold votes together and enact any major legislation—or, indeed, to do anything that takes compromise and deferral, and thus requires the luxuries of time and relative political security.[106]

Compounding the problems created by those changing power relationships is the declining level of policy experience that term limits fosters—the legislative amateurism that it indeed celebrates.[107] Some of that might have been mitigated by the presence of a highly professional staff, which California once had, but because Proposition 140 also required a 40 percent reduction in legislative personnel and funding—a provision, perhaps needless to say, that was unaffected, and unchallenged, in any court case—that professional staff has been reduced to a fraction of its size and, because there are fewer senior jobs, leading to considerably more turnover, to a fraction of its experience.

Here again, good impulses produced unintended consequences. By general, if not unanimous, agreement, there had for years been too many highly paid political hacks on legislative payrolls, men and women earning six-figure salaries and cushy pensions to organize fund-raisers, staff campaigns, and service lobbyists. But, to no one's surprise, Proposition 140 did little to reduce the number of political operatives, who know how to win elections and who, in the constant search for money, are more needed than ever. The damage, rather, was done in the nonpartisan Legislative Analyst's office, which studies and evaluates the fiscal effects of the budget and all money bills and which lost 60 percent of its staff, and in the rolls of the policy experts attached to various legislative committees. Those experts—in budgeting, water law, taxation, environmental law, education, transportation, and all the rest—had, for the better part of a generation beginning in the mid-1960s, been the people who made California's legislature a model of professionalism for the nation. Until 1990, someone from the Legislative Analyst's office appeared—and testified as an impartial expert witness—at hearings on all major revenue and appropriations bills; after 140 passed and the office's budget was cut, that was no longer possible.

Not surprisingly, there has also been been a marked decline in the quality of the work done by committee policy staff, another element of Jess Unruh's once-proud creation, partly because they are now so shorthanded, partly because the turnover makes jobs less secure, and partly because many of the new members couldn't care less. They don't miss what they've never known. Where once committee bill analyses were, for the most part, relatively objective statements that laid out the arguments on a bill, pro and con, raised unanswered questions, and tried to suggest the likely effects, they now tend increasingly to be taken verbatim from the lobbyists pushing or opposing the measure, or simply from fantasy.[108] Because term limits leaves everyone insecure, said one member, "this place has become a totally risk-averse environment, which is why you have so much stridency and so little achievement."

The net effect, almost certainly, will be more clout for lobbyists, who are never termed-out and who know the issues; for the governor and the executive branch, who still have budgeting and policy-making expertise; and for bureaucrats in the agencies. Art Agnos, a former California legislator and former mayor of San Francisco, and subsequently the Clinton administration's Western regional director for the Deparment of Housing and Urban Development, recently remarked that the real effects of term limits is that "no one will be in office long enough to touch the bureaucrats . . . They tell us political appointees—the politocrats—that while we're the A team, they're the B team: 'We be here when you come and we be here after you're gone.'"

VII

Term limits, whatever its ultimate form and legal fate, is a nice fit in the California pattern: first, a search for a quick-fix autopilot remedy for perceived legislative failure—a self-enacting political solution that exempts citizens and voters from the need to engage themselves in individual elections; second, a tangle of unintended

consequences; and, third, further exacerbation of the tension between reform and frustration, and between the voters and the
courts. In the classic Newtonian checks-and-balances theory of the
nation's constitutional framers, the three branches of government
checked one another. In the growing emphasis on plebiscitary action, and the shrinking role of the legislature in major policy-
making, the only institutional check on the exercise of majoritarian
will is the judicial system, and, in light of the spectacular deference
of state courts to "the will of the people," the federal courts in
particular.[109]

And that, of course, is precisely what's been happening. Many
of the major measures enacted by initiative in California have been
challenged in court, and as the ballot brush has gotten broader in
recent years, the courts have become increasingly engaged. By early
1997, a half-dozen initiatives were in some stage of judicial review,
among them Propositions 140 (term limits); 187 (immigration);
209 (affirmative action); 208 (the campaign finance-reform law
approved by the voters in November 1996); and 198 (an "open
primary" measure, approved in March 1996, allowing voters to pick
and choose candidates from any party in primary elections).[110]
Although many of them were likely to be ultimately upheld by the
courts, whenever a measure is even temporarily blocked by some
trial judge, its supporters vociferously complain that democracy
and the popular will are being frustrated by an unelected elite in
black robes, thereby generating further exasperation with formal
governmental institutions. When Congressman Tom DeLay, who is
several notches to the right of Speaker Newt Gingrich, started talk-
ing about impeaching federal judges early in 1997, Thelton Henderson was one of three names on the hit list.

What gets forgotten is that the voters—the majority of the
minority that votes—are as required to observe constitutional
rights when they make laws as are legislatures and governors, and
it's precisely where there are no other checks and balances—no
system of legislative hearings; no studies or expert witnesses; no
requirement that majorities in two houses, plus a governor, be in
agreement; no possibility, in most cases, that errors and inequities

can be amended through further legislative action—that judicial review is most needed.

The case was made most forcefully by the late Julian N. Eule, who, until his death in 1996, was a professor and associate dean at the UCLA Law School, who argued (in a 1990 article in the *Yale Law Journal*) that where the "constitutional filtering system has been removed, courts must play a larger role—not because direct democracy is unconstitutional, nor because it frequently produces legislation that we may find substantively displeasing or short-sighted, but because the judiciary stands *alone* in guarding against the evils incident to transient, impassioned majorities that the Constitution seeks to dissipate."[111] That "harder look," Eule said, is particularly necessary where minority rights are affected (as they clearly are in the cases of the measures dealing with aliens and affirmative action).

Eule, of course, is not the last word in this field. Since initiatives are constitutionally sanctioned processes, his critics argue, they should be treated like any other form of lawmaking. Nor were the federal trial court judges in the California cases—Mariana Pfaelzer on the immigration measure, Henderson on CCRI, Claudia Wilken on term limits—the last word in the cases they were dealing with. Henderson and Wilken have already been reversed, and they probably won't be the last. (Certainly also, they are powerless to do anything about the foolishness and unintended consequences of the measures that voters approve, provided only that they don't offend the Constitution.) But their interposition in these cases at least indicates the dangers, particularly to minorities, of the process, even instances where an initiative is blocked, reinforcing the point made by Derrick Bell: that "far from being the pure path to democracy," direct democracy, carried out in the privacy of the voting booth, may well have "diminished the ability of minority groups to participate in the democratic process [because] it enables the voters' racial beliefs and fears to be recorded and tabulated in their pure form . . ."

Pete Wilson reinforced the argument from the other side when he said that, regardless of what the courts finally do on the provisions in Proposition 187 denying schooling and other services to illegal aliens, the vote on such an initiative is itself a declaration of social intent and political demands that are hard for politicians to neglect. It sends a powerful message to people on all sides of the political spectrum, as 187 surely did, about what kind of society the voters want their state and nation to be.

And in that respect, measures like 187 have worked very well indeed. Even before it passed, California began to get more money from the Clinton administration to house illegal alien prisoners, and stricter controls, often instituted with considerable fanfare, at the border. Border controls were beefed up even more after its passage, though probably to no great effect in a situation where the only real determinants of the ebb and flow of population are economic. And if Bill Clinton heard the message, so did the new Republican Congress, which voted to deny even legal aliens food stamps and other major benefits in the 1996 federal welfare reform bill.

But those who heard it most quickly and clearly, of course, were the aliens themselves, and that produced two very different results. Shortly after the passage of Proposition 187 (in some cases even before), California school administrators, the operators of community clinics, and others in the social welfare system reported that despite the court order blocking its implementation, there was a sharp and, from the perspective of protecting public health, a dangerous decline in the number of people seeking medical and other social services in California. And that, of course, is precisely the outcome that the sponsors of measures like 187 wanted. But it also helped generate that surge of new citizens and, very possibly, a substantial block of new Democratic voters, particularly in California. Add that one to the lengthening list headed "ironies" and "unintended consequences."

PART FOUR
The Next America

‹›

I

The returns are not all in. California again is the driving engine of national economic growth and likely to remain in that position until well into the next century. Because of foundations laid forty years ago, and in some cases even before that, it is at the forefront of the world's leading-edge technologies and of its creative energy. It has replaced the declining job bases in aircraft and defense-related industries with sharp increases in what the Center for the Continuing Study of the California Economy (CCSCE) calls "future high growth sectors": computers, communications equipment and electronic components, medical instruments, motion picture production, and a range of related entertainment and information-based industries founded on the synergism among increasingly sophisticated software, Hollywood artistry—what the Disney people sometimes still call "imagineering"—and space-age computer design and graphics.[1] It leads the nation in foreign trade—the neighboring harbors of Long Beach and Los Angeles are the country's busiest, accounting for roughly one-fourth of all U.S. ocean trade; the San Jose metropolitan area (Silicon Valley) is the nation's largest exporter of goods and services. The state's climate and varied landscape—fires, floods, smog, drought, and earthquakes (so far, at least) notwithstanding—remain powerful magnets for immigrants and tourists.[2]

But if the revitalized California economy is a model for the nation and the world, and if the lives of the successful and the glamorous continue to be simultaneously the sources of worldwide fascination, horror, and envy, its increasingly dysfunctional governmental and fiscal public institutions, the depleted state of its public infrastructure, services, and amenities, the growing gaps between its affluent and its poorer residents, and its pinched social ethos hang like dark clouds in the sunny skies of the state's recovery. What had been El Dorado's perfectionist-driven willingness to take large, and perhaps excessive, risks with great public enterprise has turned into a crippling search for security bordering on paralysis.

The hold of those latter-day insecurities was nowhere more evident than in the state's response to the state Constitution Revision Commission that had been (reluctantly) appointed by the governor and leaders of the legislature to study California's increasingly unmanageable governmental structure. In the summer of 1996, the commission made a set of cautious but nonetheless sound recommendations: allow the legislature to pass the budget and other fiscal bills by majority vote, and do away with the two-thirds supermajority that California alone requires; restore more fiscal authority and accountability to local agencies; shorten and simplify the ballot by reducing the enormous number of elected state officials; modify legislative term limits to permit six two-year terms in the assembly and three four-year terms in the senate; permit the creation of regional governments to replace the thousands of local governments and districts that now overlap, willy-nilly, across the California landscape; revise the initiative process to give the legislature a larger role in reviewing initiatives before they go on the ballot and in amending bad measures after they pass. California is the only state in the union that does not permit some form of legislative revision or amendment after an initiative statute has been on the books for a fixed number of years. In one draft, the commission even called for the creation of a unicameral legislature with 120 members, thereby permitting the creation of slightly smaller districts, which, in theory, would make it somewhat easier for voters to know their representatives.

The commission was hardly the first to urge changes. Just two years earlier, another group, the Business-Higher Education Forum, which included executives from the state's leading corporations as well the leaders of most of the state's major educational institutions, concluded that the whole system was broken.[3]

> [It] is our belief that California can no longer ignore investment in public infrastructure and human capital and maintain a strong economy. Investments in education, research and development, transportation and communications systems, a new business plant and equipment are the sources of growth in the economy. To continue on our current path has the following implications for California:
>
> The state will balance its budget . . . but local government will be saddled with increasing costs.
>
> We will continue to erode the long-term growth potential of the California economy.
>
> The quality of life will continue to decline in California with increasing transportation problems, rising crime and social unrest, and continued out-migration of business and jobs.

Such reports had produced a long list of reasonable reform proposals: the creation of a split property tax roll under which owner-occupied homes would retain all their Proposition 13 protections but commercial property would pay on the basis of current property values, thereby putting all business on an equal tax footing. They proposed broadening the sales tax to certain retail services, as many other states have done, and allowing local voters to approve school bonds by a majority vote instead of the two-thirds majority that the law requires. They urged measures to allow tax loopholes, which can now be put into law by simple majorities, to be closed by simple majorities, not the supermajorities that Proposition 13 requires. They called for the restoration of some local fiscal autonomy, including local authority to levy income taxes, possibly as a surcharge on the state income tax. Some even urged increases in the upper-income tax bracket from 9.3 percent to 10 percent for those earning over $115,000 a year ($230,000 for couples) and 11 percent for those earning over $230,000 ($460,000 for couples), which is what it had been during the tight years of the recession. All, however, had been either ignored by the legislature or rejected by the voters.[4]

At the time the Constitution Revision Commission reported, therefore, it represented what looked like far and away the most promising hope for enacting some fundamental change in the state's hopelessly complicated state and local fiscal and governmental structures. But the legislature paid no attention to the recommendations—took no action, scheduled only perfunctory hearings, had no debates, and, of course, made no move to submit any of it to the electorate. On the one hand, no member was willing to do anything that looked like it might change the protections of Proposition 13—now, as in 1978 when it was passed, the third rail of California politics. On the other, there was little desire to revise the school spending mandates of Proposition 98.

Most of the state's fiscal conservatives had once held (correctly) that Proposition 98 was an arbitrary and excessively rigid constraint on the state's ability to make budgetary choices and to respond to the needs of the moment. But Proposition 98 had also developed its uses for conservatives. By the time the commission report was presented, an initiative that had been a liberal reform designed to force the hands of a parsimonious Republican governor had become, if not a useful device for his Republican successor, at least a vehicle that happened, like a broken clock that's inevitably correct twice a day, to deliver precisely what suburban voters at that moment especially seemed to want: more money for smaller classes in the public schools. If that took place at the expense of rape crisis centers, mental health clinics, and health and welfare services for the poor, and if it constrained all rational budgeting, this time at least it was more likely to discomfit the state's urban Democrats than its Republican governor and its suburban Republican legislators.

What the plebiscitary system had in fact been doing—for the most part probably inadvertently—was not all that different from what established WASP power groups tried to do earlier in American history: divide and shift governmental authority where it would be harder for the elected representatives of new social and ethnic groups to get at it, and still harder for those representatives to amass the concentrated power to control the ordinary institutions of government. It's what the Boston Yankees did just a century ago when they transferred power from a city council that was becoming increasingly Irish to a newly created Finance Commission and other remote bodies, and to the Massachusetts legislature, where they still held sway and from which, for a time, they tried to run the city.[5]

Term limits promises seats to groups that have been shut out, but in combination with all those plebiscitary restrictions, it nearly guarantees that none of them will soon be able to dominate things the way a Jess Unruh or a Willie Brown, the particular target of California's term-limits movement, once did. Indeed, the whole rationale of the system—the direct expression of "the will of the people"—strongly implies that the larger (still overwhelmingly white, still predominantly middle-class) electorate can impose its will on local majorities, and particularly the urban ethnic groups whose representatives aggressively pursue their interests. They might prefer to tax themselves, and their affluent neighbors, at a higher rate and for more services than the older white middle class, soon to become a numerical minority, would like. The common result is that simple majorities alone, and local majorities in particular, can no longer dominate the political process.

Even if the new ethnic and economic groups eventually get real representation in the legislature or at city hall, under this system there are not many important things they can do without agreement from the old majorities. In the 1840s, John Calhoun, seeking to protect slavery, wanted to grant an effective veto in all federal affairs to the southern states: He called it the doctrine of the concurrent majority.

While the comparison with the antebellum South or with Boston and other cities may not be entirely apt, it seems close enough. It may be only a matter of time before the new immigrants, like the Irish and Italians of a century ago, capture effective control of the institutions that run their state and communities. But in the meantime, the gap between California's economic dynamism and its political incompetence will become wider and wider. The tension, as John Kenneth Galbraith once described it, between private affluence and public squalor could reach levels that are no longer socially or economically tolerable.

It goes almost without saying that California represents the first major test of the democratic viability and potential of a major society that is not merely diverse but where white Europeans—the creators and, until now, always the possessors, of the system—constitute a distinct minority of the population. For better than twenty years, California seems to have been in retreat from the consequences of that prospect, forging both physical and institutional barriers against it. In the process, the state's voters have sought to create a system of government by autopilot. In the name of checking corrupt and unresponsive legislators and bureaucrats, it is both obviating the need for the diligent exercise of citizenship and reducing the chance for the new groups, already limited, to exercise real political power anytime soon. If that tied public services and institutions into increasingly unmanageable knots that make life more difficult for all residents and turned what had been ebullience and optimism into a maze of fences, limits, and caution, it merely seemed to reconfirm the original charge: that government was pretty useless and fatally self-serving.

II

In the past couple of years, there have been signs that Californians may at last be willing to restore some funding to a public school system that has suffered twenty years of deterioration and neglect. There are also hopeful signs in the ongoing discussions of a "Consensus Project," among representatives of public employee unions, developers and other real estate interests, the Chamber of Commerce, the California Taxpayers Association, the universities, the cities and counties, as well as liberal tax reform organizations on ways to restore some order to the California mess. There is a "broadly shared agreement," in the words of Burt McChesney, a lobbyist for the California Association of Realtors, that "currently nobody in the state has authority to do anything." California has been starving its public infrastructure, says another group member. It cannot compete with low-cost regions like Arizona or New Mexico, where both land and labor are cheap, and must therefore be a high-productivity state with high levels of both public and private investment. The hope was to offer something for the ballot for November 1998 that would restore some fiscal authority to local government and end some of the state's fiscal distortions.

But so far, no concrete proposals have emerged that have any promise of surviving in California's political climate. And, as the Center for the Continuing Study of the California Economy warned, the state "does not have a long term public investment strategy—no list of priorities and no plan for funding."[6] Nor is there any sign yet of a broader shift from the fee ethic back to a communitarian ethos. And while California voters recently approved an initiative raising the state's minimum wage, there is as yet no indication that the state is ready to restore a workable tax structure, either at the state or the local level, much less one that would be adequate to the state's needs. On the contrary, both recession and recovery have become rationales, even among Democrats, for further tax cuts. And, as seems clear from the tepid interest in structural government reform in California, there is not yet any strategy for finding ways of making the state's larger governmental system work again.

There is no predicting how long California will continue to remain locked in its path, much less how far or how devotedly the rest of the nation will follow. As Americans, we have always had a healthy suspicion of government. But in the past two decades, that suspicion has risen to new and sometimes paranoid proportions. More and more of us talk like Howard Jarvis: Ronald Reagan's facile dismissal of government as "the problem," not the solution, has become the staple of political debate and talk-show discourse, a posture that serves to exonerate both civic laziness and political ignorance. And what has become a banal attitude about representative government has likewise become increasingly commonplace for the related institutions of constitutional democracy: the courts, the schools, the press. Voting and serious newspaper readership decline together. The communitarian civic ideal that both represent is giving way to "markets," a fee-for-service ethic and the fragmented, unmediated, unedited exchange of an untestable mix of information, gossip, and personal invective.

The new media may insure against the power of Big Brother to dominate communications, but they also amplify the power of shared ignorance to unprecedented levels of magnitude: What used to be limited to gossip over the back fence is now spread in milliseconds to a million listeners during the evening commute, and to thousands over the Internet. And at the fringes, there are the militias and the "patriots," collecting weapons and supplies, training in the hills, and hunkering down against the black helicopters and the coming invasion of United Nations troops. One no longer need elaborate the connection between that kind of extremism, the new media, the amplified rhetoric about alleged White House murder plots (retailed, depending on the occasion, by both the left and the right), and the surrounding paranoia about government that have become commonplace in the past decade. Oliver Stone's movies about presidential assassinations and Jerry Falwell's videos about the alleged murder of Vincent Foster work the same territory.

The domesticated (civic) version—also running parallel with the unmediated broadcast of public rumor and suspicion—is the growing penchant toward constitutional quick fixes and other mechanical all-purpose solutions, combined with the certainty that we are all egregiously overtaxed. The hardiest perennial of them has been the proposal for a constitutional amendment requiring a balanced budget—what Leon Panetta, a fully certified budget hawk, who was U.S. Budget Director at the time, once labeled "the ultimate doomsday machine."

The salient feature of the amendment, and certainly the one for which California ought to provide a loud warning, was not its potential to render the nation helpless in the face of recession or other emergency. It was the section that, in the face of a zero-deficit requirement that could only rarely have been met, would most likely be its operative provision: the power of Congress to pass an *unbalanced* budget with a three-fifths majority in each house. That provision, combined with the requirement that the federal debt limit may only be waived by a similar supermajority, would almost certainly become the common (and unavoidable) way of approving appropriations. This would give political minorities effective veto power—as is the case in California—and enable the most determined and irresponsible groups to exact concessions on pain of (among other things) budgetary gridlock and government shutdown.[7]

As a formal proposal, the amendment is probably dead for the moment, killed by the Democrats' ability to tie an even larger political sacred cow, Social Security, around its neck. But for the past five years, it has been so much a driver for the national agenda that even Democrats like Bill Clinton have embraced the principle of a five-year phasedown to a zero-deficit federal budget, which, in this age of tax cuts and tax limitations, means a stringent cap on all federal spending. When the backloaded provisions ultimately kick in around the year 2002, long after Clinton is gone from office, those caps may well turn out to be not just intolerable, but the prelude to a fiscal mess greater than the supply-side debacle of the Reagan years. Which is to say that the doomsday machine worked.

The list goes on: a proposed constitutional amendment requiring a two-thirds supermajority, again like California's, to increase revenues (but maintaining the present system by which tax loopholes can be approved by simple majorities), congressional and legislative term limits, the old Gramm-Rudman budget triggers, various other supermajority tax and spending requirements, the flat tax, rigid criminal-sentencing mandates not subject to case-by-case evaluation or judicial discretion, and flirtation at the fringes with proposals that routine political decisions about budgets and other legislation be submitted for "interactive" response from those with access to computers and the Internet.

Tracy Westen, the president of the foundation-funded Center for Governmental Studies in Los Angeles, has constructed a whole "digital election scenario" for the election of 2004, which (in his not altogether wild fantasy) includes some thirty-five voter initiatives on every conceivable subject. All have been circulated for "signatures" on line, along with a spectrum of arguments pro and con, available at the click of a voice-activated mouse, from every conceivable source. In combination with the large number of new elective offices for everything from drug commissioner to gay rights commissioner, those measures will confront the voter with 200 individual ballot decisions.[8]

Among Westen's futurist initiatives is one urging Congress to approve an amendment of Article V of the U.S. Constitution so that the language guaranteeing every state a Republican form of government is modified to permit the states to replace representative democracy with direct democracy. Westen points out that all the electoral and campaign technology in this politopia—the individually targeted campaign ads, the interactive "discussions" with candidates, the proposal for electronic voting—already exists, and while he seems not entirely enchanted by the prospect, there is almost nothing in it that hasn't already been prefigured in California. And since "state legislatures seem to be fighting more and doing less . . . and leaving the real legislation to the people . . . it seems the trend toward 'democracy by initiative' is inevitable." In Canada there briefly appeared a nascent fringe organization, the Democratech Party, which wanted to submit all governmental decisions to the public through electronic referenda. "Representative government assumes that the people need to elect someone to represent them in a faraway representative assembly," said an official Democratech statement. "But with modern instantaneous communications the people can make their own decisions, relegating politicians to the scrap heap of history."

If that sounds like a self-refuting parody of Rush Limbaugh, the march to the plebiscite seems to be embraced by some of the West's (otherwise) most sober political observers. A couple of years ago, for example, *The Economist* mused about the possible benefits of a system in which parliamentary democracy was replaced by Swiss-style direct democracy, where the voters "trudge to the polls four times a year" to ballot on all manner of plebiscitary questions. Such a process (in the writer's view) eliminates the ability of lobbyists and other special interests to buy the outcome because, "when the lobbyist faces an entire electorate . . . bribery and vote buying are virtually impossible [because] nobody has enough money to bribe everybody."[9]

California is a capital-letter cautionary tale that, whatever it's called, the process of bedazzling voters with sound bites, slogans, and nuanced bias works as handsomely in the initiative process as it does in electoral politics. Offers that sound like something-for-nothing (say a 60 percent property tax cut, a guaranteed level of education funding, or a state lottery offering prizes both for schools and the lucky winners) may not be bribes, but they are the nearest thing to it. And when they work at the ballot box, they often do so with far more lasting effects.

The larger danger, of course, is precisely the nondeliberative quality of the California-style initiative, particularly in a society that is far less monocultural than the Swiss and doesn't have the luxury of slow Alpine trudges to reflect on what it's about to do. There is nothing structured into the process—no hearings, no rules of procedure, no formal debates, no professional staff, no informed voice—to present the downside, to outline the broader implications, to ask the cost, to speak for minorities, to engineer compromises, or to urge caution and invoke the lessons of the past. Indeed, if the past decade of initiatives in California demonstrates anything, it's that the "will of the people" majoritarianism that is one essential part of the ethos of direct democracy almost inevitably reinforces an essentially indifferent, if not hostile, attitude toward minority rights. All those dangers would be exacerbated, of course, by electronic or other forms of absentee balloting, where voters would no longer be required to go to the local school or church or social hall and encounter their fellow citizens participating in the same civic ritual, and thus be reminded that they are, after all, part of a larger community. But the dangers are there, however the thing is done.

To say all that, probably, is merely to say awkwardly what the framers of the Constitution said better in Philadelphia, what Hamilton, Madison, and Jay said in the *The Federalist*, and what scores of delegates said in 1787–88 in the various state conventions leading up to ratification, even before they had witnessed the Terror of the French Revolution: Unchecked majorities are a danger to liberty almost as great as oligarchs and absolute monarchs. But for the moment, the drift seems to be mostly in California's (if not Switzerland's) direction. In November 1996, voters in twenty states voted on a total of ninety initiatives, which appears to be an all-time record—a decade ago, there were forty-one—on everything from hunting rights to taxes to gambling to logging regulations and sugar production, to laws legalizing medical marijuana use (which were approved in both Arizona and California).

But far and way the most common, generated by U.S. Term Limits in fourteen states and passed by voters in nine in 1996, was an "Informed Voter" measure—sometimes dubbed "the Scarlet Letter" initiative—that instructs all legislators and members of Congress in that state to support the constitutional amendment limiting members of the House of Representatives to three two-year terms and members of the Senate to two six-year terms and requires state election officials to indicate on the ballot, next to the name of each congressional incumbent and each member of the legislature, whether he or she "DISREGARDED VOTERS' INSTRUCTION ON TERM LIMITS." It also requires those who are not incumbents to indicate whether they have signed a pledge supporting the amendment. Those who do not will be similarly identified on the ballot. For Paul Jacob, who heads U.S. Term Limits, no modification or compromise reform permitting longer terms is acceptable. The watchword is "No Uncertain Terms."[10]

Jacob's very inflexibility helped derail a more moderate term-limits amendment when it came up in the House (for a second time) early in 1997. It would have allowed six two-year terms in the House and two six-year terms in the Senate. When Jacob denounced it as a sellout and ran ads against its supporters, he helped make certain that no term-limits amendment was approved, thus helping to assure his organization a long, healthy life.[11]

The Scarlet Letter initiative is probably unconstitutional. In Arkansas, one of the nine states that passed it in 1996, the state supreme court struck it down as a violation of the procedures the U.S. Constitution sets forth for amendment even before voters went to the polls. Because the drafters of the Constitution, in the words of the Arkansas court, "wanted the amending process in the hands of a body with the power to deliberate upon a proposed amendment . . . all proposals of amendments . . . must come

either from Congress or state Legislatures—not from the people."
The U.S. Term Limits measure, instead, "is an indirect attempt to
propose an amendment [that would] virtually tie the hands of the
individual members of the [legislature] such that they would no
longer be a deliberative body acting independently in exercising
their individual best judgements on the issue."[12] That phrase about
the legislature ceasing to be a deliberative body is one that can
apply more generally to the initiative process.

There are scattered indications that the rabid antigovernment
fervor of the early nineties may have peaked. (One of those indications, in the view of Nancy Rhyme, who tracks the issue for the
National Conference of State Legislators, is that only nine of those
fourteen states passed Scarlet Letter.) Certainly term limits are not
likely soon to be written into the U.S. Constitution. But the issue
will not go away, either in the two dozen states that, during the past
decade, have written them into their constitutions with respect to
their own elected state officials (and often local officials as well), or
in national politics. On almost the very same day that term limits
failed (again) in the House early in 1997, the Scarlet Letter,
funded almost entirely by U.S. Term Limits and a handful of out-
of-state term-limits organizations, qualified for the next California
ballot, a reminder to politicians that the voters remain determined.
(U.S. Term Limits kicked in $300,000 to that "informed voter"
measure but won't, of course, disclose where *its* money comes
from.)[13] In June 1998, California voters approved the Scarlet Letter initiative, 53–47, notwithstanding its sponsors' own acknowl-
edgment in the official ballot pamphlet that it was probably unconstitutional.

Nor has the initiative process lost any of its allure. Some twenty-
four states now have some form of initiative and/or referendum in
their constitutions, nearly all of them adopted during the Progressive Era.[14] Mississippi joined the list in 1992, and recently there
have been moves in a number of additional states, among them
Rhode Island and Texas, states that had never seriously considered
such things before, to write the initiative process into their constitutions. That pressure comes not from Hispanics or other newly
enfranchised political groups, many of which vigorously oppose

those constitutional changes as openings to yet more measures like Proposition 187, but from Ross Perot's United We Stand America and other organizations that are overwhelmingly white and middle class. And in the states that already have the initiative process, there is increasing pressure to use it, some of it generated by the dynamics of political reform itself. In California in 1996, the consultants, confronted by yet another voter-enacted measure limiting campaign spending, were certain that it would drive still more politicians to find (or gin up) ballot issues to help generate name identification, energize voter registration drives, and otherwise get around the expenditure and fund-raising restrictions on ordinary campaigns for office.

The celebratory history of direct democracy is centered on its inclusiveness. But in our politically more sophisticated (if not more cynical) age, defense of the initiative is itself far less disinterested than had once appeared. The groups that embrace and cheer it are not just "the people" fighting the 'interests" or "the politicians," much less battling "Satan" and "Mammon," as the editor of the *Sacramento Bee* so charmingly put it in the heyday of the Progressive Era. They are often established political interest groups trying to further their cause or repulse the advances of other groups by extraordinary means. More important, each enlargement of the process reduces that much more the power and accountability of legislatures—and thus the general ability to govern, to shape predictable outcomes. And while it may well further the Jeffersonian objective of tying government down and thus preventing mischief, it also vastly reduces the chances that it will produce great leaders and the visionary statecraft that they are sometimes associated with. In the battle over the initiative, the framers would be the first to recognize that it is not that our politics have become too conservative; it is that, perceived in the Burkean sense, they are not nearly conservative enough.

III

In the summer of 1996, the City of Anaheim and the Walt Disney Company jointly announced plans for a $1.4 billion expansion of

Disneyland and the surrounding Disneyland Resort. Plans included a second theme park to be called "Disney's California Adventure," complete with a new hotel, a promenade described as larger than St. Peter's Square in Rome, plus a new 200,000-square-foot complex of shops and restaurants. The project would allow the company to do what Walt Disney had always hoped for: gain control of the land around the park to make it a self-contained resort destination, like Disneyworld in Florida, and thus capture the revenues from hotels, food, and memorabilia that might otherwise slip into other pockets. (What the announcement did not say is that Disney had threatened to pull out of Anaheim if it did not get a set of tax breaks and other public subsidies for the new project, primarily in the form of various public works projects eventually totalling some $546 million.)[15]

The new fifty-five-acre park, said the announcement, "celebrates the fun and variety of California, its people, its accomplishments and its unique places—from the glamor of Hollywood to the exhilaration of soaring above Yosemite Valley to a California gleaming beach-front"[16] that is to include, in the words of one sardonic observer, "ersatz lagoon, boardwalk and lighthouse." Using a specially designed glider suspended in front of a huge projection screen, it was also to feature a "hang-gliding tour of the Golden Gate Bridge," trails through five acres of simulated wildernesss consisting of man-made geyser fields, caves, forests, and other "nature areas." There was also to be a tribute, the Los Angeles Times said, "to the immigrants and artisans of California," by way of "a village of working factories and farms whose craftsmen will demonstrate bread baking, chocolate making and other crafts"; and a historical show—"to be a very emotional experience," in the words of a Disney executive—devoted to working men and women "of all races, ethnicities and religions who helped build the state."[17] The new theme park, Disney's announcement said, "will capture California's Golden State of Mind." In working out the theme for this new theme park, said Disneyland president Paul Pressler, "we really have set out to try to capture a bit of what the California dream is all about."

Most of this canned enthusiasm is neither unusual or worrisome. Those promoting California, a place that was imagined long before it was ever seen, were always more likely to sell the dream than the reality, even as real people continue to pursue the purest form of the dream. (To this day, the perennially hopeful are panning for gold in the rivers of the Mother Lode, an effort that is said to be especially promising just after the great torrents of floodwater in wet winters scour up new material along their banks.) For his part, Walt Disney himself always had a penchant for offering the most saccharine version of whatever he was portraying, whether it was the sanitized barnyard of the Mouse and the Duck or the monstrous mechanical Abe Lincoln that the imagineers erected at the 1965 New York's World's Fair. The Matterhorn did not fall because a replica was stuck in the middle of Anaheim, nor, as far as anyone knows, did the Disney version seriously depress tourism in Switzerland. In any case, when it was built, it wasn't that easy for most American families to get to the Matterhorn.

But when the replica is erected no more than a few minutes from the real thing—when the theme-park immigrants are barely ten minutes drive from Santa Ana's living barrios, with their strings of *mercados* and *tiendras*, and no more than fifteen minutes from Westminster's Little Saigon, and when the real University of California at Irvine, where the children of thousands of those Vietnamese now prepare to become the next generation of doctors and programmers and engineers, is no more than twenty minutes down the freeway, social sanitation becomes not just an enhancement, an "authentic reproduction" to replace the increasingly scarce or inaccessible real thing. It becomes the essential purpose of the enterprise; it not only reduces the California dreaming to a sanitized absurdity but renders it invisible. Maybe it's true, as the architecture critic Ada Louise Huxtable observed, that "surrogate experience and synthetic settings have become the preferred American way of life." And to the extent it's true, "it is California that sets the trends and establishes the values for the rest of the country . . . The standard is no longer real versus phony but the relative merits of the imitation. What makes the good ones better is their improvement on reality."[18] Now, in the Disney version, California will join Disney's other artifacts as a safe and sanitized surrogate for its vital self. It's still too early to know whether it will also be an improvement on reality.

Real hang gliding and white-water rafting are not for everyone, and it's a haul across town to seek out what's left of the "real" Hollywood, though the studio tours keep packing them in. But when the dream itself is gated, fenced, and reduced to such shrunken hypersecure proportions—landscape, beach, Golden Gate, Hollywood—even the wax-museum image of California is an extraordinarily pale shadow of what the real thing was not much more than a generation ago—and what it still sometimes is not so far away. Not long ago, Disney tried to develop a Civil War theme park in Virginia—and came within a shadow of establishing itself on the site of some real battlefields: Is the real California dream now no more than a subject for a museum exhibit, something to be dimly recollected in the clean, secure confines of a self-contained theme park? As a symbol of the new high-tech California, with its gated communities and its fee-ethic citizenship, it is perfectly in place. But as a representation of what resonated around the country even thirty years ago—of what Americans expected of the Golden State, of what the Golden State expected of itself, and of what is often still taking place just a few miles down the road—it is very little indeed.

IV

If California seemed to be a national model of high civic investment and engagement in the 1950s and 1960s, so it has become the lodestar of tax reduction and public disinvestment of the 1980s and 1990s. That it is now again becoming a fully certified example of economic success makes the dangers all the greater. Frederick Jackson Turner, having declared the frontier closed, observed that "the age of the Pacific Ocean begins, mysterious and unfathomable in its meaning for our own future."[19] Having now become the leading port of entry for a vast, rich stock of Asian and Latino cultural products, ideas, and practices, from the bean burrito and the guacamole salad to the tofu diet, from the works of Frida Kalho and Francisco Zuniga to the I Ching, tai chi, Hiroshige's paintings, and Zen, will the state now also become the conduit for the Pacific

Rim economic ideas and patterns of a developing world? Will it grow in the style of what radical free-market economists like Milton Friedman admire so much in East Asia (and, once, in places like Hong Kong, particularly)—economies whose driving force is an unforgiving combination of high employment and high incomes at the top, and the hard lash of long hours and subsistence wages, "free market" schools, and a nearly total absence of social welfare services at the bottom?

In the spring of 1997, even as California's economy was booming, the state Industrial Welfare Commission, which is dominated by appointees of Governor Pete Wilson, moved to end the state's long-standing regulation that requires most employers to pay workers overtime after they work eight hours on any given day. The change, which flew the flag of freedom and competitiveness, drew the strong opposition of labor unions and of the Democrats in the legislature, and promised to become a major issue in the election of 1998, but it was also a sign of the new economic pressures.[20] At the same time, President Bill Clinton, calling once again for higher educational standards (also in the name of competitiveness), implicitly urged the nation to match Singapore, Korea, Hong Kong, and Japan in math and science achievement test scores, but without specifying the unforgiving rewards and penalties that drive students in those nations—and in Japan, for that matter—to get those scores.[21]

The whole nation has seen the growing gap between the incomes of those in its upper brackets and those at the bottom of the wage scale; but here again, the curious California recovery, where the gaps have grown even more pronounced, has led the way. Those gaps, according to a major study conducted by UCLA's School of Public Policy and Social Research, cut cross ethnic lines (as might be expected), with many well-educated immigrants from Asia and the Middle East quickly taking high-wage jobs in the professions—according to one estimate, one in three engineers in Northern California is an immigrant—while uneducated refugees and other Southeast Asian newcomers struggle at the bottom.[22]

Although the conclusion is controversial, the UCLA study also found that those low-wage immigrants from Asia and Latin America have taken jobs from poorly educated black residents, who are themselves increasingly separated from black professionals and other successful African Americans.[23] That those developments are accompanied by regressive shifts in taxes from the haves to the have-nots, even as most social services are reduced, only strengthens the impression and intensifies the concern. What intensifies it even more is that the new California economy sits atop such a large immigrant population, some legal, some not, whose presence, at least in the short run, not only depresses wage scales at the lower end but reduces the incentive to provide infrastructure and public services that would probably have been offered as a matter of course to groups considered genuinely "American."

All of which leads back to the unique two-sided test that California represents. On the one side: How soon will those immigrants, or their children and grandchildren, qualify in the national ethos as full-fledged Americans? How fast will American society write them into the dream—or better yet, when will the dream be sufficiently colorized to accommodate them? On the other: At what point will they become sufficiently acculturated and sufficiently engaged and sophisticated in politics that they can fully assert their rights as taxpayers and citizens? How fast can the economy and society absorb them—and particularly those who came with little education and few skills?

There have been encouraging signs since the election of 1996, both in California and nationally, that the virulent immigrant bashing and the related forms of wedge politics that Governor Pete Wilson worked so hard are on the wane. Both the national and the state Republican Parties, reviewing their alienation of minority voters, particularly Hispanics, and analyzing the demographics, have acknowledged their need to broaden their party's base, and have issued what border on mea culpas for their campaign messages in recent years. Mike Schroeder, the incoming chairman of the California GOP, an uncompromising hard-line conservative, cited one GOP television ad picturing Latino children that urged voters not to let "them" take over the state. "It might as well have said, 'I'm Bob Dole, don't vote for me,'" he told a reporter. "It was insulting. If I was Hispanic, I wouldn't have voted for Bob Dole either."[24]

Schroeder's mea culpa was at least partly undermined by his role as what one observer called Represenative Bob Dornan's "pit bull lawyer." Dornan, perhaps the most pugnacious right-winger in Congress, had been beaten in his 1996 reelection bid by a Hispanic activist named Loretta Sanchez and launched a protracted campaign, fraught with ethnic overtones, challenging the standing of hundreds of newly enfranchised Latino voters in an effort to reverse the outcome. The effort failed. Even Dan Schnur, who had been Pete Wilson's press secretary through the 1994 election, later acknowledged that "if you talk about cracking down on illegal immigration, you have to . . . support legal immigration. If you criticize racial preferences, you have to outline what alternative programs are going to look like."[25]

But the distance between earnest declarations about outreach and changing the party's essential political orientation in California remains huge. A great many Latinos were turned off by the Republican Party's tactics and, more generally, by its support of anti-immigrant and anti-affirmative-action legislation in the last few years, and there are some encouraging signs of increasing Hispanic political engagement, particularly in recent off-year school bond elections. The campaigns for Propositions 187 and 209, and the push to drive legal aliens from welfare rolls and other benefits, have also energized a wide spectrum of immigrant-rights groups—the Interfaith Coalition for Human Rights, the Chinese American Voters Education Committee, Hermanidad Mexicana National, the Citizenship Action Network, La Raza Centro Legal, the Asian Pacific American Legal Center—to offer a growing array of citizenship classes and other programs to help immigrants to become naturalized. The AFL-CIO is making new efforts to organize immigrant workers in the garment industry, in computer manufacturing, and in thousands of low-wage service-sector jobs.[26] If there is to be hope for a revitalized politics and a restoration of economic equity, it will largely have to come from such efforts.

But their success so far is marginal at best, both in the workplace and in the voting booth. In a labor market like California's, with its surplus of unskilled workers, and with the legacy of deep distrust for unions that many Latin American immigrants bring from the old country, it's easy to shut unions out. And in the face of a pathetically weak party structure, the most effective tool used in registering older immigrant groups in the cities of the East is missing. Thus the representation of California's foreign-born residents on the voter rolls remains as low as it does on the rolls of the unions. In 1992, 10 percent of those who voted in California were Hispanic; in 1996, it was 11 percent. In the meantime, the proportion of voters who were over fifty had increased from 36 to 42 percent, while the number whose incomes were over $60,000 had increased from 31 to 36 percent.[27] And what's true for the voter rolls is more emphatically true for the broader challenge that California's growing spectrum of colors, cultures, and backgrounds represents for the New America. On the one hand, it requires the nation to manage its immigration fairly and effectively; on the other, it tests its capacity to tolerate and assimilate, or at least to accommodate, its multiculturalism in such a way that the nation's European-based political institutions can function successfully. The more culturally diverse the society becomes, the more urgent is the need for an effective single political system that appears sufficiently legitimate to those diverse groups that it can successfully mediate among them and allocate power and social resources fairly.

For all the disputes about immigration, progress has to come simultaneously on all fronts if it's to come at all. Effective assimilation builds confidence in a reasonably open immigration policy. Enforceable immigration controls reinforce the chances of successful assimilation. But since the new immigration comes—perhaps as pure coincidence, more likely as cause—at the same time as the broader disaffection with government and the accompanying revolt against taxes, the test becomes particularly difficult. It also comes as the "globalization" of the California economy creates a concommitant new kind of "citizenship," a growing class of people whose ties with the communities in which they happen to live become ever more attentuated.

That, too, is a familiar pattern in the developing world. It has often been confidently predicted that Los Angeles will eventually become the first "world city," both in its techno-economics and in the mosaic of its population and culture, what Mayor Richard Riordan calls "the capital city of the future." But it may be a future like none ever envisaged in America. In the apparently unbridgeable gap between the people on the streets and barrios, and those in the picture-window suites, Los Angeles bears worrisome resemblances to Caracas and Singapore, to Warsaw and Seoul, and, until recently at least, to Hong Kong. The elites behind those picture windows have more in common with their offshore counterparts than they do with their compatriots down below and beyond the gates.

A generation ago, California was the place in the world best prepared to minimize those gaps—through high-quality public services in every area imaginable; through huge investments in roads, water systems, parks, and other infrastructure; and particularly through high-quality, cost-free education for virtually everyone. The community college tax-credit "scholarships" that Bill Clinton proposed in 1997 for the middle class through the second year of college, California offered every resident, rich and poor, through four years of college in the year 1960.[28] Even now, after several rounds of fee increases, California's four-year institutions still charge no more than the national average, and its community colleges far less, than the national average. But it has ceased to be the model that it once was; in the debates over such issues, no one proposes, much less assumes, that California be exceptional. The public debate in everything from K–12 education to welfare and library support now is only about how close the state might, with some effort, get to the national average.

Given all that, can California/America still color the dream and the vision of the good society that, not so long ago, went with it? It is not just an idle red-white-and-blue question. The new kids now crowding into the schools and universities of California— black, brown, Asian—will constitute the majority of the state's workforce, and a good part of the nation's, in the next decade, and forever after; they are the people who will have to pay the taxes to provide the public services and fund the Social Security and Medicare of those who now imagine they own the country.

In March 1995, historian (and California State Librarian) Kevin Starr posted a panegyric to the state on the library's home page on the Internet, which spoke about how, again and again, the nation had called on California "to seek out the American future, test it, to try its options, rejecting what doesn't work and building upon what does."[29]

> In recent times, the American people have turned to California and asked it to create a technology revolution, and California responded—in Silicon Valley, in San Diego, on the campuses of our great universities. The American people have turned to California for new models of lifestyle, new ways of enjoying and celebrating the gift of life, and California responded with an outpouring of architecture, landscaping, entertainment, sport and recreation, a new relationship to the outdoors—all of which expanded and enhanced leisure in these United States.

And now, once again, Starr wrote, "the United States is testing its future through California. Looking at California, as they have always looked at California, as a bellwether state, the American people are asking a series of questions which now become the California challenge: Can the American economy restructure itself in the aftermath of the Cold War? Can the American people turn to positive effect the cultural diversity of a nation in the process of being transformed through legal immigration?[30] Can the American people maintain their standards of living and education? . . ."

To which he provided uniformly positive answers: "Yes, California is saying, Americans of every cultural background can learn to live with and more importantly to respect each other. Yes, California is saying, the American people can still find homes and jobs, and a good education. Yes, California is saying . . ." But the very fact that the questions were being asked in such anxious tones, protesting, it seemed, far too much—and by a man who had made a career of celebrating the California phenomenon—suggested more than casual pro forma doubt. *Things had better work here . . .*

In truth (and perhaps in sadness), because of its population, its resources, and its enormous economic wealth, California may still be the best place to set and test the American future, which, of course, is what makes the stakes so high. If the public commitment is so far lacking—to those kids, and to the success of the larger society—there is hardly another place about which one could even imagine anyone raising the kind of questions, however hyperbolic in form, that Starr addresses to his state. Texas, which has a large Hispanic population, has not engaged in the immigrant bashing that California has. Latinos are much further integrated into its political structure—there is hardly a town south of San Antonio that's not run by Latinos—and its official engagement with Mexico under Republican governor George W. Bush in promoting trade and cultural exchange is far greater and warmer than California's has ever been under Pete Wilson. As Wilson was pushing his state to deny education to illegal aliens, Texas was welcoming residents of border cities in northern Mexico to its public universities. Twenty years ago, in an action that was held to be unconstitutional by the Supreme Court, the Texas legislature tried to give local school districts the right to exclude illegal alien children from the public schools. Now, in Texas polls, substantial majorities say they believe children should be educated in the public schools regardless of the immigration status of their parents.[31] In California in the spring of 1994, as the debate over Proposition 187 was heating up, 55 percent of registered voters told the pollsters that children of undocumented immigrants should not be allowed to attend public schools.[32]

And yet no one has ever described Texas, or Florida, another state with a heavy proportion of new immigrants (and with a significantly higher level of spending on schools), or any other state, as the nation's bellwether for the future—as the test of whether an increasingly diverse nation being transformed through immigration can use that transformation to positive effect, or of whether, under such conditions, it can continue to successfully govern itself as a democratic republic.[33] And while it is nowhere written that any state or region has to play such a role, be such a symbol, be charged with such a test, there is also the awful possibility that as a nation we no longer really expect the thing to be done at all. What is certain is that without California, there is no national model, no place that, because of its unique history, geographic fortune, and cultural makeup, can combine promises of the good life with the social and economic affirmation that California once provided—and, just perhaps, could provide again.

NOTES

‹›

NOTES FOR PART ONE:
INTRODUCTION

1. Because the initiative and referendum are so often confused, a brief definition may be in order. The *initiative* is a law or constitutional amendment initiated by the voters, generally by collecting a specified percentage of signatures of the electorate. The *referendum* in California is a similar process designed to negate an act of the legislature. It is used occasionally, but not nearly as often as the initiative has been during the past twenty years. In both cases, if enough valid signatures are turned in, the measure then goes on the ballot for voter approval.

2. Jean Ross, director of the California Budget Project, interview, April 28, 1997.

3. The law was passed and signed in April 1913, after Wood-row Wilson, then barely sworn in as president and trying to maintain good relations with Japan, sent Bryan to California to try to persuade Johnson to block the bill. Johnson had opposed Wilson when Johnson was the candidate for vice-president with Teddy Roosevelt on the Bull Moose ticket in 1912. Wilson, who had done his own Japanese-bashing during the election campaign, was therefore poorly positioned to ask Johnson for any favors on that score. In any case, the pressure behind the bill was almost irresistible. It passed overwhelmingly, and Johnson, who had been quietly working both sides of the issue, signed it. See Spencer C. Olin, Jr., *California's Prodigal Sons: Hiram Johnson and the Progressives, 1911–17* (Berkeley: University of California Press, 1968), pp. 80–91.

4. California historian Kevin

Starr points out that contrary to Turner's postulation of the West as a frontier of open land, California was, from the beginning, an urban, cosmopolitan configuration which "had more in common with Melbourne, Sydney and Hong Kong . . . than it did with the rural Far West." Starr, "Moving Beyond the Turner Thesis," California State Librarian's Weekly Column, December 15, 1995 (http://library.ca.gov/).

NOTES FOR PART TWO:
THE GOLDEN MOMENT

1. "California," *Look*, September 18, 1962, p. 30.

2. *Newsweek*, September 10, 1962; *Look*, September 26, 1962; *Life*, October 19, 1962; *Ladies Home Journal*, July 1967; *Time*, November 7, 1969; *Saturday Review*, September 23, 1967.

3. "California," op. cit., p. 31.

4. The zen cultists and the nude beach references are from *Time*, November 7, 1969, p. 61; the teenager quote is from *Newsweek*, September 10, 1962, p. 31; the lounge lizards are on p. 36.

5. "California: The Experimental Society," *Saturday Review*, p. 28.

6. It was reissued in 1984 by Pantheon Books as *The WPA Guide to California* and still remains both one of the great documents on California and a shining reminder of the quality of the work of the Federal Writers' Project.

7. "The California Woman: What Happens When Old Rules Are Left Behind?" *Ladies Home Journal*, July 1967, p. 76.

8. *Look*, p. 96.

9. *Factories in the Field: The Story of Migratory Farm Labor in California* (Santa Barbara, CA: Peregrine Publishers, 1935).

10. *Look*, p. 31.

11. U.S. Bureau of the Census, "Mother Tongue of the Foreign Born . . . ," *Census of the Population, 1960. California, General Social and Economic Characteristics*, Table 41. Prepared by the Geography Division in cooperation with the Housing Division, Bureau of the Census, Washington, D.C., 1975.

12. Kevin Starr, *Endangered Dreams: The Great Depression in California*, (New York: Oxford University Press, 1996), p. 318.

13. Committee to Re-Elect Governor Brown, *Record of Achievement: Administration of Edmund G. Brown, Governor, 1959–1962*, pp. 49–50.

14. Brown used that figure in testimony before Congress the previous year, then dropped it when Northern California legislators complained that the whole thing was a subsidy to Central Valley farmers and city dwellers in Los Angeles. Ironically, the proposed Peripheral Canal, the most recent major project for the California Water Project, approved in the administration of Jerry Brown, was

rejected by voters in a referendum in 1982.

15. Brown: Special message on water to the Legislature, January 22, 1959. See also Committee to Re-elect Governor Brown, op. cit., pp. 4–11.

16. Edmund G. Brown, *Oral History*, MS. in the California State Library, Sacramento, p. 278. Also Jack Burby, "Governor Pat Brown, A Personal Memoir," *California Journal*, (April 1996): 34–36.

17. "Political Giant 'Pat' Brown Dies," *Sacramento Bee*, February 17, 1996, p. 1.

18. Reagan took the oath of office at midnight on January 1, so for all practical purposes Brown's term ended in 1966.

19. Office of the Chancellor, California State University, *Fact Sheet*. University of California, *Profile*. Clark Kerr, "The Idea of a Multiversity" (first of the Godkin Lectures), in *The Uses of the University*, 4th ed. (Cambridge, MA: Harvard University Press, 1995), pp. 1–34.

20. Kerr, *The Uses of the University*, p. 6.

21. Ibid., p. 101.

22. Kerr interview, May 26, 1995. Kerr, *The Uses of the University*, p. 67; Sheldon Rothblatt, ed., *The OECD, the Master Plan and the California Dream* (Berkeley, CA: Center for Studies in Higher Education, UC Berkeley, 1992).

23. I first saw California schools in the fall of 1964, when I spent four weeks in various districts researching a book on schools in different regions around the country, *Voices in the Classroom* (Boston: Beacon Press, 1965).

24. Thor Severson, "State Drops to 35th in Scholastic Standards," *Sacramento Bee*, March 31, 1958. p. 1; "Lack of Fundamentals Is Charged by Critic," *Sacramento Bee*, March 27, 1958, p. 1. Many of these stories sound precisely like the things that were published a generation later, though where it had once been the threat of the Russians beating our academic and technological brains out, in the 1980s it was the Germans and the Japanese.

25. U.S. Department of Education, *Digest of Education Statistics, 1993*, Washington, D.C., 1993, p. 87.

26. *Digest of Education Statistics*, pp. 162–163; see also California Department of Education, *Fact Book, 1995–96*, pp. 46–47.

27. Stephen E. Ambrose, *Nixon: The Education of a Politician, 1913–1962* (New York: Simon and Shuster, 1987), pp. 667.

28. Ibid., p. 671.

29. Joan Didion, *Slouching Toward Bethlehem* (New York: Delta, 1968), p. 172.

30. E.g., John Jacobs, *A Rage for Justice: The Passion and Politics of Phillip Burton* (Berkeley: University of California Press, 1996), pp. 81–83.

31. Brown, *Oral History*, p. 282; Roger Rapoport, *California Dreaming: The Political Odyssey of Pat & Jerry Brown* (Berkeley, CA: Nolo Press, 1982), pp. 63–65.

32. *Violence in the City—An End or a Beginning: A Report by the Governor's Commission on the Los Angeles Riots*, pp. 1, 3.

33. Ibid., p. 3.

34. California Advisory Commission to the U.S. Commission on Civil Rights, *Reports on California: Police–Minority Relations in Los Angeles and the San Francisco Bay Area*, 1965.

35. *Violence in the City*, pp. 4–5.

36. Nathanael West, *Day of the Locust* (New York: Random House, 1939). Quoted from *Miss Lonelyhearts and Day of the Locust* (New York: New Directions, 1962), p. 184.

37. Didion, op. cit., pp. 220–221.

38. Edmund G. Brown, *Oral History*, p. 486.

39. The point was made by David Bowman, John Ellwood, and Eugene Smolensky of the Graduate School of Public Policy at Berkeley in an unpublished paper circulated during the 1993 recession, "Removing the Current Recession from the State's Budget Deficit: California's Structural Deficit," n.d.

40. Lou Cannon, *Reagan* (New York: 1982), pp. 147–186.

41. "Interests, not people, are represented in Sacramento," wrote Carey McWilliams in 1949, in a passage that still gets quoted endlessly by California political writers. "Sacramento is the market place of California where grape growers and sardine fishermen, morticians and osteopaths bid for allotments and state power. Today there is scarcely an interest-group that has failed to secure some form of special legislation safeguarding its special interests." Carey McWilliams, *California: The Great Exception* (Santa Barbara, CA: Peregrine Press, 1976), p. 213. McWilliams, when he was at *The Nation*, had been the first to write a national piece exposing Artie Samish.

42. "Not by Dancing or Fireworks," *San Francisco Chronicle*, December 28, 1962, p. 26.

43. McWilliams, *California: The Great Exception*, p. 25.

44. *Time*, November 18, 1991, p. 42.

45. The criticism of the workers compensation system was certainly correct; because the system was so corrupt, it was costly to employers and niggardly to workers with serious injuries. But it paid off lavishly to the lawyers and doctors who manipulated the system. In the early 1990s, the legislature and governor finally managed to agree on reforms and cleaned the system up. On taxes, as explained elsewhere in this book, they were crying wolf.

46. Center for the Continuing Study of the California Economy, *California Population Characteristics*

(Palo Alto, CA: Author, 1995), p. 11.

47. Jordan Bonfante, "The Endangered Dream," *Time*, November 18, 1991, p. 42.

48. *New York Times*, October 28, 1991, p. 1; also *New York Times*, November 17, 1991, p. E4; October 16, 1991, p. A16; July 31, 1992, p. A1; August 24, 1993, p. A1; August 25, 1993, p. A1; November 26, 1993, p. A1; December 19, 1993, p. 1. Reinhold, who died in 1996, was nonetheless a fine reporter, and a writer of intelligence and grace who was highly respected by his colleagues.

49. The phrases come from "California in the Rear View Mirror," *Newsweek*, July 13, 1993, p. 24. What was closer to the truth was not that skilled blue-collar workers were leaving, but that much of the in-migration was bimodal—composed in part of low-skilled foreign immigrants (although their rate of in-migration slowed during the recession) and of college graduates and other highly educated professionals and skilled technicians. William Frey, *Interstate Migration and Immigration for Whites and Minorities. 1985–1990: The Emeregence of Multi-Ethnic States* (Ann Arbor, MI: University of Michigan Population Studies Center, 1993); and Frey, *Immigration and Internal Migration "Flight"* (Ann Arbor, MI: University of Michigan Population Studies Center, No. 94–306, 1994).

50. Bonfante, "Endangered Dream," *Time*, November 18, 1991, p. 42.

51. Department of Justice, *1993 Statistical Yearbook of the Immigration and Naturalization Service*, Table 4. *Census (California), Social and Economic Characteristics*, Table 32, 33, Washington, D.C., 1993. Hans Johnson, in a major study conducted for the Public Policy Institute of California, concluded that the flow of illegal immigrants varies sharply over time, rising (as might be expected) when the California economy is strong (and especially if conditions in Mexico are difficult), and falling when it's weak. The great flow of the 1980s, he reported, slowed to a trickle in the recession of 1990–93. But the number also seemed to have been driven by the amnesty of the Immigration Reform and Control Act, which prompted the newly legalized aliens to bring over a substantial number of relatives who entered the country illegally. Hans Johnson, *Undocumented Immigration to California* (San Francisco: The Public Policy Institute of California, 1996).

52. Ibid., pp. 102–105. Robert Suro, *Watching America's Door: The Immigration Backlash and the New Policy Debate* (New York: Twentieth Century Press, 1996), p. 38.

53. California Department of Finance, Demographic Research Unit, 1995 Population Projection

Series, *Total Population By County, By Year, By Race/Ethnicity.*

54. "Despite their proliferation," in the words of a recent RAND review of the literature, "recent studies on the net fiscal costs of immigration do not provide a reliable estimate of what those net costs are. Moreover, without reaching a consensus on a host of data, accounting and conceptual issues, we doubt that additional studies will provide a definitive answer to the policy questions raised about immigration." George Vernez and Kevin McCarthy, *The Fiscal Costs of Immigration*, RAND, February 1995, pp. vi-xiii.

55. Los Angeles County Internal Services Division, *Impact of Undocumented Persons and Other Immigrants on Costs, Revenues and Services in Los Angeles County*, 1992; Louis Rea and Richard Parker, *Report by the Auditor General of California: A Fiscal Analysis of Undocumented Immigrants Residing in San Diego County*, August 1992; Rea and Parker, *Illegal Immigration in San Diego County: An Analysis of Costs and Revenues*, September 1993. Both were sharply criticized for serious methodological flaws. See, e.g., Rebecca Clark and Jeffrey Passel, *How Much Do Immigrants Pay in Taxes? Evidence from Los Angeles County* (Washington, D.C.: The Urban Institute, 1993).

56. James P. Smith and Barry Edmonston, eds., *The New Americans: Economic, Demographic and Fiscal Ef-* *fects of Immigration* (Washington, D.C.: National Academy Press, 1997), pp. S-9, S-10.

57. The first significant study of the emerging Latino middle class in Southern California, by Gregory Rodriguez of Pepperdine University, showed that 50 percent of households with U.S.-born heads of household exceeded the median income level for the region in 1990, lower than the levels for whites and Asians, but considerably higher than those headed by blacks or foreign-born Latinos. Nearly two-thirds of Latinos who entered the country in the 1960s lived in owner-occupied homes. Patrick McDonnell, "New Latino Middle Class on the Rise, Study Finds," *Los Angeles Times,* October 10, 1996, p. A1.

58. It also generated a shock in Pasadena, which had expected no more than an average of 15,000 people per game at the Rose Bowl, where the Galaxy plays its home games. When those 70,000 people showed up for the team's opening game in 1996, Pasadena's city council began to hear the reverberations from traffic-sensitive residents. But since the city was getting 7 percent of each ticket sold, plus various surcharges and bonuses, the complaints are likely to be manageable. Shawn Hubler and Richard Winton, "Soccer Surprise Stokes Debate on Rose Bowl," *Los Angeles Times,* April 15, 1996, p. A1; Damon Hack, "Gaining a Foothold:

First Season Surpassing MLS'
Hopes," *Sacramento Bee*, August 8,
1996, p. D1.

59. "A Welcome for Immigrants
Turns to Resentment," *New York
Times*, August 25, 1993, p. 1.

60. The most dramatic illustration was the the victory of Loretta
Sanchez over long-term Congressman Robert Dornan, by all estimates the most vitriolic and
combative right-winger in the
House, in an Orange County district that is now more than 50 percent Hispanic. A number of
legislative districts were also captured by Hispanics for the first
time, thereby increasing Hispanic
representation in California's
eighty-member assembly from seven
to fourteen. But the percentage of
California Hispanic voters in 1996,
while larger than in 1994, barely
exceeded the percentage in 1992.

NOTES FOR PART TWO:
GOOD-BYE EL DORADO

1. Interviews with Sacramento
County Executive Bob Thomas and
other county officials, May 1996;
interview with Liz Gibson, California State Library, June 1996; interview with Steve Szalay, executive
director of the California State Association of Counties, June 3, 1996;
letter from Helen Whitney, chair of
the Lake County Board of Supervisors to Governor Pete Wilson, May
28, 1996; various budget documents from Los Angeles, Merced,

and other counties; Matt Lait
"Bankruptcy Over; Recovery Not,"
Los Angeles Times, June 9, 1996; and
Davan Maharaj, "Bankruptcy Judge
Approves Complex O.C. Recovery
Plan," *Los Angeles Times*, May 16,
1996.

2. George Skelton, "Earthquake:
The Long Road Back," *Los Angeles
Times*, January 20, 1994, p. A3.

3. That history is itself a central
part of this story and will be told
more fully in later sections. But to
give it context, it would be better
first to fast-forward to California
now, and describe briefly the
changed state of California's public
services and infrastructure, and its
wider social geography—a portrayal of the seismic shifts that a
California Rip Van Winkle who had
fallen asleep in the heyday of the
Pat Brown years would have found
on waking thirty-five years later.

4. *Proposition 13: Its Impact on
California and Implications for State
and Local Finance*, California Budget
Project, April 1997, p. 11.
(www.cpb.org).

5. California Department of Finance, *California Satistical Abstract*,
1995, Table P-2, p. 184; Table P-12,
p. 188. (www.dof.ca.gov.). In 1997,
the California Budget Project calculated that in 1992–93, total state
and local taxes in California came
to $112 per $1,000 of personal income and ranked twenty-sixth in
the country, which had an average
tax burden of $116 per $1,000 of

personal income. California Budget Project, *Quick Facts: How Does California Compare?*, April 1997, p. 2. (www.cbp.org).

6. Goldberg, op. cit. p. 13. The California Budget Project calculates the numbers somewhat differently, showing a 14 percent decline in California revenues betwen 1976–77 and 1992–93 and a slight increase in average revenues, as a percentage of personal income, in other states. But those differences hardly affect the larger point: that California slipped from being a high-tax state to an average-tax state.

7. The most comprehensive recent comparison of the states in education—resources and results—is Craig D. Jerald, "Prop. 13, rising enrollment, and economic woes have hit California's schools hard," *Education Week,* January 1997. Also see California Department of Education, *Fact Book, 1996–97: Handbook of Education Information,* pp. 54–55.

8. U.S. Office of Education, National Center for Education Statistics. The most recent figures, for 1992–93, show California spending $4,780 per child; in the same year, Connecticut spent $7,980, New Jersey $9,415, New York $8,902, and Pennsylvania $6,890. The comparisons for 1994–95 are from California Department of Education, *Fact Book, 1995–96,* p. 45. The numbers for 1997–98 are from the gov-

ernor's budget proposals. See, e.g., Office of the Governor, *Budget Summary Highlights, 1997–98,* p. 15. The ten-year comparison is from an analysis by school lobbyist John Mockler, which no one has disputed.

9. Jim Sanders, "For a Shabby Learning Experience, Try School Library," *Sacramento Bee,* January 21, 1990, p. A1; *Digest of Education Statistics,* Table 82, p. 90, and Table 95, p. 105.

10. Los Angeles is only third among the nation's cities in the percentage of foreign-born residents (38 percent in 1990), and fourth in the percentage of people (50) who speak some language other than English at home. But no state has as many in the top ten in either category. Among those with high percentages of non-English speakers, it has four: Santa Ana, San Jose, San Francisco, and Los Angeles.

11. Sid Thompson (since retired as superintendent) interview, May 21, 1996.

12. For the 1996 numbers, U.S. Department of Education, National Center for Education Statistics, National Assessment of Education Progress, *The Reading Report Card,* 1992 and 1994; and *Trends in Academic Progress,* prepared by the Educational Testing Service, 1992. Also see NCES: *Digest of Education Statistics,* 1993, Tables 117, 118, pp. 120–123. (www.ed.gov/NCES/NAEP). As to

why California's ethnic minorities also scored lower than their counterparts in other states, one can only speculate. It probably results in part from poor teaching and lack of resources, but does it also come in part from the compounding effects of unusually large *concentrations* of limited-English speakers and other academically disadvantaged kids from different backgrounds in California classes? The answer is anyone's guess.

13. Led, ironically, by Marion Joseph, the liberal Democrat who had managed the successful campaign of Wilson Riles to unseat Max Rafferty, who had been a champion of phonics.

14. Jeff Leeds, "State Fails to Stop Compton Schools' Slide into Decay," *Los Angeles Times,* January 26, 1997, p. A1.

15. *School Facilities: America's Schools Report Differing Conditions* (Washington, D.C.: U.S. General Accounting Office, GAO-HEHS-76-103), and *School Facilities: Profiles of School Conditions by State* (Washington, D.C.: U.S. General Accounting Office, GAO-HEHS-96148); Jim Sanders, "Schools Fall into Disrepair: Desks Totter, Roofs Leak Across Many Campuses," *Sacramento Bee,* July 2, 1989, p. B1.

16. Amy Pyle and Lucille Renwick, "L.A. School Bond Appears to Win," *Los Angeles Times,* April 9, 1997, p. A1; Ted Rohrlich, "Record Percentage of Latinos Turn Out to Vote, Exit Poll Finds," *Los Angeles Times,* April 9, 1997, p. A3.

17. California Legislative Analyst (LAO), *Analysis of the 1996–97 Budget Bill,* p. I–9. Also see LAO, *Bond Debt Update,* May 20, 1996. (www.lao.ca.gov.). The Analyst's number, $10.5 billion, is described as "an estimate only," since no plan exists. Marian Bergeson, Wilson's secretary of education and child development in 1997, put the figure at $17 billion, as did Chairman Leroy Greene and the staff of the state senate's Education Committee. The Analyst also points out that the total state needs for all purposes, about $25 billion by 2000–01, far exceeds the state's capacity to fund those bonds. But by late 1987, legislative sources put the price tag for schools alone at $40 billion. Assemblyman James L. Brulte, "The Facts About California's Financing Gap for New School Construction," unpublished, July 31, 1996.

18. *No Room for Johnny: A New Approach to the School Facilities Crisis,* California Little Hoover Commission (Commission on California State Goverment Oraganzation and Economy), June 1992, pp. 55, 56. In 1996, the legislature passed a bill, AB3176, creating a study committee to review the process. It was to report its findings by July 1997.

19. See, e.g., Nick Anderson, "Increased Spending Transforms School Board Elections," *Los Angeles*

Times (Orange County ed.), March 17, 1997, p. A16.

20. *California Spending: A Comparison of State and Local Spending Priorities,* California Taxpayers Association, July 1996, Table 2. One particularly revealing indication is that in an age when privatization of municipal services has become so fashionable, the firefighter unions in many cities, recognizing that new building-safety practices are reducing the call for ordinary fire fighting, have successfully lobbied city councils and boards of supervisors to let them take over ambulance services previously provided by private firms, even though the cost of the firefighter paramedics, which is pegged to firefighter salaries, is much higher than when it was provided privately. Like school board members, council members are increasingly beholden to the political contributions of municipal employee unions for campaign funding.

21. Peter Schrag, "The Declining School Board," *Sacramento Bee,* December 16, 1987; Schrag "Message from LA," *Sacramento Bee,* June 14, 1989.

22. Tyrone Vahedi, who was running the "Educational Efficiency Initiative" campaign, said if the damages were incurred in connection with some direct service to a child, it would be a classroom expense; otherwise, it's an administrative expense. But given the measure's uncertain wording, the lawyers and courts may well say something else.

23. Riordan, who is sometimes believed to be contemplating a run for higher office in California, and thus might be particularly interested in cultivating the UTLA (as well as in getting a little extra political attention), had also been a close personal friend of former UTLA president Helen Bernstein. Bernstein was killed when she was hit by a car in the spring of 1997.

24. The problem of union power in local elections is equally acute in the community colleges, where, in the words of one community college president, board members often "bargain with the very unions that helped elect them . . ." Even union officials acknowledge that in Los Angeles, the union contributes about $100,000 to each favored candidate in elections. "That's more money than anyone else has, and that's why our candidates usually win." Quoted in *Cross-Currents,* published by the nonpartisan California Higher Education Policy Center, Winter 1997, p. 13.

25. In 1996, State superintendent Delaine Eastin called for the addition of a third year of science and the inclusion of algebra and geometry as absolute minimums for all students. But since she has no authority to impose those requirements, since the state seems mired in ambivalence about state man-

dates and standards, and since resources are still so short, the chances of anything happening soon are small.

26. Honig, who drew widespread opposition from conservatives for his public fights with Republican governor George Deukmejian over school funding, and from the religious right over his efforts to clamp down on private schools of creation science, was indicted and tried on a conflict-of-interest charge involving a counseling program run by his wife. He was convicted early in 1993 and forced to resign from office. He has since become a leader in the statewide campaign to upgrade California's primary school reading program.

27. That may be true for the relatively select group who go to the University of California— theoretically the top 12.5 percent of the state's high school graduates. Barry Munitz, the chancellor of the much larger Califiornia State University system, sees the picture very differently. The quality of preparation in K-12, he said early in 1997, "is in bad shape," and those in the schools now are "a lost generation."

28. The requirements of Proposition 98 (1988) are discussed more fully elsewhere in this book. The measure, as amended by a subsequent ballot measure (Proposition 111), provides that when state revenues decline, as they did in the early 1990s, the state can reduce funding to K-14 education below the basic Proposition 98 guarantees, but must bring it back to what it would have been when revenues recover. Under that restoration provision, the schools actually received over 60 percent of the additional post-recession revenues for fiscal years 1996-97 and 1997-98.

29. "They want class size reductions," Wilson reportedly said, "and we're going to give it to them."

30. In the fall of 1993, the U.S. Offfice of Education reported California's teacher–pupil ratio at 24. That number is based on all teachers who are employed in schools, not just those in the classroom. By the same count, the national average was 17.4. Only Utah, at 24.7, had larger classes. The number for New York is 15.2; for New Jersey, it's 13.6. National Center for Education Statistics, U.S. Department of Education, *Digest of Education Statistics,* 1995, Table 63, p. 76.

31. See, e.g., *Policy Brief: Class Size Reduction,* Legislative Analyst's Office, February 12, 1997.

32. See, e.g., California Budget Project, *How Does California Compare?,* Sacramento, 1996, p. 24. (www.quiknet.com/~cabudget); U.S. Department of Education, *Digest of Educational Statistics,* 1993, Table 153.

33. Robin Greene, "A Happy Trade-Off—High Taxes, Fine Schools," *Los Angeles Times,* June 22, 1996, p. B7.

34. Phone interview with Susanna Sweeney, California Consortium of Educational Foundations, October 1996. Also Jan Ferris, "In an Era of Tight Funds, Schools Increasingly Pass the Hat," *Sacramento Bee*, February 16, 1997, p. A1.

35. The difference, as some California officials point out, comes almost entirely in the difference in the local share, which, of course, derives from the property tax limitations imposed by Proposition 13. The state contribution in New York and California is almost the same.

36. "Quality Counts: A Report Card on the Condition of Public Education in the 50 States," *Education Week*, January 22, 1997, pp. 24, 74–77.

37. Again, it should be pointed out that under Deukmejian, per-pupil funding increased in California, but far less than it did elsewhere, and far less than the changing needs of the schools required.

38. The decline between 1980 and 1990, 2.7 percent, was minor at the University of California, but significant at the California State University (down 8.7 percent) and in the California community colleges (down 7.7 percent). William Pickens, *Financing the Plan: California's Master Plan for Higher Education, 1960 to 1994* (Report Prepared for the California Higher Education Policy Center), May 1995, pp. 26–28.

39. *UC by the Numbers: A Portrait of Undergraduate Students at the University of California*, "Freshman Enrollment by Family Income," May 28, 1996. (www.ucop.edu/sas/btn/btn23.html). In 1991–92, according to the UC statistics, 24 percent of UC freshmen came from families with incomes under $30,000. In 1995–96, that had risen to 28 percent. Meanwhile, the percentage of students from families with incomes over $70,000 had declined from 39 percent to 37 percent, though it's highly likely that the percentage with incomes over $100,000 or $120,000 (who were not counted separately) had in fact increased. In any case, the UC profile hardly reflected the state's population, much less the downward-shifting demographics of the state's high school classes.

40. Lieutenant Governor Gray Davis, a Democrat with mighty ambitions for higher office, threatened to run an initiative freezing all higher education fees until the year 2002. That seemed to get Wilson's attention.

41. William Pickens, *Financing the Plan: California's Master Plan for Higher Education 1960 to 1994* (San Jose, CA: California Higher Education Policy Center, 1995), p. 21.

42. Warren H. Fox, statement submitted to the state Senate Budget and Fiscal Review Committee, March 12, 1997.

43. California Legislative Analyst, "Higher Education," *Cal Guide: A Profile of State Finances and Programs,* January 1995, p. 5.

44. Michael A. Shires, *The Future of Public Undergraduate Education in California* (Santa Monica, CA: RAND, 1996), p. xix.

45. Kerr interview, May 26, 1995.

46. Donald Kennedy, "Making Choices in the Research University," *Daedalus* (Fall 1993): 139.

47. Interviews with UC officials, May 1994; also see "Report on Voluntary Early Retirement Incentive Program for Faculty and Its Effect on Academic Programs," Report of the UC Regents Committee on Educational Policy, May 19, 1994.

48. Letter from Atkinson to Wilson, January 29, 1996: "There is no question in my mind that it is the constitutional duty of the Board to set policy for the University, and the role of the President to implement that policy. I have a legal as well as a moral duty to do so."

49. California higher education spending declined 18.1 percent between 1990–91 and 1994–95. The national figure is 10.7 percent. California Budget Project, *How Does California Compare?* July 1996. (www.cpb.org/reports/cacompare.html).

50. Jess Bravin and Kevin Welner, "Reforming California Higher Education Through the Initiative Process," paper given at the Pacific Sociological Association, March 22, 1996.

51. James Richardson, "What Price Glory?," *UCLA Magazine* (February 1997): 30.

52. Courtney Leatherman, "Heavy Reliance on Low-Paid Lecturers Said to Produce 'Faceless Departments,'" *Chronicle of Higher Education,* March 28, 1997, pp. A12–13.

53. The university claims that fees still cover only about one-third of the cost of each undergraduate's education. But some studies of institutional cross-subsidization—the shift of state funds from undergraduate instruction to graduate and research programs—suggest that in fact fees pay close to 80 percent of the real cost. Charles L. Schwartz, a retired UC Berkeley physics professor, has been particularly persistent in analyzing UC budget data on such questions, and often persuasive in his conclusions.

54. Interview, April 1995.

55. *Furman v. Georgia,* 408 U.S. 238 (1972).

56. Cannon, op. cit., p. 167.

57. California Legislature, *Report to the Prison Reform Conference Committee,* June 12, 1996. II-1. The law doubles the normal sentence for any second felony, and imposes a mandatory sentence of twenty-five years to life for any third felony.

58. Peter W. Greenwood, C. Peter Rydell, Allan F. Abrahamse, Jonathan P. Caulkins, James R.

Chiesa, Karyn E. Model, and Stephen P. Klein, *Three Strikes and You're Out: Estimated Benefits and Costs of California's New Mandatory Sentencing Law* (Santa Monica, CA: RAND/MR-509-RC, 1994); Shires, op. cit., p. xviii. Also Shires's memo to author, May 25, 1995.

59. The California Postsecondary Commission put 1994–95 undergraduate enrollment at 1,722,466, of whom more than 1.3 million were enrolled in the community colleges. It estimates enrollment in 2004–05 to reach 2.2 million, of whom more than 1.7 million will be community college students—provided the resources are there to handle them. See *Tidal Wave II: An Evaluation of Enrollment Projections for California Higher Education,* The California Higher Education Policy Center, September 1995.

60. Shires, op. cit,. p. 52.

61. What they have not been able to do is reduce the additional load on the courts, as the potential second- and third-strikers, who might once have plea-bargained for a sentence, demand jury trials. Since the mid-1980s, criminal jury trials increased roughly 50 percent; in the first year of the Three Strikes law, they rose 12 percent, making the delays for civil trials even longer. See *State Court Outlook: California Courts in Crisis,* The Judicial Council of California, 1996. The sponsors of the Three Strikes measure, among them the state's district attorneys and other law enforcement groups, tried to circulate another intiative petition to deny judges the small area of discretion they've carved out for themselves, but the drive failed.

62. *California Population Characteristics* (Palo Alto, CA: Center for the Continuing Study of the California Economy, 1995), p. 116.

63. List from California Department of Corrections. The state's first prison, San Quentin, was opened in 1852. Five have gone "on line" since 1994.

64. Office of the Legislative Analyst, *Policy Brief: Addressing the State's Long-Term Inmate Population Growth,* May 20, 1997, p. 8. The Legislative Analyst suggested committing some short-term and elderly offenders in jails and community detention facilities to lower that number, but that would require significant changes in sentencing policy. And even with those changes, the state would still need seven new prisons. In 1995, the projected need was for twenty-four new prisons, but because of the reduced crime rate and slowing rate of increase in prison population, the projections have been reduced.

65. Even discounting for a certain amount of hyperbole on the part of prison officials, the fear always remains that sooner or later, the crowding, whatever the figure, will set off a deadly riot and/or

bring on a federal court order requiring the state to release or transfer prisoners.

66. California Legislative Analyst, *The 1996–97 Budget: Perspectives and Issues*, p. 87. See also *Governor's Budget Summary, 1996–97*, p. 123. The quotes are from statements Gomez made at an annual legislative retreat at Berkeley in February 1996.

67. *Governor's Budget Summary, 1997–98*, pp. 88, 124, 127. (The projection for the University of California, in full-time-equivalent students, was 153,000; for prisons, 159,823 inmates. An additional 9,400 inmates were projected for the state Youth Authority.) Also see California Department of Corrections, "CDC Facts," April 1, 1997. (www.cdc.state.ca.us/factsht.html).

68. Kathleen Connolly, Lea McDermid, Vincent Schiraldi, and Dan Macallair, "From Classrooms to Cell Blocks: How Prison Building Affects Higher Education and African American Enrollment," San Francisco, Center on Juvenile and Criminal Justice, October 1996, p. 2.

69. Interview, May 30, 1996.

70. Susie Cohen, interview, June 12, 1996.

71. California Mental Health Directors Association, "Redesigning Mental Health," November 1995.

72. Thousands of additional books were saved by volunteers, most from groups like the American Association of Retired Persons, who stored them in their homes until a decision could be made about what to do with them.

73. Peter Hecht, "Library Fee to Go Before Voters," *Sacramento Bee*, August 10, 1995, p. B3.

74. Catherine Bridge, "County Gives to Libraries After Suit," *Sacramento Bee* (Neighbors ed.), February 8, 1996, p. N1.

75. Liz Gibson, *Status of California Public Libraries, 1995–96* (Sacramento, CA: The California State Library, 1996), p. 21, Appendix G–5, G(1)1.

76. Reagan would proclaim his success in reducing the state's welfare rolls, which stemmed at least in part from the fact that the recession, which had driven them up, ended. But the Democrats' price was a higher schedule of benefits protected by those COLAs. Cannon, op. cit., pp. 177–185.

77. Senate Committee on Budget and Fiscal Review, *Overview of the 1996–97 Budget Bill*, January 1996, p. SI–6; Robert B. Gunnison, "Wilson OKs Welfare Cuts for Kids, Poor," *San Francisco Chronicle*, November 26, 1996, p. A1.

78. With the recovery of the past couple of years, caseloads have begun to decline sharply, and total welfare expenditures have declined even more. Office of the Legislative Analyst, *Cal Facts*, January 1996, p. 59.

79. In an important study by the

Public Policy Institute of California, Thomas MaCurdy and Margaret O'Brien-Strain calculated that of the families receiving AFDC, many have members who receive part of their annual income from work. But 432,000 (45 percent) of those families are highly dependent on welfare programs; 262,000 of them have no income other than public assistance. "The sheer size of this group," one of the authors said, ". . . presents the most crucial challenge for policy makers in the effort to reform state programs." See *Who Will Be Affected by Welfare Reform in California?* (San Francisco: The Public Policy Institute of California, 1997), pp. 129–130. The quote, by O'Brien-Strain, is from a PPIC press release, February 11, 1997.

80. Cathleen Ferraro, "Millions More Want Jobs Than the Stats Show," *Sacramento Bee*, September 1996, p. A1.

81. In the summer of 1996, before Congress voted to continue some benefits for legal aliens that had originally been scheduled for elimination under the federal welfare law, the Legislative Analyst estimated that the reduction in benefits would cost California $6.7 billion over a three-year period. *Policy Brief*, "Federal Welfare Reform (H.R.3734): Fiscal Effect on California," Legislative Analyst's Office, August 20, 1996.

82. Eugene Smolensky, Eirik Evenhouse, and Siobhan Reilly, *Welfare Reform: A Primer in 12 Questions* (San Francisco: The Public Policy Institute of California, 1997).

83. Jared Bernstein, "The Challenge of Moving from Welfare to Work," The Economic Policy Institute, 1997. (http://epinet.org/ibbern.html).

84. Jim Newton, "Riordan Wades into U.S. Welfare Debate," *Los Angeles Times*, May 8, 1997, p. B1. Under the original welfare bill, more than 240,000 California aliens had faced cutoffs. After Congress agreed to restore benefits to elderly disabled legal aliens, that number dropped to an estimated 70,000. California Department of Social Services, *Fact Sheet*, "Supplemental Security Income/State Supplementary Payment," January 9, 1997.

85. In January 1997, when Republican governors, realizing how much the cuts in benefits to legal aliens would cost their states, asked Congress to restore at least some of them, Pete Wilson of California was not among them. Robert Pear, "G.O.P. Governors Seek to Restore Immigrant Aid," *New York Times*, January 25, 1997, p. 1.

86. Interviews with Muriel Johnson and other county officials, August 2, 1996. "Counties Fear Financial and Social Impacts of Federal Welfare Reform," *Los Angeles Times*, August 2, 1996, p. 3; "Deep Cuts for State's Poor Seen," *Los Angeles Times*, August 2, 1996, p. 1;

"Counties Ask State to Be Last-Ditch Provider for Poor," *Los Angeles Times*, August 9, 1996, p. A3.

87. Interview with Assemblywoman Dion Aroner, cochair of the legislative committee that drafted the state's welfare reform bills, May 15, 1997.

88. John Jacobs, "Movement on Welfare Reform?" *Sacramento Bee*, March 25, 1997, p. B6.

89. *Governor's Budget Summary, 1997–98*, pp. 106–07; Senate Office of Research, *California Rankings*, 1995, p. 70.

90. The most glaring is the denial of prenatal care to illegal aliens, most of whose babies will be born in this country and thus automatically become American citizens. As a wide range of medical groups have pointed out, that's a false economy that's likely to cost the state far more in care for those children than it will ever save.

91. *Governor's Budget Summary*, p. 110; California Senate Office of Research, *Rankings*, p. 68.

92. Institute for the Future, *The Future of California's Health Care* (San Francisco, 1997), p. 11. (www.iftf.org/).

93. California Senate Office of Research, *California Rankings: Comparing California to the Other States in the Nation*, 1995, pp. 63, 64, 70, 74.

94. Institute for the Future, op. cit., p. 5.

95. Claire Cooper, "Private Justice for Rich Spurs Cries of Protest," *Sacramento Bee*, May 3, 1991, p. A1; Aissatou Sidime, "Serving on the Bench as a Business," *Sacramento Bee*, July 29, 1991, p. C1.

96. Margaret A. Jacobs, "Renting Justice: Retired Judges Seize Rising Role in Settling Disputes in California," *Wall Street Journal*, July 26, 1996, p. 1.

97. Joel Kotkin, *California: A Twenty-First Century Prospectus* (Denver, CO: The Center for the New West), February 28, 1996, p. 15.

98. Frederick Rose, "The Outlook: California's Recovery Gains Strength Slowly," *Wall Street Journal*, June 17, 1996, p. 1. In fact, even in 1995, when the resurgent California economy grew more vigorously than the national economy, California wages and salaries grew at a somewhat slower rate. The difference was property income, including interest dividends, which grew much more rapidly than the nation's.

99. The federal government has been trying to enlist the operators who comply with wages and hours laws, as well as major retailers, to take responsibility for their suppliers, apparently with some success. But the problem is not likely to disappear. Phone interview with Labor Secretary Robert Reich, April 1996. In 1994, according to a Labor Department survey, more than 90 percent of California garment manufacturers violated health and

safety codes, half failed to pay minimum wage, and almost 70 percent did not pay proper overtime. More than half were not in full compliance in verifying the immigration status of their workers. Stuart Silverstein, "Labor Abuse Rampant in State Garment Industry," *Los Angeles Times*, April 15, 1994, p. D1. Also see James Flanigan, "Economic Experts Say County Can Weather Welfare Reform," *Los Angeles Times*, August 2, 1996, p. 1.

100. The Center for Continuing Study of the California Economy, *California Economic Growth, 1996–97* (Palo Alto, CA, 1997), p. V–5.

101. Jennifer Sherman, Don Villarejo, Anna Garcia, Stephen McCurdy, Ketty Mobed, David Runsten, Cathy Saiki, Steven Samuels, and Mark Shenker, *Finding the Invisible Farm Workers: The Parlier Survey* (Davis, CA: The California Institute for Rural Studies, 1997).

102. Don Villarejo and Dave Runsten, *California's Agricultural Dilemma: Higher Production and Lower Wages* (Davis, CA: The California Institute for Rural Studies, 1993), pp. viii, 23.

103. Steven Greenhouse, "U.S. Surveys Find Farm Worker Pay Down for 20 Years," *New York Times*, March 31, 1997, p. A1.

104. Interview with Connell, May 1996. Ilana DeBare "Silicon Valley Scales New Peaks," *Sacramento Bee*, August 11, 1996, p. 1.

105. Deborah Reed, Melissa Glen Haber, and Laura Mameesh, *The Distribution of Income in California* (San Francisco: The Public Policy Institute of California, 1996), pp. v–xv. Similar data were generated by State Controller Kathleen Connell in "The Wage Gap and California's Recovery," *Controller's Quarterly* (May 1996): 5–7.

106. "What Are the Fastest Growing Jobs in California?," data compiled from California Employment Development Department and the U.S. Bureau of Labor Statistics. California Budget Project Report, March 17, 1996. See also Louis Uchitelle, "Welfare Recipients Taking Jobs Once Held by the Working Poor," *New York Times*, April 1, 1997, p. A1.

107. *California Statistical Abstract*, 1995, Table I-9, p. 127; U.S. Bureau of the Census, *1990 Census of Population and Housing*, prepared by the Geography Division in cooperation with the Housing Division, Washington, D.C., 1990.

108. Technically, they merely deferred payments for a year; but the effect of the court rulings was to force the state to come up with an additional $1 billion, counting interest, that it did not budget for.

109. Jean Ross, director of the California Budget Project, "How Has California's Business Tax Burden Changed," testimony to the Senate Revenue and Taxation Committee, February 5, 1997. (www.cpb.org). Wilson ran a full-page ad in

the Western edition of *New York Times* (July 16, 1996, p. A9), headlined "Who Just Enacted This Year's Largest Tax Cut for Business?" The answer, of course, was California. "The last time corporate taxes were this low in California," it said, "Ronald Reagan was governor."

110. Citizens for Tax Justice and the Institute on Taxation and Economic Policy, *Who Pays? A Distributional Analysis of the Tax Systems in All 50 States*, Washington, June 1996, p. 4. (www.ctj.org); phone interview with Etlinger, March 4, 1997.

111. "What Happened to the Tax Increase?" California Budget Project analysis, January 1997.

112. Edward J. Blakely and Mary Gail Snyder, *Fortress America: Gated and Walled Communities in the United States* (Cambridge, MA: The Lincoln Institute, 1995), pp. 1, 5; Blakely interview, July 1996.

113. Mike Davis, in his brilliant, sardonic (and sometimes exaggerated) *City of Quartz* (1990) has a fully elaborated theory that contemporary Los Angeles architecture and design is driven by the impulse to make public spaces as unliveable as possible for the poor and homeless. See, e.g., "Fortress L.A.," pp. 221–263.

114. Tom Gorman, "It Has It All—Even a Wall," *Los Angeles Times*, August 19, 1996, p. A3.

115. George Sternlieb, "Things Aren't What They Used to Be," *Jour-*

nal of the American Planning Association, Fall 1990, p. 494.

116. Blakely and Snyder, op. cit., pp. 2, 7.

117. William Fulton, "Another Legacy of Proposition 13—A Crazy Quilt of 'Cocoon' Citizens," *Los Angeles Times*, December 1, 1991, Opinion, p. 1.

118. The key issue is whether the advocates of various voucher proposals—free-market advocates, Christian conservatives, educational reformers of various stripes—can ever get themselves together to agree on a plan, and whether one or more of the state's conservative deep pockets, of whom there are many, can be persuaded to put up enough money to take on the unions.

119. "California's AFDC Benefit Levels and Expenditures Are Close to Average When Its High Child Poverty Rate and Cost of Living Are Considered" (Washington, D.C.: Center on Budget and Policy Priorities, June 11, 1996).

120. James Flanigan, "San Diego Offers Lesson on Art of the Comeback," *Los Angeles Times*, July 31, 1996, p. 1.

121. Iris Lav, Edward B. Lazere, and Jim St. George, *A Tale of Two Futures: Restructuring California's Finances to Boost Economic Growth* (Washington, D.C.: Center on Budget and Policy Priorities, 1994), p. viii. The percentages of capital spending come from the California

Council for Economic and Environmental Balance. See Mary Beth Barber, "Is California Driving Business Out of the State?," *California Journal* (May 1993): 10.

122. *Cal-Tax Research Bulletin* (Sacramento: The California Taxpayers Association, January 1986), p. 6; California Senate Offfice of Research, *California Rankings*, 1995, p. 130.

123. Document Prepared for Senator Mike Thompson by the State Senate Budget and Fiscal Review Committee, November 10, 1995.

124. It also made for a lot of political jockeying about who should pay for the lion's share of the work—the users of the bridge (i.e., Northern Californians) through increased tolls, or the state's motorists generally through their regular gas taxes.

125. It's also conceivable that the three-year recession in the early 1990s, which saw a significant decline in vehicle mileage in California, may have deferred some pressure for road improvements, which, with an improved economy, may now return.

126. Stephen Levy, interview, May 16, 1996.

127. *California Rankings*, p. 131.

128. "California's Growing Taxpayer Squeeze," California Department of Finance, October 1991.

129. California Department of Finance, *California Statistical Ab-*

stract, 1995, pp. 22, 78, 79; *California Statistical Abstract*, 1970, p. 158. (www.dof.ca.gov).

130. Lav et al., op. cit, p. 101; *California Statistical Abstract*, 1995, Table D-7.

131. California Legislative Analyst, *The 1996–97 Budget: Perspectives and Issues*, p. 99.

132. Cannon, *Reagan*, p. 166.

133. Voting data compiled by Mark DiCamillo of the Field Institute, a nonpartisan San Francisco-based public opinion research organization. School enrollment projection from the California State Department of Finance. (www.dof.ca.gov).

NOTES FOR PART THREE:
THE SPIRIT OF 13

1. Howard Jarvis (with Robert Pack), *I'm Mad as Hell* (New York: Times Books, 1979), p. 277.

2. On Churchill, ibid., p. 269. On the Goldwater fund-raising episode, see Jack Anderson column, *Washington Post*, July 25, 1978.

3. Leo Rennert, "Elusive Hayakawa Funds," *Sacramento Bee*, October 14, 1976, p. 1.

4. Dan O'Neill, "'Shady' Dealings by Jarvis Alleged," *Sacramento Bee*, July 25, 1978, p. A3.

5. Advertisement for U.S. Steel in *Architect and Engineer*, August 1943, quoted in Merry Ovnick, *Los Angeles: The End of the Rainbow* (Los Angeles: Balcony Press, 1994), p. 275. Ovnick provides a comprehen-

sive survey of Los Angeles residential architecture from the first settlements to the present.

6. Mike Davis, *City of Quartz* (New York: Vintage, 1992), p. 174. The tax revolt brought a perverse echo of Henry George, who, in *Progress and Poverty*, propounded the single tax proposal just a century earlier (1879). George, a San Francisco journalist, sensed, albeit with a very different perspective from Jarvis's, the crucial importance of land and land values in economic and social relations. As should become clearer later in this section, in its treatment of commercial property, Proposition 13 discouraged development, rewarded speculative holdings, and thus turned the single tax idea on its head.

7. Lo is now at the University of Missouri in Columbia. He made the comment at a conference on Proposition 13 at UCLA in May 1994.

8. The best account of this whole episode is still Robert Kuttner, *Revolt of the Haves* (New York: Simon and Schuster, 1980), pp. 31–44. See also David O. Sears and Jack Citrin, *Tax Revolt: Something for Nothing in California* (Cambridge, MA: Harvard University Press, 1982).

9. Clarence Y.H. Lo, *Small Property Versus Big Government* (Berkeley, CA: University of California Press, 1990), p. 77.

10. Lo, op. cit., p. 87.

11. Davis, op. cit., p. 170.

12. Also on the ballot was one of Watson's initiatives that would have limited property taxes. It failed 34–66.

13. Roger Rapoport, *California Dreaming: The Political Odyssey of Pat & Jerry Brown* (Berkeley, CA: Nolo Press, 1982), p. 156.

14. Cannon, op. cit., p. 155; John Vickerman, interview and notes, December 3, 1996.

15. Analysis, from State Board of Equalization Annual Reports for the period 1967–68 to 1978–79, provided by John Vickerman, who was a senior budget analyst with the state Legislative Analyst's Office during this period. Vickerman also observed at the time that a combination of economic factors in the housing market, and particularly the inflation in the prices of new homes, hit first-time home buyers much harder than others, and hit current homeowners who do not move least. But "oddly, it is this last group which is raising the loudest cry . . . for more property tax relief." Vickerman, "Notes on Property Tax Relief Bills Before the California Legislature," talk to the San Francisco Chapter of the National Association of Business Economists, April 21, 1977.

16. Lo, op. cit., p. 15.

17. "Illegal Aliens Take Free Ride on Gravy Train," *Sacramento Bee*, September 17, 1978, p. F5.

18. In his 1970 race for the state Board of Equalization, he advocated a 1 percent property tax limit. Schools, he said, should be taken off the property tax altogether and funded through the sales tax. See *Sacramento Bee*, May 24, 1970, p. A13.

19. Fox was altogether different from the old man in personality. He was not a rabble-rouser and was able to negotiate with other groups even as he stoutly pursued his organization's objectives.

20. *An Analysis of Proposition 13, the Jarvis-Gann Property Tax Initiative* (Sacramento: Legislative Analyst's Office, 1978), pp. 86–87.

21. Kuttner, op. cit., p. 55.

22. Jarvis, op. cit., p. 48.

23. George Deukmejian, who served in both houses before becoming governor, pointed out with no little sentimentality (as have a number of other old hands) that, before lobbyists were prohibited from wining and dining politicians, there was a lot more bipartisan conviviality in Sacramento's watering spots, and, thus, a lot more ability to work comfortably with members of the other party than there has been in recent years. It's improbable that political reform is the major cause, but who's to say it hasn't contributed?

24. California State Senate Forum on the Future of California, March 21, 1996 (Tape 2 of videotape at California State Library).

25. Under the "threshhold circuit-breaker," homeowners were required to pay all property tax up to a specified percentage of their household income; the state would reimburse a portion of the tax above this amount. In addition, low-income senior citizens, who were already getting some relief, would get an additional break.

26. *Los Angeles Times*, September 16, 1977.

27. "Special Report," *California Journal*, May 1978, pp. 3–7.

28. "Jarvis Rips Riles on Initiative," *Sacramento Bee*, February 23, 1978, p. B1.

29. The list comes from the official filings for the various Jarvis organizations at the Office of the Secretary of State in Sacramento and represents the most common categories from a sampling of the thousands of people named as contributors.

30. *Serrano v. Priest*, 5 Cal. 3d 584 (1971); *Serrano v. Priest*, 18 Cal. 3d 728 (1976).

31. Stephen M. Rhoads, Ann Sutherland Frentz, and Rudolph S. Marshall, Jr., "AB 65: California's Reply to *Serrano*," paper presented at the annual meeting of the American Education Finance Association, March 14, 1978; William A. Fischel, "How *Serrano* Caused Proposition 13," unpublished paper, subsequently revised and published under the same title in *The Journal of Law and Politics*, Fall

1996, pp. 607–36. See also Fischel, "Did *Serrano* Cause Proposition 13?," *National Tax Journal*, vol. 42 (1989), p. 465.

32. *Serrano v. Priest* (Serrano I), 5 Cal. 3d 600.

33. Fischel, *How Serrano Caused Proposition 13*, op. cit., pp. 10–11. Fischel also argues that many local districts could not reduce rates when their property values increased because under the post-*Serrano* equalization formula their state aid was reduced in response to those increases. Had they cut local taxes they would have defaulted on prior contractual commitments. But the issue of *Serrano* rarely came up in the debates, so this part of Fischel's case is not conclusive. What's more persuasive is that *Serrano* undercut potential arguments in affluent communities, which had opposed early property-tax-cutting measures, against Jarvis-Gann. As Fischel points out, there was a wide political swing in affluent places such as Beverly Hills between the (negative) vote on the Watson initiative in 1972 and the support for Jarvis-Gann in 1978.

34. The Field Institute California Poll, Release #975, June 2, 1978. It's always possible that, in light of the fact that the whole establishment opposed Jarvis-Gann, many poll respondents were embarrassed to acknowledge their support of Proposition 13 at the time, thereby skewing Field's results. There have been similar patterns in polling on other isues where one side, the popular side, was also the side opposed by most of the respectable establishment.

35. John Vickerman, the senior budget analyst in the Legislative Analyst's Office at the time, said much later that Pope might have averted the problem, but "he just didn't know how to juggle the numbers."

36. Alexander Pope, "The Assessor's Perspective," *University of Southern California Law Review* 53 (1979): 155.

37. Bill Butcher, quoted in Kuttner, op. cit., p. 71.

38. David O. Sears and Jack Citrin, *Tax Revolt: Something for Nothing in California* (enlarged edition) (Cambridge, MA: Harvard University Press, 1985), pp. 98, 101, 148. There is also a Field California Poll taken a week before the election showing similar results; "Heavy Tide on the Order of Seven to Four Running in Favor of Prop. 13," (San Francisco: The Field Institute, June 2, 1978); the Sears and Citrin retrospective "Tax Revolt Survey" of 1,788 people is available through UCDATA at the University of California, Berkeley. It was conducted eighteen months after the vote (and is thus somewhat suspect); it shows parents and nonparents as having supported 13 in equal proportions (in both cases by percentages that were higher than the actual vote).

39. The individual corporate sums are taken from a before-the-fact estimate by the Assembly Revenue and Taxation Committee, *Facts About Proposition 13: The Jarvis/Gann Initiative*, February 15, 1978, p. 34.

40. *Annual Report of the California State Board of Equalization*, Sacramento, 1980, p. 39.

41. Kenneth T. Rosen, "The Impact of Proposition 13 on House Prices in Northern California: A Test of the Interjurisdictional Capitalization Hypothesis," *The Journal of Political Economy* 90 (1982): 200 (reprint No. 22 of the UC Berkeley Institute of Business and Economic Research). Rosen cautions that the tax cuts occurred without any "substantial corresponding reduction in services" in those early years because the surplus was available to bail out local communities. "Thus these results, while strongly confirming the theory of property tax capitalization, must be viewed as tentative because of the remaining uncertainty regarding future service cutbacks in local communities."

42. Arthur O'Sullivan, Terri A. Sexton, and Steven M. Sheffrin, *Property Taxes and Tax Revolts: The Legacy of Proposition 13* (Cambridge, UK: Cambridge University Press, 1995), p. 137. Douglas Jeffe and Sherry B. Jeffe, "Proposition 13: Ten Years Later," *Public Opinion* (May/June, 1978): 18.

43. Interview, December 9, 1996.

44. See, e.g., Peter Theroux, *Translating LA: A Tour of the Rainbow City* (New York: Norton, 1994), pp. 135–137. There are, in fact, strange similarities between the effects of Proposition 13 and rent control generally in artificially favoring existing occupants of housing at the expense of those seeking housing, and thus the old over the young, established groups over new groups. The same arguments that opponents of delisting use in New York (generally on the left) are used by the defenders of Proposition 13 in California ("You want to throw all those worthy folks out on the street . . . ?").

45. Brown, perhaps the most protean of politicians, would remake himself several more times, as a contemplative resident of a Zen monastery in Japan, as a penitent working (briefly) with Mother Teresa in caring for the destitute in Calcutta, as chairman and chief fund raiser for the California Democratic Party, as a virulent critic of the evils of money in politics who would run for president "free of the contradiction and hypocrisy [of] previous campaigns," as a sort of Cassandra warning endlessly of political evil, and then again as a candidate for mayor of Oakland in 1998. Jerry Brown's preferred rite, Garry Wills once said, "would be all Ash Wednesday, with no Easter."

46. Orville Schell, *Brown* (New York: Random House, 1978), p. 262.

47. Legislative Analyst's summary of Proposition 13, on the official June 1978 California Ballot Pamphlet.

48. "TRB," *New Republic,* October 23, 1995, p. 6. Fox also liked to cite columnist Richard Reeves, who once implied that the brutal murder of twelve-year-old Polly Klaas in Northern California might have been prevented if the police had had state-of-the-art communications and identification equipment that might have allowed them to identify the abductor, who had a long criminal record, when they fortuitously stopped (and released) him shortly after the girl's kidnaping and before she was killed. It was budget cuts prompted by Proposition 13, Reeves suggested, that precluded timely purchase of such equipment.

49. Jarvis, op. cit., p. 286.

50. Lenny Goldberg, *Taxation With Representation: A Citizen's Guide to Reforming Proposition 13* (Sacramento, CA: California Tax Reform Association and New California Alliance, 1991), p. 53.

51. Sears and Citrin, op. cit., p. 251.

52. "Jarvis, Gann Split Bitterly Over Follow-Up," *Sacramento Bee,* November 17, 1978, p. A1.

53. Jarvis, *I'm Mad as Hell,* p. 136.

54. Kuttner, *Revolt of the Haves,* p. 93. Kuttner cites press accounts. Cranston, nonetheless, could take pleasure two years later when he easily beat the hapless Gann, who had run against him for the senate.

55. "Jarvis Brings Prop: 13 Concept to Paris, London," *Sacramento Bee,* December 5, 1978, p. B1.

56. Terri A. Sexton and Steven M. Sheffrin, "Five Lessons from Tax Revolts," *State Tax Notes,* December 18, 1995, pp. 1763–64. In the spring of 1996, Oklahoma voters were thought to favor an initiative that was almost a carbon copy of Proposition 13, but by a surprising 67–33 margin they rejected it.

57. Jack Citrin, "Jarvis Leaves a Whole New Ball Game; California Tax Revolt Transformed All the Rules of Politics," *Los Angeles Times,* August 22, 1986, Section II, p. 5.

58. See, e.g., James Mayer, "Making Measure 47 Work," *Oregonian,* November 10, 1996, p. 1.

59. Although the full story of how plebiscitary populism was commercialized has never been told, a more extensive treatment appears in the next section of this book. See also Tracy Webber, "The Darth Vaders of Direct Mail," *Los Angeles Times,* March 3, 1996, p. 1.

60. The work of Butcher-Forde is described more fully in the next section.

61. The observation comes from, among others, Gerald Meral, head of the California Planning and Conservation League, which conducts frequent polls of voter attitudes on a range of issues.

62. This could of course only be a problem in the strange system

that Proposition 13 created. If a home was still assessed, say, at 1975 values, while the new one would be assessed on the basis of its acquisition cost, the official assessment on a relatively modest place could be far higher than that on the more sumptuous former residence. Seniors in such situations are not required to pay any more property tax on the new place than on the previous one.

63. See Alvin D. Sokolow and Peter M. Detwiler, "State–Local Relations in California," in Platon Rigos, Dale Krane, and Mel Hill, eds., *Home Rule in America: A Fifty State Handbook*, (Washington, D.C.: CQ Press, Forthcoming).

64. By pegging increases in the spending cap to increases in personal income, which effectively eliminated any effective spending cap. But by then, of course, the pinch had long shifted to the revenue side.

65. Beneath Deukmejian's astringent conservatism, there was a pervasive sentimentality about low-tuition public universities. Gardner privately tried repeatedly to get Deukmejian to accede to increases in UC's then-low fees, but Deukmejian always refused (Gardner, in interviews with the author).

66. Maureen DiMarco, who for six years served as Governor Pete Wilson's Secretary of Education and Children's Services before being forced out in the fall of 1996, and who was one of the handful of

people who actually understood the complex formulas of Proposition 98, was among the first to make that observation. Because Proposition 98 automatically allocates a fixed chunk of state revenues to the schools, it turns one of the state's most powerful employee organizations, the California Teachers Association, into a rabid opponent of any tax cut. But it also undercuts the incentives of all other groups to support any tax increase for the state general fund.

67. The data were compiled by John Mockler, probably the most respected school lobbyist in California. In 1987–88, the schools got $3,621 per child. In 1997–98, they got $5,010; in constant dollars, using the consumer price index, that comes to $3,476. And Mockler's figures do not deviate greatly from other data.

68. The California Teachers Association, "the 800-pound gorilla" among the state's educational lobbies, has been engaged in a virtually endless public media campaign for the better part of a decade, often in pursuit of objectives that put it at odds with other education groups, and sometimes even with other school employee unions.

69. Robert L. Manwaring and Steven M. Sheffrin, "Litigation, School Finance Reform and Aggregate Educational Spending," unpublished paper, presented at the International Institute of Public Finance, March 1996.

70. As in a memo from the California Taxpayers Association to the state Senate Budget and Fiscal Review Committee, January 18, 1995.

71. See, e.g., *Cal Facts*, California Legislative Analyst's Office, 1996, pp. 17–18; *Cal-Tax Research*, The California Taxpayers Association, May 1996, p. 6. That seems to be true even if certain fees are included, but since fees as a whole are hard to categorize and evaluate (how does one count charges at public universities, or hospitals?), comparisons are difficult.

72. Legislative Analyst's Report, *Understanding Proposition 218*, December 1996. (www. lao. ca. gov). For provisions and the preelection analysis of 218, see California Ballot Pamphlet for the November 5, 1996, general election. (Available on line at www.ss.ca.gov.)

73. See, e.g., John Wildermuth, "New State Tax Law Rattling Budgets," *San Francisco Chronicle*, December 17, 1996, p. 1; Eric Young and Tony Bizjak, "Moody's Reduces City's Bond Rating," *Sacramento Bee*, December 25, 1996, p. B1.

74. "Sane Decisions and Their Defeat," *Sacramento Bee*, January 25, 1997, p. B6.

75. Phone interview with Burt McChesney, a lobbyist for the California Association of Realtors, March 1997.

76. Wilson, at a meeting of the Advisory Board of the Public Policy Institute of California, and in conversations with the author, September 13, 1996.

77. William Fulton, "Another Legacy of Proposition 13—A Crazy Quilt of 'Cocoon Citizens,'" *Los Angeles Times*, December 1, 1991, Opinion section, p. 1.

78. Interview, May 1996. See also "Developers Can't Bail Out Schools," *Sacramento Bee*, May 16, 1993, p. FO1.

79. Eventually there will be seventy-one miles of such roads, most following existing freeway routes, which were developed by a consortium of private entrepreneurs, including a French company, and augmented by developer fees and state bonds. Users obtain a transponder that automaticaly bills their accounts when they use what are sometmes called "the Lexus lanes" but appear to be used far more often by more plebian vehicles. But in rush-hour circumstances, such as those on the Riverside Freeway, the paying customers speed past the bumper-to-bumper traffic on the adjacent lanes. It is, as the critics say, another form of privatization like "private housing enclaves with their own private police," but it is also, as the backers point out, a reflection that there is less and less tax money available, and that the taxpayers, though paying far less per mile in gas taxes than they did a generation ago, steadfastly refuse to approve any increases.

80. That partial break is small against the policies of retirement communities in Arizona that exclude all children, in part so that, as provided by Arizona law, they need pay no school taxes. That's not permissible under California law.

81. See "Deja vu in Elk Grove," *Sacramento Bee*, January 16, 1987, p. B6; "Trying Again in Elk Grove," *Sacramento Bee*, April 24, 1987, p. B10.

82. *Nordlinger v. Hahn*, 505 U.S. 1 (1992).

83. See California Business Higher Education Roundtable, *California Fiscal Reform: A Plan for Action* (Oakland, CA: University of California, 1994), p. 14.

84. *Nordlinger v. Hahn*, 505 U.S. 1 (1992).

85. *Allegheny Pittsburgh Coal Co. v. Webster County*, 488 U.S. 336 (1989).

86. O'Sullivan et al., op. cit., p. 138. Like a lot of others, O'Sullivan and his coauthors call for repeal of those dynasty provisions allowing property to be passed from generation to generation without reassessment, and the sooner the better, "before intergenerational transmission of property without reassessment becomes a common practice in California." In the meantime, they serve only "to dramatize the inequities built into the existing system." The same recommendation was made in 1994 by a task force of the California Business-Higher Education Forum in *California Fiscal Reform: A Plan for Action* (Oakland, CA: University of California, 1994), p. 35.

87. Jarvis, op. cit., p. 73.

88. O'Sullivan et al., op. cit., p. 142.

89. In 1996, when Oklahomans rejected a property tax reduction measure that was almost a carbon copy of Proposition 13, one of the major arguments against it was that it would discourage new businesses from moving into the state because they would not benefit from the rollback and would have to pay taxes on the acquisition value of their properties. See "Oklahoma Property Tax Rollback Plan Fails," AP wire story, March 13, 1996.

90. See Lenny Goldberg, *Taxation With Representation: A Citizen's Guide to Reforming Proposition 13* (Sacramento, CA: California Tax Reform Association and New California Alliance, 1991), pp. 69–70. Goldberg also points out the bizarre way in which corporate property does not change ownership. If one company buys another, the courts have held, a change has occurred. If there is a near-total turnover in common stock over a period of time, or even if four people each buy a 25 percent share at the same time, ownership is deemed not to have changed.

91. Interview, June 1994; reinterview, May 20, 1996. For a more op-

timistic view of this process, see Dean J. Misczynski, "The Fiscalization of Land Use," in John J. Kirlin and Donald R. Winkler, eds., *California Policy Choices*, vol. 3 (Los Angeles: University of Southern California School of Public Administration, 1986), pp. 73–106. Misczynski argues that since, in the old era, public facilities could be built with money that was "free" from the point of view of local officials (usually with state money, and sometimes with federal money), "the cost of those facilities did not have to assume a very large role in local land use decisions." The new constraints, he argues, at least force consideration of the costs of local development and thus make for "a stronger result" than planning without regard to fiscal considerations.

92. William Fulton, "In Their Race for Sales-Tax Income, Cities Often Wind up as the Losers," *Sacramento Bee*, September 4, 1995, p. B7.

93. Doug Kaplan, "Overmalled, Underschooled," *Los Angeles Times*, December 9, 1996, p. B5.

94. Alvin D. Sokolow, "State Rules and the County-City Arena: Competition for Land and Taxes in California's Central Valley," *Publius: The Journal of Federalism* (Winter 1993): 61.

95. Data on incorporations from League of California Cities.

96. *Fullerton Joint Union High School District v. State Board of Educa-*tion, 32 Cal. 3d. 793 (1982). For an overview of the issue, see Peter M. Detwiler, "Suburban Secession: History and Context," paper delivered at the Envisioning California Conference, Pasadena, September 28, 1996. Detwiler is consultant to the California Senate Committee on Housing and Land Use. (peter.detwiler@sen.ca.gov).

97. Lockyer's bill, however, required that before any Valley secession could take place, it would have to get approval, not only of its voters, but of the voters in Los Angeles as a whole. That, of course, was not acceptable to the secessionists, but short of a change in party control, it's probably all they'll get.

98. Simi Valley, in fact, is not in the San Fernando Valley, or even in Los Angeles County, but it is close enough, in geography and in spirit, to explain why the two are often identified together.

99. Sara Catania, "America's Safest, Richest City," *Los Angeles Daily News*, May 25, 1996, p. 1.

100. See *Los Angeles Times*, May 26, 1996, p. M1.

101. Interviews conducted July 1994, May 1996.

102. In the recession of the early 1990s, the joke about growth management in Governor Pete Wilson's office was that they wished they had some growth to manage. But the pressure for slow growth or no growth continued even through the recession.

103. Lo, op. cit., among others, found frequent overlaps between the tax protesters and the slow-growthers, not only in Southern California, but in other states. See Lo, pp. 60–63; 86–87; 179–80.

104. Lo, op. cit., p. 215.

105. The phrase comes from Fred Silva, who for many years was a public policy analyst in the California legislature. Most recently he served as staff director of the California Constitution Revision Commission, which attempted to deal with these issues but whose recommendations were largely ignored. The commission's proposals are discussed more fully in later sections of this book.

106. In 1987, Margaret Thatcher, then disassembling Britain's welfare state, had said almost the same thing: "There is no such thing as society. There are individual men and women, and there are families."

NOTES FOR PART THREE: MARCH OF THE PLEBISCITES

1. Jim Shultz, *The Initiative Cookbook: Recipes and Stories from California's Ballot Wars* (San Francisco: The Democracy Center, 1996), p. 3.

2. Kevin Starr, *Inventing the Dream: California Through the Progressive Era* (New York: Oxford University Press, 1985), p. 254.

3. George E. Mowry, *The California Progressives* (Berkeley, CA: Uni-versity of California Press, 1951), p. 141.

4. Richard Coke Lower, *A Bloc of One: The Political Career of Hiram W. Johnson* (Palo Alto, CA: Stanford University Press, 1993), pp. 13–18.

5. Text in Franklin Hichborn, *Story of the Session of the California Legislature of 1911* (San Francisco: James H. Barry Co., 1911), Appendix, p. v.

6. Mowry, op. cit., p. 120.

7. Quoted in Thomas E. Cronin, *Direct Democracy: The Politics of Initiative, Referendum and Recall* (Cambridge, MA: Harvard University Press, 1989), p. 52.

8. Lower, op. cit., p. 18; Mowry, op. cit., pp. 140, 148.

9. Richard Hofstadter, *The Age of Reform* (New York: Knopf, 1956), p. 266. The paraphrase is from Croly's *Progressive Democracy* (New York: Macmillan, 1914).

10. "Anti-Democracy in California," *New York Times*, October 18, 1911. Quoted in California Commission on Campaign Financing, *Democracy by Initiative: Shaping California's Fourth Branch of Government* (Los Angeles: Center for Responsive Government, 1992), p. 42n.

11. *Sacramento Bee*, April 5, 1913, p. 32. Those were the days when editors and editorial writers left no doubt where they stood: no qualifications, cost-benefit analyses, or other prevarications. McClatchy, a close friend of Johnson, was, like

him, a vigorous supporter of Progressive reform.

12. Another incentive to gather more signatures than required is that registrars first proceed by a sampling technique. If more than 110 percent of the sample is valid, the measure qualifies. If the sample shows that between 95 and 110 percent of the signatures are valid, then each signature is individually verified. If the sample falls below 95 percent, the measure does not qualify.

13. The delta is a large area of wetlands, sloughs, and other waterways east of San Francisco Bay (and feeding the bay) that remains largely unknown, even to many Californians. It is fed by both the Sacramento and San Joaquin rivers and remains a critical area for fish and other wildlife.

14. Carey McWilliams, "The Initiative: A Vehicle for Eccentric Reform," *Los Angeles Times*, April 2, 1978, section V, p. 7. McWilliams, one of the shrewdest observers of California political history, declared that the initiative and referendum fit the traditional attitude of California voters, who "become impatient quickly, demand attention to pressing problems and will not put up with legislative procrastination beyond a certain point. As a signal-flashing device in a state with weak party organizations, the intiative serves an important purpose, but not without real risk." He had no

idea when he wrote those words in 1978 of what was about to come.

15. Shultz, op. cit., p. 2.

16. "The Insurance Initiatives: No, No, Five Times No," *Sacramento Bee*, September 26, 1988, p. B10. The ultimate responsibility, as the paper said, was the legislature's, whose failure to act on the state's escalating insurance premiums caused this mess to be "dumped in the public's lap." But in this game, "the public can't win and should refuse to play."

17. Since there were dozens of campaign committees—Citizens for No-Fault (California Insurers for Proposition 104 and 106); Californians Against Unfair Rate Increases (No on 100 and 103); Committee for Fair Lawyers Fees (Yes on 106); Californians for Honest Insurance Reform (For 100); Voter Revolt Against Unfair Insurance Rates (For 103)—and since money sometimes passed between some of them, it's nearly impossible to calculate the exact amount. The records are available in the Archives of the Secretary of State in Sacramento. See also Center for Responsive Government, *Democracy by Initiative*, pp. 290, 391, 395.

18. Interview with Harry Snyder, West Coast regional director of Consumers Union, April 14, 1997.

19. Dan Bernstein, "Insurance Chief Defends Record," *Sacramento Bee*, January 26, 1997, p. A1.

20. Eric Young, "Audit Faults

Insurance Department," *Sacramento Bee*, March 14, 1997, p. D3.

21. *Democracy by Initiative*, p. 67.

22. Daniel Lowenstein, now a professor of law at UCLA, and a member of the California Fair Political Practices Commission in the late 1970s and early 1980s, made a persuasive case, on the basis of a review of measures that had passed and failed in prior years, that because the proponents of a measure have to carry their case, the ability of opponents to confuse the issue is often enough to defeat it. In some respects, that is probably a good thing. Lowenstein, "Campaign Spending and Ballot Propositions: Recent Experience, Public Choice Theory and the First Amendment," *UCLA Law Review* 29 (February 1982): 29.

23. Intel contributed $500,000, Hewlett-Packard $250,000, to the No-on-211 campaign; spokesmen for both complained publicly that they had not been consulted on the transfer and would not have approved of it. Ilana DeBare, "Firms Upset as 211 Funds Are Diverted," *Sacramento Bee*, November 5, 1996, p. E1.

24. John Gunther, *Inside U.S.A.* (Philadelphia: The Curtis Publishing Co., 1947). (Reissued by the New Press, New York, 1997, p. 16.)

25. Spencer C. Olin, Jr., *California's Prodigal Sons: Hiram Johnson and the Progressives* (Berkeley, CA: University of California Press,

1968), p. 44. Cross-filing was later abolished. But under an initiative approved by voters in March 1996, it was to be replaced, the courts permitting, by open primaries in which voters may pick and chose candidates from any party—e.g., one of the Republicans for governor, one of the Democrats for attorney general, etc.

26. Much to the delight of Garry Trudeau, as the readers of Doonesbury no doubt recall.

27. As soon as Proposition 99 passed, the former allies were engaged in political combat on how the proceeds were to be allocated. Proposition 99 provided guidance on the rough distribution among antismoking campaigns, health care, and certain environmental programs that had been written into the measure, but left to the legislature the detailed appropriations. That battle, both in the legislature and in the courts, continues to this day.

28. John Jacobs, *A Rage for Justice: The Passion and Politics of Phillip Burton* (Berkeley: University of California Press, 1995), p. 88.

29. The abortion prohibitions were consistently blocked by state courts as violating state constitutional privacy protections, and have never been enforced. Here, too, therefore, there was an extralegislative resolution of the issue.

30. Walter Zelman, "California's

Stalemated Government," *Sacramento Bee*, August 5, 1990, p. B7.

31. Bruce Cain, the associate director of the Institute of Governmental Studies at Berkeley, who first made those distinctions, also points out that the state's political glass ceiling tended to keep able urban politicians, who might otherwise have run for higher office, in the legislature, where, like Brown, they rose to positions of power.

32. The era of legislative purity had, in fact, been relatively short. As noted in Part II, in the 1940s and 1950s, the capitol had been dominated by special interest lobbyists and particularly by the expansive Artie Samish, who represented liquor and gambling interests, and once posed with a puppet on his knee that he called "Mr. Legislature." Carey McWilliams had first written about him in *The Nation* in July 1949, but it was an exposé in *Colliers* by Lester Velie a month later that prompted the grand jury investigation that led to his indictment, conviction, and imprisonment. The removal of Samish hardly ushered in an age of political purity; it was in those days still a part-time, poorly paid legislature, many of whose members had no hesitation about being wined and dined by lobbyists. But it helped lay the groundwork for a series of open meeting laws and, in the 1960s and 1970s, a set of other political reforms—in law and

climate—that no longer tolerated corruption as blatant as Samish's.

33. See, e.g., James Richardson's *Willie Brown: A Biography* (Berkeley, CA: University of California Press, 1996), pp. 319–323.

34. Quoted in Shultz, op. cit., p. 34.

35. *Democracy by Initiative*, op. cit., pp. 131, 391.

36. Dan Bernstein, "Lottery Initiative Was One Consultant's Roll of the Dice," *Sacramento Bee*, August 5, 1996, p. A1. The final reports for Proposition 104 filed with the California Secretary of State's Office shows Reilly getting a direct fee of $1.25 million, but that hardly covers all commissions on advertising and other campaign expenses.

37. Kelly Kimball, who is CEO of Kimball Petition Management, one of the largest in the business, which he runs with his brother, Fred. Phone interview, March 18, 1997.

38. Kimball, quoted in Daniel H. Lowenstein and Robert Stern, "The First Amendment and Paid Petition Circulators," *Hastings Constitutional Law Quarterly* (Fall 1989): 198.

39. The federal decision, *Buckley v. Valeo*, 424 U.S.1 (1976), has stood in the way of all mandatory expenditure limits. The state court decision was *Hardie v. Eu*, 18 Cal. 3rd 371 (1976).

40. *Meyer v. Grant*, 108 U.S. 1886 (1988). The court's logic, as Lowenstein and Stern point out, was flimsy. The Colorado statute, they

argue, "did not prohibit any form of speech, and the Court's decision privileged not communication, but the access to the ballot of those with financial resources, to the detriment of those without such resources." Stern and Lowenstein, op. cit., p. 176.

41. Charles M. Price, "Signing on for Fun and Profit: The Business of Gathering Petition Signatures," *California Journal* (November 1992): 547. The Price piece is a good overview of the industry and its practices.

42. *Democracy by Initiative*, op. cit., p. 141.

43. *Democracy by Initiative*, op. cit., p. 151n. Ultimately, when Butcher-Forde failed to provide the needed signatures, they were dismissed and the work given to another firm of petition circulators.

44. In the heyday of the Jarvis organization in the early 1980s, the list had more than 320,000 names, most of them the very committed elderly people who had been the vanguard of Proposition 13. That number, as noted in the previous section, has since declined to about 180,000, and their average age is well over sixty-five. Under the unprecedented multiyear contract that Jarvis signed with Butcher-Forde in 1983, they also were to receive commissions ranging from 15 to 17 percent on all campaign costs, and an astounding fee of 25 cents for every letter in every mailing they sent out.

45. Tracy Weber, "The Darth Vaders of Direct Mail," *Los Angeles Times*, March 3, 1996, p. A1.

46. Ibid., p. A23.

47. Peter Schrag, "Initiative Madness," *New Republic*, August 22, 1988, p. 18.

48. During the decade between 1982 and the 1990s, the dominant firms in the business, Kimball Petition Management of Los Angeles and American Petition Consultants in Sacramento, were responsible for qualifying about three-fourths of the measures that reached the ballot. Price, op. cit., pp. 545–48.

49. *Democracy by Initiative*, op. cit., p. 159.

50. Bruce Cain, Sara Ferejohn, Margarita Najer, and Mary Walther, "Constitutional Change: Is It Too Easy to Amend Our Constitution?" in Bruce E. Cain and Roger G. Noll, eds. *Constitutional Reform in California: Making State Government More Responsive* (Berkeley, CA: Institute of Governmental Studies Press, University of California, 1995), pp. 265–290.

51. Cain, op. cit., p. 289.

52. Mathew D. McCubbins and Michael F. Thies, "The Straitjacket Called 'Initiative,'" *San Diego Union Tribune*, December 24, 1994, p. B–5. Both authors are political scientists at the University of California, San Diego. McCubbins was the founder of a committee of UC

scholars on revision of the California constitution.

53. The most recent interviews with Meral took place November 26, 1996, and March 17, 1997.

54. See, e.g., Daniel M. Weintraub, "Public Land Advocates Take Initiative Path on Bond Issue," *Los Angeles Times*, May 24, 1987, p. 3.

55. "Ten Reasons to Oppose Proposition 70," flier from Citizens for Honest Park Planning, 1988.

56. Dan Walters, "Law Will Stop Seamy Practice," *Sacramento Bee*, October 21, 1991, p. A3.

57. From the official text in the California Ballot Pamphlet for the June 1988 primary election.

58. Peter Schrag, "Broker of Strange Bedfellows," *Sacramento Bee*, November 3, 1993, p. B6.

59. Phillip Isenberg and Janet Williams, *Case Study on Proposition 99: The Cigarette Tax* (paper prepared for a course Isenberg taught at California State University, Sacramento), November 20, 1995. Isenberg chaired the legislative committee that worked out the details of the appropriations of the funds raised by the tobacco tax initiative.

60. Interviews with, and documents from, Meral.

61. Felicia Cousart, "Arts to Zoo Tax Passes Easily," *Fresno Bee*, March 3, 1993, p. A3. Ultimately a court threw the whole tax out because it delivered the money to private or semipublic organizations that had

no direct accountability to the voters and taxpayers.

62. *California's Fiscal Outlook: The LAOs Economic and Budget Projections 1996–97 Through 1998–99*, November 1996. (www.lao.ca.gov.).

63. Derrick Bell, Jr., "The Referendum, Democracy's Barrier to Racial Equality," *Washington Law Review* 54 (1978): 15.

64. Wilson's ballot ventures weren't uniformly successful. In 1992, he qualified a measure, Proposition 165, that would have reduced welfare benefits and given him power to unilaterally reduce the budget in times of fiscal emergency. A group of liberal organizations qualified a measure, Proposition 167, at the same time that would have closed tax loopholes on a number of industries and otherwise raised taxes—on oil, insurance, and a number of other well-heeled interests. Proposition 167 probably never had a chance, but it drew so much business money against it—which was largely its purpose—that Wilson was unable to get any funding to support his measure. (It also gave businesses an excuse to refuse Wilson's solicitations for an issue they really didn't want to become identified with in any case.)

65. The Gorton statement was made in a conference with the editorial board of the *Sacramento Bee* shortly after the 1994 election.

66. Office of the Secretary of

State, *California Ballot Pamphlet for the November 8, 1994 General Election*, p. 34.

67. Opponents charged that Proposition 187 was partially supported by the Pioneer Fund, founded in 1937 to study race and eugenics, whose original charter called for encouragement of "reproduction of inviduals descended primarily from white persons who settled in the original 13 states," and which had since been accused of funding racist research. The alleged "direct link" between 187 and Pioneer was through the annual support that the Fund gave to FAIR, which had totalled roughly $600,000 between 1988 and 1994. Nelson insisted that FAIR had nothing to do with the drafting of 187, but Nelson, FAIR's man in California, was certainly active in campaigning for it. See, e.g., Paul Feldman, "Group's Funding of Immigration Measure Assailed," *Los Angeles Times*, September 10, 1994, p. B3. The secretive Prince himself often told the story of how an illegal Canadian immigrant had bilked him out of $500,000 in a construction project. But the immigrant was not living here illegally, the amount was much smaller, and the controversy eventually led to a second fight between Prince and his lawyer (and to a judgment against Prince), and to an effort by Prince to start an initiative campaign to have all lawyers reexamined every four years. Gebe Martinez and Doreen Carvajal, "Creators of Prop. 187 Escape Spotlight," *Los Angeles Times*, Orange County Edition, September 4, 1994, p. A1.

68. In its 1982 decision in *Plyler v. Doe*, 457 U.S. 202, the U.S. Supreme Court held that a Texas law permitting local school districts to deny schooling to illegal aliens violated the equal protection guarantees of the Fourteenth Amendment, which speaks of "persons," not citizens. But since it was a 5–4 decision by a substantially different group of justices, some of the backers of Proposition 187 held strong (and, judging from the composition of the court in 1994, not entirely ill-founded) hopes that *Plyler* could be reversed.

69. See, e.g., Roberto Suro, *Watching America's Door: The Immigration Backlash and the New Policy Debate* (New York: The Twentieth Century Fund, 1996), pp. 40–41.

70. *Yick Wo v. Hopkins*, 118 U.S. 356(1886); *Takahashi v. Fish and Game Commission*, 334 U.S. 410 (1948); *Oyama v. California*, 322 U.S. 633 (1948).

71. Suro, op. cit., pp. 37–41; Joel Brinkley, "Eighties Policies Are Now Haunting California," *New York Times*, October 15, 1994, p. 1; Paul Jacobs, "Wilson Often Battled INS, Letters Show," *Los Angeles Times*, September 25, 1995, p. A3; James Bornemeier, "Charting Wilson's Transformation on Immigration,"

Los Angeles Times, November 2, 1994, p. A3.

72. And, here, too, Congress came to regret, and ultimately modify, some of the self-defeating cuts that it had enacted, particularly those in SSI (Supplemental Security Income). Nonetheless, when the bill went into effect, Wilson moved so fast to cut off benefits that a federal judge blocked Wilson's order because it failed to meet procedural requirements. Getting aliens off the rolls, the judge held, was not an emergency and did not justify the haste with which the governor had been proceeding.

73. *Regents of the University of California v. Bakke*, 438 U.S. 265 (1978).

74. The SAT runs from 200 to 800 on each of two parts, verbal and math, though the scores on the two are often totalled by college admission officers. The median for the college-bound population is supposed to be 500 on each; it had, in fact been drifting down for a generation until, in 1995, the College Board "recentered" the scoring to restore the curve for today's generation of students.

75. See, e.g., John Bunzel, "Affirmative Action: How It 'Works' at Berkeley," *Public Interest* (Fall 1988): 21. Bunzel, a former chairman of the U.S. Civil Rights Commission, though sharply critical of Berkeley's affirmative action policies, did not support CCRI, because he regarded

it as too broad. There is a vast amount of material on UC admissions, but perhaps the most conclusive is UC's own charts and tables on scores of various ethnic groups and its internal reports to the regents in the spring and summer of 1995 warning of the dire consequences that would follow if race preferences were ended in UC admissions. See *The Use of Socio-Economic Status in Place of Ethnicity in Undergraduate Admissions: A Preliminary Report*, University of California, Office of the President, May 1995. Perhaps more telling are the tables and admissions matrix in a letter from the Office of Civil Rights of the U.S. Department of Education clearing Berkeley (incredibly) of violations of federal civil rights law, even though it showed that Berkeley automatically gave preferences to affluent blacks and Latinos from out of state over poor Asians and whites living in the state. See letter from John E. Palomino, OCR, to Chang-lin Tien, Berkeley chancellor, March 1, 1996 (OCR Docket 09–89–2099). Also see Ben Wildavsky, "UC Campus Debates Affirmative Action," *San Francisco Chronicle*, May 16, 1995, p. 1, which shows the median SAT gap between Asians and blacks at Berkeley to be about 200 points; Robert Lerner, and Althea K. Nagai, "Racial Preferences at U.C. Berkeley," Washington, D.C., Center for Equal Opportunity, October 15, 1996;

Peter Schrag, "So You Want to Be Color-Blind: Alternative Principles for Affirmative Action," *American Prospect* (Summer 1995): 38–43; Peter Schrag, "Regents' Exam," *New Republic*, August 14, 1995, pp. 11–12; Peter Schrag, "Son of 187," *New Republic*, January 30, 1995, pp. 16–19.

76. Various interviews with Custred and Wood during the course of the CCRI campaign. One of those bills was AB 2150, sponsored by Speaker Willie Brown and passed by both houses of the legislature in 1992, which would have required the universities to include in their evaluations of administrators their success in achieving graduation rates that were ethnically proportional to the graduation rates of California high schools.

77. See Peter Schrag, "Flip Wilson," *New Republic*, October 2, 1995, pp. 14–18.

78. Jackson briefly embarrassed Wilson, who didn't know how to respond, by calling on all to stop for a minute of prayer. But the promised street protests fizzled, and the regents, though forced to move into a more secure room, finished their business on schedule.

79. Peter King, "The Curtain Pulled Back for a Moment," *Los Angeles Times*, September 9, 1996, p. A3.

80. Student government leaders at California State University at Northridge had by then also invited former Louisiana Klan leader David Duke (who said he did not support CCRI) to a campus "debate" on affirmative action.

81. "If you talk about cracking down on illegal immigration," said Dan Schnur, who had served as Wilson's press spokesman through the 1994 campaign, "you have to act in support of legal immigration. If you criticize racial preferences, you have to outline what alternative programs are going to look like." See Mark Z. Barabak, "GOP Seeks New Image Among Latinos," *Los Angeles Times*, March 30, 1997, p. A3.

82. The precedent cited by Henderson was *Washington v. Seattle School District*, 458 U.S. 457 (1982), in which the U.S. Supreme Court, in a narrow 5–4 decision, struck down a Washington State initiative that prohibited districts like Seattle from busing children to promote racial integration (but not for other purposes). In effect, the Court held, the Washington measure treated the affected minorities differently from other groups with respect to their ability to use the local governmental process to secure remedies for de facto segregation and other perceived injustices.

83. *Coalition for Economic Equity et al. v. Pete Wilson et al.* U.S. Ninth Circuit Court of Appeals, Nos. 97–15030, 97–15031 (April 8, 1997).

84. Among them, *Plyler v. Doe*, discussed more fully above.

85. Among others, *Adarand Construction v. Pena*, 115 S. Ct. 2097 (1995); *Shaw et al. v. Hunt* S. Ct. 94–923 (1996); *Kirwin v. Podberesky*, 38 F.3d 147 (1994).

86. Connerly first broached these ideas at a seminar at the Graduate School of Public Policy, University of California at Berkeley, March 31, 1997. Two months later, as the effects of the ban on race preferences became clearer, he began to voice his concerns in public. But there is not much chance that 209, now part of the California constitution, will soon be amended.

87. *Hopwood et al. v. State of Texas et al.*, 78 F. 3d 932 (1996). The panel, all conservatives, did not even need to reach the issue of *Bakke* itself, since the admissions practices of the University of Texas Law School that were under attack in the case clearly violated *Bakke* and could, as Justice Jacques L. Wiener held, have been overturned without reaching the constitutional issue. But the other two members of the panel, Justices Jerry E. Smith amd Harold R. DeMoss, Jr., proceeded to do so anyway.

88. And on this point, the judges were hardly alone. See, e.g., Stuart Taylor, Jr., "Why the Courts Will Uphold 209," *Legal Times*, December 9, 1996.

89. Jeffery Rosen, "Stare Indecisis," *New Republic*, December 23, 1996, pp. 14–16.

90. Justice Powell's concept of permitting the consideration of race as one "plus factor" in college admissions was itself a fudge, a straddle between the principled sides that had evenly split the *Bakke* court. It was never satisfactory as a bright legal line, but it seemed to reflect the nation's own ambivalence on affirmative action.

91. Nancy Rhyme, "Term Limits," *National Conference of State Legislatures*, 3 (June/July 1995): 2–3.

92. One elaborate affair, which took place at the time of the 1984 Democratic Convention in San Francisco, is wonderfully described in Richardson, op. cit., pp. 315–317.

93. George F. Will, *Restoration: Congress, Term Limits and the Recovery of Deliberative Democracy* (New York: The Free Press, 1992).

94. All recent campaign reform measures have been struck down in the courts. One, Proposition 208 (1996), is still on appeal.

95. Two of the staffers have pleaded guilty. As this book went to press, Baugh, who pleaded not guilty, had not yet been tried. See, e.g., Mary Lynn Vellinga, "Powerful PAC's Influence Helped Spur Orange Scandal?," *Sacramento Bee*, March 31, 1996, p. A6. Also see "Assemblyman Pleads Innocent to Perjury and Corruption Charges," *Sacramento Bee*, Associated Press dispatch, April 22, 1996.

96. George Skelton, "A Terminal

Case of Mad GOP Disease," *Los Angeles Times*, March 18, 1996, p. 3.

97. Daniel Weintraub, "California Leaders Look at Limits," *State Legislatures* 20 (July 1994): 40.

98. Dan Bernstein, "Assembly Still Dealing with Freshman Jitters," *Sacramento Bee*, March 17, 1997, p. A1.

99. Douglas G. Brown, "Term Limits and the Changing Legislator–Staff Relationship," unpublished talk at the Western Legislative Conference, Lake Tahoe, Nevada, June 22, 1995, p. 2.

100. Weintraub, op. cit., "California Leaders Look at Limits."

101. Timothy Hodson, Rich Jones, Karl Kurtz, and Gary Moncrief, "Leaders and Limits: Changing Patterns of State Legislative Leadership Under Term Limits," paper presented at the annual meeting of the Western Political Science Association, March 1995.

102. In addition, it costs the taxpayers of each affected district an estimated $300,000 to $500,000 to run each of these special elections.

103. Interview, November 1995.

104. In 1991, the California Supreme Court, by a 6–1 majority, had upheld Proposition 140, despite a strong dissent by Justice Stanley Mosk, the sole holdover from the Pat Brown era, who held that 140 was a violation of the California constitution, which allows the use of the initiative to "amend" but not "revise" the constitution.

Proposition 140, in Mosk's words, "would fundamentally alter a fundamental component of the state constitutional system by effecting a substantial change in the nature and character of the Legislature." The legal argument is unimportant here, but the substantive observation about the changes wrought by the measure are hard to dispute. In a footnote, Mosk noted "in passing" that 140 could also be invalid as a bill of attainder under the U.S. Constitution because it singles out one class of people for disqualification for legislative office, something that heretofore had been imposed only on those convicted of certain crimes. *Legislature of the State of California v. Eu*, SO19660, October 10, 1991. Concurring and Dissenting Opinion by Mosk, J., pp 17, 19.

105. *Bates v. Jones*. U.S. Ninth Circuit Court of Appeals No. 97-15864 (1997). The court heard the case on an expedited basis in order to clarify the issue before the 1998 campaign season formally began.

106. See, e.g., Arlene Levinson, "So Much to Do, So Little Time," *State Legislatures* 21 (July–August 1995): 36.

107. The argument has been formally made by a number of commentators. See, e.g., Mark Petracca, "Rotation in Office: The History of an Idea," in Gerald Benjamin and M. Malbin, eds., *Limiting Legislative Terms* (Washington, D.C.: CQ Press, 1992), pp. 19–51.

108. These observations often come from committee staff members themselves, who, for understandable reasons, don't wish to be named.

109. California's constitution permits amendments by initiative, but not "revision," on the sound theory that attempts to rewrite the whole constitution at the ballot box are a likely avenue to disaster. It also requires initiatives, like other legislation (excepting only the budget) to deal with a single subject. But both restrictions are hard to define and have been consistently ignored by the California Supreme Court, whose members must be reconfirmed by the voters every twelve years. In the 1980s, as discussed earlier, three members of the court were removed by the electorate because it regarded their decisions, particularly on the death penalty, as too liberal. The only instances when the state supreme court is prone to interpose itself is when the powers of the courts themselves are at risk. Thus the court in 1996 in effect nullified a part of the Three Strikes law that precluded judicial discretion in certain mandatory sentencing decisions. Since Three Strikes grants such discretion to prosecutors, the supreme court held, the same discretion may also be exercised by the trial judge.

110. In addition, federal and state courts, in separate actions and for different reasons, struck down a pair of competing finance reform measures, Propositions 68 and 73, that the voters approved in June 1988.

111. Julian N. Eule, "Judicial Review of Direct Democracy," *Yale Law Journal* 99 (1990): 1503.

NOTES FOR PART FOUR:
THE NEXT AMERICA

1. *California Economic Growth* (Palo Alto, CA: Center for the Continuing Study of the California Economy, 1997), pp. V16–V24. Between 1979 and 1995, California's share of U.S. high-technology jobs increased from 17 percent to 20 percent and now accounts for 26 percent of high-tech value-added activity in the U.S. economy.

2. In light of the world's shifting trade routes, including the increase in the volume of Asian goods shipped westward across the Indian Ocean and through the Suez Canal, the dominance of Long Beach and Los Angeles, from which a large fraction of goods are then transshipped by rail to the East Coast, is hardly assured; see Frederick Rose, "Shifting Trade Routes Affect American Ports," *Wall Street Journal*, September 16, 1996, p. 1. But for the moment, that seems a minor cloud on California's bright economic horizon.

3. John Ellwood, Steven Sheffrin, and John J. Kirlin, *California Fiscal Reform: A Plan for Action* (Oakland,

CA: University of California—California Business–Higher Education Forum, 1995), p. 4.

4. A near-exception was the increase in the upper-income tax bracket, which was on the ballot as Proposition 217 in November 1996, when, after a particularly dubious set of campaign fund transfers by the leaders of the California Chamber of Commerce, it was narrowly defeated. Recommendations for change have come from all sorts of groups, among them various university groups, the League of Women Voters, and individual legislators. Those in this list come mainly from the task force reports in *California Fiscal Reform: A Plan for Action*, op. cit.; *Reforming California's Budget Process: Preliminary Report of the California Citizens Budget Commission*, Los Angeles, 1995; and Lenny Goldberg, op. cit., pp. 77–116.

5. For a full elaboration of the way the Yankees handled the oncoming Irish in Boston, the best account is still William V. Shannon, *The American Irish* (New York: Macmillan, 1963).

6. *California Economic Growth*, op. cit., pp. 5–6.

7. Ironically, the groups that insist most vehemently that measures like the balanced budget amendment are "the will of the people" gloss over the fact that their single most important provisions are those that block effective majorities in Congress from carrying out that will.

8. Tracy Westen, "2004: A Digital Election Scenario," Los Angeles, Center for Governmental Studies (unpublished paper), 1996. (Westencgs@aol.com). It has since been revised and published in *Elections in Cyberspace: Toward a New Era in American Politics*, by the Communications and Society Program of the Aspen Institute and the American Bar Association (Washington, D.C.: The Aspen Institute, 1997).

9. "The Future of Democracy," *Economist*, June 17, 1995.

10. Which is also the name of the organization's semimonthly newsletter. The states that passed the measure are Alaska, Arkansas, Colorado, Idaho, Maine, Missouri, Nebraska, Nevada, and South Dakota. Associated Press summary, November 7, 1996. U.S. Term Limits, *Term Limits Election Results*, November 7, 1996. (www.termlimits.org).

11. Adam Clymer, "Term Limits Rejected by House, Bringing Campaign to Dead Halt," *New York Times*, February 13, 1997, p. A1. The large turnover in Congress in 1994 probably took enough steam out of the campaign so that the required two-thirds vote was always in doubt.

12. *Donovan v. Priest*, 931 S.W. 2nd 119 (1996).

13. The organization will provide a list of its National Finance

Committee, all of whose members are said to have kicked in $1,000 or more, but refuses to provide the names of its largest contributors.

14. The exceptions are Florida (1970) and Illinois (1972).

15. The Anaheim elementary school district, worried about the resulting surge in enrollment, asked for subsidies from the project to fund new facilities, but ultimately settled for a one-time payment of $1 million. The high school district, instead of getting cash, is trying to get commitments from the company for help in job training, art instruction, and other services. Robert C. Johnston and Kerry A. White, "Despite Rhetoric, Businesses Eye Bottom Line," *Education Week*, March 19, 1997, pp. 1, 34.

16. Press packet, slides, and other enclosures, from the City of Anaheim and the Disneyland Resort, July 1, 1996.

17. Marla Dickerson, "Disney Park to Celebrate Golden State," *Los Angeles Times*, July 18, 1996, p. A1.

18. Ada Louise Huxtable, *The Unreal America: Architecture and Illusion* (New York: The New Press, 1997), p. 75.

19. Quoted in Carey McWilliams, *Brothers Under the Skin* (Boston: Little Brown and Co., 1943), p. 16.

20. The Commission proposed to replace it with the federal standard, which required overtime pay only after an individual had worked over forty hours in a week. The Democrats said they were willing to give workers various flex-time options, as Wilson demanded, provided it was at the worker's discretion and not subject to unilateral imposition by the employer.

21. No other nation was mentioned, but Clinton's initial model for the U.S. math test he proposed was TIMSS, the Third International Math and Science Study, which was dominated by Singapore, Korea, Japan, and Hong Kong. (The Czech Republic also scored high—sixth in math and second in science.) That there is still considerable doubt about the comparability of the scores from one country to another, and that the regional and class differences within nations are far greater than the differences among them, is not at issue here. But clearly a major factor in the differences is that high scores in some places have far more direct consequences for the student (and perhaps her parents) than they do in this country. At the moment, it is the Asian nations that are leading the pack. For the TIMSS scores: http://www.csteep.bc.edu. For the Clinton testing materials: http://www.ed.gov/NCES/NAEP.

22. Roger Waldinger and Mehdi Bozorgmehr, eds., *Ethnic Los Angeles* (New York: The Russell Sage Foundation, 1996). Also see Patrick J. McDonnell, "Study Says Economic

Gap Cuts Across Ethnic Lines," *Los Angeles Times*, December 10, 1996, p. B1.

23. There are studies proving almost every conclusion on this issue, most of them weak. See, e.g., Richard Vedder and Lowell Galloway, *Immigration and Employment: New Evidence* (Arlington, VA: The Alexis DeTocqueville Institution), March 1994; Leon Bouvier, *Fifty Million Californians?* (Washington, D.C.: Center for Immigration Studies, 1991), pp. 41–51. But almost any assertion that the presence of an excess of workers willing to take jobs at low, often subminimum wages does not depress the market at the lower end faces a huge intuitive hurdle.

24. Phil Garcia, "New State GOP Leader to Woo Ethnic Members," *Sacramento Bee*, February 21, 1997, p. A1.

25. Mark Z. Barabak, "GOP Seeks New Image Among Latinos," *Los Angeles Times*, March 30, 1997, p. A3.

26. See, e.g., Ken Chavez, "Increasingly, Civic Awareness Takes Root in Immigrants," and "AFL-CIO Looks to Immigrants to Boost Membership," *Sacramento Bee*, May 4, 1997, p. A1; and May 5, 1997, p. A1.

27. "A Review of Voting and Political Demography in 1996," *California Opinion Index*, San Francisco, The Field Institute, February 1997.

28. The "scholarships"—tax credits of $1,500 for the first two years, tax deductions of up to $10,000 for everything else up to the fourth year—are, of course, benefits primarily for the taxpaying middle class and secondarily for the colleges, which will soon soak at least part of them up in increased tuition charges. They are not refundable for those who pay little or no tax.

29. http://library.ca.gov/california/cahdream.html.

30. The reference to "legal" immigration is a curious nod to Governor Pete Wilson, who appointed Starr and who insisted that in his support of things like Proposition 187, he was not demeaning legal immigrants. But in fact, the nation was being transformed through all manner of immigration.

31. See, e.g., "Two states of mind about those southern neighbours," *Economist*, July 13, 1996, pp. 25–27.

32. The Field Poll, which was conducted in two parts, the first in April, the latter in May.

33. In the past couple of years, New Jersey under Governor Christie Todd Whitman was widely designated as the laboratory-of-the-day for the effects of a large state tax cut. But that test has been done in California, and perhaps elsewhere, with consequences that should have long ago been clear, and that New Jersey seems slowly to be discovering.

BIBLIOGRAPHY

‹ ›

Cain, Bruce E., and Roger G. Noll, eds., *Constitutional Reform in California* (Berkeley, CA: Institute of Governmental Studies Press, 1995).

California Budget Project, *How Does California Compare?* (Sacramento, CA: July 1996).

California State Department of Finance, *California Statistical Abstract* (annual editions, 1970–1997) (Sacramento, CA).

Cannon, Lou, *Reagan* (New York: Putnam, 1982).

Center for the Continuing Study of the California Economy, *California Population Characteristics* (Palo Alto, CA: 1995).

——, *California Economic Growth* (1996–97 ed.) (Palo Alto, CA: 1996).

Cronin, Thomas E., *Direct Democracy: The Politics of the Initiative, Referendum and Recall* (Cambridge, MA: Harvard University Press, 1989).

Daniels, Roger, and Spencer C. Olin, Jr., *Racism in California: A Reader in the History of Oppression* (New York: Macmillan, 1972).

Davis, Mike, *City of Quartz* (London: Verso Books, 1990; Vintage ed., 1992).

Didion, Joan, *Slouching Toward Bethlehem* (New York: Farrar, Straus and Giroux, 1967; Delta edition, 1968).

DuBois, Philip L., and Floyd Feeney, *Improving the California Initia-*

tive Process: Options for Change (Berkeley, CA: The California Policy Seminar, University of California, 1991).

Goldberg, Lenny, *Taxation With Representation: A Citizen's Guide to Reforming Proposition 13* (Sacramento, CA: California Tax Reform Association and New California Alliance, 1991).

Green, Stephen, ed., *The California Political Almanac* (Sacramento, CA: California Journal Press, 1995).

Hichborn, Franklin., *Story of the Session of the California Legislature of 1911* (San Francisco: James H. Barry Co., 1911).

Jacobs, John, *A Rage for Justice: The Passion and Politics of Phillip Burton* (Berkeley, CA: University of California Press, 1995).

Jarvis, Howard, with Robert Pack, *I'm Mad as Hell* (New York: Times Books, 1979).

Johnson, Hans, *Undocumented Immigration to California, 1980–1993* (San Francisco: The Public Policy Institute of California, 1996).

Kahrl, William L., *Water and Power: The Conflict Over Los Angeles' Water Supply in the Owens Valley* (Berkeley, CA: University of California Press, 1982).

Kerr, Clark, *The Uses of the University* (4th ed.) (Cambridge, MA: Harvard University Press, 1995).

Kirlin, John J., and Donald R. Winkler, eds., *California Policy Choices*, vol. III (Los Angeles: University of Southern California School of Public Administration, 1986).

Kotkin, Joel, and Paul Grabowicz, *California, Inc.* (New York: Rawson, Wade, 1982).

Kuttner, Robert, *Revolt of the Haves* (New York: Simon and Schuster, 1980).

Lav, Iris, J., Edward B. Lazere, and Jim St. George, *A Tale of Two Futures: Restructuring California's Finances to Boost Economic Growth* (Washington, D.C.: Center on Budget and Policy Priorities, 1994).

Lo, Clarence Y., *Small Property Versus Big Government* (Berkeley, CA: University of California Press, 1990, 1995).

Lowenstein, Daniel, *Election Law: Cases and Materials* (Durham, NC: Carolina Academic Press, 1995).

Lower, Richard Coke, *A Bloc of One: The Political Career of Hiram W. Johnson* (Palo Alto, CA: Stanford University Press, 1993).

McWilliams, Carey, *Brothers Under the Skin* (Boston: Little Brown and Co., 1945).

———, *California: The Great Exception* (New York: Current Books, Inc., 1949; Berkeley, CA: University of California Press, 1999).

———, *Factories in the Field* (Santa Barbara, CA: Peregrine Press, 1972).

Magleby, David, *Direct Legislation: Voting on Ballot Propositions in the United States* (Baltimore: Johns Hopkins University Press, 1984).

Mowry, George E., *The California Progressives* (Berkeley, CA: University of California Press, 1951).

Olin, Spencer C., Jr., *California's Prodigal Sons: Hiram Johnson and the Progressives, 1911–17* (Berkeley, CA: University of California Press, 1968).

O'Sullivan, Arthur, Terri A. Sexton, and Steven M. Sheffrin, *Property Taxes & Tax Revolts: The Legacy of Proposition 13* (Cambridge: Cambridge University Press, 1995).

———, *The Future of Proposition 13 in California* (Berkeley, CA: The California Policy Seminar, University of California, 1993).

Ovnick, Merry, *Los Angeles: The End of the Rainbow* (Los Angeles: Balcony Press, 1994).

Rapoport, Roger, *California Dreaming: The Political Odyssey of Pat and Jerry Brown* (Berkeley, CA: The Nolo Press, 1982).

Reed, Deborah, Melissa Glenn Haber, and Laura Mameesh, *The Distribution of Income in California* (San Francisco: The Public Policy Institute of California, 1996).

Reisner, Marc, *Cadillac Desert: The American West and Its Disappearing Water* (New York: Viking, 1986).

Richardson, James, *Willie Brown* (Berkeley, CA: University of California Press, 1996).

Schell, Orville, *Brown* (New York: Random House, 1978).

Schmidt, David., *Citizen Lawmakers: The Ballot Initiative Revolution* (Philadelphia, PA: Temple University Press, 1989).

Sears, David O., and Jack Citrin, *Tax Revolt: Something for Nothing in California* (Cambridge, MA: Harvard University Press, 1982, 1985).

Sheffrin, Steven M., and Maria Dresch, *Estimating the Tax Burden in California* (Berkeley, CA: The California Policy Seminar, University of California, 1995).

Shires, Michael, *The Future of Public Undergraduate Education in California* (Santa Monica, CA: The Rand Institute on Education and Training, 1996).

Starr, Kevin, *Inventing the Dream: California through the Progressive Era* (New York: Oxford University Press, 1985).

———, *Endangered Dreams: The Great Depression in California* (New York: Oxford University Press, 1996).

Suro, Robert, *Watching America's Door: The Immigration Backlash and the New Policy Debate* (New York: The Twentieth Century Fund, 1996).

Theroux, Peter, *Translating LA: A Tour of the Rainbow City* (New York: Norton, 1994).

INDEX

<>